PRAISE

MW01194901

"Readers interested in Canadian and American immigration history will appreciate the depth of Vermette's research and the fascinating story he tells." —*Publishers Weekly*

"First, let me say simply that this is a terrific book, the best synthesis of Franco-American history written to date.... Both the research and prose are wonderful.... Everyone with an interest in Franco-Americans should read this book." —Leslie Choquette, *Résonance*

"I was struck by the ease with which [Vermette] is able to organize data-dense material and interpret it into natural and compelling prose. As a non-fiction writer, he has a kind of narrative patience I greatly admire, an ability to make his argument with a light touch, through the strength of his research and writing rather than with explicit or bellicose assertions... [H]e is a persuasive and entertaining storyteller. *A Distinct Alien Race* is a great gift to those of us with Franco-American ancestry, and to other readers it offers a thorough introduction to a large but often invisible ethnic group that has shaped New England and the U.S. more generally." Abby Paige, Performer and Author of *When We Were French*

"David Vermette's *A Distinct Alien Race* is an important study that goes well beyond just recounting an economic and social history of New England and Quebec. Vermette, an excellent and engaging writer/researcher, exposes an area of the past that has been somewhat dismissed and even discounted by both American and Quebec/Acadian historians who study the enormous French-speaking Canadian emigration from Quebec and the Maritimes to the textile industries of Massachusetts, Vermont, New Hampshire, and New York from the 1840s to the 1930s." —Sandra Stock, *Quebec Heritage News*

"Meticulously researched and overflowing with facts, yet so well written that it's difficult to put down, the book tells a story few Americans are aware of." Emilie Noelle Provost, *The Bean Magazine* (Lowell, Mass.)

A DISTINCT ALIEN RACE

David Vermette

A DISTINCT ALIEN RACE

THE UNTOLD STORY OF FRANCO-AMERICANS
Industrialization, Immigration, Religious Strife

**Baraka
Books**

Montréal

Cover photo: Joseph Beaudoin ("Jo Bodeon"), a "back-roper" in the mule room, Chace Cotton Mill, Burlington, Vermont, 1909. Lewis Wickes Hine (Library of Congress).
Back cover photo: Adrienne Pagnette, 14 or 15, doffer, Winchendon Mass, 1911. Lewis Wickes Hine (Library of Congress).

Map p. 95 by Julie Benoît

© David Vermette

ISBN 978-1-77186-149-6 pbk; 978-1-77186-168-7 epub; 978-1-77186-169-4 pdf; 978-1-77186- mobi/pocket

Second printing with corections

Book Design and Cover by Folio infographie
Editing and proofreading: Arielle Aaronson and Robin Philpot

Legal Deposit, 3rd quarter 2018

Bibliothèque et Archives nationales du Québec
Library and Archives Canada

Published by Baraka Books of Montreal
6977, rue Lacroix
Montréal, Québec H4E 2V4
Telephone: 514 808-8504
info@barakabooks.com

Printed and bound in Quebec

Trade Distribution & Returns
Canada and the United States
Independent Publishers Group
1-800-888-4741 (IPG1);
orders@ipgbook.com

"The French number more than a million in the United States...

"The number of their children is unimaginable for Americans...

"They are kept a distinct alien race, subject to the Pope in matters of religion and of politics. Soon...they will govern you, Americans."

[*British-American Citizen* (Boston), December 28, 1889]

CONTENTS

INTRODUCTION

"French or English?" asked the priest.

"English," my mother replied.

An expression of disappointment moved briefly over the priest's face as he opened his English prayer book.

It was January 1983, and we were burying my father. The priest had come to read the prayers at the gravesite. It was a few weeks after my 19th birthday. The funeral was in Massachusetts, but my father was buried with my mother's family at St. Joseph's Cemetery in Biddeford, Maine. Following the two-hour drive to Biddeford, I found myself in a cemetery spanning acres of land. With few exceptions, the tombstones jutting up from the frozen ground had old-fashioned French names carved upon them: *Onésime, Odélie, Hyacinthe.* Not only the names were French, but all of the text on many of these tombstones, thousands of them, was in that language.

A gray day such as this carves a deep groove in the gray matter of a young person. One groove went deep, carved by curiosity about the French-speaking people represented by rows upon rows of neat graves. Who were these people, with their 19th-century French names, dropped as if by parachute into this community in Maine? What does it mean that I am standing here among them?

At that moment, I knew little about the people in the cemetery. I grew up in a suburb outside of Boston where my family, like the others in our community, spoke English. My family visited Montréal when I was very young. I knew that our ancestry was French-Canadian and that my grandparents had the accent consistent with that background. The odd names and fractured English of my parents' relatives was a point of family humor. My grandmother had shown me funeral cards for her relatives, about the size of a playing card with a head shot, some brief facts about the deceased, and a prayer written in French. The cards said these relatives came from "Saint-Cyrille-de-L'Islet, P.Q." That might as well have been on another planet. I was aware of the referendum on Québec independence in 1980 and I knew there was some connection between me and the people to the North. I knew my family ate certain foods and used certain words dubbed "French." There my knowledge ended. Here was a culture, substantial portions of which my family preserved, but I had little context for it.

Inspired by the events in the graveyard, at my first opportunity I visited the library and tried to find any available book on our French-Canadian ancestors: their history, culture, and language. I had to know how and why they came to New England and about their origins before they came.

Students learned nothing about the honored dead in the Biddeford cemetery in the public schools I attended. Québec and Canada might as well not exist for all we learned about them. And despite the numerous French names in my neighborhood in Massachusetts, none of these families seemed to know much about their past. Even if they did, I did not hear them speak of it. It was a mystery long forgotten or well hidden.

To learn anything about the French-speakers in the graveyard I had to educate myself. I learned enough French to read books, papers, and documents in that language. I also discovered a general literature about Franco-Americans of New England. For the most part, it is read by Franco-Americans themselves or by specialists in the region's history.

I never lost the thread I picked up at the Biddeford graveyard, but I did put it down for years and decades at a time. Developing a career as a researcher and writer working with authors, businesses, and consulting firms taught me how to turn information into stories. At the beginning of this century, I began to apply these skills to the mystery of my family's origins after my sister bought and restored a 200-year-old Acadian farm house on Prince Edward Island with ancestral connections to my maternal grandmother's family. My sister's interest in our Acadian heritage sparked my renewed interest in our more numerous ancestors from Québec. I repaired to archives and libraries, returning to my mystery with skills and experience.

Day becomes night very quickly in the research library, with patrons intent on their microfilms. How can I convey the exhilaration of putting together shards of information to recreate the lives of the long dead, a process as tedious as the result is satisfying? Over time my research expanded as I started to assemble a history, not of a single family, but of a town, and then of a people. Slowly, an image emerged of my historically-constructed self, through the telescoping lenses of family, region, religion, and race. I began to publish pieces based on this work and discovered a Franco-American community that welcomed me into a discussion spanning generations.

As my research developed, I was asked to present my findings at conferences, universities, and historical and genealogical societies. Traveling to the relevant parts of Canada, I explored the parishes of my ancestors, visited museums and sites of interest, and questioned the cousins who live in these lands today. I also formed relationships with academics in the field, and with Franco-American activists, writers, and artists, both in person and online. I blogged and joined the confluence of the like-minded on social media.

This book is a product of my investigation of the Franco-Americans of New England who worked in the cotton textile industry in the later 19th and early 20th centuries. I have taken a people on the margins of the society of its day and placed them at the center of U.S. history. *A Distinct Alien Race* is not a complete, sequential survey of Franco-American history. I have omitted many pertinent people, places, and events. My account of a portion of a broader Franco-American story will expose many readers for the first time to a forgotten episode in U.S. immigration and labor history. I expect the reader will see familiar themes in North American history from fresh perspectives.

Overview

Between 1840 and 1930, nearly one million French-speakers entered the U.S. from parts of today's Canada. Most came from the province of Québec, the only Canadian province with a French-speaking majority. A smaller group came from the land the French once knew as *Acadie* [Acadia], in today's Canadian Maritimes. A few came from other Canadian provinces to the west of Québec. The largest number of these immigrants settled in New England, the six-state region that borders French-speaking areas of Canada. Jobs in the textile industry, centered in New England in this period, attracted many of them to the region. Many also worked in shoe factories, pulp and paper mills, brickyards, shipyards, in forests, and on farms. In 1930, faced with a growing economic crisis, the Hoover Administration changed immigration guidelines rendering it more difficult for working-class Canadians to find employment across the border.[1] These changes at the border put a hard stop to the era of French-Canadian and Acadian emigration to New England.

These Franco-Americans tended to form neighborhoods in the industrial towns of New England, sometimes called Little Canadas, where they replicated institutions they knew in Québec and the former Acadia. These neighborhoods persisted for the better part of a century before economic changes caused them to all but fade away. Today their descendants comprise about ten million U.S. citizens, about 20 percent of whom still live in New England. Fully one-half of the descendants of the 17th and 18th century French settlements in North America now live in the United States.

The story I discovered in the Biddeford graveyard is tentacular. It reaches into numerous pools of history, touching on contemporary issues such as industrialization and its discontents; cross-border immigration; the nature of U.S. citizenship; and the fear of the Other.

Industrialization and its discontents: Franco-Americans were among the earliest immigrants to the U.S. recruited for the explicit purpose of serving as industrial workers in factories. By the beginning of the 20th century, 44 percent of the nearly 133,000 cotton textile workers in New England had at least one French-Canadian born parent.[2] The remaining 56 percent were divided unevenly between numerous other nationalities including immigrants from Ireland, Germany, Italy, Poland, Austria, Russia, Portugal, Greece, and elsewhere. New England's textile workforce was dominated by Franco-Americans with a score of other nationalities represented. New England drove the U.S.'s industrialization; cotton textiles drove New England's industrialization; and, after 1865, Franco-Americans drove the textile industry.

The Franco-American textile workers were *the other side of the cotton*. The agricultural side of the story, with its Southern plantations, slave-labor and share-croppers, is an established historical narrative. Less well known is the labor history of the manufacturing side of the process, the tale of the Franco-Americans who milled the cotton into cloth. The Franco-Americans were subjects of the Cotton Kingdom, a component of the systems that created the U.S. cotton economy and sustained it through the 19th and early 20th centuries. This book examines the conditions in the industrial towns before labor unions; before safety nets; before clean water, public health, or housing regulations.

Cross-Border Immigration: Franco-Americans came to the U.S. not by ship but over land. There was no Ellis Island, no Statue of Liberty to greet them. As a Romance-language-speaking, predominantly Roman Catholic group, who came from a country contiguous with the U.S., Franco-Americans resemble today's Mexican-Americans more than any other immigrant community. Like the immigrants from south of the border, the Franco-Americans' ancestors were established in parts of the territory of the United States before there was a United States. In both groups, many families first crossed the border as migrant workers eventually settling in their respective border regions.

Today, the Southwestern border region raises issues that worried Northeasterners in the late 19th and early 20th centuries: bilingualism; demographic concerns such as birth rate and family size; questions about the newcomers' potential political clout; and their alleged challenge to the perceived Anglo-Protestant identity of the United States.

The nature of U.S. citizenship: In one view, the United States is an English-speaking country, with institutions based on Protestant Christianity. Advocates for this view expect immigrants to conform to Anglo-Protestant norms. Others see the U.S. as a political structure that exists apart from linguistic or religious identity, as an open legal container that may support many different linguistic or religious groups.

The French-speaking *Canadien* identity in the 19th and early 20th centuries was *transnational*, crossing international, state, and provincial borders. Franco-Americans tested the boundaries of U.S. citizenship by attempting to maintain their transnational identity while also claiming loyalty to the United States.

Fear of the Other: In the late 19th century, elements in the U.S. press, clergy, and academia saw the emigration of hundreds of thousands of French-speaking Roman Catholics into New England as a threat to the political institutions of the United States. Catholics in this period were a countercultural religious group in a region identified with its Puritan origins. Alarmists viewed Catholics as a potentially violent and dangerous fifth-column.

Not only were they suspect on account of their religion, but Franco-Americans were even called a separate *race* from their English-speaking neighbors. In a region where the overwhelming majority of the population was white-identified, language and religion, as opposed to skin pigmentation, became the main pretext for othering minorities.

The history of Franco-Americans also illumines recurrent themes in the history of Québec and of Canada. The exodus toward New England has been called "the seminal event in nineteenth century French Canadian history."[3] The British Empire and its proxy governments in Canada did little to stem this emigration tide. By 1901, one out of every three French-speaking *Canadiens* lived in New England.[4] And yet the tale of the Franco-Americans is almost as unknown north as south of the border. This book explores the emigrants' background in Canada and the causes of the flight from Québec. Most accounts hold that economic considerations motivated the emigrants while overlooking social and political factors. The emigrants had opinions about the political future of Québec, and their move across the border was tied to these views. I also explore continuing cross-border contacts, as well as the significance of the Franco-Americans for Québec today.

Throughout this book, I use my father's hometown of Brunswick, Maine as a touchstone, to ground these themes in a specific case.

Moving from general trends to a particular instance exposes the humanity within the events. My focus shifts from the general to the particular; from the macro to the micro; from regional history to families and individuals.

Some cautions: first, there were many different Franco-American experiences. They came from various parts of today's Canada that each had its economy and geography. Not all Franco-Americans lived in a Little Canada or worked in textiles. The various state and local governments under which Franco-Americans lived, as well as the policies of the corporations for which they worked, produced a variety of working-class experiences. Some Franco-Americans lived in towns that became magnets for successive waves of immigration from overseas; others lived in communities where they were the only immigrant group of any size. Franco-Americans also held a range of views about questions that defined their community.

Franco-Americans often share a remarkably consistent set of tendencies, experiences, and collective memories that *no individual possesses in their entirety*. The generalizations made about Franco-Americans and others in this book should be read in this light. Also, this book cites texts where members of one group characterize another, in ages past when few observers were reticent about expressing their prejudices. The opinions about Franco-Americans and others cited in this book may be offensive to modern readers. Quotations from these sources do not necessarily reflect the author's views.

I did not proceed from an assumption that Franco-Americans were either heroes or villains. I had no interest in placing them in airtight groups labeled "oppressors" or "oppressed," an exercise in brute simplification that ignores the fact that the same people who may be oppressed with respect to one group may be oppressors of another. If this book complexifies more than it simplifies, then I have succeeded.

Since this history is little-known to many English-speakers, we'll need a vocabulary for this *terra incognita*.

Definition of Terms

Even to give a name to the people who are the subject of this book is difficult. Over time, they have accepted many names, and some of the terms do not enjoy universal acceptance.

Since the 1960s, the French-speaking population of Québec has favored the self-description *Québécois* (feminine: *Québécoise*). Our ancestors who departed Québec in the late 19th and 20th centuries did not use this term. They called themselves *Canadien* (feminine: *Canadienne*).

In using the terms *Canadien* or *Canadienne*, our grandparents did not refer to all of the inhabitants of Canada, but specifically to the French-speaking, predominantly Roman Catholic people of their country, with roots in the 17th and 18th century French presence in North America. Fairly or not, for them, a *Canadien* spoke French. In the French-speakers' world, the English-speakers of Canada were not Canadians but *les Anglais* [the English]. In the mid-19th century, the term *Canadien-français* [French-Canadian] also came into use as a rough equivalent to the term *Canadien*.

It is tempting to call the Franco-American subjects of this book *the Québécois of New England*. But that term would be both inaccurate and anachronistic. Today's term *Québécois* is not equivalent to the term *Canadien* as used in the 1865-1930 period discussed in this book. While *Canadien* was a transnational, continent-wide identity, the term *Québécois(e)* describes the inhabitants of the territory of Québec alone. In this book, I will use the term *Canadien*, italicized, with its French spelling, to designate the French-speaking people of Québec, and the provinces to its West, before 1960.

We also need to distinguish *Canadiens* from *Acadians*. The Acadians are the French-descent people whose homes were in today's Canadian Maritimes in the eastern parts of the country. In the 17th and 18th centuries, *Canada* and *Acadia* were two separate geographies. Acadians and *Canadiens* have different histories and different accents. Acadians are careful to preserve the distinction between themselves and the French-speakers of Québec and elsewhere in Canada.

Today, Acadians live mainly in New Brunswick, Nova Scotia, Prince Edward Island, the Magdalen Islands of Québec, and parts of Maine. Some Louisianans, particularly in the Southwest part of the state, also claim Acadian heritage. Although I do allude to the Acadians who came to the New England mill towns in the late 19th and early 20th centuries, my story concerns mainly the immigrants from Québec who comprised about nine-tenths of the Franco-American population.

The term *Franco-American* came into vogue shortly before 1900 to describe the French-speaking people who emigrated from today's Canada to the northeastern United States. Community leaders coined the term "Franco-American" as a means of uniting the *Canadien* and Acadian elements in New England.[5] This term was used almost exclusively in New England, New York, and Québec. The emigrants to other regions of the U.S. continued to call themselves "French-Canadians." Even in New England, the term "Franco-American" was more often on the lips of the elites than of the working-class. Today, many in New England continue to call themselves "French-Canadian," "Acadian," or just "French."

I use the term *Franco-American* to designate *Canadiens* and Acadians who emigrated to New England for the most part in the 1865-1930 period and who intended to remain in the U.S., whether they were born south of the border or not. For the sake of brevity, I designate this era, from the end of the Civil War to the Great Depression, as *our period*.

It would be reasonable to assume that the term *Franco-American* might also include immigrants who came directly from France to the United States. It might also include the Huguenots, most of whom came to the thirteen British colonies in the 17th century. Justly or not, the term Franco-American, as used in New England, has tended to omit these groups.

The misunderstanding that our people are *French* is a persistent difficulty for non-Franco-Americans, today as in the past. We are of French descent for the most part, but the Québécois, Acadians, and Franco-Americans of today are centuries removed from Europe. Changes in France after 1789 set the French on a trajectory untraveled by their cousins across the sea. The geography of North America, contact with indigenous peoples, and the long history under the

British Empire, created among these groups of French-speakers new, North American identities. Old-stock Québécois and Acadians of today are no more French than Mexicans are Spanish, Brazilians are Portuguese, or a Mayflower descendant in Massachusetts is English.

Period sources, not well versed in the history, frequently refer to Franco-Americans as "the French." The term, in the historical context discussed in this book, does not necessarily designate the people of France. But even the statement "Franco-Americans are not French" is controversial. Whether New England's Franco-Americans should identify with France or with Québec was a point of contention in the early 20th century.[6]

The use of the term *race* in the sources cited in this book demands an explanation. I stand with the 1950 UNESCO statement on race: "'race' is not so much a biological phenomenon as a social myth."[7] Uses of the term "race," calculations of the number of "races," etc. evolve in response to social change. Before 1940, the term *race* in the U.S. was used in at least two senses. The first sense of the term reflects loosely our current North American usage, where one's race is determined by phenotype, especially by skin color. We think in terms of a taxonomy where "white" is a race, with various ethnicities, such as Irish, Polish, or German ranged under it. However, in our historical period, a "race" could also mean any population united by a common language and cultural heritage. Per this second usage, the term *race* was indistinguishable from the term *ethnicity*.

This two-fold definition is evident in the work of the U.S. Congress's Dillingham Commission. In the first decade of the 20th century, the U.S. Congress appointed this commission to investigate immigrants and their employment across industries. The commission made recommendations that led to the restriction of so-called "undesirable" immigrants. Among the voluminous documentation the Commission produced was a *Dictionary of Races or Peoples* published in 1911. The *Dictionary*'s authors acknowledge the ambiguity of the term "race":

> Race is determined by language in such phrases as "the races of Europe," but by physical qualities, such as color, hair, and shape of head, when we speak of "the five great races" or grand divisions of mankind. In either case an attempt is made to bring into a common class all who have the

same inheritance. But the term "race" is sometimes used in other senses. Thus we may reach wider and wider "races" each including the preceding, as when we speak of the English race, the Teutonic race, the Aryan or Indo-European race, the Caucasian race, and, finally, the human race. Not only is there this popular looseness in the use of the word, but its scientific acceptations in the most exact of studies, namely in national census taking, is also variable.[8]

The first of the Dillingham Commission's definitions, in which race is "determined by language," is apparent in an 1885 article in the *New York Times* bearing the headline *"Race Prejudices in Canada."* This article describes a movement among English-speaking elements in the province of Ontario to form groups "against the French Canadians." The newspaper states that such groups are "calculated to stir up race differences."[9] The "race prejudices" in question in 1885 reflect conflicts based on distinctions not of skin color but of language.

When the authors of the Dillingham Commission's *Dictionary* discuss the definition of race based on phenotype, they settle on five races determined by perceived skin color: "white, black, yellow, brown and red." However, they also found that the precise "scientific acceptation" of the word "race" was unsettled. Although racial classifiers had been hard at work since Linnaeus in the 18th century, various taxonomies listed anywhere from 4 to 63 races of humankind. And despite the division of humanity into five races, the *Dictionary* continues to use the term with "popular looseness."[10] For example, the brief entry on "French-Canadian" in the *Dictionary* uses the term "race" to describe the French or French-Canadians three times.[11]

In the Dillingham Commission reports, and other documents from our period, "American" is also regarded as a "race." The term "American" is often used to designate only U.S.-born, white-identified, English-speaking Protestants. They were regarded as the "true" Americans, with even other "white races," as well as all non-white races, excluded from this group.[12]

Today, we tend to racialize all Americans of European descent as "white," but this was not accepted universally in our period. The racial status of southern and eastern Europeans, in particular, was in flux. In his 1914 book, *The Old World in the New*, sociologist Edward Alsworth

Ross cites a physician who claims, "the Slavs are immune to certain kinds of dirt. They can stand what would kill a white man."[13] A study of ethnic groups in Burlington, Vermont published in 1937 states that some of that city's Yankees were unclear as to whether they would classify Italians and Greeks as "white."[14] Attacks on Greek-Americans in South Omaha by white-identified Nebraskans in 1909 were called "race riots."[15]

As the Dillingham Commission's *Dictionary* notes, the "national census-taking" was not always clear on the boundaries of whiteness, and the census authorities could remove a group from that category. For instance, Mexican-Americans were racialized as "white" in the U.S. Census until 1930. In the 1920s, with the restriction of immigration on the national agenda, U.S. residents of Mexican origin lost their status as "white," at least as far as the Census was concerned. In 1930 a "racial" classification "Mexican" appeared and just as quickly disappeared from the census after that.[16] The term "Hispanic" appeared as an ethnic designation in 1980.[17]

For legal purposes, governments designated Franco-Americans in our period as "white." They are identified as such in the racial classifications in official documents such as the census, naturalization petitions, and military draft cards. However, they were often described as a separate "race" according to the secondary definition of the term, where it designated any coherent group that speaks its own language. Franco-Americans are spoken of as a "race," in this sense, in both English and French (Fr: *"la race"* = Eng. *"race"*). Did Anglo-Protestants in the U.S. regard Franco-Americans as belonging to their race, or to *a distinct alien race*? The answer remained ambiguous throughout our period.

A Sprint Through 250 Years of History

Nations inhabited the northeastern parts of what we call North America before there were *Canadiens*, Acadians, or Franco-Americans. Scholars classify these indigenous peoples by language groups: Iroquoian, Algonquinian, and Inuit. These nations were diverse in terms of how they made their living, and in their customs and beliefs. They were not static but changed over time. Today, such terms as "Native Americans" and "First Nations" are used to gather under a single category a myriad of peoples over eons. But these nations are only "native" or "first" in relation to the settlers from Europe.

From a Franco-American perspective, the backstory begins with Jacques Cartier, who traveled up the St. Lawrence River for France in 1534. He made two subsequent voyages to North America. Born a year after Columbus's first voyage west, like that earlier mariner, Cartier also sailed westward in search of gold and a passage to Asia. He found neither. Early French attempts at settling North America failed until Samuel de Champlain sailed at the beginning of the 17th century. Before the days of Champlain, the French, along with other Europeans, began to sail westward for the fish, but the French stayed for the furs. French settlement of what became Acadia began by 1604. Champlain founded Québec City along the St. Lawrence River in 1608.

During the 17th century, the French interest in what Europeans called the New World was mainly commercial. Since furs were the chief commodity, and this trade involved commerce with indigenous peoples, the French had to learn the languages and ways of the native North American nations. Their commerce involved the French in the military and diplomatic affairs of these nations from the first years of Champlain's voyages. Converting the indigenous peoples to Roman Catholicism was another aim of France in North America. These efforts, however distasteful to many 21st century observers, also required communicating with the native peoples in their languages. The vast land the Europeans labeled on their map *Nouvelle-France* [New France] was a fur company with a Catholic Mission attached. Or perhaps it was a Mission with a fur company in tow.

In the 16th and 17th centuries, the French mapped out three main territories in *Nouvelle-France* over which they exercised a sphere of influence. There was *l'Acadie* in today's Canadian Maritimes; *le Canada*, from the St. Lawrence Valley westward and laying claim to the Ohio Valley and Great Lakes region; and *la Louisiane*, the area in today's U.S. Midwest, from south of the Great Lakes to the Gulf of Mexico. These regions describe a great arc across the continent that followed the waterways from the Atlantic Ocean, to the rivers St. Lawrence and Ottawa, to the Great Lakes, to the Mississippi, and southward to the Gulf. In the 18th century, the French built a series of trading posts and forts to begin to connect these vast territories with one another and to entrap the growing English colonies along the Atlantic coast, containing them to the east of the Appalachians.

In Canada, there was a clear distinction between *the French* and *the Canadiens* by the 1680s.[1] Those dubbed *Canadiens* were the French speakers born in Canada and intending to stay there. *The French* were the ruling class, the military and administrative personnel who were born in France and would tend to serve their terms in Canada and return to Europe. Observers began to note differences in manners and mores between the French and the *Canadiens* in the 18th century.[2]

Relatively few French-speakers lived in New France, beyond several concentrations in each region. The focus on trade did not encourage the development of larger, more densely populated settlements as in the Anglo-American colonies of this period. Agriculture developed, especially in the St. Lawrence Valley and the upper portions of Louisiana after 1650, but it did not become the defining economic activity of the *Canadiens* until the British took Canada in the mid-18th century.

Despite the vast territories designated as New France on maps of colonial North America, the French did not exercise sovereignty over this entire region. For the most part, indigenous nations retained their sovereignty, and the French exercised their influence through alliances and trade with these nations. The French and *Canadiens* were able to have a sphere of influence in North America only because of their alliances with indigenous peoples. Mi'kmaq scholar Dr. Daniel N. Paul describes early contacts between his people and the Acadians as a "mutually beneficial and respectful relationship" which had allowed "the French settlers to begin to establish themselves in Acadia...without opposition from the Mi'kmaq. During this period, the two peoples established many social exchanges. Inter-marriage was quite common, and each adapted to many of the customs of the other." Doctor Paul also states that the fortunes of both groups changed after the British took possession of Acadia in the early 18th century.[3] However, relations between the French-speaking settlers and indigenous peoples were not always amicable. The French waged wars against the Fox in upper Louisiana and the Natchez in lower Louisiana, and there was sporadic warfare with the Haudenosaunee ("Iroquois") in Canada.

In 1701, after long, skirmishing warfare, the Haudenosaunee and the French negotiated a treaty known as the Great Peace of Montréal. This diplomatic triumph was largely the work of a Wyandot ("Huron") leader at Michilimackinac called Kondiaronk (the Muskrat). The peace conference lasted months, and some thirty indigenous nations signed the treaty along with the French. The text of the treaty survives. Written in a neat, 18th century French, it includes the pictograms representing the various native North American nations, their communities or leaders. Among Canadian First Nations, the treaty still holds.

In the 19th century, U.S. historian Francis Parkman claimed that the French and *Canadiens* "embraced and cherished" the indigenous nations.[4] Today, other voices deny that there were any important differences between the French and other Europeans on the continent with respect to relations with the indigenous peoples. They insist that force defined these relations.[5] Both views are too

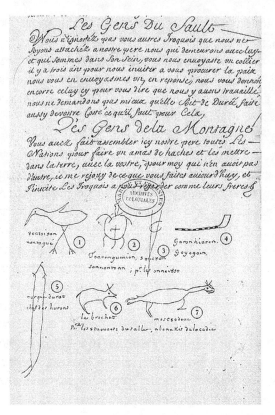

FIGURE 1: The *Great Peace of Montréal*, 1701. A page from the treaty.
French text with pictogram signatures of several First Nations.

simple. To tell a whole truth about this history, a truth that would embrace and cherish the unvarnished accounts of the First Nations, would confound stereotypes and contemporary political verities on all sides. A telling that neither romanticizes nor demonizes is likely beyond the capacity of our world to hear it. But this is another book.

The French and *Canadiens* pushed deep into the interior of the continent in the era of New France. The explorations of La Vérendrye and son, from the 1730s through the 1750s, pushed westward to the modern-day Dakotas and Wyoming, to Manitoba, and the Saskatchewan River. French-speaking settlements in the Great Lakes and the

Mississippi Valley were in place before there was a United States. In the first half of the 18th century the land they knew as *le Pays des Illinois* [the Illinois Country] or *Haute-Louisiane* [Upper Louisiana] in today's U.S. Midwest, had farms supplying the lower Mississippi. *Canadiens* lived in these regions when the U.S., expanding westward, acquired them. Everywhere they went in the West, through the 18th and 19th centuries, the French and *Canadiens* left their mark in the names of places such as Detroit, Chicago, Vincennes, Des Plaines, Des Moines, Baton Rouge, New Orleans, Coeur d'Alene, Nez Perce, Boise, and numerous others.

United States histories speak of an event called "the French and Indian War." But there were numerous wars and skirmishes between France and England for hegemony in North America throughout the 17th and 18th centuries. European wars reached across the Atlantic and involved the British colonists and their French-speaking counterparts in them. These wars pitted the British colonists, sometimes allied with the Haudenosaunee, against the French, *Canadiens,* and their indigenous allies. The Ohio Valley was a particular bone of contention in the West. Whether Maine was to be a northeastern outpost of the Massachusetts Bay colony or part of Acadia was in dispute in the East. Acadia traded hands between Britain and France several times, eventually coming under British rule in 1713. The mainland portion of Acadia became known as *Nova Scotia.*

These conflicts between the two empires culminated in the Seven Years ("French and Indian") War of the 1750s and 1760s. Britain, France, and their allies fought the Seven Years War in Europe, the Americas, India, the Caribbean, the Philippines, Africa, and on the high seas. It was a world war in all but name. In North America, the fighting involved tens of thousands of regular troops and militia. Beginning in 1755, the war saw British forces deport the Acadians of Nova Scotia, subjects of the British king. In the main, New Englanders who coveted the lands the Acadians had settled in Nova Scotia, inspired the deportation. The Acadians were loaded onto ships and scattered throughout the thirteen colonies, to England, to France, and to as far afield as the Falkland Islands. Their villages were destroyed. Many Acadians died in shipwrecks and disease. A similar deportation from another Acadian settlement, *Île Saint-Jean,* occurred in 1758. The island came under British rule in the war and was later dubbed *Prince Edward Island.*

Some of the Acadian deportees found their way to Louisiana, but British forces did not send them there. The Acadians who arrived in Louisiana went there on their own initiative from secondary locations, where they had landed after the deportation of the 1750s, notably from Saint-Domingue (today's Haiti), from France, from the colony of Maryland, and other regions. Some Acadians escaped the Deportation and went to Canada. Others returned to the former Acadia after the war. Today, *New Brunswick* is the Canadian province with the greatest number of Acadians, and it is the only officially bilingual (French/English) province.

Meanwhile, the out-numbered French-led forces were winning the North American phase of the Seven Years War until 1758 when their great fortress of Louisbourg fell. The following year, British General James Wolfe sailed up the St. Lawrence, leaving destruction in his wake. Wolfe's invasion, with 20,000 troops, culminated with the battle of the Plains of Abraham in which the capital of New France, Québec City, was taken by the British.[6] The French-speakers rallied in 1760, won the battle of Sainte-Foy, near Québec City, and intended to retake the capital. Whether or not help would arrive from France was a decisive factor. If the ship arriving over the horizon after the spring thaw was French, then the fight continued. If it was not, then the war in North America was won for the British. The British ship appearing over the horizon in the spring sealed the fate of New France. Later in 1760, the second most important town in Canada, Montréal, capitulated to the British.

By the Treaty of Paris of 1763, which ended the war, France ceded its sphere of influence in Canada to Great Britain. The treaty also made France cede Louisiana to Spain. The vast Louisiana territory would return to France briefly at the beginning of the 19th century before its sale to the Jefferson Administration in 1803. The 1763 treaty made the *Canadiens* bits of a French colonial enterprise peeled off from one Empire and assigned to another. Officialdom, and some of the landowners, and others with connections in France, left Canada and returned to Europe. People in more modest economic circumstances, some tens of thousands of *Canadiens*, who had generations of ancestors buried in North America by 1763, had no means to move to a France they had never seen. They remained in Canada and took the oath of allegiance to the British King.

Before 1763, under the French Regime in Canada, the *Canadiens* had had little say in their government. They did not create the policies of French colonialism. They were no more than subjects of the French Empire. Now, under the British Empire, these agents of French colonizers became the colonized. Thus, in the 18th century, due to the fortunes of war and the diplomatic rivalries of the great powers, two small communities of French-speakers, first the Acadians (1713) and then the *Canadiens* (1763), came under the control of not only a foreign power but a hated rival. The British Empire could have attempted to deport the inhabitants of Canada, as it had done with the Acadians. Or it could rule them by military government, as it did in the earliest years of British Canada. Or the British Crown could show magnanimity and include the *Canadiens* in the institutions of limited self-government enjoyed by its other subjects.

The power to be magnanimous or severe rested far away, in London. No matter how benign the terms of conquest, no matter how gracious the gestures, no matter how much the British Crown conceded regarding language, religion, or laws, nothing could mitigate the fact that foreigners *granted* the *Canadiens* these privileges. They were imposed from without and not secured from within. And a Sovereign who grants largess by its own will has the power to withdraw it by the same token. The fate of Canada was most decidedly not in the hands of the farmers, laborers, merchants, tradespeople, women, and children who remained in Canada when the smoke of battle cleared, and the well-connected or wealthy had returned to France. The fact that the *Canadiens* were eventually offered constitutional government, on the British model, and granted rights and privileges within that system, has never erased in its entirety the feeling of powerlessness that comes with having received grace dispensed from a foreign throne. This feeling is a key to understanding all subsequent Québec nationalism.

Whether we characterize the events in Canada of the 1760s as an abandonment by France of its American colonies or as a British conquest of them is irrelevant. It was both. But for British military action and intent to take the territory, Canada might still be French. France's half-heartedness in defending its American sphere of influence also played its part in the outcome of 1763. What is most important for our history is that the image of the *Canadiens as a conquered people* became embedded within the psyches of *both* the English- *and* the French-speaking inhabitants of what evolved into today's Canada. Proud of its victory, English-Canada was happy to celebrate Wolfe's Conquest of Canada in the era before such triumphs of imperialism engendered embarrassment.

The British wanted Canada for two reasons. First, they wanted to control the fur trade, which was centered in Montréal and faced west toward the Great Lakes. Second, Britain wanted to remove the threat the French, the *Canadiens*, and their indigenous allies posed to its thirteen colonies to the south. When the British government levied taxes on the thirteen colonies to help pay for the war it had fought in North America to protect them, it kicked a hornet's nest. A chain of events followed, leading to Emerson's "shot heard round the world" and the famous Declaration of Independence of July 1776.

In the brief period between 1763 and the American Revolution, the British expected *the Province of Quebec*, as they had renamed the former Canada, to become much like their other North American colonies. They expected that settlers from their thirteen colonies and Great Britain would migrate to Canada. Thus, the small population of less than 100,000 *Canadiens* in the Province of Quebec would assimilate to the British majority. The *Canadiens*, however, led by the clergy and a small group of landowners and professionals who had remained after the British Conquest, had no intention of assimilating. They maintained their language, religion, and culture.

The *Quebec Act* of 1774 recognized that *Canadien* assimilation to the language and ways of the English was not forthcoming for the time being. The French fact in the colony was normalized. The Quebec Act was a measure to secure the loyalty of the *Canadiens* as the colonies to its south became increasingly restive. It was a stopgap, pending further efforts toward the assimilation of the *Canadiens* into the British Empire.

The Quebec Act restored the pre-1763 borders of Canada, which included the Great Lakes region and the Ohio Valley. It recognized French civil law, while it established English criminal law in the Province. As a consequence of the restoration of the French civil code, it also affirmed both the tithe for the Roman Catholic clergy and the traditional privileges of the land-holding *seigneurs* [landlords]. Except for the imposition of English criminal law, these provisions reinstated Canada's *status quo ante bellum*.

The Quebec Act enraged many inhabitants of the thirteen colonies who numbered it among the British Parliament's *Intolerable Acts*. Congress cited the Quebec Act as a grievance in the U.S. Declaration of Independence.[7] The language in the Declaration veils the real burr under the American Patriots' saddles. Many Anglo-American colonists were incensed that a Protestant King of Great Britain had not only *tolerated* but *established* the Roman Catholic Church in a province under British rule. Many New Englanders viewed the British government's policy of accommodation to Catholics as the prelude to the invasion of a *Canadien* "papist" horde with the aim of enslaving Protestant America.[8]

No less a figure than Samuel Adams, among many others, sounded this alarm: "Much more is to be dreaded from the growth of Popery in America, than from Stamp Acts or any other acts destructive of civil rights; Nay, I could not help fancying that the Stamp Act itself was contrived with a design only to inure the people to the habit of contemplating themselves as the slaves of men; and the transition thence to a subjection to Satan is mighty easy."[9]

When the fighting broke out between the thirteen colonies and their mother country, *Canadiens* were on both sides of the war. Congress sent an embassy northward, including Benjamin Franklin and the Maryland Jesuit John Carroll, to win the *Canadiens* to their cause. Congress also wrote an official communiqué to the *Canadiens* pleading their case and inviting them to join the British colonies' Revolution. However, anti-Catholic rhetoric in a parallel communiqué from Congress to the people of Great Britain soured communications between the *Canadien* elite and Congress. The clergy and the large property owners, their privileges secured by the Quebec Act, were on the side of the British Monarchy. Many of the common folk in the towns and rural parishes supported the Revolution.[10] For most of the *Canadiens*, the war of 1775 was a civil war between English factions. The *Canadiens* would wait it out and see in which direction the winds of war listed.

Some *Canadiens* joined the Continental Army. My fourth great-grandfather Charles Racine was most likely press-ganged into joining the regiment of Moses Hazen, an English-speaking Montrealer born and raised in Massachusetts. Congress gave a commission to Hazen to raise a regiment of the Continental Army in Canada. Since it was not the militia of any of the thirteen states, Hazen's group was called *Congress's Own*. Racine's enlistment, voluntary or otherwise, occurred during the U.S.'s disastrous invasion of the Province of Quebec in 1775-76. At least parts of Hazen's regiment, largely *Canadien*, were at Valley Forge, the Battle of Germantown, and at Yorktown.

After the success of the American Revolution, many of the supporters of the British Crown from the thirteen colonies came, in exile, to Canada. In the U.S., they're known as *Tories*, in Canada as *Loyalists*. They came especially to today's Ontario, where generations of Anglophones thought it an honor to claim descent from a Loyalist. These so-called United Empire Loyalists were the root of English-Canada. After the arrival of the Loyalists in the 1780s, Canada was the scene of a shotgun wedding. The groom was a particularly pro-British, monarchist, Protestant population, eager to distinguish British North America from the United States. The bride was a French-speaking, Catholic population determined to preserve its uniqueness. It was bound to be a rocky marriage.

In 1791, a divorce between majority English-speaking "Upper Canada" (Ontario) and majority French-speaking "Lower Canada" (Québec) was made official. There was, however, an important English-speaking minority in Lower Canada as well as a significant French-speaking minority in Upper Canada. British legislation of 1791 established in both colonies elected legislative assemblies, with strictly limited functions. The Governor chosen by London, with an appointed executive and legislative council, held the real political power in the two colonies of Upper and Lower Canada.

The Napoleonic Wars made Canada useful to Great Britain for its timber, especially for ship-building. Toward the end of this period of warfare, the U.S. invaded Canada once again in the War of 1812 with no more success than in its previous attempt in the 1770s. At the Battle of Chateauguay, a force of *Canadien* troops, under the command of a *Canadien*, along with a contingent of Mohawk allies, turned back a numerically superior force of the U.S. Army in southwestern Québec in October 1813.

In the early 19th century, a political movement among the *Canadiens*, which became known as *les Patriotes* [the Patriots], worked to gain for the people of Lower Canada their rights as British subjects. This movement advocated what was known as *responsible government* in the province, a government in which the Executive branch was responsible to the elected Legislative branch. The *Patriote* movement also opposed the corruptions of an aristocratic clique that tended to control affairs in Lower Canada. The refusal of London to respond effectively to the demands of the *Patriotes* led to open rebellion against British rule in 1837-38. What began as a movement for political reform in 1837 became radicalized by 1838. In that year, a contingent of *Patriotes* published a Declaration of Independence of the Republic of Lower Canada. There was also a parallel rebellion in Upper Canada, but the movements had different leadership and were only loosely affiliated.

The fighting during the Rebellion in Lower Canada was regional and intermittent. In most engagements, Queen Victoria's army crushed the poorly armed rebels. Reprisals during and after the Rebellion included wanton destruction of property, the decimation of entire villages, the deliberate desecration of churches, execution of the leaders, and deportations to the penal colony of Australia. The repression during and after the Rebellion was disproportionate to the military threat the rebels posed. The leader of the *Patriotes* in 1837, Louis-Joseph Papineau, had fled the country for the United States. He tried to find aid for Lower Canada's cause in the U.S. and in France but to no avail.

In the aftermath of the Rebellions, London dispatched Lord Durham to Canada to analyze the causes of the troubles and to make recommendations for ameliorating the political situation in British North America. For Lord Durham, the issue in Lower Canada was not political but "racial," using the term in its 19th century sense. The problem, he thought, was the attempt to make "English" and "French" races co-exist within the same colony. Durham referred to the *Canadiens* disparagingly, and incorrectly, as "a people with no history and no literature," a statement that sent pens scratching all over Lower Canada just to prove him wrong.[11]

Lord Durham's solution to rebellious Lower Canada was cultural assimilation – to erase the *Canadiens* as a people. The means he recommended to accomplish this end was to unite Upper and Lower Canada to create one British colony under a single Parliament. Thus, the French-speakers would eventually become a minority within Canada, controlled by a politically dominant, English-speaking majority. Placed in the minority, the *Canadiens* would, in Lord Durham's words, "abandon their vain hopes for nationality."[12]

Following Lord Durham's recommendation, the British Empire united the two provinces of Upper and Lower Canada in 1840. The latter had a modest budget surplus while Upper Canada was in debt.[13] The Upper province amassed its debt while improving its infrastructure. When the Provinces united, Lower Canada (now dubbed Canada East) was also made liable for the debt of Upper Canada (Canada West). Effectively, Québec paid for Ontario's early 19th-century infrastructure. The new colonial entity created by the union of the two Canadas came to be known as United Canada.

After the defeat of the Rebellions, and in light of the stated British policy of cultural assimilation, a slow drain of population toward the U.S. began in a few regions of Québec. Whether it was economic instability or the traditional wanderlust of the *Canadiens*, a small number of families departed Lower Canada for the U.S. as early as the 1820s. A seasonal migration of young men to the U.S. had grown sufficiently in the 1830s to attract comment in Lord Durham's 1839 report.[14] By 1849, the exodus from the province southward invited the Parliament of United Canada to launch an investigation. Another such inquest followed in 1857.

In 1848 the British governor granted *responsible government* to United Canada, but further constitutional changes were not far behind. In 1867, United Canada joined the British colonies of Nova Scotia and New Brunswick in a new Confederation established by the British North America Act. This Act of the British Parliament established the political entity we know as Canada today. What had been United Canada was divided again into two provinces, called Ontario (the former Canada West) and Québec (formerly Canada East). Under this Confederation, each province had its own legislature and executive (called a *premier*). The new constitution also convened a Federal Parliament, finding its home at Ottawa, consisting of an elected House of Commons and an appointed Senate. A Prime Minister, with his cabinet, constituted the executive power at the Federal level. A Governor-General, appointed by the British Crown and representing it, had to assent to laws passed by the Canadian Federal Parliament. Eventually, other provinces to both the East and West were added to the Confederation until it became, like the U.S., an entity stretching from sea to shining sea. For the remainder of the 19th century, Canada was a (more or less) self-governing entity within the British Empire.

The British North America Act of 1867 granted the *Canadiens* a measure of political power and autonomy within their own domain: *the province of Québec*. For 150 years, they have had some control over their fate, within a Parliamentary system of government. The Anglophone people of the country are not alone responsible for everything that has occurred in Canada. The elite of Québec gained political power under the British Empire's rule, and they knew how to use it. Nonetheless, they wielded power within a structure imposed from without. No referendum or plebiscite sanctioned the several constitutional changes that occurred in British North America in the century between 1763 and 1867.[15] Subsequent developments in Canada tended to confine the *Canadiens* within Québec.

The 30-year period of political upheaval, from the Rebellions of 1837 to the Confederation of 1867, formed the context for the first wave of emigration of the *Canadiens* toward New England. The wages paid by textile mills across the border was the main draw for poorer families in a second stage of emigration that began with the end of the U.S. Civil War.

Before the Civil War, textile manufacturing had become an industrial juggernaut in the Northeastern U.S., a train ride away from Québec. Many of the children and grandchildren of the same Massachusetts families that took control of commerce after the U.S. gained its independence invested in cotton textile manufacturing in the following generation. But for the merchants of Boston, and the textile industry in which they invested, there would have been little call for labor from across the northern border. Loyal republicans in politics, these merchant princes of Boston became subjects of a great global potentate: *King Cotton*.

Two elements create woven textiles: the *warp*, stationary threads stretched vertically across the loom, and the *woof*, the threads that migrate horizontally between them. The warp and the woof yarns have distinct characteristics, but they integrate to create countless colorful fabrics. Two yarns weave the fabric of our tale of Franco-Americans in New England. The warp consists of the merchants and industrialists who created the industry, while the workers who came into the mills from rural Québec form the woof.

To place the Franco-Americans within U.S. history, we must spend no little effort to spin the warp threads and to stretch them tight across the frame. Our tale begins, then, not with the workers who came from Québec to New England, but with the merchants who created the textile industry. Only when we have understood the textile industrialists – their sources of capital and labor, and how they industrialized New England – may we weave the woof threads tightly. With the patience of a weaver, the complete fabric, the yarn I began to spin that January day in the Biddeford graveyard, will emerge, plaited from threads of distinct types.

SECTION ONE

FROM SHIPS' CAPTAINS
TO CAPTAINS OF INDUSTRY

CHAPTER ONE

HEAD OF THE MERCANTILE COMMUNITY OF BOSTON

On August 2, 1841, the Boston Exchange Company laid the cornerstone of its new building on State Street. The Merchant's Exchange, as this edifice was called, became the epicenter of the city's commerce. Sometime home of the Boston Stock Exchange, in the mid-19th century this merchant's complex housed insurance companies, banks, a post office, a telegraph office, and a hotel. The second floor served as headquarters for six railroad companies. The Exchange had offices of engravers and a Board of Brokers. It also had a glorious, domed reading room where the merchants gathered their intelligence.[1]

A week before the event, the Building Committee of the Boston Exchange Company sent a letter to the dean of Boston merchants, Thomas Handasyd (pronounced "Handy Side") Perkins, inviting him to preside over the ceremonial laying of the cornerstone. The Committee chose Perkins for this honor as one who had "long and honorably sustained the position of *head* of the mercantile community of Boston."[2] Writing in 1845, U.S. Supreme Court Justice Joseph Story concurred with the committee's assessment of Perkins's stature among merchants. Addressing Perkins, Story wrote, "You justly stand at the head of our commercial community; and you have achieved this enviable distinction by a life of successful enterprise."[3] When

Perkins died in 1854, Abbott Lawrence, from a family of renowned Boston merchants, said to a gathering of his peers, "I feel as you feel that we have lost our guide, our great exemplar in the mercantile profession."[4] Perkins was the merchants' role model, the biggest fish in his particular harbor.

The records left by Perkins and his associates are a portal into the world of the 19th-century Boston merchants who created the New England textile industry, including their sources of funding and the values and business practices they left to posterity. This template for the nation's commerce has outlasted by many years the granite stone Perkins help to lay on State Street in 1841.

Perkins, like many merchants of his day, did not specialize in any single commodity. His occupation was to buy anything in one place that he could sell at a profit somewhere else. Most of his dealings were overseas, especially in the West Indies, Europe, and China. At various times he traded in flour, horses, fish, furs, slaves, and opium. As his business matured, Perkins invested his profits from overseas trade in bedrock U.S. industries including mining, iron manufacturing, banking, and resort hotels.

Among his other interests, Perkins was among the players in the New England textile industry as an owner and as an investor. In the early 1820s, he was a founder of the Elliot Manufacturing Company, a cotton mill in Newton, Massachusetts. As a founder of the Appleton Company, he was also on the ground floor of the prototype of textile mill towns: Lowell, Massachusetts.[5]

Perkins's memo book records his investments in textiles and related businesses in 1845. He owned stock in ten cotton and woolen mills in Lowell to the tune of $480,750. He held a $212,300 stake in the Chicopee, Cabot, Perkins and Dwight textile manufacturing operations in Western Massachusetts. He had $116,000 in Manchester, New Hampshire's Amoskeag, Stark and Manchester mills and $11,000 invested in a Nashua, New Hampshire cotton mill. Mills in Salem, Massachusetts and Salmon Falls, New Hampshire, and a machine shop and a bleachery ancillary to the textile trade, attracted another $77,500 of Perkins's capital.[6] All told, Perkins held over $800,000 in textiles and related stocks. It is safe to assume that a large share of Perkins's money in 1845 was invested in textiles, since, upon his demise nine years later, his fortune totaled $1.6 million.[7]

Born in Boston on December 15, 1764, Perkins had a knack for showing up wherever history was made.[8] He was a boy when he saw the frozen blood of the victims of the Boston Massacre in the street. At age twelve he heard the Declaration of Independence, fresh off the presses, read publicly in Boston in July 1776. He departed what is now Haiti a few years before the slave rebellion there, but his brothers who remained behind wrote letters to him with the news. Perkins was in China when the ship *Columbia* arrived. It was the first U.S. ship to circumnavigate the globe. Doing business in Europe during the French Revolutionary Wars, Perkins dined most Saturdays in Paris with the U.S. ambassador and future president James Monroe (he was quite taken with Mrs. Monroe). He agreed to smuggle Lafayette's son out of France and into the U.S. after the Marquis fell afoul of the French Revolution and found himself in an Austrian prison. Perkins was in Paris to see heads fall into the baskets as the guillotine did its business. And he saw and did all of this before he turned thirty-one.

Perkins's grandfather had been a fur trader. His mother Elizabeth (Peck) Perkins was a successful merchant with international contacts. His father James Perkins had a checkered career as a joiner and then as a merchant, selling oil, fish, gunpowder, and Native American slaves. On occasion, James Perkins found himself on the wrong side of the law. He was arrested for breaking and entering but acquitted. On another occasion, he was convicted of passing counterfeit money and fined accordingly. Thomas Perkins was eight years old when his father died, leaving a large family about £350, most of it in merchandise, and one "Negro woman valued at less than £27."[9]

At age 21, he collected an inheritance from his grandfather, the fur trader, and traveled to Saint-Domingue. Thomas's brother James was employed by a merchant house there and was trading on that island. Saint-Domingue's major products were sugar and coffee for European and North American tables produced by armies of slave laborers. Cotton cultivation to supply Britain's mills was another cash crop. When the Perkinses began to do business of their own in Saint-Domingue, the French colony was the habitation of 37,000 Europeans and 425,000 African slaves, while the island imported slaves at a precipitous clip of greater than 40,000 per year in this era.[10] The mortality rate among slaves was higher than in the U.S. contributing to the brisk demand.[11]

When the Perkins brothers co-founded the firm of Perkins, Burling & Perkins in 1786, one of their first moves was to enter the island's slave trade. A letter from Thomas Perkins to Daniel Sargent of Boston, dated July 27, 1786, states, "We have already made some advances in establishing…a place for the disposition of slaves in this quarter as will be attended with safety & advantage to the proprietors."[12]

The Perkinses sold slaves from one Caribbean port to another, a business the Perkins brothers claimed they were "particularly well situated to effect."[13] The Perkinses were middlemen in the slave trade. They would meet ships on their arrival in Saint-Domingue from the African Coast and buy slaves on spec or per the orders of third parties. They would then hold the slaves pending sale.[14] The Baker Library at Harvard University holds the papers of Samuel Cabot, Jr. who, much later, became a partner in one of the many incarnations of the Perkins firm. Among these documents is an account for the most notorious of slave ships: *Amistad*.[15] This ship was traveling from Havana to another Cuban port when slaves seized control of the vessel.[16]

Thomas Perkins returned to Boston in 1788 and another brother, Samuel, took his place in the firm. Thomas turned his interests toward trade in Asia, but he partnered with his brother James again in 1792. They became Boston agents for a shipowner named Daniel McNeill who owned several vessels plying the slave trade between Africa and the Caribbean, and between several West Indies ports.[17]

The following letter from the Perkins company files alludes to the trans-Caribbean transportation and sale of slaves. It draws an image of the matter-of-fact transactions of the slave trade in this period.

October 6, 1792

To Perkins, Burling & Co.:

This money you will appropriate to the purchase of the Slaves & other articles specifi'd in the enclosed Memo. (for us as agents of Dan'l McNiel [sic] from the Cape [in Haiti] to Havanna [sic] & from there here). If you cannot readily buy the Slaves in the road, we hope you will find some new Negroes from on shore, who know nothing of the language, and will answer to admit the vessel....We are to fit out his vessel (Brig' *Katy*) for the Coast, & send a number of vessels to take away the Molasses he has consigned to us: they will take the Cape on their way, in "order to get the Slaves for admission." For this business we are to receive 5% on outfit, & 5 on sales.[18]

The brig *Katy* never made it to its destination after loading up with slaves. It went down into the sea sometime in 1793 and was lost. The ship had a capacity of approximately 130 slaves, and these enslaved people along with the crew of the *Katy* suffered a silent death beneath the ocean.[19] Another document from the Perkins letters, addressed to Samuel Perkins, mentions the loss of the *Katy* most casually.

1793

To S. G. Perkins:

If you cou'd buy more Slaves at 150 or 200 dollars, such for instance as went down in the *Katy*, & charter a vessel to take them down to Havanna, all on a/c [account] of the *Sachem*, it w'd do well....They are worth 250 to 270 Ds.[20]

McNeill most likely penned the following 1792 memo from the Perkins company papers addressing a Captain Robert Adamson. Adamson was master of McNeill's vessel the *Willing Quaker* bound for Africa for slaves. McNeill gives detailed instructions for the proper selection and "handling" of the human cargo.

He is to take care that they [the slaves] are *young & healthy, without any defects* in their Limbs, Teeth & Eyes, & as few females as possible. Every attention is to be paid them that they are *well fed, well used, kept clean & dry*. For if once they get disheartened they will *die like Sheep. Suffer no person to strike them on any account*, & always keep your men Slaves in Irons, & see the Gratings Locked at Sunset...[P]roceed to Surinam & there dispose of your Women Slaves....[I]f you can get $50 a head you may dispose of the whole.[21]

McNeill also wrote a letter accompanying this voyage of the *Willing Quaker* to a personage he called King Nembana at Sierra Leone demanding "the balance due me of seven Slaves."[22]

To ply such a trade, it helped the merchants to have "ideas convenient to their business." These are the words of Joseph Ingraham, a ship's captain the Perkins firm engaged. He confessed to mixed feelings when he encountered a ship from Liverpool, then one of the world centers of the slave trade.[23] The captain of the British ship, bound for the African coast to transport 500 slaves, invited Ingraham to dinner. When the British captain offered the first toast to "the land of liberty," Ingraham perceived the irony.

"I could scarce conceal my feelings at hearing such a toast given on board a ship bound to enslave five hundred poor wretches," Ingraham confessed. "However, perhaps they possess'd ideas convenient to their business, which I have often witnessed in the West Indies, namely that Negroes were a lower order of Human beings, born to be slaves."[24]

Not everyone in that period shared ideas "convenient to their business," however. In 1788, the Massachusetts state legislature passed a law that was by no means ambiguous in its prohibition of the slave trade: "Whereas by the African Trade for Slaves, the lives and liberties of many innocent persons have been...sacrificed to the lust for gain...Be it therefore enacted" that no one, "either as master, factor, supercargo, owner, or hirer...cause to be imported or transported any of the inhabitants of any state or kingdom in that part of the world called Africa as slaves or servants."[25] Although the Perkins firm's trans-Caribbean slave commerce in the 1790s may have escaped illegality, its involvement in the transatlantic trade was in violation of the spirit of Massachusetts law. Havana, however, was far away and the firm evaded the law by sailing under colors other than the Stars and Stripes.[26]

Perkins and associates had an *instrumental* view of the law: it could be ignored at will or leveraged to commercial advantage. One scholar quipped, "the Perkinses felt that unfair laws demanded creativity, not obedience."[27] As for those who wrote and enforced the laws, in the words of Samuel Eliot Morison, the Eastern Massachusetts merchants looked at politics "as from the quarterdeck of an East-Indiaman" and regarded their elected representatives as "little more than their political chantey-men."[28] Perkins became close to "political chantey-men" of national stature. Later in his career, he would spend the night at Mount Vernon as a guest of George Washington. Perkins would also guide John Quincy Adams as the President toured the entrepreneur's railway and his granite quarry in the town of Quincy, Massachusetts. Perkins became *de facto* leader of the Massachusetts Federalist Party in the early 19th century and somehow found the time to serve as a state legislator. He received a nomination to serve his district in the U.S. House of Representatives but declined the honor. He also refused an appointment as Secretary of the Navy because his fleet was larger than the U.S. government's.[29]

The Massachusetts state law prohibiting the slave trade was a minor disincentive for Perkins. But when the slave rebellion broke out in Saint-Domingue, the Perkins's company there suffered a loss. The state's prohibition, as well as the slave rebellion, signaled that the "execrable commerce" in slaves, as Thomas Jefferson once termed it, was becoming too risky.[30] The slave trade in the West Indies was a side business for the Perkins firm and the wars of the French Revolution generated new opportunities for them.

But the commitment of the New England merchants to the slave trade was indirect as well. The West Indies were suppliers of consumer products and of raw materials for refinement, while they were also markets for New England produce. New England imported coffee and sugar, as well as molasses for distilling rum, while it exported fish consumed by slaves. The merchants were not alone in their dependence on this transatlantic economy. Artisans such as shipwrights, ropemakers, timbermen, nail makers, coopers, and others whose livelihood depended on the ships coming in and out of the region's ports from the West Indies, were enmeshed in the slave-labor economy.[31] Slave-based agriculture embedded itself in the entire Atlantic economy of the era.[32]

The West Indies adventures were formative for the Perkins brothers. The colonial powers on the islands had laws restricting trade, allegedly to the benefit of the mother countries. The Perkins firm's moves to evade these restrictions involved smuggling, bribery, and subterfuge, what historians have called "the shadow trade."[33] These "shadow" methods had been in the U.S. mercantile playbook since Colonial times, but Perkins and his generation were poised to take them global.[34]

The Merchant Princes and the Old China Trade

A global economy is nothing new. Before 1800, Boston merchants were doing business worldwide. Insurance rate quotations from 1796-97 show merchant vessels bound from Boston to the following locations: various European ports; the Cape of Good Hope; Isle de France (today's Mauritius); Medeira, Canaries, and Cape Verde Islands; Persia; India; China; Jamaica and other West Indies Islands; Nova Scotia and Newfoundland; Québec; New Orleans (not yet a part of the U.S.); Saint Augustine and the Bahamas; and United States ports.[35]

Immediately after the U.S. wrested its independence from Great Britain, merchants of Boston and other "United States ports" coveted the lucrative trade goods of China. Tea was the most important of these commodities, although silks, ceramics and other Asian goods were also prized. As early as 1788, Thomas Perkins served as a supercargo (i.e., a supervisor of the cargo) on board a ship bound for China.[36] Officially, foreigners in China could trade only through commissioned dealers, known as Hong merchants, in the port known to the English-speakers as Canton.

For the Boston merchants, the China trade entailed vast distances in both space and time. It required patience and capital. Only the savviest firms, such as the Perkins group, could afford to finance these lucrative voyages. But first U.S. merchants had to solve a problem: finding something they had that the Chinese wanted. While American consumers had an appetite for Chinese goods, the Middle Kingdom didn't have as much use for what the westerners were offering. For a time, New England ginseng proved popular. The Chinese believed it was an aphrodisiac. The merchants offered the East Asians cotton and varieties of exotic wood. The Perkins firm traded furs and skins from the Pacific Northwest at Canton, including prized sea otter pelts. For a period, the Perkins firm had a contract with the Montréal-based fur-trading concern, the Northwest Company, to carry its furs to China.[37] But soon that market became crowded and sea otter scarce.

What the Chinese *would* accept was cold, hard cash, i.e., silver. But the U.S. was poor in precious metals and merchants had to trade their goods in Britain or South America to gain the specie required for the

China trade. One strategy was to trade U.S. goods in Britain to purchase interest-bearing bills issued by London banks and redeemable in cash. The U.S. merchants then negotiated these bills in China. At last, U.S.-based merchants found a trade good for which there was a seemingly insatiable market in China: opium.[38] The best variety of that product, however, was grown in India and that was in the British Empire's sphere of influence. The British East India Company had a virtual monopoly on the opium trade, acting as an intermediary between India and China.

China prohibited the importation of opium in 1729 renewing its commitment to enforce the ban in 1811, but the British East India Company plied its trade surreptitiously.[39] They traded opium through allegedly independent merchants that afforded the company plausible deniability. There were also the established methods of "the shadow trade," smuggling and collusion with local officials. Looking for a way past the British monopoly, U.S. traders encouraged a new source of supply for the drug in Turkey. Consumers regarded the Turkish variety as inferior, but U.S. merchants managed to open a market for it in China beginning in 1804.[40] When the ship *Entan*, sailing out of Baltimore, carried about three tons of opium from Smyrna in western Turkey to Canton in 1805, an "opium rush" commenced.[41]

During the first years of the 19th century, the Perkins brothers established an office in Canton under the name of Perkins & Co. John Perkins Cushing, Thomas Perkins's teenage nephew, became the company's trusted representative in China. Shortly after Cushing's arrival at Canton, Perkins & Co. wrote to their young manager asking for "information respecting the article of Turkey Opium; its value in China, etc."[42]

The Perkins company acquired the drug through an agency based in Smyrna. Opium obtained in Turkey for around $2.50 per pound could sell for approximately $7 to $10 in China.[43] The Turkey-to-China trade had hardly started when it was interrupted by the War of 1812. In 1814, with the U.S. and Great Britain at war, a Perkins ship captured two British vessels carrying opium and headed for Canton. The Americans broke through a British blockade of the Chinese trading port and sold their captured cargo.[44] This incident marked a new phase of the China trade which would continue for decades.

Opium was not the only product Perkins and the other Boston merchants were trading in China, but its share grew by an order of magnitude. From only 2 to 4 percent of U.S. exports to China in the period between 1805 and 1807, opium stood at between 10 and 30 percent by 1816 to 1818.[45] The Perkins concern was, for a time, among the largest opium dealers in China. Perkins & Co. owned between 50 and 75 percent of the Turkish opium crop during some seasons, and its clout controlled the price for the U.S. traders at Canton.[46] On but one voyage the Perkins's ship the *Augusta* turned a profit of $50,000 carrying 120,000 pounds of Turkish opium.[47]

Some observers minimize the Northeastern merchants' role in the opium trade, arguing that it was small in percentage terms.[48] This argument fails to appreciate their engagement in the trade in its global context. In the opium trade, the U.S. faced its formidable competitor, Great Britain. In the early 19th century, the British Empire was the superpower. The United States was a small, promising experiment.

A few numbers make the case. In 1800, the U.S. conducted its second Federal Census. The year 1801 was a census year in Britain. These counts show that Great Britain had about twice the population of the United States, 10.5 vs. 5.3 million. London had a population of one million in 1801. Boston in 1800 was a village of 25,000. At the start of the 19th century, no U.S. city had one-tenth the population of London. In 1801, Liverpool (78,000) had a much larger population than the U.S.'s most populous city, New York (60,000 in 1800).

With its larger urban areas, expanding empire, and economic clout, one would expect to see the British dominate the American traders in most categories, especially in the opium trade given the East India Company's attempt to monopolize it. To the British merchants, their U.S. counterparts were like a mosquito on their flanks: tiny, but sufficiently persistent and annoying to distract the larger animal's attention. That the Americans had a share in it at all, and that it earned fortunes for influential individuals, are the salient facts, and not the relative size of the U.S. share of that market.

The Perkinses were by no means the only old money families involved in the opium trade. John Jacob Astor, a well-connected man associated with the fur trade and Manhattan real estate, was involved in the business, and introduced the drug to New York City. Warren Delano, Jr., President Franklin Roosevelt's grandfather, was an able opium trader. The Forbes, Peabody, Cushing, and Cabot families were also among these dealers.[49]

In 1829, one of these competitors, Russell & Company, acquired the Perkins firm in Canton and the merged entity became the largest U.S. opium dealer in China.[50] When Perkins & Co. at Canton counted its profits, they amounted to the precise figure of $1,127,432.49 for the partners. In 1831, John Perkins Cushing returned home with a personal fortune estimated at $700,000.[51] He invested the largest share of his China nest egg in New England's burgeoning textile industry.[52]

By investing in textile manufacturing, the Perkinses, Cabots, Lowells, and allied family firms created a way out of their dependence on risky overseas trades. Merchant capital, gained, directly or indirectly, in the Atlantic slave economy and in the China trade, provided the funds to establish the factories and to buy the raw cotton, grown increasingly on the plantations of the U.S. South.[53] Manufacturing would provide more steady returns than maritime trade; pooling capital would reduce risk.[54] As the 19th century wore on, smart money, like Perkins's, was betting on it.

CHAPTER TWO

A TEXTILE INDUSTRY FOR NEW ENGLAND

Just before Christmas 1807, President Thomas Jefferson signed into law *"An Act laying an Embargo on all ships and vessels in the ports and harbors of the United States."*[1] War consumed the two European superpowers, Great Britain and France, and the neutral U.S. was caught between them. At various times, both European powers tried to prevent U.S. merchant ships from supplying its rival, while Great Britain forced U.S. sailors into service on her ships. The U.S. responded by closing up shop.

The Embargo Act was no Christmas gift for the New England merchants. Their goods for export rotting in warehouses, the merchants had capital, but no place to put it. Unaccustomed to twiddling their thumbs, the Boston merchants in their counting houses on and around State Street had an opportunity to think. The fact that the U.S. was cut off from importing manufactured goods put a lightbulb over the heads of some of them: *"Why are we not manufacturing our own goods for our own markets?"*[2]

The U.S. had small factories run by skilled artisans but not on any scale to compete with England. But where there were corporations in the U.S., they tended to be in New England. In 1800, New England represented less than a quarter of the population of the U.S., but had nearly 60 percent of the country's corporations, although many of these firms were building infrastructure rather than manufacturing commodities.[3] In 1810, two Boston merchants named Francis Cabot Lowell and Nathan Appleton went to Great Britain where they would discover how the U.S. could compete with the mother country at her own game of manufacturing.

During the 18th century, Lancashire in Northern England became the center of a textile revolution. Britons such as James Hargreaves, Richard Arkwright, Samuel Crompton, and Edmund Cartwright invented and perfected machines that automated processes for spinning and weaving cotton into cloth.[4] Cartwright's water-powered loom was the most impressive of these innovations. By the end of the 18th century, Britain exported 61 percent of the cotton cloth she manufactured.[5] Cotton textile manufacturing dominated the U.K.'s economy into the late 19th century, and the owners made fortunes.[6]

From the worker's perspective, the mills in Lancashire and neighboring Cheshire merited the adjectives the poet William Blake used to modify them: *dark* and *satanic*. William Moran describes what Francis Cabot Lowell may have seen on his British junket: "Children, as well as adults, seized from poorhouses and forced to work. Others were recruited from the poverty-stricken masses living in the streets... Overseers wielding lashes forced the mill workers to labor until they dropped from exhaustion. The only escape was the pauper's grave."[7] Lowell, with a decent bone in his body, thought he could have the profits absent the brutality. He would create a kinder Lancashire in Massachusetts.

The British textile industrialists protected their technology and trade secrets by force of law. Lowell's wealth and prominence afforded him access to the inside of the English textile mills, but he could make no drawings or diagrams to take Stateside. The usual tale says that Lowell debriefed his associate Appleton on what he had seen, repeating what he had learned until he knew the textile operations and the workings of the machinery by heart.

Others were already working toward the idea of a domestic textile industry. Samuel Slater, bankrolled by Moses Brown, began work on a cotton yarn mill in Pawtucket, Rhode Island in 1790.[8] Local women working at home or in small shops wove this factory-produced yarn into cloth. This procedure of "putting out work," as it was known, was later called the Slater System. Slater's mill was the first of many in the Blackstone River Valley region, a corner of New England not far from where the states of Massachusetts, Rhode Island, and Connecticut meet. In the 19th century, the Blackstone Valley would develop into a major Franco-American center.

The Brown family of Rhode Island was in the transatlantic slave trade, a specialty of the Union's smallest state. Moses Brown became a slavery opponent and attempted to dissuade other merchants from engaging in the trade.[9] His mills, under the aegis of Samuel Slater, made much use of child labor. Some sources claim that Slater's operations had dedicated "whipping rooms" where floor managers called "overseers" were known to beat children who weren't working hard enough.[10] You could take the traders out of the slave trade, but old habits persisted.

Francis Cabot Lowell and a small group of associates, however, had something more ambitious than Slater's mill in mind.

From Waltham to Lowell

On February 23, 1813, the Governor of Massachusetts approved "an Act to incorporate The Boston Manufacturing Company." Named in the act were Francis Cabot Lowell, Benjamin Gorham, Uriah Cotting, and Lowell's brother-in-law Patrick Tracy Jackson. Nathan Appleton, Israel Thorndike, and Israel Thorndike, Jr. were other men associated with the firm. The Boston Manufacturing Company was authorized "for the purpose of manufacturing Cotton, Woolen & linen goods, at Boston in the County of Suffolk, or within fifteen miles thereof."[11]

On September 4, 1813, an agreement was drawn up "between the Associates of the Boston Manufacturing Company," dividing the firm's stock into 100 shares. Five men – Lowell, Jackson, the two Israel Thorndikes, and Appleton – owned half the company.

"It is proposed to make weaving at first, the principal object of attention," this same agreement notes.

> From some experiments which have been made it is believed that this important part of manufacturing, can be performed wholly by water, at much less expense than the usual manner, & that a very considerable

number of looms might be employed in weaving cloths for other factories. Connected with this it is supposed that the spinning of cotton, & woolen yarns, will be found profitable.

The company found its water power on the Charles River in nearby Waltham, Massachusetts and built a brick mill there by 1814. The Waltham mill became the first integrated factory in the U.S., containing under a single roof the complete range of textile manufacturing operations. Raw materials entered, and finished goods exited.

Treasurer was the key title in the company. An agreement of the Boston Manufacturing Company of October 1814 defined this executive's role. The agreement empowered the Treasurer to receive and pay all monies, make contracts, incur debts, and make purchases on the company's behalf, including buying and selling stock. In addition to managing "the pecuniary concerns" of the company, the Treasurer was to "superintend & regulate" the "general affairs of the company." The Treasurer reported to the company directors.

As the New England textile industry evolved, it was standard practice for the Treasurer to reside in Boston while an official called an Agent, living near the factory, managed the day-to-day affairs of the mill. In modern parlance, the Treasurer was the Chief Executive Officer (CEO) while the resident Agent was the Chief Operating Officer (COO).[12]

By 1815, the Waltham factory was in full operation. In its first seven years, sales rose from $3,000 to $345,000.[13] The firm improved upon the technology and operations Lowell had seen in England. Increased operational efficiency allowed the company to lower its prices and the market grew. Stockholders received annual dividends that ran from 8 to 28 percent.[14]

The success of the Waltham mill became the matrix of the *Boston Associates*, a shorthand historians use for an aggregation of investors who came to dominate the textile industry. Economic historian Winifred Barr Rothenburg quantifies the web of interests woven by this small group of businessmen in the three decades after the founding of the Boston Manufacturing Company:

By 1845, the Boston Associates would become 80 men with interests in 31 textile companies controlling one-fifth of the total capacity of the American textile industry. Meanwhile, seventeen of them would serve as directors of seven Boston banks commanding over 40 percent of the city's authorized banking capital, twenty would be directors of six insurance companies carrying 41 percent of the state's marine insurance and 77 percent of its fire insurance, and eleven members would serve on the boards of five railroads operating in New England.[15]

The Boston Associates acquired their capital in much the same businesses in which Perkins earned his: the West Indies and China trades. Earlier in his career, Francis Cabot Lowell was involved in overseas trade with China, India, and Europe, often dealing in the New England stand-bys of fish, timber, and flour. He ran a rum distillery importing molasses from the Caribbean, a hypotenuse of the triangle trade. He speculated on land in Maine, and, with Uriah Cotting, led the development of Boston's India Wharf. The India Wharf construction project created a new infrastructure for the city including a sea wall, a long wharf, and a warren of stores and warehouses.[16] As the name implies, India Wharf was designed to funnel the wealth of the Indies onto the shores of Massachusetts. Asia acted in the 19th century with the same magnetic pull that caused Columbus to sail west centuries prior.

Before the Revolution, Israel Thorndike partnered with Moses Brown trading in textiles and fishing gear.[17] When the Revolutionary War came, Brown & Thorndike were the second largest investors in privateers at Beverly, Massachusetts during the American Revolution.[18] The partners were also players in the China trade and other Asian ventures. Both partners served in the Massachusetts legislature. Later in his career, Thorndike reportedly had more of his money placed in manufacturing than any other investor.[19]

Patrick Tracy Jackson was engaged in both the West and East Indies trade. Lowell's close associate Nathan Appleton began his career in partnership with his brother, buying goods in Boston at auction and selling them to country merchants.[20] The brothers then expanded into European trade during the Napoleonic Wars. Appleton later served the industrialists' interests in the state and federal legislatures. His success in the textile industry enabled him to act as a patron to his son-in-law, the poet Henry Wadsworth Longfellow, who made the Deportation of the Acadians the subject of his celebrated *Evangeline*.

Paul Moody, working closely with Lowell, shared the credit for many of the operational improvements in the Waltham mill. Moody was one of a succession of men with mechanical skills and experience who operationalized the Boston investors' capital. Moody learned how to weave as a young man and worked in a nail factory as well as in a wool mill. He was a machinist in New Hampshire and Maine before he established a cotton mill in partnership with several others at Amesbury, Massachusetts. Coming to Waltham at the founding of the Boston Manufacturing Company facility there, it was Moody who set up the machinery at the factory and who patented many improvements on the designs Lowell had stored in his cranium in England.[21]

Cut off from commerce with Britain by the War of 1812, following on the heels of the Embargo Act, the domestic textile industry flourished. When peace came, the goods stored in British warehouses during the war flooded the market, and U.S. textile firms faced devastating competition. The glut of cheap goods was deliberate. British manufacturers intended to strangle the infant U.S. textile industry in its cradle.[22]

Lowell supported a steep tariff imposed on imported textiles to protect U.S. competitors from the free market. He traveled to Washington, D.C. to lobby for the optimal tariff.[23] The formula he supported, passed by Congress in 1816, protected cheaper cotton goods, mainly coarser fabrics, while allowing the British to have the market in finer, more expensive products. Scholars debate the efficacy of the tariff.[24] Whether it produced the desired effect or not, Lowell and his supporters intended to shelter the fledgling textile industry's chosen market segment behind a government-mandated fortress.

Safely protected by Washington, the Boston Associates built on their success in Waltham. They made plans to harness the water power of the Merrimack River at East Chelmsford, Massachusetts. The Merrimack had sufficient water power to fuel many mills and sustain an entire textile town to weave profits out of cotton and wool. Lowell died in 1817 and didn't live to see a new Lancashire rise on the Merrimack.[25] Appleton and Jackson took the lead in developing the prototypical mill town named for their deceased partner: *Lowell*.[26] By 1839, nine textile manufacturing firms were operating out of Lowell.[27]

Lowell and his associates did not believe that the U.S. would develop a permanent working class, as in England, where workers spent their entire lives toiling in the mills.[28] In his memoirs, Patrick Tracy Jackson described the labor policy at Lowell: "The business could...be conducted without any permanent manufacturing population." Jackson noted that the *operatives*, as the line workers were called, did not "form a separate caste, pursuing a sedentary employment, from parent to child, in the heated rooms of a factory; but are recruited, in a circulating current, from the healthy and virtuous population of the country."[29]

The Era of the Mill Women

Young, single women, from the farms of New England, formed the "healthy and virtuous" current that flowed through the Lowell mills. Spinning and weaving had been a traditional role for women at least since Homer's Penelope wove during the day and unraveled her work by night. Wherever there was yarn, at home or in a factory, it was often women who were spinning and weaving it. By 1827, 90 percent of the operatives in the Lowell mills were women.[30] Most were from 16 to 25 years old, born in the United States, white-identified, Protestant, and literate.[31] As a rule, a woman would work in the mills for no more than five years, long enough to earn a dowry, or help pay down a mortgage on the family farm, or to send a brother to school.[32]

As late as 1845, a local historian of Lowell confirmed that Jackson's "circulating current" still flowed. He claims that the textile workforce in Lowell continued to consist of young women "well educated in virtuous rural homes." This observer also states that Lowell had "no permanent factory population" referring to this fact as a "wide gulf which separates the English manufacturing towns" from their Massachusetts counterpart.[33]

The mill masters built tenements to house their overwhelmingly female workforce. In many cases, an older woman chaperoned the tenants. The mill owners enforced a strict code of conduct. A Congressional Report written in the early 20th century describes the mill owners' attempt to "make the factories resemble, as closely as possible, big boarding schools." Chaperones kept tabs on the employees' "general conduct" and made sure they attended "public worship" on Sunday at the Protestant church of their choice. [34]

Lowell offered opportunities for education and edification to the factory women. Eminences such as Ralph Waldo Emerson and John Quincy Adams lectured to the so-called "mill girls" at Lowell.[35] Presidents Andrew Jackson and John Tyler had to come in person to see the factory town of Lowell and its distaff workforce.[36] "They are very pretty women, by the Eternal!" exclaimed Old Hickory.[37] Charles Dickens also visited and judged Lowell to be most un-Dickensian.[38]

Harriet Hanson Robinson wrote a memoir of her life as a mill operative in 19th century Lowell. She portrays the young women as well-informed, as they debated the events of the day: "By reading the weekly newspapers the girls became interested in public events; they knew all about the Mexican war, and the anti-slavery cause had its adherents among them."[39] Producers as well as consumers of the written word, the young women of the looms published a literary magazine called the *Lowell Offering*.

Robinson also cites a Harvard professor's opinion of the bookish factory operatives, published in the *Atlantic Monthly*:

> During the palmy days of *The Lowell Offering* I used every winter to lecture for the Lowell Lyceum....The Lowell Hall was always crowded, and four-fifths of the audience were factory girls. When the lecturer entered, almost every girl had a book in her hand, and was intent upon it. When he rose, the book was laid aside, and paper and pencil taken instead....I have never seen anywhere so assiduous note-taking...as in that assembly of young women, laboring for their subsistence.[40]

Powered by its young women and its falling water, the textile industry expanded rapidly. It became a feeding frenzy, not unlike Silicon Valley in our day.[41] By 1840, Lowell had the second largest population in the state. Investors had put eight million dollars into the town's textile mills by that year, and this sum would increase to twelve million by 1850.[42]

The jutting, Northeastern corner of the U.S., cut into six small states by 1820, began to market its cotton goods all over the world. At last, East Coast merchants found a domestic product that even China coveted: cotton textiles woven by women from the farmsteads of rural New England.[43] Waterville, Lewiston, and Biddeford, Maine; Manchester and Nashua, New Hampshire; Burlington and Winooski, Vermont; Fall River, Chicopee, and Lawrence, Massachusetts; Woonsocket, Pawtucket, and Central Falls, Rhode Island; Thompson, Putnam, and Norwich, Connecticut, wherever a river could turn a waterwheel, a mill town sprang up from the villages of stony New England.

The industry's diffusion was not the work of the Boston Associates alone. In 1810, before Lowell's success in Waltham, there were already 269 cotton mills in the U.S., and not all of them were in New England.[44] Businesses the Associates built from the ground up, as in Waltham and Lowell, were more exceptional than usual. Disputing the contention that cotton manufacturing began near Boston and emanated from there, French historian François Weil emphasizes "the importance of local dynamism to regional industrial development" in New England in the earlier 19th century. "The growth in the number of cotton-manufacturing companies...was not brought about by a single group of Boston capitalists," writes Weil. "Instead, industrial development was the work of investment networks that were initially local."[45]

The Waltham mill was not the first U.S. cotton mill, but the operations on the Charles and the Merrimack, with their automation and integrated operations, boarding houses, and cash wages paid, were a watershed. As the industry matured in the second third of the 19th century, Lowell became a model and Boston capital gobbled up the locals, especially to the city's west and north.

Why New England?

By the mid-19th century, New England was the most intensively industrialized part of the country. The neighboring Mid-Atlantic region of the U.S. had three times New England's population by the century's midpoint. And yet New England "had invested 75 percent more capital, employed 75 percent more workers, and produced 45 percent more output per manufacturing firm than the Mid-Atlantic."[46] Cotton textiles led the charge. By 1860, cotton goods were the U.S.'s largest industry in terms of "capital invested, workers employed, and net value of its product."[47]

The merchants' liquid capital was a driver of New England's rapid industrialization. The merchants were able to manage risk and organize complex long-term business operations. With its economy based on trade, the Embargo and "Mr. Madison's War" of 1812 hit coastal New England particularly hard. That gave a segment of the region's merchants a strong motive to pivot from trade to industry.

Geography helped. Most of the mills were near the coast or on nearby rivers making it relatively easy to bring raw materials in and ship product out. New England also had an abundant energy source. The same rocky, rambling terrain that made New England less suitable for agriculture than the South or Midwest also gave these regions many rivers with waterfalls harnessed to power the mills. Some scholars argue that it wasn't the rivers. Other parts of the U.S. also had them. The difference maker for New England was the concentration of technological and managerial know-how, during the extended period throughout the 19th century, when the industry was innovating most rapidly.[48]

Finally, New England had the labor force: the young women. The traditional role for young women on the farm in New England was to spin and weave yarn, and to make candles and other crafts. Mass-produced goods in a market economy began to replace these home handicrafts.[49] Industrialism built on itself by disrupting the role of young women on the farm, which in turn encouraged them to fill manufacturing jobs in the growing textile industry. Educated, single women, with a diminishing rural role, seized their opportunity when the mill towns offered them the chance for adventure and some power in the market. Robinson's memoir speaks to the attraction that financial independence and intellectual stimulation had for the era's women.[50] When there was a viable alternative to life on the farm, they were drawn into the factory towns.[51]

These early factories were labor intensive. That meant the mills needed the women more than the women needed the mills and this explains the relatively civilized conditions of factory life before 1845.

"Help was too valuable to be ill-treated," wrote Robinson.[52] Families were usually not dependent on the women's wages, and the mill women were neither as poverty-stricken nor as desperate as immigrant factory workers of a later generation. And yet, on average women were paid less than men. New England had its sufficient, domestic cheap labor pool. The search for alternate sources of inexpensive labor would preoccupy the textile industry until the end of its New England-dominated phase in the 1920s.

New England, and specifically the Boston Associates, had another important asset: Daniel Webster.[53] An icon of eloquence, Webster was the lawyer's lawyer. Originally from New Hampshire, and a product of its Dartmouth College, Webster served that state in the U.S. House of Representatives. At Francis Cabot Lowell's behest, Webster relocated to Boston, eventually establishing himself south of the city in the town of Marshfield. Thomas Perkins's name topped the brief list of signatures on an 1822 letter offering Webster the nomination for Boston's district in the U.S. House of Representatives.[54] This letter marked the beginning of his illustrious career of service to the Bay State. Webster served Massachusetts as a lion of the U.S. Senate for a generation. He was twice Secretary of State and a perennial Presidential contender – the latter, at least, in his own mind.

Webster was also an attorney for the Boston Associates and pressed their interests in Washington. The Senator supported their tariffs and argued their cases in court. Webster's services in the interest of the Boston merchants were priceless, but the merchants weren't shy about putting a price on them. Perpetually in financial trouble, the Boston merchants were happy to aid the Senator known as "Black Dan" in exchange for services rendered.[55]

Webster represented the Associates before the Spanish and French Claims Commissions. The Spanish commission (1821-1824) settled claims arising from French and Spanish depredations against U.S. shipping and other property during the undeclared war with France (1798-1800). The French Claims Commission (1831) was convened to settle similar grievances against France arising from the Napoleonic Wars. In the case of the Spanish commission, the U.S. government agreed to assume the claims against Spain up to a limit of $5 million. Webster was paid five cents on every dollar he recouped for the businessmen he represented. The commission granted the Boston Associates or Associate-controlled insurance companies about 20 percent of the total sum paid by the government on these claims, a transfer of public money into private hands. If the round figure of a million dollars paid to the Associates is correct, then Black Dan came away with $50,000.[56]

There was a spike in capital investment in the Lowell textile mills concurrent with the disbursements from the Spanish and French Claims Commissions. There is no way to prove that the monies disbursed to the merchants by these commissions were invested in Lowell, but these funds may have liberated capital that found its way into the industry.[57]

But the importance of governments to the development of the U.S. textile industry goes beyond individual deals or individual senators. Sven Beckert's work shows that industrial economies in general, and the cotton textile industry in particular, depend on strong, responsive states and they developed first only under such governments. Governments chartered the corporations. Corporations depended on the State's legal superstructure to protect their private property rights, including their intellectual property, and to enforce their contracts. Governments invested in transportation infrastructures that enabled commerce and in education systems, like the public schools that tutored the women who published the *Lowell Offering*. Modern, centralized states, characterized by the rule of law, were not passive containers for industrial societies. They enabled them.[58]

Service to the fledgling U.S. Government built fortunes for some Boston merchants. The Cabot family became one of New England's wealthiest by fighting the U.S. Congress's war on the high seas as a private navy in the Revolutionary War. Members of the family then invested this fortune in one of New England's earliest attempts at cotton manufacturing. After Lowell's success, a subsequent generation of Cabots, in association with the Perkins group, entered the textile game. They fed the growth of the town of Lowell and acquired a portfolio of mills throughout New England. The mills controlled by this line of Cabots became magnets attracting to New England generations of workers from Québec.

CHAPTER THREE

ENTER THE CABOTS

A line of the renowned Cabot family of Massachusetts descends from the progenitor John Cabot (1680-1742), through his son Joseph (1720-1767), and then through the generations of Francis (1757-1832), Frederick (1786-1869), and then another Francis (1825-1905). Although not nearly as well-known as the likes of their distant cousin, Francis Cabot Lowell, this line of the Cabots would become proconsuls in the Empire of Cotton.

The founder of this house, John Cabot, was born on the Channel Island of Jersey and came to Salem, Massachusetts in 1700, eight years after that colonial settlement's notorious witch trials. John Cabot founded the mercantile tradition of the family, at least on the western side of the Atlantic. This Cabot married his sons off to other merchants of Salem and built the foundations of a dynasty.[1]

Before the American Revolution, the Cabots of the North Shore of Massachusetts, first at Salem and then at Beverly, engaged in the unglamorous activity of exporting local produce while importing finished goods, such as textiles, iron, and cordage. They traded their imports at retail or wholesale.[2] Slaves were among the "commodities" the Cabots traded in the 18th century. In Hugh Thomas's detailed tome on the slave trade, the Cabots are one of only six Boston-area families he implicates by name as merchants in the transatlantic slave trade.[3]

Having relocated from Salem to Beverly before the Revolutionary War, the sons of Joseph Cabot operated under the company name of

J. & A. Cabot. These Cabots were trading chiefly with Spain, exporting fish from New England and occasionally rice from Charleston or tobacco from Virginia.[4] Undistinguished merchants in the colonial epoch, the sons of Joseph Cabot, especially Andrew, John, and George, made the first, substantial family fortune as privateers in the long war for independence that followed the hostilities at Lexington and Concord.[5]

Privateers were armed vessels with a government commission, called a letter of marque, authorizing the bearer to seize enemy merchant ships and sell their cargos, and often the ship itself, for profit. The owners took the greatest share of these prizes, with the officers and crews of the ship as well as the government taking a piece of the proceeds.[6] Special courts adjudicated the prizes and parceled out the booty to those who could prove they had a claim to it. Both Congress and state legislatures authorized privateers. The Massachusetts government began licensing such vessels as early as November 1775.[7]

Privateers made up the bulk of the infant U.S.'s armed, seafaring presence during the War of Independence. Between 1776 and 1782, the Continental Navy sailed no more than 34 ships in any one year.[8] No less than 350 privateers sailed from Essex County, Massachusetts alone.[9] The Cabots of Beverly had an ownership stake in at least 41 such vessels.[10]

The Cabot's ship the *Franklin* sailing out of Salem is an example of the scale and activities of a privateer of the era. This vessel of two hundred tons had a crew of one hundred men and sported eighteen mounted guns. On the 17th of November 1778, the *Franklin* seized a vessel capturing about 300 pounds of fish. On the 21st of the same month, the American privateer seized an English ship bound for Antigua capturing a load of "dry goods." On the 25th, she took yet another British prize of unknown cargo.[11] The revenues of shipowners, captains, and crews alike depended on remaining active, alert, and belligerent.

As a *de facto* ship of war, risks and rewards were great. A prize could earn £20,000 pounds and up to £30,000 if gold were aboard but more than half the ships privateers seized, the British recaptured.[12] A contemporary named Trumbull, sailing into Beverly aboard the Cabot's privateer the *Cicero*, reported seeing eleven other ships owned by the Cabots moored there, all of which were captured or destroyed within a year.[13] The risks were far greater than losing a prize or a ship. While the official U.S. Navy lost 832 seamen in the war, the small seaport town of Newburyport, Massachusetts alone lost 1,000 men at sea in privateering.[14] But the Cabots were undaunted, and the shipwrights of the North Shore were industrious.

In some cases, governments compensated privateers for their losses, at least in part. When some Cabot-owned vessels participated in the catastrophic engagement against the British on the Penobscot River in Maine in 1779, the State of Massachusetts agreed to reimburse the owners.[15] The state's compensation allowed Andrew Cabot to purchase, at a reduced price, land owned by the Oliver family, Loyalists to the British crown from Cambridge, Massachusetts who had fled to Halifax.[16]

"The wealth acquired by the Cabots from privateering was reputed at the time to be very large and caused bitter envy in some quarters," writes Cabot family historian L. Vernon Briggs.[17] Deracinated Tories were galled. In 1780, a certain Samuel Curwen, a Salem Tory who escaped the rebellious colonies for England, wrote to a fellow exile in Wales: "It is a melancholy truth that while some are *wallowing* in undeserved wealth that plunder and rapine have thrown into their hands, the wisest, most peaceable and most deserving are suffering want...The Cabots of Beverly, who, you know, had but five years ago a very moderate share of property, are now said to be *by far the most wealthy* in New England."[18]

Briggs cites "shrewdness and natural ability" as the essential qualities in the Cabot's wartime success.[19] The Cabots tended to have two other characteristics that made their first fortune and were no less vital to their subsequent enterprises: a strong stomach for risk and *sang-froid* in acts of aggression. They were dogged in pursuing an advantage despite setbacks. There was always a silver lining for the Cabots, except when there was a gold lining.

The First Cabot Mill

The connection between the Cabots and cotton dates to the earliest attempts at textile manufacturing in the U.S., even before Francis Cabot Lowell's adventures. In 1788, the Cabots invested their privateer profits, as well as their post-war gains from overseas trade, in a factory to manufacture cotton cloth. John, Andrew, and George Cabot, along with Lowell's future associate, Israel Thorndike, were stockholders in a corporation known as the Beverly Cotton Manufactory.

As per usual for the Massachusetts merchants, these men were politically connected. Several among them had served in the Massachusetts legislature. George Cabot represented the Bay State in the U.S. Senate from 1791 to 1796 and was a friend of both President Washington and Secretary of the Treasury Alexander Hamilton.[20] In 1789, Washington himself visited Beverly to inspect the cotton mill.[21]

Unfortunately for the Cabot group, lack of skilled labor, unfamiliarity with the technology, and other difficulties drove the enterprise into the red. In a letter to Hamilton of September 1791, George Cabot itemized a loss to the firm of $10,000. On March 16, 1790, Cabot sent a petition to the U.S. Congress requesting "the patronage of Government to their undertaking, and that an additional impost may be laid on the importation of cotton goods."[22] Nothing much came from this petition. The Cabots and associates turned to the Massachusetts government which granted them indirect aid in the form of land and lottery tickets for the sale of land that covered about $4,000 of the corporation's loss.[23]

From the very beginnings of U.S. manufacturing, businesses turned to governments for a bail-out, or some form of aid, when markets didn't behave as they wished. They did not hesitate to call on government power to hedge against risk or to tilt a market in their favor. The relationship with Washington would last for ages after the Cabot group gave up on the Beverly experiment in 1798 and sold the operation.[24]

Francis Cabot: From Salem to Natchez

Francis Cabot, George Cabot's younger brother, was just 19 years old when the thirteen colonies declared their independence from Great Britain, but he joined his brothers in their wartime ventures. Francis Cabot was a part owner of the *Pilgrim*, one of the most successful of the privateers, as well as other such vessels including the *Franklin* and the *Spanish Packet*.[25]

Francis Cabot was born on June 14, 1757, in Salem.[26] He moved to Beverly with his family in 1768. After the Revolutionary War, Daniel Shays led a farmer's rebellion in the rural, western part of Massachusetts. Francis Cabot held the rank of Major under Revolutionary War hero Benjamin Lincoln in the resistance to Shays' uprising. Francis Cabot would also serve in the modest capacity of Private under General Andrew Jackson at the Battle of New Orleans in the War of 1812.

In 1780, Francis Cabot married Anna Clarke, also known as Nancy, who gave birth to five children. The first U.S. Federal Census in 1790 finds Francis Cabot back at Salem, where he was a sales agent for the products of his brothers' cotton mill.[27] Nancy Clarke Cabot died young, in 1788. Francis left his children in the care of their grandparents and departed for what was then called Federal City, now known as Washington, D.C. In October 1791, Cabot bought a lot in the new capital at the first public sale of lands, but appears to have struggled to find a place for himself there.[28]

His former commander Benjamin Lincoln wrote a letter to President Washington on Cabot's behalf dated June 10, 1791. Lincoln recommends Cabot to Washington for an "opening in the public line." Lincoln mentions Cabot's service as his aide during Shays' Rebellion and vouches for him as "a Gentleman of a respectable family, brother to Mr [George] Cabot one of our Senators in Congress."[29]

Apparently, the Father Of His Country was unable to help Cabot find a government position since Cabot moved to Philadelphia by 1793. Sometime after 1795, he moved again to Natchez, a settlement founded by the *Canadien* Jean-Baptiste Le Moyne de Bienville as *Fort Rosalie*, in what became Mississippi. There Cabot plied his merchant's trade until his death in 1832. During Cabot's tenure there, Thomas Perkins's partner in the West Indies trade, Walter Burling, brought a superior strain of cotton from Mexico that would make Natchez a center of the Cotton Kingdom.[30] By the time of Francis Cabot's death, Natchez was dependent on the cotton economy and on the slaves who grew and harvested the white gold.

Frederick Cabot and the Turn Toward Textile Manufacturing

It was up to the next generation of Cabots to take the promise of the Beverly cotton factory, and of the raw cotton coming through points south, and turn it into profits. Frederick Cabot, Francis and Nancy Cabot's son, was born on February 20, 1786, in Salem. He was no more than two years old when his mother died and still a small boy when his father left the family for southern adventures. John and Sarah (Pickering) Clarke, his maternal grandparents, raised Frederick Cabot.

By age 21, Frederick joined the drift of the family from the Massachusetts North Shore toward Boston. He began his professional career as a merchant in the state capital operating under the firm name of Cabot & Lee with offices on Kilby Street.[31] The Lee in question was Frederick's cousin. Into the 1820s, Frederick worked with various partners importing dry goods, mainly from Great Britain, and selling them on commission. At this date, in the U.S. context, "dry goods" meant chiefly textiles or items made of them. Dry goods were a third major category of commodity in addition to groceries and hardware.

Frederick Cabot began his professional life in a niche not dissimilar to that which his forbears had occupied in Salem before the Revolutionary War: importing manufactured goods and selling them at retail or wholesale. His experience in the sales end of the textile business – his knowledge of the numerous types and qualities of cloth and their various markets – would serve him well when he entered the manufacturing side of the trade in the 1820s.

The firm of Cabot & Lee lasted until about 1816 where the Boston Directory shows Frederick doing business on his own out of a new location on Broad Street.[32] By 1817, Cabot had partnered with another

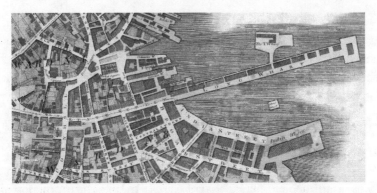

FIGURE 2: Detail from a map of Boston in 1814 at the beginning of Frederick Cabot's career, showing India Wharf (bottom right), as well as India, State, Broad, Central and Kilby Streets. (Map reproduction courtesy of the Norman B. Leventhal Map Center at the Boston Public Library)

cousin, Edward Clarke. The new firm dealt their dry goods out of Market Street.[33] By 1820, the firm of Cabot & Clarke moved to 4 Central Street, which intersected with India Street, providing access to India Wharf on the Boston waterfront.[34]

On October 23, 1821, Frederick Cabot married his first cousin, Marianne Cabot, the daughter of Samuel Cabot, Sr. and the former Sally Barrett. The endogamous link back to the Samuel Cabots was a union between a moderately prosperous and a very prosperous branch of the same family. The Cabots had a knack for marrying into money, even if that meant marrying another Cabot.[35]

From the early days in Salem, kinship networks fostered commercial alliances among the Cabots and other members of the merchant class. Sibling exchanges – for example a brother and a sister from one family marrying a brother and a sister from another – and marriages to cousins of one degree or another, were a means of creating class solidarity. Such unions also kept fortunes within families and allowed less wealthy branches to maintain their financial position.[36]

Through these kinship bonds, as well as socializing institutions such as Harvard, the wealthy merchant class formed a compact, self-conscious social unit that protected the group's economic and social capital. Terms used to describe these networks, such as *Essex*

Junto, the *Boston Associates*, or *Boston Brahmins* were means of designating, from different perspectives, in different generations, much the same group of families. Such terms captured the cohesion of this group, their self-sameness and their tendency to act in concert.

Boston was a small town where the same relatively small number of families dominated trade, politics, finance, philanthropy, and the professions. The era's notion of conflict of interest was murky. The Perkins group, for example, was a hydra with many heads, running multiple entities with relationships to one another. Perkins managed the corporation that built the Bunker Hill monument in the Boston neighborhood of Charlestown. He also led the company that quarried the stone for the project, and he was the founder of the railroad that carried the stone to the building site. Thus, Perkins was a contractor for the monument project; he was a supplier for that contractor, while he was also the customer for both services. This didn't seem out of order in 19th century Boston.

This network of merchant families also spent lavish sums on medical, charitable, and educational institutions. Perkins contributed to Boston's Museum of Fine Arts, the Boston Athenaeum, Maclean's psychiatric hospital, Massachusetts General Hospital, and his eponymous Perkins School for the Blind, all of which still exist. Wealth was not only for personal edification or enjoyment, the descendants of the Puritans believed, but also for the endowment of institutions that survive the individual and serve the community.

Contrary to stereotype, which would portray Boston's as the most exclusive and impenetrable upper class in the urban Northeast, in practice the city's "society" was porous. Members of wealthy families from modest beginnings were allowed to marry into the established merchant class. In other Northeastern centers such as New York City or Philadelphia, the equivalent class tended to become a fixed group of families over the course of the 19th century. Like an organism under the influence of natural selection, the Boston group retained enough cohesion from one generation to the next to maintain its features while it also incorporated useful mutations. The new blood helped the Brahmins to survive the economic, social, and political upheavals of the 19th and early 20th centuries and enabled Boston to maintain its economic and intellectual influence even as New York City eclipsed the Hub as the largest Northeastern port and financial center.[37]

By marrying his cousin, Frederick Cabot was drawn into the Samuel Cabot line, allied by marriage and in business, with Thomas Perkins. As a young bachelor, Frederick's cousin Samuel Cabot, Jr., had been working in Philadelphia while his mother back in Massachusetts served as his matchmaker. Mrs. Cabot eventually succeeded in marrying Samuel off to Perkins's daughter Eliza, the most eligible bachelorette in town. Samuel Cabot, Jr. then formed a company with the sons of James and Thomas Perkins called Cabot & Perkins. In 1820, Frederick Cabot's offices were a stone's throw from those of Cabot & Perkins at 31 India Wharf.[38]

Neither James nor Thomas Perkins, Sr. produced a suitable heir to the business. James, Jr. was an alcoholic. Thomas Perkins, Jr. was an eccentric and impulsive character. The son-in-law, rather than the son, proved his worth to the older generation of Perkinses.[39] Samuel Cabot, Jr. became his father-in-law's partner and *de facto* inheritor of the Thomas Perkins mantel. As Thomas Perkins, Sr. aged, Samuel Cabot, Jr. took on the day-to-day decision-making for the business.[40]

The Elliot Manufacturing Company

Frederick Cabot entered the manufacturing side of the textile market through the Cabot/Perkins family connection. His name appears along with those of Samuel Cabot and James Perkins in the June 12, 1823 act of the State legislature incorporating the Elliot Manufacturing Company, "for the purpose of manufacturing cotton goods" at Newton, Massachusetts.[41]

The Boston Directory throughout the 1820s continues to list Frederick Cabot as a dry goods merchant, in partnership with his cousin/brother-in-law Richard Clarke Cabot and William Whitney.[42] However, in this period Frederick became engaged in the business of textile manufacturing, first with the Perkins group at the Elliot mill, then in Lowell, and later in New Hampshire and Maine.

Thomas Perkins's father-in-law Simon Elliot owned several mills and factories on the Upper Falls of the Charles River in Newton, to

Boston's west. Perkins inherited a piece of this property after his father-in-law's death. In November 1814, the Perkins brothers purchased for $20,000 the share of the Elliot property owned by Thomas's brother-in-law, with its several buildings and water rights. The Perkins brothers intended to establish a cotton mill on the property, but they judged the business conditions unfavorable in the wake of the War of 1812. They did little with their holdings of 57 acres in Newton until the 1820s, when the Perkins associates established the Elliot Company.

The first officers elected by the directors of the company were Thomas Perkins, President; George H. Kuhn of Boston, Treasurer; and Frederick Cabot, resident Agent. The Perkins/Cabot group had a tall hurdle in their path – there is no evidence that any of them had a minute of experience running a textile mill. Perkins plunged into this new enterprise as he had earlier invested in an ironworks in Vergennes, Vermont despite having little knowledge of iron production. The iron concern was a disappointment – it turned a profit only when it had a government contract to forge cannonballs for the War of 1812 – but Perkins and his group were undeterred.[43] In Newton they had a ringer: Otis Pettee, a skilled and experienced machinist from Foxborough, Massachusetts.[44]

The Boston Associates were dependent on the Otis Pettees and Paul Moodys of their day, men from a background as middle-class tradesmen or mechanics who were willing to get their hands dirty and make the machines do their master's bidding. Pettee had already founded a thread factory in his hometown and had worked for a competing textile mill in Newton before falling in with Perkinses and Cabots. Pettee seems to have associated closely with Frederick Cabot since both men are named in an Act of the state legislature to incorporate a "religious society" that ran a "meeting-house" in Newton.[45]

A poster displayed throughout the mill outlined the routine Cabot and Pettee oversaw at the Elliot Manufacturing Company:

Machinery will be put in motion at five o'clock in the morning from March twentieth to September twentieth, and all workmen or operatives are required to be in their places ready to commence work at that hour. A half-hour is allowed for breakfast – from half-past six to seven. At twelve o'clock, three-quarters of an hour is allowed for dinner, and at seven o'clock in the evening the day's labor will end. From September twentieth, during the winter months, to March twentieth, breakfast will be taken before commencing work, and the wheels will be started at early daylight in a clear morning; cloudy or dark mornings artificial light will be used; the dinner hour the same as in summer; the afternoon run will continue until half-past seven in the evening, with the exception that Saturday's work will end with the daylight.[46]

Pettee established a shop at the Elliot mill that built machinery for cotton manufacturers. He held patents for technical improvements he had made in this line. After managing technical operations at the Elliot mills for several years, Pettee spun off the machine shop as a separate business in 1831.

The Elliot Manufacturing Company was relatively short-lived. By 1840, the stockholders were at odds, and Pettee, now a wealthy man, had the satisfaction of buying his former place of employment for $40,000. He returned the company to profitability under the name of the Elliot Mills.[47] Years before 1840, however, Frederick Cabot had moved on to other ventures.

The Lowell Manufacturing Company

In the later 1820s, Frederick Cabot joined the frenzy of capital investment in Lowell. An act of the Massachusetts legislature of February 8, 1828, incorporated the Lowell Manufacturing Company "for the purpose of manufacturing woolen and cotton goods." The act names as incorporators Frederick Cabot and his partners in the Boston dry goods business, Richard Cabot and William Whitney.[48]

The act of incorporation authorized the company to own real estate valued at $100,000 with a capital stock of half-a-million dollars, and three subsequent Acts of 1832, 1846, and 1850 increased the authorized capital by $1.5 million.[49] Since Frederick Cabot disappears from the Boston Directory as of 1830, and had a son born in 1831 at Dracut, Massachusetts, a town adjoining Lowell, it's likely that Frederick relocated to the Merrimack Valley to oversee operations at the new mill.[50]

The Lowell Manufacturing Company occupied a four-story building, about 200 feet long, with several outbuildings that served as storehouses, as a dyeing facility, and for other operations. The manufacture of coarse cotton fabric occupied most of the space in the mill in its early years. These cottons were known at the time as "Negro cloth" for what one 19th century source euphemized as "plantation wear."[51] The slaves referred to these inexpensive cottons as "Lowells."[52] The Cabots took the produce of slaves and transformed it into cloth for slaves' garments. Slaves became both producers and consumers in the Empire of Cotton. In modern business jargon, the Lowell Manufacturing Company achieved vertical integration.

Carpet weaving claimed the remainder of the manufacturing space in the Lowell mill. Alexander Wright was the mill's superintendent and expert on carpet production. A Scotsman by birth, Wright came with his family to the United States at age fifteen, arriving in the first ship that came to Boston following the War of 1812. The son of a chemical bleacher, at age twenty Wright founded a shop for weaving carpets in Medway, Massachusetts. In 1827, Frederick Cabot, along with George Lyman and Patrick Tracy Jackson, purchased Wright's carpet weaving operation in Medway. They then sold it to Cabot's Lowell Manufacturing Company and brought Wright and his crew to Lowell. Wright played in Lowell a role similar to Pettee's in Newton. Carpets became the product that differentiated the Lowell Manufacturing Company in the marketplace. The Lowell Manufacturing Company lasted until 1899 when it merged with another carpet manufacturer.[53]

But Frederick Cabot moved on once again. Cabot and family relocated to Philadelphia for a period in the 1830s.[54] He then reappears in the Boston Directory in 1839, back where he began, on Kilby Street in Boston, working as a commission merchant under the firm name of De Witt, Cabot & Company.[55] Cabot's partner Alexander De Witt was a State and Federal solon. Later he would serve in the Massachusetts legislature as a member of the American Party, associated with the anti-immigrant, anti-Catholic Know Nothing movement, which dominated the state government for a time in the 1850s.[56] There was a recession in 1837 which may have spurred Cabot's return to his previous occupation in wholesale and retail sales. If there was a financial setback in this period, it was temporary.

The Kennebec and Norway Plains Companies

In the 1840s, Frederick Cabot focused again on textile manufacturing. At this later stage of his career, Cabot became treasurer of two companies: the Kennebec Company of Augusta, Maine and the Norway Plains Company of Rochester, New Hampshire.[57] Eventually, these communities would attract Franco-American labor. In each of them, Cabot worked in concert with enterprising locals: Reuel Williams in Maine and John Sturtevant in New Hampshire.

Of the same generation as Frederick Cabot, Reuel Williams was born on June 2, 1783, in what is now Augusta. He was one among twelve children of Captain Seth and Zilpha (Ingraham) Williams. He was admitted to the bar at age 21. He supported the separation of Maine from Massachusetts, and the former became the twenty-third state of the Union per the Missouri Compromise of 1820. Williams served in the Maine State legislature from the 1820s through the 1840s.

Williams succeeded in lobbying to have Augusta named the Maine state capital and was also involved in negotiations toward settling the northeastern border between the United States and the British North American possessions. The question of the northeastern border of the U.S. was finally resolved by Secretary of State Daniel Webster in the Webster-Ashburton Treaty of 1842. The line agreed upon, separating Maine from New Brunswick, divided Acadian communities living on either side of the new border, creating a considerable Acadian presence in Northern Maine.

In 1837, Williams was appointed by the Maine legislature to the U.S. Senate resigning in 1843 to devote himself to his private sector interests. He was a player in the various railroad projects in his home state. He was also a partner in the project of damming the Kennebec River at Augusta to capture its water power.[58]

On February 28, 1838, the Maine legislature approved an Act incorporating the Kennebec Company of Augusta, with Williams's name topping the list of five incorporators. The company had a very broad charter to manufacture "cotton, wool, iron, steel and paper" products and an initial capital of up to $500,000.[59] It was not until 1846, however, that cotton manufacturing was operating at the Kennebec Company.[60]

The Kennebec Company is an example of how Boston capital inundated textile firms founded by locals. Separate returns published by the State of Maine list the principal stockholders in the company in 1845 and 1848. In 1845, the Boston-based firm of Chace, Motley & Mills, led by Frederick Cabot's associate Caleb Chace, was the largest shareholder, but Williams held the second largest number of shares. Local Mainers make up the bulk of the shareholders. By 1848, while Williams was the largest stockholder, only about one-half of the shareholders were local. Boston investors, including Cabot, Chace, and Chace's firm, owned a generous portion of the company. When the Kennebec Company began to manufacture cotton goods in 1846, Boston capital pounced.[61] And by 1848, Frederick Cabot was Treasurer of the Kennebec Company.[62]

Around the same time, Cabot also became Treasurer of the Norway Plains Company.[63] The state legislature of New Hampshire chartered this firm in July 1846.[64] John D. Sturtevant, the son of a farmer, was the man most responsible for this company, among the first to manufacture woolen blankets.

Sturtevant was born on the Fourth of July 1816, at Center Harbor, New Hampshire, the son of Perez and Dorothy (Kimball) Sturtevant. His ancestors were among the early settlers of Plymouth Colony. By age 16, he was apprenticed to a cloth-dresser, working in the summer months and going to school in the winter. He worked in textile manufacturing in the mills of Vermont, New Hampshire, Virginia, and Massachusetts. By 1840, he was superintendent of the Whitney Blanket Mills in Lowell. When that company folded, Sturtevant bought one of the mills and went into the woolen manufacturing business for himself.

Returning to New Hampshire, Sturtevant and a partner bought the former Gonic Manufacturing Company in Rochester, but the partnership soon dissolved, and Sturtevant formed the Norway Plains Company there with a capitalization of $60,000. Sturtevant held about a third of the stock.[65] Around 1848, Frederick Cabot became Treasurer of this company, a title he held for the remainder of his active business career. An 1849 directory of New England's business-men lists Cabot as both Treasurer and President of the Norway Plains Company, while Sturtevant had the title of Agent.[66]

Frederick Cabot retired in the late 1850s and moved to the town of Brookline, Massachusetts, just outside of Boston. He informed the enumerator of the 1860 U.S. Federal Census that his worth in real and personal estate was about $100,000.[67] Cabot's wealth of some six-figure amount was no mean sum by the standards of 1860.

Comparing the value of a dollar between one era and another is an inexact procedure. Rather than comparing Cabot's dollars to ours, perhaps a better measure of his wealth in 1860 is to consider the evidence on pages 530 through 534 in the Boston Directory for that year. Advertisements for 42 banks appear on these pages. Of these institutions, 16 have capital in the seven figures, but only five of the banks possess capital in excess of $1 million. The others have capital in the six figures, the same order of magnitude as Cabot's worth. The more modest institutions include the Mechanics Bank with capital of $250,000, Bank of the Metropolis at $200,000 and the Broadway Bank with $150,000. And the Boston of 1860 was a major financial center of the United States. Cabot was worth as much as a bank in a smaller town.[68]

Frederick Cabot died at age 83 on June 16, 1869, at the Massachusetts Infant Asylum. His death record in the state archives lists his occupation as "Gentleman" and the cause of death as "Old Age."[69] The executrix of his will, his widow Marianne, pledged a probate bond of $300,000 suggesting that Cabot's estate was much larger at the time of his death than it had been in 1860.[70]

But in the decade before his demise, toward the tail end of his lucrative career, Cabot made one more move in the textile business. He purchased, along with a relative and a business associate, an ill-starred cotton mill in the small, leafy college town of Brunswick, Maine.

CHAPTER FOUR

TEXTILES IN BRUNSWICK
The First Half-Century

Cotton manufacturing in what is now the State of Maine began in the town of Brunswick the year after President Jefferson's embargo opened a market for domestic manufacturers. In 1809, a group of local merchants founded the Brunswick Cotton Manufactory Company on the falls of the Androscoggin River, near the site of a colonial-era fort. This facility spun cotton yarn. The men behind this concern were local merchants Ezra Smith, William King, and Dr. Benjamin Porter.[1]

Ezra Smith was a retailer from Topsham, just across the river from Brunswick, who was part of the group that built the sluice on the Androscoggin to capture the water power.[2]

William King was a prosperous lumber merchant of nearby Bath, who was to become the first Governor of Maine. Like his colleague in state government, Reuel Williams, King was a leader in the movement to make Maine the twenty-third state. When he co-founded the mill in Brunswick, King understood cotton's potential. In 1802, he had sent the first ship from Bath to New Orleans for a load of cotton, and the mid-coast region of Maine became a local center of the cotton carrying trade.[3]

Doctor Benjamin Porter was a surgeon by training and a veteran of the Revolutionary War. Porter was King's brother-in-law and business partner in both the lumber trade and a retail store in Brunswick. Like King, Dr. Porter was a politician. He was a State Senator from Lincoln

County in the Massachusetts legislature before Maine achieved statehood.[4]

Local tradesmen Robert Eastman and James Jones built the machinery for the Brunswick Cotton Manufactory. Eastman was a maker of clocks and watches in Brunswick. He also invented machinery for cutting clapboards and later owned a machine shop. James Jones was a blacksmith in town.[5]

Local capital supporting local machinists made the first steps toward establishing a cotton industry in the town. Only later, when locals had captured the water power and built the manufacturing infrastructure, did Boston capitalists appear on the scene. Brunswick's early experiments in cotton manufacturing support Weil's contention that local groups were responsible for the development of textile operations that Boston capital later acquired. And despite auspicious beginnings, before Boston arrived on the banks of the Androscoggin, local industrialists faced nearly a half-century of disappointment. The tangled web of transactions that is the story of the first half-century of textiles in Brunswick deserves a recital. These details reveal the machinations of the 19th century New England textile industry and how a local enterprise came into the orbit of the Boston Associates.

The Brunswick Cotton Manufactory Company was not a commercial success. In 1812, a new company was formed called the Maine Cotton and Woolen Manufacturing Company. This corporation built a new mill and bought the former company's building, transforming it into a storehouse. This company had 1,248 cotton spindles and produced 100,000 yards of cotton cloth "in a season." It also had two hundred and forty woolen spindles, nine woolen looms, and carding and fulling machines. The company employed about a hundred workers.[6]

Its success was short-lived. On December 13, 1825, fire broke out in Brunswick, on a day when the thermometer read -13 degrees F (-25 C) and swept away thirty buildings including the cotton and woolen mills. Losses in the fire totaled $90,000, with only $1,800 of the factory's loss covered by insurance.[7]

Undaunted, a new group of investors revived hopes for textile manufacturing in Brunswick after the conflagration. In a series of real estate transactions, all registered with Cumberland County on February 17, 1829, a group of four local entrepreneurs, including the President of Brunswick's Bowdoin College, purchased the land adjacent to the former Brunswick Cotton Manufactory. Other real estate transactions with local investors indicate that the drivers behind this enterprise were selling shares in a new textile company, incorporated on February 6, 1834, as The Brunswick Company.[8]

In this relatively early, quaint stage in U.S. corporate history, shares in the company were conveyed via real estate. A shareholder owned a fraction of the real and fungible property of the company and their stake was conveyed via deed. For example, in one such deed a local businesswoman named Narcissa Stone paid into the future company $250 and received "one undivided twenty fourth part" of the land, buildings, and water privileges.[9]

In a document received by the county on June 3, 1834, the small group of investors sold its property, and a partially constructed stone building, to the new Brunswick Company for $25,500.[10] This property then traded hands several times through the remainder of the 1830s and 1840s.

In a document filed September 19, 1835, William Willis of Portland bought the mill from the Brunswick Company for $40,000.[11] The ever-vigilant Boston Associates now enter the picture. In a document filed on September 16 of that year, William Appleton of Boston bought the property of the Maine Cotton and Woolen Factory for $8,600 from a committee appointed to sell it, which included George Bond of Boston.[12] William Appleton was a member of Perkins's clique and a first cousin of Francis Cabot Lowell's close associate Nathan Appleton. He was among the founders of Lowell as one of the principals in that town's Merrimack Manufacturing Company. A banker as well as a merchant, he served Massachusetts in the U.S. House of Representatives.[13]

Willis bought Appleton's Brunswick property for $12,000 but only with the latter's financial support.[14] Willis obtained a mortgage from Appleton on that property. Next, Willis sold the mill as well as the property he obtained from Appleton to the Brunswick Company for five dollars.[15] These transactions brought into the Brunswick Company the property owned by the earlier Brunswick textile firms.

By 1836, Nathaniel F. Deering, a businessman, lawyer, and author from Portland became Treasurer of the Brunswick Company with I. A. Beard, a local newspaper editor, serving as Agent.[16] With the likes of William Willis, Deering, Appleton, and Bond in the frame, by the mid-1830s, the control of the Brunswick textile business began to drift southward, toward the larger communities of Portland and Boston.

The Brunswick Company ran into financial difficulty in the late 1830s. In November 1839, the company took out a mortgage for $50,000 from a group including several of its own officers and stock-holders.[17] In 1840, there was a settlement with numerous creditors where the trio of Ebenezer Everett of Brunswick and George Bond and William Brigham of Boston became trustees of the property in the interest of the creditors. Claims against the Brunswick Company amounted to $120,000.[18] At last, the property was sold in 1841 for $50,000 to Everett, Bond, and Brigham and the same group, in a document filed the same day, paid off the company's mortgages for another $50,000.[19]

George Wheeler's 1878 history of Brunswick claims that Bond and Brigham were acting on behalf of a Boston-based firm called Whitwell, Seaver, & Co. which appointed the duo of Augustine P. Kimball of Boston and John Dunning Coburn of Brunswick to manage the company.[20] Everett and Brigham put the mill up for auction in 1843 and the partnership of Kimball & Coburn bought it for the cut rate of $34,400.[21]

Kimball & Coburn had the financial backing of Appleton's son-in-law Amos A. Lawrence of Boston.[22] Lawrence was a scion of the family of textile barons who lent their name to a northern Massachusetts mill town and a university town in Kansas. Kimball & Coburn appear to have had trouble paying the mortgage since Lawrence proceeded to foreclose on the property.[23] But the partners re-negotiated the terms of the loan, and received the property back from Lawrence, free and clear, in 1845.[24] Their troubles in paying Lawrence signal that the partnership of Kimball & Coburn, like its predecessors, could not make the business pay. By a document filed on May 14, 1847, they obtained a mortgage on the mill from Charles Thompson, a merchant of Topsham, for $33,600.[25] This transaction is the beginning of yet another in the succession of textile manufacturing companies on the Androscoggin at Brunswick.

A new outfit, the Warumbo Company, was duly incorporated in the State of Maine on July 3, 1847. Kimball and Coburn are two of the four men named in the act incorporating this company.[26] The Warumbo Company, like its predecessors, didn't last long. Its property remained leveraged, and its problems were compounded by the death of Coburn in June 1849 at the age of 33.[27] Thompson purchased the floundering mill from the Warumbo Company for the bargain basement price of $2,500 in June 1852.[28]

Boston then intervened decisively. Frederick Cabot and Caleb Chace along with Cabot's cousin John Clarke Lee of Salem, bought the mill from Thompson for $42,000 on February 17, 1853.[29] Cabot and associates organized a new corporation called the Cabot Company on March 4, 1853, and Cabot, Chace, and Lee sold the mill to this new corporate entity at cost on September 16 of that year.[30] This company existed, in one form or another, for nearly a century.

The principals named in the act incorporating the Cabot Company were Frederick Cabot, Ebenezer Everett, and George F. Shepley. Everett was a local attorney involved in earlier iterations of the Brunswick mill. Shepley was a lawyer and State's attorney based in Portland, best known for his service in the Civil War as military commandant of occupied New Orleans, and as military governor of Louisiana and then of Richmond, Virginia.[31]

Immediately, the new Cabot Company began to buy small parcels of land near the mill. The company installed new machinery, and a novel arrangement of this equipment increased the mill's capacity.[32] In 1855, the company built "two large double tenement boarding houses" to accommodate its expanded workforce; many more tenements followed as there were several expansions of the mill throughout the 19th century.[33] In November 1855, the company voted to issue stock to pay for the new machinery.[34] In 1856, the directors elected Frederick's son, Francis Cabot, Treasurer. The elder Cabot remained a company director and major stockholder.[35]

But the failure of stockholders to pay into the company impeded its progress. A nationwide financial crisis in 1857 may have been a factor. At a meeting of November 1857, the company voted to offer new shares. If this measure proved inadequate, then the directors agreed to sell the property. In December, Sereno Nickerson, a fishmonger with roots on Cape Cod, bought the mill at auction in Boston for $45,000.[36] On January 18, 1858, the state of Maine approved a second iteration of the Cabot company, under the name of the Cabot Manufacturing Company. The act of incorporation names Frederick Cabot, Benjamin Greene, and Sereno Nickerson.[37] A few weeks later, Nickerson, later to become one of the U.S.'s most prominent Masons, sold the mill to the new Cabot Manufacturing Company at cost.[38]

Frederick Cabot retired after the formation of the new Cabot Manufacturing Company, leaving his son Francis as Treasurer. Benjamin Greene, resident Agent since 1855, remained. Greene became a Director and served as Agent for 35 years.[39] At last, after half a century, the management of a textile mill in Brunswick stabilized around the duo of Francis Cabot and Benjamin Greene.

Cabot and Greene

With Cabot as Treasurer operating from Boston, and Greene as Agent managing affairs on-site in Brunswick, textile manufacturing in the town thrived. Before the arrival of the Cabots, almost everyone who invested in their Brunswick predecessors lost money. The Cabot Manufacturing Company broke that cycle. It became an award-winning business that employed thousands of men, women, and children.[40]

By the time he assumed control of the new Cabot Manufacturing Company in 1858, Francis Cabot had already enjoyed a colorful life.[41] He was born on June 16, 1825, in Newton, Massachusetts, when his father was managing the Elliot Manufacturing Company there. Francis graduated from Boston Latin School in 1839. The following year, at age 15, after just a few months at the college, Cabot was expelled from Harvard after he drove a carriage through Harvard Yard in the company of an expelled senior, a caper a descendant described as "rakish conduct."[42] Cabot found work as a clerk but spent too much time among billiard players and "professional gamesters" for his father's liking.[43] Frederick Cabot had the 20-year-old Francis shipped out to see the world from the deck of a New Bedford, Massachusetts whaler called the *Florida*, sailing for the North Pacific. It was to be a three-year hitch.

Possessing a bookish streak not unknown among the Cabots, young Francis took on board volumes of Shakespeare, the 17th century philosopher Spinoza, the English poets, and the Bible.[44] He memorized passages from this material while ensconced in the crow's nest of the whaler. At sea, Cabot sojourned for a time in Hawaii. The Cabots passed down the story that Francis had served as tutor to the King of Hawaii's daughter sometime around 1848. The royal family of Hawaii wanted Cabot to take the hand of the young woman, continued the family lore, but he had other plans.[45] He returned to New Bedford from Hawaii in January 1849 aboard the ship *Cortez*.[46]

Cabot appears back in Boston by 1851, where he worked with his father's firm when the elder Cabot was Treasurer of the Norway Plains Company.[47] Next, Francis tried his hand at business in New York, but returned to New England by 1856. He appears in the Boston Directory for that year as a commission merchant, while he also began his career in upper management with the mill in Brunswick.[48] On November 12, 1856, Cabot married Mary Louisa Higginson in Brattleboro, Vermont. Higginson claimed descent from a sister of the poet Chaucer. The couple produced ten children, eight of whom reached adulthood.

By 1857, Francis formed his own Boston-based company, Francis Cabot & Co., along with his brother John Higginson Cabot and John Eliot Parkman.[49] Parkman was the younger brother of the historian Francis Parkman, the chronicler of New France.[50] Francis Parkman's brother partnered with a man whose business in Brunswick would entice thousands of the descendants of New France to cross the border.

The firm of Francis Cabot & Co. traded in India. A biographical sketch of John Higginson Cabot in a Harvard alumni publication claims that this firm was doing business in Calcutta.[51] An historian of India's mercantile history finds that in this period foreign traders were interested primarily in two goods available in Calcutta: indigo and opium.[52]

The 1858 Boston Directory lists Francis Cabot as both a partner in the firm of Francis Cabot & Co. and as Treasurer of the Cabot Manufacturing Company.[53] Francis operated both businesses out of his office at 40 Central Wharf in Boston. By 1859, the firm of Francis Cabot & Co. was no more. Francis, whose occupation in the Directory is listed only as "Treasurer," was now working from an office in the Merchant's Exchange building. Francis Cabot was also Treasurer of the Boston Exchange Company, the firm that operated the Merchant's Exchange.[54] Like father, like son, Francis was now firmly ensconced in the textile business and will run his interests from Room 16 at the Merchant's Exchange for the next 30 years.

In 1860, Cabot moved with his family to nearby Brookline, a refuge for Boston's wealthier families. Renting a house at first, in 1864 Cabot bought a plot of land in Brookline and built a Victorian monstrosity of a residence on Heath Street where he and his family would live for the rest of his days. In 1889, Francis Cabot moved his office to 70 Kilby Street in Boston, an address not far from his previous location in the Merchant's Exchange building.[55]

Like his father and many other Boston textile barons, Francis Cabot was not content to control one textile mill. He ran a portfolio of such mills. Earlier in his career, he inherited his father's position in the Norway Plains Company. He appears among the group that founded the Winthrop Mills in Maine, and he was also among the incorporators of the Fisher Manufacturing Company of Grafton, Massachusetts.[56] The Waumbeck Mills, at Milton Mills, New Hampshire, and the Clinton Mills Company of Norwich, Connecticut were also in Francis Cabot's textile portfolio.[57] He also served as Treasurer of the Old Boston National Bank.[58] Despite these varied business interests Cabot still found time to study philosophy and read romantic poetry.[59]

Frederick Cabot's former associate, John D. Sturtevant, also had an interest in most of these enterprises, including the operations in Winthrop, Maine; Milton Mills, New Hampshire; and Norwich, Connecticut. Sturtevant's son-in-law and Cabot relative, Amasa Clarke, also had a leadership role in several of these firms.[60] The Cabots and their relatives, along with Sturtevant and Chace, became a nucleus around which spun textile mills all over New England. Every town that had a textile operation controlled by the Francis Cabot group spawned a Franco-American community.

Benjamin Greene was cut from a different cloth than Francis Cabot.[61] Whereas Cabot was born to wealth and success, Greene was from a solid background among small tradespeople. He was born on April 13, 1818, in Eastford, Connecticut, the son of Robert Greene and the former Sarah Hurlbert. His father was a mason (with a small "m").[62]

Greene began his career in the textile mills of his hometown. He later found employment in the mills of Southbridge, Massachusetts and Richmond, Virginia. By 1850, he held the position of Agent in a large cotton mill in Webster, Massachusetts before coming to Brunswick in 1855.

Greene married Emily Morse who died in 1858 and then Susan Holmes who also pre-deceased her husband in 1881. Per the 1900 U.S. Federal Census, Greene was married for a third time to a woman named Hattie, some 40 years his junior. He had one child by his first wife and three by his second.

In addition to serving as Agent of the Cabot mill, Greene also became, at one time or another, a proprietor of a grocery and dry goods store in Brunswick, a director of the Brunswick Water Power Company and was, for 35 years, a director of the town's First National Bank. Locals regarded Greene's store, operated in cooperation with the Adams Brothers of Brunswick, as the company store of the Cabot mill, but Greene denied it.[63] His combined business activities made Greene, per his obituary in the local paper, "the richest man in town."

In 1874, Greene built a splendid mansion in Brunswick, a two-and-a-half story, Italianate structure at a cost of over $34,000. Greene imported carpenters and artisans from Italy to decorate his home with marble, stucco, and frescoes. He had brought to Maine oak flooring manufactured in Louisiana.[64]

When the Cabot Company first came to Brunswick in the early 1850s, it followed the Lowell model, well-known to Frederick Cabot. The mill was a five-story granite structure, including basement and attic, built in 1834 on the pattern of the Hamilton mill No. 2

FIGURE 3: Benjamin Greene, Agent, Cabot Manufacturing
Company in 1876. (Pejepscot Historical Society)

in Lowell.[65] And like the mills in Lowell, the Cabot mill employed
young women, as did the mill's previous incarnation under Kimball
& Coburn.[66]

Cabot and Greene changed the pattern. First, they continued to
purchase real estate around the mill as part of an aggressive program
of expansion. To fill positions in their growing enterprise, they would
turn to the *Canadiens*. Although earlier Brunswick textile companies
had employed a tiny number of *Canadiens* dating back to around 1850,
it is Cabot and Greene who preside over a large influx of workers from
Québec after the Civil War. These workers became the spine of the
company and drove Cabot's and Greene's prosperity. By the early
1900s, Franco-Americans comprised 90 percent of the mill hands in
Brunswick and numbered in the thousands.[67]

FIGURE 4: Benjamin Greene House (1908). (Pejepscot Historical Society)

By attracting these *Canadien* Catholics to move south, Cabot and Greene changed the demographics of the town, as they participated in a regional social experiment. Brunswick – and New England – would never be the same.

SECTION TWO

THE OTHER SIDE
OF THE COTTON

CHAPTER FIVE

FRANCO-AMERICANS
RESCUE KING COTTON

In 1861, Francis Cabot was Treasurer of the Boston Exchange Company.[1] In this capacity, he oversaw the Merchant's Exchange building, the edifice for which Thomas Perkins laid the cornerstone twenty years prior. Cabot also ran his textile interests from an office in the building. His headquarters were at the nerve center of Boston's industrial and mercantile elite.

That same year finds my great-great grandfather Joseph Vermette living in the parish of Saint-Gervais-de-Bellechasse in what was then known as Canada East. Saint-Gervais is a small, rural parish in Québec on the south shore of the St. Lawrence River not far from Québec City. Joseph is of the same generation as Francis Cabot, just three years younger than the textile mogul. Per the Canadian Census of 1861, he is a day-laborer (Fr. *journalier*).[2] For a day wage, this class of laborers toiled in construction, in road repairs, as occasional farm workers, in transportation, or at other odd jobs.[3] Six generations of Joseph's Vermette ancestors had been family farmers or laborers in this region of Québec.

Per the census, Joseph and his wife Marie-Louise have six children living with them at Saint-Gervais. The couple has another child, the eldest girl, who is living on her uncle's farm in the same parish. Joseph's brother had inherited the Vermette family farm there. Joseph, his wife, and their brood are living with another family of three in a one-story wooden house, eleven people under the same roof. Joseph owns one horse, one cow, and a vehicle that all together are worth $25. He owns no real estate. By contrast, his peers on that same page of the census own property valued at between $300 and $500. Joseph cannot read or write. During this period, there are Joseph Vermettes all over Québec: poor, landless, illiterate laborers.

Over the next twenty years, three of Joseph's sons will cross the border, and come to Brunswick to work in the Cabot mill. These sons of Joseph Vermette become distant satellites in Francis Cabot's orbit. Two half-sisters will follow Joseph's sons to Brunswick. Two other sons of Joseph Vermette will find their way to the United States. These two brothers, much younger than the three who come to Brunswick, live for a time in Worcester, Massachusetts, before one moves to Claremont, New Hampshire and the other to New York City. In 1940, the New Yorker, Theodore Vermette, is living in the neighborhood now known as Bed-Stuy.[4] When these children of Joseph Vermette cross the border, they are part of a movement of nearly one million people.

The emigration movement from Québec to New England unfolded in several stages over the ninety-year period before 1930. The suppression of the Rebellions of 1837-38 accelerated what had been a seasonal migration toward the United States. Refugees from the Rebellions established small pockets of a *Canadien* presence in Vermont and upstate New York.[5] One of their number, Ludger Duvernay, founded the U.S.'s first *Canadien*, French-language newspaper *Le Canadien Patriote* [*The Canadien Patriot*] in Burlington, Vermont in 1839.[6] The refugees from the rebellion did not establish a permanent presence on the southern side of the border, but they had worn a beaten path between Québec and the northeastern United States.

The emigration movement began in the region around Montréal, the city of Québec, the county of Dorchester, and the Eastern Townships region (now known as *l'Estrie*) that bordered the United States.[7] Québec's Richelieu Valley region was both a hotbed of the Rebellion of 1837 and an early center of the movement toward New England before the Civil War.[8] The parish of Saint-Ours in the Richelieu Valley was a major source of emigrants to the U.S. both before and after the rebellions. Parishioners of Saint-Ours appear among the early emigrants to several communities in New England including Woonsocket, Rhode Island; Southbridge and Worcester, Massachusetts; and Brunswick.[9]

The first of my ancestors to live in the U.S. was Prudent Racine of Saint-Charles in the Richelieu Valley. In an 1839 report, Racine's name appears on a "LIST of REBELS" who fortified the *Seigneur's* manor house at Saint-Charles in November of 1837, against the approach of Queen Victoria's troops.[10] The *Patriotes* of 1837 lost the subsequent Battle of Saint-Charles, and the town was destroyed, and its church desecrated.[11] After the demolition of Saint-Charles, Prudent Racine and family wandered south, living here and there in the Eastern Townships region of Québec.

In the late 1840s and early 1850s, Racine, his wife Elinore and their large family, settled for a few years in Richford, Vermont, a town bordering Québec where they appear in the U.S. Federal Census of 1850, with the French names characteristically mangled. Prudent and family returned to Québec in the later 1850s, settling in the town of Roxton Falls. Prudent was a *journalier* at Roxton Falls per the Canadian census of 1861, at the same time that Joseph Vermette has that same occupation in Saint-Gervais. Several of Prudent Racine's children, including two of my great-great-grandmothers, eventually moved to the United States.

Vermont and Maine were the first two New England states with a significant Franco-American presence in the period from 1840 to 1860.[12] Geography favored the movement from the Richelieu River Valley into Vermont. The Richelieu River originates at Lake Champlain and empties into the Saint Lawrence. The Richelieu-Lake Champlain route opened the way to Vermont and points south. This route was well-established before the days of the railroads.

Another well-traveled route, before the railways, connected Québec to Maine. The Old Canada Road traversed a corridor defined by the Kennebec and Chaudière rivers. This was the route Benedict Arnold traveled when he invaded Québec from the south during the Revolutionary War. In the 19th century, this road saw traffic to and fro, crossing the border near Jackman, Maine. Emigrants from the

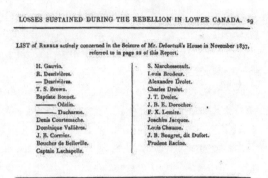

LIST of Rebels actively concerned in the Seizure of Mr. *Debartzch's House* in November 1837, referred to in page 22 of this Report.

H. Gauvin.	S. Marchesseault.
R. Desrivières.	Louis Brodeur.
— Desrivières.	Alexandre Drolet.
T. S. Brown.	Charles Drolet.
Baptiste Bonnet.	J. T. Drolet.
——— Odelin.	J. B. E. Dorocher.
——— Ducharme.	F. X. Lemire.
Denis Courtemache.	Joachim Jacques.
Dominique Vallières.	Louis Chausse.
J. B. Cormier.	J. B. Bougret, dit Dufort.
Boucher de Belleville.	Prudent Racine.
Captain Lachapelle.	

FIGURE 5: Rebellion of 1837, Prudent Racine, final name on a "LIST of Rebels" at Saint-Charles-sur-Richelieu.

Beauce region of Québec, in particular, traveled this road to find work in forests, on farms, in construction projects, and, later, in the factories of the Kennebec River region of Maine.[13]

There were no controls on the border in this era. Traffic flowed freely. In this pre-Civil War phase of the movement, individuals and some families moved between Québec and New England, between one mill town and another, and between various parts of Québec, as workers followed their hopes for better wages over the horizon.

Many of the travelers on these routes were young men seeking temporary employment and many returned to Québec.[14] This migration continued an established pattern. In rural Québec, it was common for men to find work in the logging industries during the winter. They would return from the forests to their families in the spring to work their farms.[15] Since they were accustomed to traveling from the homestead to the logging concessions in Québec, it seemed a small step to venture across the frontier, to the border regions of New England. A variation on the familiar pattern emerged: workers toiled for a portion of the year in the factories of the U.S. and then returned to Québec in the farming seasons.[16]

As time went on many of these migrant workers remained in the U.S., but a reputation as wanderers pursued them. A close observer taking notes circa 1890 found that Franco-Americans divided into three groups: those who came from Québec to New England intending to

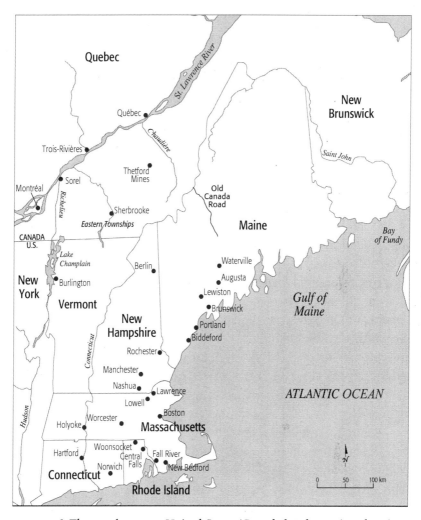

FIGURE 6: The northeastern United States/Canada border region showing portions of Québec and New Brunswick, and the New England states, with select regions and communities mentioned in the text.
(Map by Julie Benoît)

stay in the U.S.; others intending to work for a time across the border and then return to Québec; and those who were in constant motion, following the four winds.[17]

Before the Civil War, there was a parallel movement of farm families from Québec to the U.S. Midwest. Many of these farmers moved to states such as Michigan, Illinois, Wisconsin, and Minnesota. A priest named Charles Chiniquy pursued a stream of *Canadien* families toward Kankakee County in Illinois, and he led other families to the region where they formed a cluster. Chiniquy left the Catholic Church to become a Protestant pastor, taking some of his flock with him. The author of salacious, anti-Catholic diatribes, when Chiniquy faced a lawsuit for slander, a young Illinois lawyer named Abraham Lincoln defended him.[18] Some of the Illinois families from Québec continued to head westward. After the Civil War, families from Québec began to travel as far as Clay and Cloud County, Kansas and beyond.[19]

Families moved from Québec to the West for the same reason that Americans from the East were making the move: available farmland. The rural Midwest offered the *Canadien* farm families an opportunity to continue the agricultural way of life they knew in Québec. Logging activity in Michigan and other states of the northern Midwest also attracted emigration from Québec in the 19th century. While many of New England's Franco-Americans remained a transient population before the Civil War, the *Canadiens* of the Midwest represented a permanent settlement in the United States. What is now the U.S. Midwest had had a *Canadien* presence since the days of New France. The 19th century Québec diaspora reinforced this older blood.[20]

The West Coast attracted its share of *Canadiens* in the first half of the 19th century, especially to the region known in the U.S. as the Oregon Country. My ancestor's brother, Hyacinthe Lavigueur, was one of these migrants to the Far West. He departed the island of Montréal in the 1820s, most likely in the service of the Hudson Bay Company, and helped to establish the parish of St. Paul in Oregon in a region still known as French Prairie. John C. Fremont, who was one among the first pair of U.S. Senators elected by the State of California in 1850, had *Canadien* roots. He was also the first Republican candidate for President of the United States.

Through the remainder of the 19th century, the Québec diaspora spread throughout the United States and Canada forming clusters of hundreds, thousands, and tens of thousands of people. These small bands, spreading from coast to coast, formed a cultural and linguistic archipelago within the United States. In every state that bordered Canada, and other states contiguous with them, there were pockets of people of *Canadien* origins.

These small French-speaking aggregations described a "T" shape across the map of the United States. The Mississippi River, with its French-speakers dating back to the days of New France, constituted the vertical bar of the T, and the areas nearest the Canadian border, the horizontal bar. This T-shape is traced in the French place names left by these travelers in the lengthy period from the 17th to the early 20th century. This expanse forms what a Franco-American writer dubbed a "ghost empire."[21] Franco-American communities also appear in unlikely places, far beyond the U.S./Canada border region. By 1935, there were 2,000 Franco-Americans in Long Beach, California. There was a *Club Franco-Américain* [Franco-American Club] in Long Beach at the time with 300 members.[22]

By the middle of the 19th century, the emigration movement began to center increasingly on the six New England states, where workers began to settle rather than sojourn.[23] In 1860, Vermont and Maine accounted for nearly two-thirds (64 percent) of the Franco-American population of New England. Still but a trickle of emigration from Québec, New England Franco-Americans numbered just 37,420 in 1860.[24] The expansion of the Grand Trunk railroad beginning in 1853 accelerated the flow.[25] Franco-Americans were among the only immigrant groups to arrive in the U.S. via railroad.[26]

With the growth of the railroad network, mill towns in Massachusetts, Rhode Island, New Hampshire, and, to a lesser degree, Connecticut, began to attract an increasing share of emigrants from the North.[27] Towns in upstate New York such as Cohoes, Plattsburgh, Troy, and Glens Falls also welcomed Franco-Americans who migrated toward that state on a pattern similar to the move into New England.[28] The change in the destination of the migrants, from rural areas of the Midwest toward Northeastern industrial centers, reflected shifts in the textile industry labor markets. These shifts began with the arrival of an increasing number of immigrant laborers in the textile towns.

A New Cheap Labor Pool for New England

Finding sources of labor was a persistent problem for textile industry management in the 19th and 20th centuries. Since the founders of Lowell did not have the benefit of a permanent working class, they faced turnover among their employees. High turnover meant that they had to continue to find new sources of labor as young Yankee women gave way to immigrant laborers. The arrival of the immigrant signaled a new era in the mill towns, where, contrary to the wishes of Francis Cabot Lowell's successors, workers could spend a lifetime in a mill. A single textile company employed generations of the same family. Depending on which line one follows, four generations of my family worked at Brunswick's Cabot mill, at one time or another.

Young women were the majority of the workers in the mills from about 1815 until the 1840s. Irish laborers came to dig canals and to work in construction in Lowell and subsequently became mill operatives.[29] In the 1840s and 1850s, an increasing number of Irish immigrants, driven to desperate poverty by the atrocity known as the potato famine, found work in New England textile mills. A small number of immigrants from Great Britain, who had experience in the textile mills overseas, as well as Germans and other northern Europeans, also began to seek employment in New England mills in the second third of the century. The turnover in employees, from native-born to immigrant labor, was rapid. In the Hamilton Mill in Lowell, the number of immigrant workers rose from less than four percent in 1836 to greater than sixty percent by 1860.[30] This transitional period, where Europeans replaced the mill women, was short-lived, lasting from circa 1845 until the Civil War. After the Civil War, *Canadiens* began to dominate the industry's labor force.

A Massachusetts Bureau of Labor Statistics report from 1885 described this transition in labor pools:

> In the beginning the daughters of American farmers and mechanics formed a large proportion of the operatives....They brought to the work a

degree of intelligence and culture which their successors have not shown because it is not now demanded. As machinery became more automatic and greater perfection of processes was attained, an operative class of less general intelligence took their place, while the young American found employments requiring greater individual skill.

Speaking broadly, the textile factory population of the State has in this way presented three successive phases as to nationality, first, American; second, Irish and English; third, and the present, French Canadian.[31]

A 1910 U.S. government study divided the ethnic history of the New England textile mills into similar phases:

The first period was that of the native Americans [sic], with a few English and Scotch, and in the second period a few Germans came in along with the Irish. But in general the three periods were that of the Americans, extending to about 1840 or 1845, that of the Irish, beginning in the forties, and that of the French Canadians, which began immediately after the Civil War.[32]

This division of the labor history of the mills into three phases is schematic. Many Irish women and men worked beside *Canadien* operatives, who worked beside "Americans" and other ethnicities by the later 19th century. And *Canadiens* worked in the textile industry before the Civil War. However, the war created a labor shortage which the *Canadiens* filled. Once established, the *Canadiens* did not relinquish their position in the mills until they closed. The dominance of the *Canadiens* in the mills, well into the 20th century was especially pronounced in the states of Maine, New Hampshire, and Vermont.[33]

Observers in the 19th century were not unaware of the socio-economic implications of this transition in the industry's sources of labor. A Massachusetts Bureau of Labor Statistics Report from 1873 recorded a prescient comment from a Lowellian:

We are gradually creating – what the founders of Lowell never looked for – a permanent body of factory employees, composed in part of American stock, but more largely of Irish and French-Canadian elements, with English, Scotch and German blood co-mingled. What this fact forebodes I will not venture to conjecture. But perhaps we are to have here a class of resident laborers similar to that of the manufacturing cities of Europe.[34]

Within our contemporary racializations, people of Irish, French-Canadian, English, Scottish, and German blood are not importantly different from one another. Recent U.S. Census forms would place them into a single category called non-Hispanic White. The same year this report was published, a newspaper in Lewiston, Maine described that town of mainly Yankees, Irish, and Franco-Americans as a cultural "mosaic."[35] Today, we would not tend to call a town dominated by so-called non-Hispanic whites a "mosaic." In 19th century Lewiston these groups were as distinct as a fish is from a lime. Places like post-Civil War Lowell and Lewiston were crucibles where the textile corporations launched an unintended social experiment in the co-mingling of what 19th century observers regarded as different "races."

In the minds of many Yankees, the presence of immigrants "co-mingling" in the mill towns made them less attractive places for their daughters. The Dillingham Commission Report, written in the first decade of the 20th century, notes that the arrival of the immigrants in the mills made the work seem "less worthy and respectable" in the eyes of the mill women who were soon an "almost negligible minority" of the workers.[36]

The report mentions other reasons, besides antipathy to immigrants, to explain the disappearance of "Americans" from mill payrolls. It cites underbidding by immigrants, especially in shops that operated on a piecework basis. The Commission also found that labor disputes offered an opportunity for foreign workers to "displace old employees" and notes a general "discontent of American working people with the conditions in the cotton mills."[37]

Increased competition in the textile industry was the underlying cause of the labor disputes and the growing discontent among workers. As competition grew, the corporations sought ways to increase production and decrease labor costs including speeding up the pace of the machinery or expecting the same number of workers to tend a greater number of machines. Cuts in wage rates especially for piecework bred antagonism between Management and Labor. Then came a downturn in the textile business in the 1850s. Nathan Appleton, at mid-century the grand old man of textiles, blamed the industry's recession on overproduction, the disruptive effect of the British war in China, and the

Tariff of 1846 that reduced federal imposts to historic lows.[38] A nation-wide economic crisis in 1857 exacerbated the slowdown in textiles. During the recession, five of the Boston Associates' mills or related businesses had gone under, while several others teetered on the brink.[39]

As the industry stumbled, "a certain social stigma" began "to be ascribed to those employed in cotton-mill work."[40] The case of Berengera Caswell, whose lifeless body was found tied to a board in a brook in Saco, Maine in 1850, caused a widely-publicized scandal. An English-speaking Canadian by birth, Caswell was working in the Amoskeag textile mill in Manchester when she formed a relationship with a man named William Long. After Long left town, Caswell discovered she was pregnant. Caswell followed Long to Biddeford, Maine, Saco's twin city, where the couple sought an abortion from a physician of dubious distinction named James Smith. The procedure produced an infection that killed the woman and Smith disposed of the body in the stream. He was later arrested and found guilty of murder, a charge the Maine Supreme Court later found should have been manslaughter. The press covered the sensational story, and tabloid-worthy novelizations of Caswell's tale came into print.[41]

Caswell's was not the only such incident, and these tragedies nursed parental suspicions about the wisdom of allowing young women the freedoms they enjoyed in the mill towns. While Harriet Robinson described the mills as an unprecedented step toward the emancipation of women, the Victorian Age grew wary of the notion of women who had their own money and the liberty to make their own decisions, beyond the scrutiny of fathers or husbands.[42]

The Civil War, following within a few years of the industry's troubles in the 1850s, destabilized the cotton industry's labor markets. The Union blockaded Confederate ports and the resulting cotton drought caused economic dislocation and social unrest in textile manufacturing regions worldwide.[43] Some New England mills, dependent on Southern cotton, closed their doors and waited out the fighting. Others had reserves of raw material to continue to operate but working hours were cut. In Brunswick, the Cabot mill ceased production for a brief period in May 1861, one month after shots were fired at Fort Sumter. It then restarted the mill on a three-quarters schedule.[44] The company had a supply of raw material on hand, thanks to a cotton storehouse built the previous year with a capacity of a thousand bales.[45]

Mills that managed to find adequate cotton supplies came roaring back by the middle of the war years, but prices were steep. The average price of cotton consumed at the Cabot mill was 12 cents per pound in 1860. By 1864, the price ballooned to $1.87.[46] The final months of the war found the industry on its knees. An informant told the Massachusetts Bureau of Labor Statistics: "In December, 1864, Sherman took Savannah, and there came a great change. It knocked everything down; everything was prostrated until April, 1865."[47]

Whatever the state of the cotton industry during the fighting, service in the Civil War gave new impetus to the emigration movement from Québec. Estimates of the number of *Canadiens* who fought in the Civil War range from 20,000 to 53,000.[48] Two sons of Prudent Racine, Philibert and Cyprien, fought with the First Battery, Vermont Light Artillery in the war, serving in the Red River campaign in Louisiana. The brothers anglicized their names. Philibert took the alias "Philip F. Root" while Cyprien became "George S. Root." Philibert had his hearing and eyesight damaged in the fighting. The brothers both survived the war and returned briefly to Canada. Cyprien then moved to Michigan, also living for a few years in Kansas. Philibert came to Brunswick where two of his sisters, my great-great-grandmothers, joined him.

Canadiens who served in the Civil War became famous in their day. The ranks included Calixte (Calixa) Lavallée, a veteran of the Battle of Antietam serving with troops from Rhode Island. A composer and conductor, Lavallée wrote the music for the Canadian national anthem, *O Canada*. Major Edmond Mallet, a veteran of the battle of Cold Harbor, became one of the first historians of the French and *Canadien* presence in the United States. Having served with distinction in the Union Army, Mallet was appointed by President Lincoln to a federal government position. Major Mallet was a friend of the Métis leader Louis Riel and a Franco-American activist.[49]

As the war dragged on, many male industrial workers joined the Union Army. Other men and women laid off by the mills, or with their hours slashed, found jobs in war production industries.[50] Still others followed Horace Greely's *dictum* and went West. When the cotton

FIGURE 7: Philibert Racine (1845-1900) alias Philip F. Root,
First Battery, Vermont light artillery, c. 1862.

mills began to recover after the war, they found their textile labor
pool had evaporated.

A 1910 U.S. Senate report reflects on this transition:

The change in nationality of cotton-factory operatives was greatly
accelerated by the Civil War, which was particularly disastrous to that
industry...[I]n June and November 1862 only about one-half the number
of spindles in New York and the New England States were in operation,
and.... at Lowell nine of the great corporations shut down their mills and
"dismissed 10,000 operatives, penniless, into the streets." "This crime,
this worse than crime, this blunder," naively remarked one historian of
the city, "entailed its own punishment...When these companies resumed
operations, their former skilled operatives were dispersed, and could no

more be recalled than the Ten Lost Tribes of Israel".....When the factories opened again it was found that the operatives...had been absorbed in other industries, such as the manufacture of woolen goods, of shoes, and of clothing, which thrived while the cotton manufacture languished. As a result, there was, after the war, an actual want of women in the factory districts, "so much so that men are now employed to do work formerly done by women."

Overseers in mills at Lowell, New Bedford, Salem, and elsewhere stated to a committee on the message of the governor of Massachusetts, who had proposed the emigration of young women to the West, that they had scoured Maine, New Hampshire, and Vermont and had "actually imported families from Canada and Europe to meet the demands of their mills."[51]

The Dillingham Commission suggested that labor unrest in Lowell was a spur to *Canadien* immigration to the town. This report dates the arrival of the *Canadiens* to "the period immediately following the civil war." It states that during the Civil War, the mills were closed "through the timidity of the owners" and the workforce "considerably scattered." Not long after the mills re-opened following the war, skilled workers known as mule spinners went on strike for a ten-hour day. The report notes that these two events – the scattering of the workforce, followed not long after by the strike – were "roughly coincident with the French Canadian immigration and it is probable that they made the opportunity for new laborers to enter the employment of the mills."[52]

As the 1910 Senate report notes, desperate managers, their workforce "considerably scattered," launched a public relations campaign to attract wage-earners into the mills. Advertisements in Canada promoted the New England mill towns, and recruiters traveled north to bring workers into them.[53] The *Canadiens* then began to settle the U.S. by invitation.

The textile corporations recruited in Québec even before the war.[54] In 1859, the Dwight Manufacturing Company of Chicopee, Massachusetts commissioned an agent named J. M. Boynton to recruit labor north of the border. The Dwight Company found that a competing agent was already recruiting in Québec around Saint-Hyacinthe and Stanstead at that time.[55] Boynton brought 50 *Canadiennes* from Québec to the Western Massachusetts operation that year. The

Dwight firm continued to follow the pattern of hiring women as entry-level operatives. Québec natives were sometimes sent north to sell the mill towns to their countrymen. A recruiter named Joseph Proulx, from Saint-Hyacinthe, canvassed at Saint-Ours. He received four dollars per head "as well as a travel allowance and a percentage on the transportation costs of immigrants."[56]

A *Canadien* named Samuel Marin recruited for the Lowell firms immediately after the Civil War. Lowellian Charles Cowley writing in 1883 noted that there were few Franco-Americans in Lowell before 1865 when some of the town's manufacturers hired Marin to recruit in Québec. Marin persuaded his people in Québec of "the advantages to be derived from a 'change of base'" inducing them to move "with their families from the Valley of the St. Lawrence to the Valley of the Merrimack." Cowley notes that more *Canadiens* had come to Lowell than any other group in the nearly two decades since the end of the war. They had established a "permanent foothold" in the town, and the movement from Québec to Lowell was ongoing. [57] Unlike the Dwight Company's agent, Lowell's Marin recruited entire families.

The synergy between the revival of the textile industry post-war, and the aggressive recruitment campaign of the mills, brought the *Canadien* immigration movement to its height. It transformed a movement that had been mainly young, male, and migrant into a permanent settlement of *Canadien* families in New England.

The recruitment efforts of the mills met condemnation by the elites in Québec. The outspoken Bishop Louis Laflèche of Trois-Rivières denounced the *Canadiens* who were selling their countrymen to foreigners. He compared them to slave traders.[58] The bishop's comparison was inapt, but some of the recruiters' practices, such as locking their future mill workers in the railroad cars so that they wouldn't renege on their commitment to "a change of base," did little to discourage such comparisons.

The recruiters did not always pay the prospective mill workers' transportation costs from Québec. In an interview for the Federal Writer's Project in the 1930s, Philippe Lemay, of Manchester, who came with his family from Québec to New England in 1864, gives this account:

The majority of French Canadian immigrants came to Manchester at their own expense. In fact, all of them did, so far as I know, and they didn't have to be coaxed, either. It is true that some companies, seeing in the type *quebecois* an honest, able workman, asking little for himself and rather unwilling to let himself be fooled by strike agitators, brought here a certain number through recruiting agents sent to Canada for the purpose....However, if their fares and other expenses were paid by the textile corporations, it was never mentioned and I don't believe it was done.

Our people didn't come to the States with money they had saved up, though, since they emigrated because they were really obliged to go where they could earn their daily bread and butter. To raise enough money to buy railroad tickets for the family and pay for food, rooms and other expenses on route, they had to *faire encan* [hold an auction], sell all their household goods at auction. That money was practically all gone when they arrived here, and all they possessed was the clothes they had on their backs.[59]

Fever for The States

From the close of the Civil War until 1900, workers from Québec came across the border in wave after wave, following the business cycle.[60] Families from the poorer classes of Québec abandoned their rural homes for the wages promised by New England factories, forests, and farms. So large was this movement of the rural poor toward the States that it became known in Québec as "the Exodus" or "the Fever for the States."

Historian Robert Rumilly describes the symptoms:

Across the province [of Québec], there was a daily exodus. Some families sold their furniture at auction, closed their house and went away. Every Sunday, at the doors of the churches, the public criers announced these sales: thus, those who were departing realized the money for their voyage. Some neighbors followed their example, and then some others: it was like a contagion, like an epidemic. In the parishes, some entire ranges were emptied out, and all the houses were closed, and all the lands were rented out, or sold, or simply abandoned. Some smaller centers were depopulated. Each run of the railroad carried *Canadien* families. The Grand Trunk transported them directly from Montréal, from Saint-Hyacinthe or from Sherbrooke, to Lewiston and Portland. The stations were full. At Saint-Jean, they sold several hundred dollars in tickets per day...[people] deserted the country of Québec as if a curse had struck it.[61]

The *Canadiens* were not alone. Anglophones from many parts of Canada also departed for the U.S. in this period. But the numbers of *Canadiens* of Québec who left their homeland were disproportionate to their *per capita* population in the Confederation.[62] The concentration of the French-speaking population in Québec made the drain of *Canadiens* visible and dramatic. English-speaking Canadians in the U.S. tended to assimilate easily to life south of the border.[63] The movement of these Anglophones across the frontier did not have the feverish character of the *Canadien* movement. It engendered less anxiety among elites on both sides of the border.

By 1870, there were more than one hundred thousand Franco-Americans in New England. As the fever spread, the balance of the Franco-American population among the states in the region shifted. While in 1860, Vermont and Maine represented about two-thirds of the Franco-American population of the region, a decade later these states' share had declined to 44 percent. By 1870, Massachusetts had the greatest number of New England Franco-Americans. In the last 30 years of the 19th century, the Franco-American population of New England would grow by a factor greater than five.[64] By 1900, one out of every ten New Englanders was Franco-American.[65]

Franco-American neighborhoods, called Little Canadas, developed in the industrial cities of New England. A network of regional mutual benefit societies – called *national societies* – and religious and social institutions supported these neighborhoods and linked them together. The Little Canadas centered around the mill, French-language newspapers, the national societies, and the so-called *national parish* church.[66]

The Catholic Church distinguishes *Territorial* parishes from *National* parishes. Territorial parishes serve all Catholics within its jurisdiction regardless of nationality or language. The vernacular language of the territorial parish (the liturgical language was Latin for all Catholics) was the common language of the country. In the U.S. that language was English. National parishes served almost exclusively a specific ethnic group, using the language of that group in sermons, announcements, in confession, etc. Along with the national parish came the parochial school, with instruction, at least in part, in the language of the parish. In many Franco-American parochial schools, instruction was in French for one-half of the school day, with the other half in English. Both of my grandfathers attended schools in Maine on this pattern.[67]

In the Little Canadas, French was the language heard on the streets, in the mill, as well as in church.[68] It was the language heard in the grocery stores, clothing stores, and other businesses that served the Franco-American population. Many mill towns had a Franco-American economy parallel to its Yankee counterpart. The owners of these small businesses often formed the vanguard of a tiny Franco-American middle class, which might also include local Franco-American professionals and the parish priest.[69]

The pace of the growth of the institutional network in the 1860s and 1870s is a measure of the Franco-Americans' presence in the mill towns as a permanent community. By 1880, New England's Franco-Americans founded as many as 63 parishes and 73 national societies.[70] By that year, there were 37 French-language newspapers in New England and another 11 in New York.[71] By 1891, Franco-Americans had 53 parochial schools with over 26,000 students in attendance; by 1908 that number grew to 133 schools with nearly 55,000 pupils, comprising 41 percent of the region's Catholic schools.[72] Through these institutions, Franco-Americans developed within their neighborhoods outposts of Québec in New England.

As the Franco-American beachheads in the mill towns became settlements, the floodgates of emigration opened wider. The 1880s were the height of the boom.[73] Beginning from a few select areas, a greater portion of Québec joined the movement as it gained momentum. Once established, *Canadien* working families themselves became uncompensated recruiters for the mills through word-of-mouth contacts. One immigration pattern saw individuals come to New England, scout the territory, and then send for the family. The established Franco-American family then recruited their relatives and neighbors back home, who then recruited their relatives and neighbors in turn.[74]

Through this pattern of migration, mill towns in New England became twinned with a town or region of Québec. Although emigrants came from many regions of the province to any given mill town, each town tended to have a critical mass of Franco-Americans who hailed from a single region. For example, Woonsocket saw many immigrants from the Richelieu Valley. Sorel was the former home of many *Canadien* immigrants of Southbridge, Massachusetts, while Salem Franco-Americans came mainly from Rimouski. Waterville, Maine was associated with the Beauce region. The town of L'Islet, the county of the same name, and three surrounding counties (Kamouraska, Montmagny, and Témiscouata) supplied many of Brunswick's Franco-Americans.[75]

Within the mill towns, there also developed secondary clusters of smaller groups of Franco-Americans from other parts of Québec. For instance, although many Brunswick Franco-Americans hailed from L'Islet, there was a smaller, secondary group from Roxton Falls, in a different region of the province.[76]

The Saviors of Textile Manufacturing

With its new Franco-American workforce, the New England cotton industry recovered after the Civil War and the region's industrialization continued apace. By 1880, New England was home to more than one-fifth of the U.S.'s manufacturing workers while it represented only 8 percent of the nation's population. New England had twice as many manufacturing workers *per capita* than the U.S. as a whole. The textile industry employed better than a third of these New England manufacturing employees, and over one-half of U.S. textile employees lived in the region.[77] New England cotton textile production represented 80 percent of the industry's entire U.S. output, a five percent increase over its share in 1860.[78]

The concentration of Franco-Americans in manufacturing was intense. By 1900, 62 percent of employed Franco-Americans in Rhode Island worked in manufacturing; the numbers were 58 percent in Massachusetts, and 57 percent in Connecticut and New Hampshire. Manufacturing employed 78 percent of all New England Franco-American women who worked outside the home; the figure rose as high as 84 percent in Rhode Island.[79] As many as three out of four New England Franco-Americans lived in towns where manufacturing was dominant.[80]

Concentrated in manufacturing in general, textiles claimed the largest cohort of Franco-Americans. The U.S. Federal Census shows that in 1900, New England was home to 54 percent of the U.S.'s cotton mill operatives. Almost one-quarter (24 percent) of all cotton mill operatives nationwide were Franco-American New Englanders. Workers with at least one French-Canadian-born parent comprised 44 percent of cotton textile operatives in New England, more than twice as many as any other ethnic bloc in the mills and many times the numbers of most. In Connecticut, a state where Franco-Americans made up only eight percent of the foreign-born population in 1900, they represented almost 48 percent of cotton mill wage-earners. In Maine, workers with at least one French-Canadian-born parent represented 69 percent of the state's cotton textile operatives.[81]

With the help of its Franco-American workforce, New England's textile leviathan not only overcame a disastrous civil war but grew in terms of both capital invested and production capacity. Between 1850 and 1890 capital invested in cotton textiles nationwide increased from $74.5 million to $354 million. The value of the industry's products rose from about $62 million to $268 million in that same period. By 1895, the textile industry, including cotton, wool, and silk goods, with the factory products that depended upon them, comprised one-ninth of all U.S. manufacturing.[82]

New England mills accounted for much of the growth in the industry's capacity. The number of spindles in the region, the customary metric of the textile industry's capacity, increased by nearly 43 percent between 1860 and 1870 and then grew by another 57 percent by 1880.[83] About four-fifths of New England's textile capacity in 1880 was located within a 60-mile radius of Boston.[84] Out of 17.1 million spindles in the U.S. in 1895, Massachusetts mills alone accounted for 7.2 million or just under 42 percent of the nation's capacity.[85] A census of Massachusetts conducted that year found that Franco-Americans comprised nearly one-third of the state's cotton mill employees, the largest ethnic cohort in the industry.[86]

Manufacturing continued to thrive in New England only because the owners and managers found a sufficiently large cheap labor pool in the *Canadien* farmers and laborers. They were ripe for the harvest in a territory located conveniently adjacent to New England. The Franco-American influx enabled New England's leading industry to maintain its market position and sustain its growth. With hundreds of millions of dollars in capital riding on textiles, Franco-Americans were the unwitting saviors of the investors and of the region's economy. So vital was cotton agriculture and manufacturing to the 19th century U.S. that it does not go too far to suggest that the Franco-American influx helped to restore the nation's economy after the war.

The saviors of the investors included numerous child laborers. The 19th century *Canadien* family was an economic unit modeled on the subsistence farm.[87] Children on a family farm worked at tasks suited to their abilities as soon as they were able. They were expected to produce as well as to consume. Our notion of a breadwinner was foreign to these families. Everyone won their bread by contributing cooperatively to the whole. Children were not only a cost-center for the family economic unit but also a profit-center. Farm tasks are endless, but they vary over the course of the day and year, and the work is mainly outdoors.[88] The work in the mills was repetitious, in conditions that were loud, blazingly hot, humid, and frequently dangerous.[89]

Putting one's numerous children into the mill was a survival strategy. Children, sometimes several in a single family, worked in the mills and turned their earnings over to the patriarch of the family, entrusted with the household's financial decisions.[90] The Dillingham Commission's research found husbands accounted for just 52 percent of household income in Franco-American families. One-third of that income came from minors.[91] Since one income was not enough to support the family, child labor was unexceptional.

Not So Docile

As Franco-Americans came to dominate the textile workforce, some owners heaped praise on these saviors of the industry, lauding their alleged innate qualities of industriousness and submission to authority. One contemporary observer opined, "The French are much better than the Irish when learned. They work steadier and are much more ambitious."[92] An 1882 Massachusetts government report noted that "the employers of labor have done much to stimulate French[-Canadian] immigration." The Management "prefer them in the mills," the report continued, "for they are industrious in the extreme, do not grumble about pay, are docile, and have nothing to do with labor agitations."[93]

"Labor agitations" in the textile mills had a long history. The women who worked in the region's textile industry in its first years went on strike in Pawtucket, Rhode Island as early as 1824. Twenty years later, the women of the Lowell mills formed the Lowell Female Labor Reform Association. Later, immigrants from Great Britain and Ireland brought with them an embryonic working-class consciousness from across the sea. English mule-spinners, skilled workers with a history of collective action in the U.K., formed a union in Fall River in 1858.[94]

There was no such history of organized labor in the agricultural districts of Québec. The *Canadiens* of 19th century rural Québec worked mainly on their own account. They were farmers, small tradespeople, day-laborers, or they worked in cottage industries. There were few corporations to strike against, and there was no European-style, industrial working class in their agricultural economy. Early attempts at unionization in Québec included the short-lived *Grande Association de Protection des Ouvriers du Canada* [Great Association for the Protection of the Workers of Canada] and the more successful Knights of Labour.[95] But the latter was active mainly in the cities and towns. The Church was the engine of social organization. The clergy preached against affiliation with organizations, such as Labor Unions, that were outside the church's purview. Franco-Americans tended to unionize slowly, only as the 19th century became the 20th. During the post-Civil War Gilded Age, Franco-Americans were thought to be a thorn in the side of organized labor.[96]

Desperate, docile, indefatigable workers, and disinclined to "labor agitations": whether these characterizations were truthful or not, they comprised a made-to-order set of traits according to the cotton industrialists. They could not have manufactured in their mills a more perfect working-class.

Unfortunately for them, Franco-Americans were not nearly as docile as reputed. Because they were slow to unionize, it does not follow that they were averse to strikes. Some sources portray the Franco-Americans as fleeing the mill towns when strikes occurred.[97] The families that departed one mill town for another at the first sign of strikes were the families intending to return to Québec. They were in the U.S. to save a quantity of cash and head home. They weren't there to take a stand. However, the Franco-Americans who intended to make New England their home fought for their perceived rights in many a mill town. Strikes were by no means unknown in Québec, so the tactic was not beyond the Franco-Americans.[98]

In Brunswick, there were at least four strikes in the Cabot mill in the six years between 1881 and 1887. In August of 1881, fifteen boys from eight to fourteen years of age walked off the job when they found out that children's wages were higher in the mills of nearby Lisbon and Lewiston. The local newspaper reports that some children were paid a dollar per week, while others made just eight cents per day. Adults followed the boys off the job. Immediately, Greene gave the residents in the company-owned tenements their 30-day notice to vacate. The local newspaper reported rumors abroad that some "French families" were contemplating leaving the town but they stayed put, and the strike came to an end in less than a week.[99] By 1881, "French family" and "mill worker" were synonymous terms in Brunswick. In all, 550 employees were involved in the 1881 strike, 175 men and 375 women. The strike gained the men an eight cents per day raise and women a ten cents per day hike.

A strike of similar duration broke out at the Cabot mill in March 1886. Women led this action. It began when speeder tenders asked for an increase in wages. As in 1881, organized labor was no factor in the strike. The women won a pay raise from $0.85 to $0.95 per day. The following year there were at least two strikes. One occurred in January and led Greene to shut down the mill for two days. Another week-long strike began on July 11. Three hundred and twenty-five weavers struck for an increase in pay. Management suspended all 700 hands in the mill for a week. The strikers won an increase of five cents per cut and work resumed. The strikes in 1880s Brunswick were a partial or total success for Labor.[100]

At Suncook, New Hampshire, Franco-Americans struck against three mills in 1881. The strikers held mass meetings, paraded in the streets with clubs, and prevented willing workers from entering the mills. The *New York Times* covered the strike on its front page, reporting that "nearly all" of the strikers were "French Canadian." The newspaper covered the arrest of the leader of the movement, "a French Canadian acting in a riotous manner" who was arrested by "special officers and taken to the station." The *Times* continues,

> [He was] followed the entire distance by hundreds of strikers throwing missiles and with drawn knives. The officers were obliged to draw revolvers and use billies many times before reaching the station. The prisoner is now under guard. It is expected there will be an attempt to release him, as the strikers make threats to that effect.[101]

Not very docile. Nor were the Franco-Americans at Norwich, Connecticut who walked out of the local mill in 1886 to protest high-handed treatment from Management. Cotton mill employees at the Baltic Mill went on strike due to fines imposed for small accidents such as spilling a drop of oil or a single broken thread in a loom. When 400 weavers were nickeled and dimed for $50 in fines, they took their grievance to their manager. He refused to hear their case, ordering them to "go out of this office and be damned." Instantly, a thousand employees were in the streets.

Besides the fines, strikers also complained of substandard wages and price gouging at the company store where the markup was 25 percent. All employees were obliged to live in the company-owned tenements. Between the rent and the company store, Management recouped much of its labor costs. Norwich residents complained that with a thousand employees on strike, the responsibility for their support would fall on the town. One local taxpayer told the *New York Times*, "The Baltic Mill is a curse to this town. We get a small tax from it...and the town has to pay more than three times the amount for the support of its poor."[102]

In Manville, Rhode Island in June 1887, two thousand predominantly Franco-American employees of three large cotton mills went on strike, shutting down operations. Their grievances included poor working conditions and reduced wages. As in Brunswick in 1881, Management gave immediate notice to its employees living in company-owned housing to quit the premises. In this case, the strike was poorly organized, and Franco-American employees started to leave the town.[103] In the winter of 1898, strikes hit New Bedford, Massachusetts; the twin Maine towns of Biddeford and Saco; and elsewhere in the region. Brunswick joined the strike and the stoppage dragged on for more than two months.[104] During the strike, the Agent of the Cabot mill received a death threat written in French.[105] Canadian authorities used the opportunity of the 1898 strikes to send agents to lure Franco-Americans back to Québec to settle in the Lac Saint-Jean region.[106]

Many strikes would follow in the 20th century, but by then Labor began to organize throughout the textile industry. During the 19th century, Franco-American-led strikes tended to be spontaneous actions.[107] But Franco-Americans before 1900 did not shy away from a fight. In the smaller textile centers, where they were the majority in the mills, as in Brunswick, Suncook, Norwich, and Manville, they defended their interests.

Franco-Americans would have many causes to defend themselves since conditions in the mill towns deteriorated after immigrants and their children became the bulk of the labor force, amid "urban crowding, squalor, and disease."[108] For the Yankee owners and managers, the Anglo-Protestant women who worked in the mills in the first half of the 19th century were *their own*. When the mills became the workplace of Irish and Franco-American women, men, and children, the concern about the employees' comfort and edification seemed less pressing. As a utopian industrial experiment, Lowell was finished by 1845 – the same moment when immigrants began to replace Yankee women.[109] Gone were the literary journal and the visiting dignitaries; there to stay for a long tenure were overcrowded tenements and slums.

Harriet Robinson returned to Lowell in her later years and described the town's decline in her 1898 memoirs. During her return visit, Robinson observed that an estimated two-thirds of the workforce consisted of "American-born children of foreign parentage." She reported the contrast between the "jubilant feeling" the young women of the looms once had and the "tired hopelessness" of the latter-day workers whom she describes as "underfed" with a "prematurely old look."

She also reports that conditions in the mills had declined markedly since her youth. Once the factories "were light, well ventilated, and moderately heated" but they had become massive complexes, with buildings crowded together such that workers gazed out the window onto brick walls and could breathe only stale air. When she revisited the room where she used to work, she found the heat "so intense" that she "could hardly breathe." She found the housing in the streets where she once lived in a "dilapidated condition" with "houses going to decay, broken side walks, and filthy streets." She deplored the "modern system of overcrowding the mill-people." She described her return to Lowell as a visit to "the ruins of an industry once clean and prosperous."[110]

Francis Cabot Lowell's intention to create a kinder brand of industrialism lasted for as long as Yankee women dominated the labor force. Although his generation's brand of paternalism is not to modern tastes, Lowell and associates nonetheless recognized the humanity of the worker. A latter-day textile manager expressed views that epitomized the change in attitude between Lowell's generation and the manager's: "I regard my work people just as I regard my machinery. So long as they can do my work for what I choose to pay them, I keep them, getting out of them all I can...When my machines get old and useless, I reject them and get new, and these people are part of my machinery."[111]

It was the *othering* of the distinct, alien races in the mills that made possible this dehumanization, the identification of human beings with interchangeable machine parts. Care and empathy extended to those within the tribe and French-speaking Catholics of Québec were not members of the Yankee tribe.

In Brunswick, as the numbers of Franco-Americans grew, the community faced public health challenges brought on by the squalor surrounding the Cabot mill, by the lack of empathy that created it. We know the story today only through the efforts of a crusading newspaper editor and a courageous Franco-American doctor.

CHAPTER SIX

FRANCO-AMERICANS COME TO BRUNSWICK

On June 13, 1889, Brunswick celebrated its 150th year. Favorite sons delivered addresses, read poems, and paraded in a procession through the streets. They then enjoyed a sumptuous banquet with turkey, larded chicken, and lobster salad; cucumbers and sliced tomatoes; strawberries and cream, macaroons, and ice cream.

Professor Charles Carroll Everett a town native and a graduate of its Bowdoin College gave the keynote address. He was the son of Ebenezer Everett an original incorporator of the Cabot Company in 1853. Charles Everett pursued graduate studies at Harvard Divinity School where he later taught, writing on the philosophy of religion.[1] In his encomium to the town, mentioning its "solemn pines," "pleasant mall," and the college yard, the professor also notes,

> It is very pleasant, early of a summer evening, to pass from the classic shades of the college to the lower end of the town, in which one finds one's self as if in another World. The bright faces and the lively jargon of the French create for the moment the illusion of being in some foreign land.[2]

The local newspaper called this "foreign land" within the Yankee town the "French Quarter." The learned professor termed it "the lower end of the town" with more justification than he knows. A half-century later, a less nostalgic speaker, referring to the conditions of sanitation in the French Quarter, wrote, "in 1880 a man from the Middle Ages would have felt at home amidst the dirt and smells of Brunswick."[3]

When did the *Canadiens* bring their "bright faces" and "lively jargon" to this elegant college town? When and how did they develop their enclave, a small outpost of "another World" in coastal Maine?

The manuscript U.S. Federal Census records the growth of Brunswick's Franco-American community. The census for 1840, the accepted date for the commencement of the immigration movement from Québec to the U.S., found no *Canadiens* in Brunswick. Almost everyone in Brunswick in 1840 spoke English. Most were of British descent and were born in Maine or another New England state. There had been little demographic change in the town since the arrival of British colonists some 200 years prior.[4]

1850

By mid-century, the picture begins to change. There was a small African-American enclave in Brunswick in 1850 but it quickly and mysteriously disappears from the town. The havoc in Ireland in the 1840s brought a Hibernian element there. A group of Irish laborers worked on the local railroad in Brunswick, but they did not form a separate neighborhood. In addition to these African-American and Irish populations, there were a few residents born in a small number of Western European countries, in the West Indies, or in English-speaking parts of today's Canada.

In addition to these populations, two families, eleven individuals, from French-Canada appear to be living together. The census lists the heads of these families as "Mitchell Blay" (Michel Blais) and "John Demouy" (Jean Demouy). These eleven people were all born in Canada, except for two-year-old Margaret Demouy who was born in Maine. Both men were "laborers." None of the adults could read or write. Both heads of households were in their fifties. The subsequent decennial Federal Censuses find neither of these families in Brunswick. No one knew it in 1850, but these two *Canadien* families, arriving in the town sometime between 1840 and 1850, formed the front end of a wedge.

1860

There are four consecutive pages in the 1860 U.S. Federal Census of Brunswick recording the residents of eight contiguous dwellings, inhabited by thirteen French-speaking families from "Lower Canada" (Québec). The occupation of all but a few of the employed members of these families was "factory operative." These appear to be residents of boarding houses associated with the recently formed Cabot Manufacturing Company and most of these *Canadiens* were employed there.

Outside of this group of families living in a cluster, there was one other couple from Lower Canada, Joseph Janelle ("Janell") and his wife, Lucie. Joseph gave his occupation as "Millman." He was a naturalized U.S. citizen, having taken the oath in 1856. He was from a parish not far away from the other *Canadien* families in the town. His naturalization papers state that he crossed the border at Derby Line, Vermont in 1838, coming to Brunswick in 1844. If he arrived in Brunswick in the 1840s, he should appear in the 1850 census, but he does not. If it is true that he came to Brunswick in 1844, then he may have been the first person born in Québec to come to the town.

In the U.S. Census, the French names of *Canadiens* were either anglicized or mangled by 19th century enumerators. It is safe to assume that the enumerator could not speak French. Most of these *Canadien* workers could neither speak English nor write their names, so spelling them for the census enumerator was not an option. Unfamiliar with *Canadien* surnames, the enumerators tended to either spell them phonetically or transform them into a familiar English name. Franco-American genealogists have developed an arcane art of resurrecting the genuine *Canadien* names out of these records. Using the microfilmed parish registers of Québec, the 19th century Canadian Censuses (where available), and following their movements within the U.S., I traced these fourteen families in 1860 Brunswick back to their Québec origins.[5]

These families originated in a small cluster of parishes east of Montréal, between the Richelieu and Yamaska rivers in Québec. Brunswick tends to confirm the finding that the Richelieu Valley was an early center of the emigration movement. With one exception, the occupation of these heads of households, before they came to the U.S., was either "farmer" or "laborer." These families were mobile. One-half of them spent time in at least one other New England mill town in addition to Brunswick, and I traced nine of these families to more than one parish in Québec. Some of them have children born in Maine as well as in Canada, while others have young children born in Massachusetts as well.

Several of these families owned real estate worth as much as $2,000 per the census. Given the transient nature of these families, and the fact that they appear to be residents of mill-owned boarding houses in Brunswick, the real estate they owned was probably in Québec, not Maine. The heads of household of these early Franco-American families were middle-aged men, in their 40s and 50s. They do not seem to be coming to New England to establish their families there. The findings of my research on Brunswick's Franco-Americans in 1860 is consistent with the image of families working in the New England mills temporarily while expecting to return to their home-steads in Québec.

Some of these families were related. One of the heads of household was the son-in-law of another. Another head of household emigrated with his adult son, whose family forms a separate household. These connections are consistent with a pattern of migration with extended family groups.

Among these families in the 1860 census, there is also evidence of child labor. Eleven-year-olds worked as factory operatives. In the coming decades, Brunswick's Cabot mill will employ even younger children. The mill remained a state leader in the category of child labor through the end of the century. Numbers gathered by the Maine Bureau of Industrial and Labor Statistics show that in 1894 the Cabot Company, a mid-sized mill, employed more children under the age of 15 than all but one of the cotton mills surveyed. In 1895, the Cabot mill employed 69 such children and led the pack in this category by a wide margin. The next largest child employer had 50 such employees, and the numbers of employed children per mill fell off rapidly after that. In 1899 and again in 1900, the Cabot mill was the largest employer

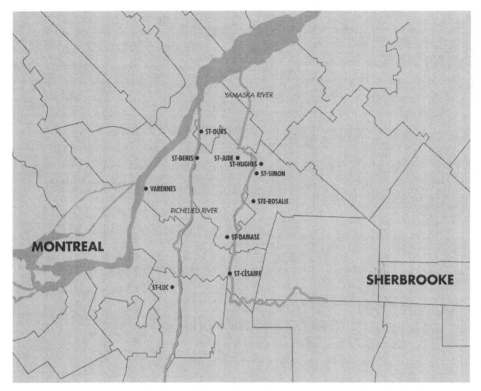

FIGURE 8: Source parishes of Brunswick Franco-American families 1860.
(Map by Erica Vermette)

of children under the age of 15 among the cotton manufacturers supplying data to the Bureau.[6]

The Franco-Americans of 1860 did not receive the warmest welcome in Brunswick, in the days of the Know Nothings. Eyewitnesses reflecting on this earliest period of Franco-American Brunswick recalled,

> Once, there was such antipathy between American Protestants, Irish and *Canadiens*, that often, in meetings on the street and even at the factory, we came to insults and blows. "We didn't dare go out at night," said a witness, "from fear of finding ourselves in some fight. Do you want to go to the post office to get your mail? We would go all together in a 'gang' to protect ourselves in case of attack. Also, we didn't think to run about, no more the young men than the young ladies. We stayed quietly in the house."

Those that we dreaded the most were the Protestant fanatics who hated Catholics and were always prepared to do some dirty deed (*mauvais coup*) to them. At Bath and Lewiston, they had burned and destroyed several times the rooms which served as Catholic chapels. At Brunswick, they did not come to these excesses of savagery, but we report that one evening, returning to Topsham and passing before a small house situated on the side of the river and occupied by two *Canadien* families, Labbé and Lévesque, some of these fanatics tried to demolish it and throw the debris in the river. They didn't manage, however, to complete the execution of their criminal plan. But a woman, who found herself then alone and sick in the house was so scared that she died a few days later as a result of this fear.[7]

1870

The 1870 census for Brunswick contains ten-and-a-half consecutive pages of French names. There are more than 65 Franco-American families in Brunswick in 1870. The Franco-American population grew nearly fourfold in the 1860s, numbering 413 in 1870. The census is explicit that most of this population, over the age of seven years, worked in the cotton mill. By 1870, almost one out of every ten Brunswick residents was a French-Canadian textile mill worker or a family member of one of them.

The Franco-American population in 1870 lived huddled together. Only three Franco-American families lived apart from the housing associated with the Cabot mill: the family of Thomas "Ruiz" (Ruest), and two families with the surname Choquet who work for the Maine Central Railroad. By 1870 a population of several hundred, in a town of several thousand, lived together in a body, spoke its own language, and worked according to its own rhythm – that of the mill.

The birthplaces of their youngest children demonstrate continued mobility within this group. The family of Joseph Benoit, recorded in the 1860 census, now has a new member, another Joseph, five years old in 1870, born in Rhode Island. I have traced this family to several parishes in Québec as well. Children among the Brunswick Franco-American families born in Canada, as well as in other New England states, suggests itinerant, mill-working families.

Despite the mobility, in 1870 there are a growing number of families that became permanent residents of Brunswick. Three of the Franco-American families in the 1860 census are also present in 1870, which dates a permanent Franco-American community in the town to the 1860s. Many of the Franco-American men and women in Brunswick by 1870 became naturalized U.S. citizens, and their families remained in Brunswick for generations. Many of their descendants still live in the area after almost a century and a half.

After the Civil War, there was a shift in the source of Brunswick's Franco-American immigrants. While the Brunswick Franco-Americans of 1860 were from the Richelieu Valley, by 1870 *Canadiens* have started to arrive from the town and county of L'Islet, and three other nearby counties on the south bank of the St. Lawrence. In the 1930s and 1940s, William N. Locke, a linguist from the Massachusetts Institute of Technology studied the Brunswick Franco-American community. He states that the first *Canadien* to come from L'Islet to Brunswick arrived via ox cart in the 1850s. The trip took three weeks. This unnamed individual then returned to L'Islet and subsequently brought three other men with him back to Brunswick. These men later returned to Lower Canada, where they were married and returned (again) to Brunswick. These men wrote home and invited their extended family and friends to join them and slowly the stream from L'Islet began to flow.[8]

If Franco-Americans of this era did not have a national parish in New England, it was not uncommon for them to return to Québec to get married or to have their children baptized in their home parish. In 1867, I see marriages recorded at L'Islet where Brunswick is the residence of the groom.[9] These marriages appear in the parish register at L'Islet the year after a major expansion of the Cabot mill in 1866.[10] The need for additional hands in the newly expanded mill produced a shift in the source of Brunswick Franco-American emigrants, from the Richelieu Valley to the L'Islet region. If the L'Islet-to-Brunswick connection originated in the 1850s, it is not yet visible in the 1860 census. The earliest workers from L'Islet at Brunswick were migrant, as Locke's account suggests, and did not form a permanent community in Brunswick until the post-war 1860s.

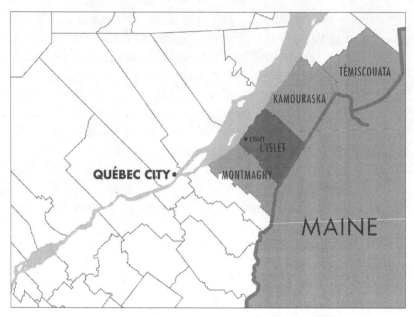

FIGURE 9: Source counties of Brunswick Franco-American
families after 1865. (Map by Erica Vermette)

1880

Between 1870 and 1880, the Franco-American population of Brunswick grew almost three-fold. Brunswick's Franco-American community numbered 1,199 individuals in 1880. From about a dozen families in 1860, the number of Franco-American families in Brunswick reached three digits by 1880. By that year, between one-in-four and one-in-five Brunswick residents is Franco-American. During the 1870s and 1880s, new families arrived in Brunswick from Québec on an ongoing basis. Possessing a core of families who had been in Maine for more than a decade, newcomers continued to reinforce the connection with Québec.

The 1870s and 1880s saw the beginnings of an institutional network that bound the Franco-American population together and served as a link between Brunswick and other Franco-American centers. In 1877, the Catholic Church established a local parish, named for Saint-Jean Baptiste [St. John the Baptist], a patron of *Canadiens*.

Today, the church is known as Saint John's. Officially, St. John's was not designated as a national parish but its members, into the mid-20th century, were overwhelmingly Franco-American. Latin and French inscriptions decorate the church. The captions on the stations of the cross, iconography that appears in virtually every Catholic Church, is in French. The parish priests, even when they were of Irish origin, were fluent in French. Most of the gravestones in the cemetery dating before 1940 are inscribed in French. The 1927 book celebrating the 50th anniversary of the parish is bilingual, with most of the text in French.[11]

Not long after the dedication of St. John's church came the parochial school. The school had lay teachers at first but soon attracted an order of nuns known as *la Congrégation des Dames de Sion* [the Congregation of the Ladies of Zion].[12] A church-linked marching band appeared in early 1881.[13] My great-grandfather was a founding member. The Saint-Jean-Baptiste Society, mainly a mutual aid organization in its U.S. incarnation, came to Brunswick by the 1880s.[14] *Les Artisans* [The Artisans], a society with a similar mission based in Montréal, had members among the town's Franco-Americans.[15]

The local newspaper in Brunswick in the 1880s began to speak of a *French Quarter* consisting of tenement housing owned, for the most part, by the Cabot Company. Not only did the Cabot mill employ most of the Franco-Americans, it housed them as well. Although the term was not used in Brunswick, this cluster of tenements and the area surrounding them was the root of Brunswick's Little Canada.

Contemporary newspaper accounts of the tenements in Brunswick's French Quarter describe two- or three-story houses with eight, two-bedroom apartments in each. The 1880 census represents the highest average household size in the 1850-1900 period, with an average of 20 people per dwelling among the Franco-Americans. But the size of a "dwelling" and the numbers of people who inhabited them varied widely. A better measure is population density. In 1886, the town's Franco-American doctor estimated that the French Quarter housed 500 persons per acre.[16]

In 1880, the French-speaking population remained in its worker housing in a discrete portion of the town. We find the Franco-

American population in the census split into two large groups of contiguous dwellings, one west and the other east of Maine Street. In the census, there are about four pages of French names in the group to the east of Maine Street and about twenty continuous pages of French names in the group to its west.

Out of this population of nearly 1,200, I find eight clerks in various retail stores, six workers in a pulp mill, four domestic servants, three bakers, three blacksmiths, three house carpenters, three workers in a paper mill, three workers in a saw mill, two dressmakers, two shoe-makers, a worker in a box shop, a railroad worker, a glassmaker, a stone mason, a marble cutter, an errand boy, an office boy, a barber, a saloon keeper, a farmer, a physician, and the parish priest. The occupation of all others employed outside the home is either "Works in Cotton mill" or "Laborer." These two occupations employed 96 percent of 1880 Brunswick's Franco-Americans.

The 1880 census records large Franco-American families in Brunswick, with as many as ten or twelve family members, from the parents to their eight and nine-year-old children, working in the mill. My great-grandmother's family was typical. Albina Ouellette (or Ouellet), my father's grandmother, was born in February 1868 in Roxton Falls, Québec. The 1880 census reports that Albina, age twelve, her father, and seven of her eleven siblings, including her ten-year-old younger brother, worked in the cotton mill.

Outside of the two main centers of the Franco-American population straddling Maine Street, we find one Franco-American woman, Marie Gamache, working as a domestic servant for Benjamin Greene. Besides Gamache, four families and one individual lived apart from the French Quarter. These families include the Marcoux, Lavallée, and Charles Gamache families with the heads of household listed as "laborers." Judging from where they lived, I believe these men were farm workers. In between these two families, Henri Boucher, a marble cutter, aged 54 lived by himself. Finally, well outside the downtown area, lived a farm family headed by Pierre Gamache.

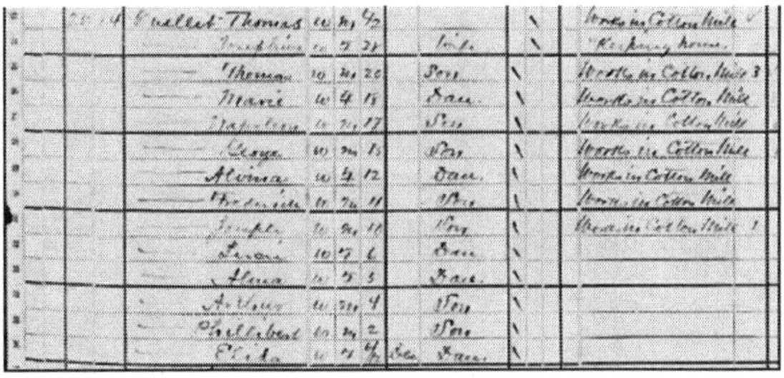

FIGURE 10: Ouellet family in 1880 census. Family has 12 children,
7 working in the cotton mill. Albina ("Alvina") at line 29.
Occupation on right *"Works in Cotton Mill."*

1900

The Franco-American population of Brunswick more than doubled in the 20 years between 1880 and 1900.[17] The 1900 census is more explicit than its predecessors in identifying national origin. As in 1880, it asks for the place of birth of the subject and his or her parents, but only in 1890 did the census begin to distinguish the subject's place of birth as either "Canada-French" or "Canada-English."

I count 2,556 Franco-Americans in Brunswick in 1900.[18] More than 2,500 souls would constitute a substantial parish in rural Québec at the time. By the beginning of the 20th century, Franco-Americans form 38 percent of the population of Brunswick, and their numbers continued to grow. By 1900, 40 percent of the French-speaking population of the town was born in the United States. By the 1920s, Brunswick was about one-half Franco-American.[19]

In 1900, there was a much greater distribution of the Franco-American population throughout the town than in previous decades. The 1900 census makes a distinction between *"Brunswick Village,"* the central, commercial portion of Brunswick, roughly the area between Bowdoin College and the Cabot Mill, and *"Brunswick Township,"* which includes the outlying rural districts. The Franco-Americans remained concentrated in a core neighborhood near the mill, but a small number now live all over the township, in the more rural areas as well as in the village.

Some of the Franco-Americans moved out of the mill housing and bought property nearby. An 1885 article in the local newspaper reports that "the French Canadians" had "recently" purchased property and were beginning to build houses in the "northwestern part of the village," the portion of the town between the mill and the Catholic Church.[20] They built homes cooperatively in this neighborhood. "The way they put together a wooden building is something of a marvel," gushed the newspaper's editor. This development began a move away from the tenements into a residential area that became the Franco-American neighborhood in the late 19th and 20th centuries.

Some of the streets in this neighborhood were 100 percent Franco-American in 1900. For instance, the residents of Oak Street, where my six-year-old grandfather was living with his family in 1900, about 150 people, are all Franco-American. The 1900 census gives language data only for those who are over ten years of age or so. Among this group, nearly 40 percent of Oak Street residents spoke only French. Men and their older sons who worked outside the home tended to know some English. In most cases, women and younger children spoke only French. French was the language of the home.

The Cabot mill remained the largest single employer of Franco-Americans. By 1900, however, the Franco-Americans had diversified into other occupations and trades, including a few in businesses of their own or working white collar jobs, as well as many more farmers and other types of laborers. Picture, by this point, a population of newcomers from Québec, not unlike their forerunners of 1870, and a more established generation of Franco-Americans, some of whom had lived in Brunswick for 30 years or more by 1900.

The currents of the U.S. mainstream began to carry some Franco-Americans by 1900. At 47 Water Street lived the Leclaire family. The occupation of 21-year-old Peter Leclaire is listed as "Soldier, Philippines." Peter fought in the U.S. Army in the Philippines conflict that followed the Spanish-American War. Franco-Americans from Brunswick fought in several other U.S. wars in the decades that followed. There was also a Franco-American student at Bowdoin College in 1900, an Alfred Laferriere, who was born in Maine of parents from

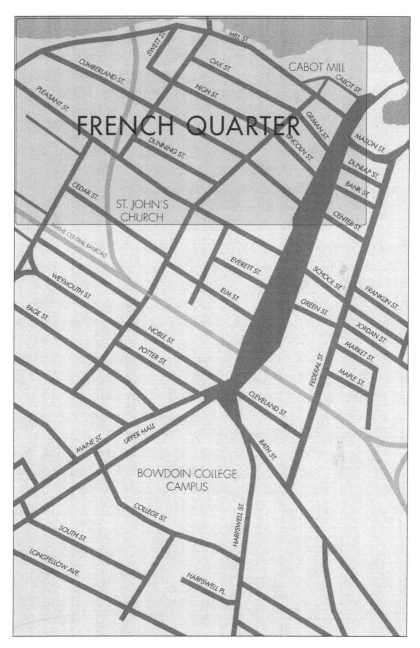

FIGURE 11: Brunswick's French Quarter c. 1900. (Map by Erica Vermette)

French-Canada. Institutions such as colleges and the military were homogenizing forces in the 20th century.[21]

By 1900, Brunswick's doors were open not only to the *Canadiens* but also to small numbers of immigrants from all over the world. In a 60-year period, Brunswick was transformed from a predominantly Anglo-Saxon Protestant locale to a town that included residents born in China, Russia, Syria, Germany, and many other parts of the globe. Typically, the newcomers lived in the more densely populated Brunswick Village, while the rural districts surrounding the town contained a more homogeneous, Yankee population.

The immigrants from Europe or Asia are not present in Brunswick in large enough numbers to form ethnic enclaves. The town bifurcates into Franco-American and Yankee populations, with small numbers of other nationalities. There are pages in the 1900 census of Brunswick that record an Anglo-Saxon population as homogenous as it was in 1840. Other pages show an equally homogenous Franco-American population. Still other pages show a cosmopolitan town open to the "huddled masses" of the American imagination.

The development of the Franco-American group in Brunswick follows many of the trends associated with the broader *Canadien* movement into New England. There was a pre-Civil War, transient population from the Richelieu Valley that gave way to a more permanent group from elsewhere in Québec following the war. As elsewhere in New England, the Franco-Americans were concentrated intensely in the manufacturing sector and were segregated in tenements and enclaves. And as elsewhere, Brunswick saw the development of a Little Canada, through the growth of a network of French-speaking institutions and through property ownership.

CHAPTER SEVEN

THE CASE OF THE CABOT MILL

Although homeownership increased after 1885, the Cabot Company continued to house most of the rapidly growing Franco-American population throughout the 19th century. The company erected slap-dash tenement buildings by the river that housed thousands of Franco-Americans. These were not the neat, brick buildings that accommodated the young women of Lowell in an earlier generation. The tenements became warehouses for workers. The company imported workers from Québec without thinking that hundreds of families, living on a small acreage, would need at least garbage and sewerage removal. The company promised to house the workers without providing essential infrastructure. Either Management did not think it through, or Cabot and Greene thought they could get away with providing inadequate housing at a negligible cost. They were correct.

Repeated outbreaks of typhoid fever and diphtheria ran through these overcrowded tenements. In 1886, a particularly lethal diphtheria outbreak spread through Brunswick's French Quarter. This disease infected at least 171 individuals, mostly Franco-American children, between May and September of that year. Better than ten percent of the Franco-American group in the town became infected with the disease. Between the spring and fall of 1886 disease claimed the lives of 44 children. Almost all of them died from either diphtheria or typhoid fever.[1]

Drinking water contaminated with excrement is a common, proximate cause of typhoid fever infection.[2] The epidemiology of diphtheria is less clear, but a 21st-century study found that the disease was correlated with "poor, socioeconomically disadvantaged groups living in crowded conditions."[3] Modern medicine finds that poverty is the major risk factor.

In the summer of 1886, Albert G. Tenney, editor of the local newspaper, the *Brunswick Telegraph*, mounted a campaign against the Cabot Company and its neglected tenements. Tenney's series of articles detailed the poor conditions in the company housing in the French Quarter:

> The houses are built in close contact; there are no yards; the sheds and privies are near by; the drainage – the sink spouts are running only a few feet or so outside of the houses where all dirty water is poured out – falling on the surface of the ground, some of which drains into the cellar and leaves one of the most prolific sources of disease. The houses have from two to three stories, some of which are divided into eight tenements; the average number of people is about twelve in each tenement (96 to a house); the number of rooms in each is from five to seven; bedrooms are small, many of which have only one window where there are two beds. This will give you an idea of the amount of dirty water and slops that are poured out on the surface, close by the block – leaving the most offensive odor that can exist. These large blocks are accommodated with only four privies – giving about twenty five people for each privy – and those privies are cleaned only once a year, and this is done during this present hot weather of July. These places have overflowed since the month of May.
>
> Swine, cows, and hens are kept in the sheds, pig-pens in close connection with wood sheds &c. – giving additional offensive odor. The wells are in the midst of this filth, some of which are not more than twenty feet distant from the sink spout and privies. Sandy soil as it is in this place there is no doubt that some of these wells receive the slops in a few days after their pouring out of doors.
>
> The collection of refuse matter in or around the dwelling houses, such as swill, waste of meat, fish and decaying vegetables, dead carcasses are all present, giving or generating disease germs, affecting the purity of the air....The above mention will show the favorable condition for any contagious disease to spring up.[4]

Doctor Onésime Paré (b. June 1854, St-Gervais-de-Bellechasse, Québec) provided the *Telegraph* with this description, as well as other information regarding the extent of the disease.[5] In his newspaper, Tenney brings forth evidence of other doctors to corroborate the facts as Dr. Paré presented them.

An eyewitness account corroborates the *Telegraph*'s general description of the tenements. In 1977, Suzanne Roy conducted an interview in French with Celestine (Fortin) Lavigne who grew up in Brunswick's French Quarter in the late 19th century. Lavigne was born in Saint-Eugène in the county of L'Islet in February 1886. Her family came to Brunswick the following year and lived in the Cabot Company housing. Lavigne went to work in the mill at age 12. She states that four families lived in the same two-story house where her family resided. Her family of twelve lived in two rooms, one upstairs, one downstairs. The family passed through a hall to get to the upper room where all of them slept. There was no heat in the bedroom, and she says that in the winter they nearly froze. She confirms that only Franco-Americans lived in the tenements. From a distance of many decades, Lavigne recalled that everyone in her childhood world was poor.[6]

The conditions in the French Quarter were not the accepted standard for this period. That's clear from Tenney's statement that the squalor in Brunswick "show[ed] a degree of brutality almost inconceivable in a civilized community." He calls it "a sight even to make a Christian swear." He feared the poisoning of the environment through the corporation's "clinging to big dividends, clutched as savagely as the miser clutches his well filled but greasy purse."[7]

Tenney called attention to the disease and squalid conditions in the tenements as early as 1881. In the July 15, 1881 edition of the *Telegraph*, Tenney notes that there had been 25 cases of typhoid fever in the Cabot housing since the beginning of that year. He also states that the Cabot Company had "received a magnificent donation from the town in an exemption from taxation for eleven years." Some readers disputed this claim, and Tenney devoted columns in his paper to proving that the Cabot Company had received either an exemption from taxation or that the town had undervalued its property for more than a decade.

FIGURE 12: Cabot Mill Tenements c. 1900. (Pejepscot Historical Society)

After citing the figures surrounding the Cabot mill's tax break, Tenney concludes,

> If the Cabot Company can, after receiving such an exemption, large or small, permit its territory to become a terror and disgrace for its filth, the centre of typhoid fever, two new cases now running in its tenement houses, all we have to say is, that men and heirs of some of the oldest families of Boston (it would not be decent to give names) have sadly degenerated from ancestral virtue.[8]

A week later, Tenney inveighed against the town's inaction in the face of the Cabot Company's malfeasance.

> The Town Board of Health will not act, though their action under the statute would not involve the town in one dollar's expense; the exempted and wealthy Cabot Company of Boston defies public sentiment, refuses to clean up what ninety-nine out of every one hundred persons in Brunswick concede is one of the nastiest holes in existence, and nobody dares go forward and complain to the Grand Jury, and have the Company indicted, after having been the direct cause of thirty cases of typhoid fever on its territory since January 1st, 1881. If this is not a conspicuous instance of corporate influence we know not what is.[9]

Faced with another outbreak of fatal diseases in the French Quarter in 1886, exasperated by the inaction of the Cabot Company and local authorities, Tenney took action. In the *Telegraph*'s July 2, 1886 edition, he reports that he had met with Dr. A. G. Young of the State Board of Health, who was in town lecturing at the Maine Medical School at Bowdoin. Tenney mentions in this same edition that the pastor at St. John's church had commented that since January 1886 he "had buried more children than he had baptized."

About two weeks later, Dr. Young made another visit to Brunswick and examined conditions in the "factory boarding houses." The doctor reported to Tenney that "matters were in a very bad condition requiring the speedy attention of the local board of health." The following week, Dr. Young visited Brunswick again, commenting that "he had never seen things in a worse condition." Tenney reported 123 cases of diphtheria over the preceding three months, and as many as four in one house.[10]

Moved to make some semblance of a clean-up, Greene ordered a crew of Franco-American employees to clean out the noxious contents of one of the privies. This load was dumped unceremoniously on the side of the road not far from the mill.[11] A representative of the local Board of Health ordered its removal. Greene replied that he would have the pile covered with soil. The Board member rejected that solution, and Greene was given 24 hours to remove it. A buyer was found for the deposit, but Greene did nothing. Tenney reports that the "filthy mass was...festering in the warm air and partial sunshine after the shower giving off an odor that was perfectly sickening, and that in the face of a large home not more than 50 feet distant, and containing how many tenements we know not – of course in the face of every traveler over the road."[12] Eventually, the town had the nuisance removed at its own expense and the Cabot Company received the bill. Tenney called for the hand of the Almighty to smite the company:

> In the name of all that is decent, in the name of common humanity we ask if the people of the village are to be treated after this heathen fashion. If so it would be better for them if the lightning of heaven should flash and consume every vestige of the Cabot Company's property planted upon our soil.[13]

But this malediction was not the end. The editor ran a weekly article in his paper about the squalor on the Cabot Company's property that extended from July until October. Several articles in this series bear a headline with the number of diphtheria infections listed as if they were casualties of war. "One Hundred and Twelve Cases of Diphtheria in two months and a half," the paper declares on July 23. "ONE HUNDRED AND TWENTY-SIX CASES IN TIIIRTEEN WEEKS," screams a block headline on August 6. "One Hundred and Forty-Two Cases since May 1st" declares the bold typeface on August 20. The September 17 headline gives the figures of 19 deaths on 148 cases in Dr. Paré's practice alone.

In the July 30 edition, Tenney recounts the arguments of local apologists for the corporation. Cabot Company champions claimed that most of the cases of diphtheria had appeared not in the tenements the company owned but in privately operated boarding houses. Tenney refutes this contention, reporting that of 87 cases cited by Dr. Paré, 60 were in the Cabot Company's dwellings. The small number of privately-owned boarding houses were near the Cabot tenements. The Cabot Company owned by far the greatest number of the tenements and had set the tone of neglect that pervaded the French Quarter.

Yankees owned the private boarding houses in question, although Franco-Americans owned a couple of the smaller houses. Of the three Franco-American-owned houses mentioned, Tenney reports that Eugene Morin's house was in bad condition. However, that owned by Alexis Sainte-Marie, a two-family dwelling, is the only boarding house mentioned as having been "in good order," while the houses owned by locals James Weeman and Horatio McKeaney were in a condition worse than Morin's. The good housekeeping of the Sainte-Marie family did not prevent them from losing two children to diphtheria.[14]

Unable to deter the editor by shifting the blame onto the owners of private boarding houses, Cabot Company defenders then asserted that personal animosity motivated Tenney's crusade against Greene. In response, Tenney referred to Dr. Young's inspections, his two visits to Brunswick in one week, and his conclusions from them.[15]

Answering the charge that personal animus motivated his crusade, Tenney is honest enough to report that there had been a rift between the newspaperman and Greene. In the 1850s, when the Cabot Company was new, the *Telegraph*'s coverage of the firm was positive.[16] The breach occurred after an incident at a town meeting where Greene had denounced Tenney for reasons the editor does not disclose. Participants in that town meeting defended Tenney, which may have embarrassed Greene and the two men became estranged. But none of this makes Tenney a liar; both eyewitnesses and documentary evidence support his account.[17]

Tenney continued to fire salvos despite his critics. He reports that the rent charged for the tenements was $7 per month, while the buildings themselves had cost between $75 and $125 apiece to build. A "commercially minded" friend of Tenney's estimated that the buildings paid for themselves every three or four years. The company constructed the tenement "blocks," as they were known, between about 1870 and 1880 and they deteriorated steadily after that. Tenney claims that he had a "scientific friend" who had inspected the premises when the editor had first called attention to the poor conditions in the company housing in 1881. This observer said that Tenney had "not reported the nuisance one half as bad as it is." Since that time, says Tenney, attempts at a clean-up had been "only partial." Conditions had worsened between 1881 and 1886.[18]

By mid-August, the conflict widened. Newspapers from Lewiston, Portland, and Boston picked up the story. Tenney printed extracts from the *Boston Herald*, the *Lewiston Gazette*, and the *Lewiston Journal*, all of which supported his campaign against the Cabot Company. The *Lewiston Gazette* wrote, "The Cabot Co. seems to be a good specimen of those soulless corporations who by their meanness and criminal neglect, their reckless disregard of human life and comfort, are responsible for scores of cases of diphtheria and nobody knows what else."[19] The Damariscotta (Maine) *Herald* praised Tenney for "looking out for the welfare of the French operatives."[20] Only the Bath *Times* threw doubt on Tenney's veracity.[21]

Answering the skeptics, Tenney suggested empirical methods: "If any one doubts whether we have overstated the filthy conditions of the Cabot Company's premises, let him go and look over the Cove hill from the sidewalk....If he is not then satisfied – both sight and smell – let him make a second visit on some hot day with a good southerly wind blowing."[22] Local factory owners began to grumble that the Cabot Company was giving all manufacturers a bad name. The *Telegraph* reported that workers in other factories near the river were greeted by a nauseating stench when the wind from the vicinity of the Cabot houses blew their way.[23] Wrote Tenney,

> We only wish that the Boston Cabot gentlemen could listen to the biting denunciations of them as notorious...for their filthy greed, by gentlemen, we can tell them who, as manufacturers, are their equals in experience, perhaps in wealth, but infinitely their superiors in all that goes to make up the true man, regardful of the lives and health of the men and women whom they employ. Some of these manufacturers...are downright wrathy over the reflection cast upon all other manufacturers by the abominable neglect of Cabot company Directors, to remedy a state of things which no man here dares to deny exists.[24]

In his August 20th edition, Tenney reported a dozen new cases of diphtheria diagnosed over the previous week, ten of them in the Cabot-owned houses, along with two cases of typhoid fever. His rhetoric against the Cabot Company and what he terms "the disgracefully neglected Cabot homes" reached a crescendo:

> [Its] record should consign to eternal infamy the management of this corporation, more heartless than the Fejees of old, who in hot blood, murdered their prisoners, then roasted and ate them. The Cabot Company has no such tender mercy for the poor slaves bound to it by the necessities of existence, they dying by slow poison germinated in the filth permitted by the company's home management to flow over the soil in reeking streams from the vaults of the boarding houses, the poor people inhabiting them being powerless to secure relief.[25]

An italicized note appended at press time to this diatribe states that Greene had invited the local Board of Health to visit the Cabot Company grounds, and make recommendations and that he would abide by them. Greene had capitulated. But the local board refused to act. Tenney reported murmurings that local politics were to blame. He describes two local Board of Health members, Despeaux and Bowker, as "tremendous politicians" who were in league with Greene.[26]

Oren Trask Despeaux was a prominent local Republican. He was not of *Canadien* decent, despite his French name. He was a descendant of Huguenots who had come to the colony of Rhode Island in the 17th century and married into the English colonists. His family had been English speaking for generations. His mother came from an old Massachusetts family. Despeaux was a Protestant and a Mason. Over time, he held several local political offices.[27] While two of the three members of the board of health, Dr. Adams and Mr. Bowker, had played modest roles in the struggle against the Cabot Company, Despeaux sided with Greene. His lukewarm response to the public health crisis baffled Tenney since Despeaux claimed that he wished to cultivate "the French vote."[28]

Greene, despite his apparent submission to the Board of Health, continued to deny any wrong-doing. He distributed a circular, under the signature of three physicians, downplaying the instances of diphtheria and suggesting that Dr. Paré had misdiagnosed some patients. Tenney declared the testimony of Greene's three doctors as "misleading" because Greene had "selected a day when few cases of sickness were then prevailing in the Cabot company's boarding houses" and asked his doctors to examine a fixed number of patients. "Very shrewdly," writes Tenney, "[the doctors] were not asked to give any testimony as to what diseases *had occurred – nothing as to the surroundings of the houses – nor to express any opinion as to what might result from the filthy surroundings.*"[29]

To counter Greene's feint, Tenney reported that there were four new cases of diphtheria in the week preceding September 3, and he brought in two physicians, a Dr. Mitchell to confirm three of the cases, and Dr. Adams to examine the other. Both physicians concurred with Dr. Paré's diagnoses. Tenney also cited a piece in the *Lewiston Journal* mentioning the "sad sight" of "the row of little graves in the [Catholic] cemetery" at Brunswick.[30] Here was a fact Greene could not obfuscate.

On September 10, Tenney reported that the State Board of Health had come in a body in the last days of August to make an official inspection of the Cabot mill premises. The Board examined the alleged cases of diphtheria. Although they were allowed into only five of the 133 tenements "occupied by the French," the State Board of Health in their report dated September 2, confirmed Dr. Paré's diagnoses. They also corroborate Tenney's and Paré's account of the conditions in the tenements in the French Quarter. Tenney states that the Board "found the methods of disposing of excreta and the common waste of dwellings to be of the worst character. The privies were all in horrible condition."

The same edition of the *Telegraph* printed figures compiled from attending physicians and from St. John's Church. They showed that 216 families lived in the French Quarter. There had been among them 171 cases of diphtheria, with 40 deaths from diseases of people of all ages from May 1 to September 3, 1886 and a total of 74 deaths in the French Quarter in the first eight months of that year. Doctor Paré provided a detailed list of burials per the Catholic Church's records. Paré cites the name, age, date, and cause of death. The doctor's list follows the manuscript vital records kept by the town of Brunswick closely, although these latter records appear to have a few missing burials of children from late July.[31]

Doctor Paré filed this list of deaths with the State Board of Health. His report to the state shows that the diphtheria outbreak began in April 1886 when there were five deaths from the disease.[32] The doctor cites 44 child mortalities between April and September (inclusive).[33] The town vital records show 32 children out of 42 total burials in this same period. The town's records, in most cases, do not state the cause of death, but a few cite diphtheria. The town vital records reveal that ten children died between April and September 1885 while in 1887, 18 children died in this same span of months. These comparisons highlight the unusually high child death toll in 1886.

Corroborating Paré's and Tenney's account, Locke provides statistics on the total number of burials from St. John's parish in Brunswick for the years 1877-1895. There is a sharp spike in the number of deaths among the Franco-American community in the years 1886 and 1887. It is unlikely that this increase in mortality is a natural consequence of the growth of the Franco-American population during these years because there were nearly half as many deaths in 1888 (41 total) as there were in 1886 (81 deaths).[34]

Doctor Paré's list of burials revealed seven instances where more than one child died in the French Quarter on the same day, between

April and September of 1886. The town vital records document five such days. In two of these instances, the body count was three child deaths in one day. In August 1886 alone, per Paré's list, there is one child death on August 7th, two on the 9th, one apiece on the 10th, the 17th, and the 21st, one each day from the 24th through the 26th, then another two on the 28th and one on the 29th. All of these deaths in August were from diphtheria, typhoid fever, or diarrhea.

Locating the places of residence of the children who died per the 1880 census shows that the deaths tended to occur within compact areas. In that census, my 12-year-old great-grandmother Albina was living with her family in what the census designates as *dwelling 25*. Two-year-old Marie Claire Sainte-Marie and her eight-year-old brother, Alexis Albert, died on the same day, April 13, 1886. The census indicates that this family lived in *dwelling 23*. "Cause of death: Diphtheria," the town records report. Ten-month-old Joseph Desjardins died on August 26; this family lived in *dwelling 27*. Nine-year-old Rosa Leblanc died on June 30; her family resided in *dwelling 29*. The census also reveals that no less than thirty-two individuals lived in *dwelling 29*.

I count six child deaths among the non-Franco-American population of Brunswick between April and September. There were more than seven Franco-American child deaths for every one among the non-Franco-American population of the town during these months. Diphtheria, in the Brunswick summer of 1886, was not an equal opportunity disease.

Child mortality, across classes and ethnicities, was high by our standards, in the state of medical science in 1886. Francis Cabot and his wife Mary Louisa buried two of their ten children, and their wealth could not prevent these deaths. However, both the statistics of burials from the 1880s and the bitter denunciations of the Cabot company's neglect by contemporaries show that a body count of more than three dozen children in half-a-year, in a single, cramped neighborhood, was extraordinary, even by 19th century standards.

Meanwhile, in early September, Despeaux granted an interview to the *Sentinel*, a paper from nearby Bath, in which he disparaged Tenney. The *Sentinel* piece did nothing to disabuse readers of the suspicion that Despeaux was in collusion with Greene. Despeaux suggested that Tenney's criticism of the Cabot Company had been selective since there were other, similar public health nuisances in the town.[35] Despeaux was also the source of a story that Greene had tried to clean up the mess from the privy dumped by the side of the road, but the Franco-American workers had prevented its removal. Tenney dismissed this allegation as ludicrous since "the French themselves had complained" of the nuisance. The editor reiterated the information he had obtained from Dr. Adams, that the town had cleaned up the mess, paid the bill, and expected the Cabot Company to reimburse the municipality.[36] Tenney also claims that Despeaux had tried to keep the State Board of Health report out of the *Telegraph*'s hands.[37]

At last, in the September 17 edition of his newspaper, Tenney declares victory. He refers to the State Board of Health report claiming that it represents "a triumphant vindication of Dr. Pare [sic] and the editor of the *Telegraph*....The *Telegraph* has at last brought the Cabot company to its knees." On September 24, Tenney reports that Greene had started to clean up the Cabot Company grounds "but how thorough the work is we are not informed." The diphtheria outbreak appeared to have subsided, as Dr. Paré had only one new case "of a mild type" to report in the Cabot Company's boarding houses. The last article in Tenney's series, dated October 1, states that there were three new cases and one death from the disease in the preceding week. But Tenney also reports that there was evidence of changes on the Cabot Company's property.

Despite Tenney's victory lap, no appreciable improvement in the Cabot Company's housekeeping occurred until Greene's retirement in 1890. Almost exactly two years after his 1886 series concluded, Tenney once again reports five cases of diphtheria with one death among them, and four cases of typhoid fever "all on French territory." Although Tenney finds the responsibility for these outbreaks elsewhere, he observes that the state of the Cabot boarding houses, as well as the privately-owned houses in the same neighborhood, was "little better than it was two years ago."[38] The town vital records continue to report the deaths of children and adults with French surnames from both diphtheria and typhoid fever into the early 1890s.

Not Only Brunswick

The State of Maine's Board of Health included its censure of the Cabot Company's home management in its *Second Annual Report* for the year 1886.[39] Brunswick's Dr. Paré is the only Franco-American physician cited in this book-length report. The *Report* shows that the public health situation in Brunswick was not unique among the state's Franco-American centers.

For example, Dr. C. W. Bailey of Westbrook attests,

> The diarrhoeal [sic] diseases of children have been very prevalent. These cases have been principally among the French population, and insanitary [sic] conditions, with overcrowding of families, seemed to enter largely into the causation. Much is needed to improve the sanitary condition of this village. Some of the things that need to be remedied are insufficient drainage, bad arrangements of water closets and privies. We have a water supply drawn from the river directly above the village, and but a few miles farther up there are large manufactories where all the wastes and excreta are dropped into the river, and still farther up a large powder manufactory with all its accompaniments of acids, saltpetre, soda and soot. It seems to me that this must render the water unfit for cooking purposes.[40]

This brief description of conditions among the "French population" in Westbrook echoes Dr. Paré's account of Brunswick's French Quarter. In Westbrook, as in Brunswick, overcrowding and pollution of the drinking water by sewage were culprits.

Elsewhere in the 1886 *Report*, Dr. S. J. Bassford of Biddeford states that whooping cough had caused a number of deaths among "the French children, but none, I think, among Americans." The doctor also reports that the public health situation in the town improved when tenement residents were given access to clean water.[41] Doctor Frederick Bacon, also from Biddeford, reported to the state, "the diarrheal diseases have been somewhat prevalent among the French children." The doctor attributes these illnesses to "bad drainage."[42] In Biddeford, some diseases were for "the French children" alone.

Moving northward to Winthrop, where Francis Cabot was Treasurer of the town's Winthrop Mills, a brief account by Dr. A. P. Snow observes that there were two deaths from "the diarrhoeal diseases of children" among "the French population, where there was a want of cleanliness about the premises. The general sanitary condition of this town is good." [43] Doctor Snow makes a distinction between the conditions among "the French population" and the general condition of the town. Doctor Daniel Driscoll, also practicing in Winthrop, found that "the diarrhoeal diseases" were "moderately prevalent," among "the Canadian population" and attributes the cause, in part, to "bad sanitary surroundings." [44]

Doctor A. M. Foster, practicing medicine in the town of Lewiston, reports that "a vast number" of the town's houses were not connected to the sewers but had "the old filthy privies, in many instances complete nuisances." He also reports that the town's garbage dump was "in close proximity to a quarter where a large part of the foreign population reside." [45] Franco-Americans were the largest cohort among this "foreign population" in Lewiston in 1886. [46]

From Waterville, another Franco-American center in Maine, Dr. S. H. Holmes reports that the "the diarrhoeal diseases of children have been frequent." "There is quite a large French population," writes the doctor, "and with them the well is often within twenty feet of hog-pens and cow-stalls, thus assuring the pollution of the water." [47] As in Brunswick, the "large French population" of Waterville kept farm animals near the wells. Franco-Americans, from a rural milieu, maintained small numbers of livestock in the industrial towns of New England. The tenement "blocks" were often built on tiny plots of land "in close contact" with one another, as Tenney noted. Any animals the tenants owned were kept within this small range. Tenement life in the industrial towns did not have enough room for both the workers and their livestock.

In these accounts, the physicians refer to the neighborhoods where the Franco-Americans dwell as neither *the poor section* of town nor as *the immigrant section* but specifically as the "French" section. It is among this population, identified not by occupation or class but by ethnicity, that the doctors report notable incidences of squalor and disease. Brunswick's unsanitary and overcrowded conditions were particularly egregious but not exceptional among Franco-American neighborhoods. They *were* exceptional by middle-class U.S. standards, as the denunciations by physicians and the press demonstrate.

Standards in many Maine mill towns did not improve into the 20th century. In 1904, journalist and novelist Camille Lessard Bissonnette came with her family from Québec to Lewiston. Her novel *Canuck* describes conditions of life and work for her heroine Victoria ("Vic") and the fictional Labranche family in a New England mill town at the beginning of the 20th century. Her detailed account resembles other, non-fictional depictions. These factors, as well as the autobiographical nature of the work, lead me to believe that her description of tenement conditions among the mill town "Canucks" is a realistic portrayal of a life she lived. Although the novel's setting is Lowell, I believe Bissonnette describes conditions she saw first-hand in Lewiston.

The novelist describes the Labranche family's four-room apartment on the fourth floor of a large block. "All traces of paint" had disappeared from the buildings in the neighborhood both inside and out. Door and window frames had been "eaten away" while putty on the windows was long gone. Panes of glass were loose or missing. There were holes in the plaster in the ceiling and the walls, through which the wooden lathe was visible. Around an iron sink crawled "cockroaches of all sizes and colors." The bathroom fixtures were covered with mildew and there was no enamel on the sink. Dirty holes in the bathroom, where the plaster had given way, had become "a haven for cockroaches." "When she first entered their new quarters, Vic wandered curiously from room to room," Bissonnette writes, "she whispered: 'So, this is the United States! And this is where I'm going to live!'"[48]

Nor was such squalor confined to Maine. In 1882, the Massachusetts Bureau of Labor Statistics published a lengthy description of conditions in Little Canada, Lowell.[49] This neighborhood, the Bureau found, was built on "made ground" between eight and fifteen feet deep, "composed of the refuse of the city and mills among which could be distinguished tin cans, bottles, swill, ash-barrels, general household refuse, and a quantity of wool and cotton waste, which the agent of the local board of health said would rot and breed disease."

The researchers observed three tenement blocks owned by "a prominent physician." An apartment they entered housed one family in two rooms. One room was 14 by 15 feet, with an 8 foot ceiling, the other but 14 by 8 feet. The apartment had three windows. The one window in the bedroom opened up on the privy "the foul air of which entered into this room, there being no opportunity for it to be carried away" because of the lack of an air shaft between buildings. The cellar, described as "dark and gloomy," was also partitioned into apartments "littered with chips and refuse." The inhabitants of a neighboring block had to carry away "refuse of all kinds and human excrement," except when the they would "throw it between the two blocks." In one of the apartments in another building, the researchers discovered an "extremely disagreeable odor." Into the space left by a broken window, the tenement dwellers had crammed an article of clothing, allowing the odor to linger. Fourteen people, spanning four generations lived in this five-room apartment.

"The general appearance of 'Little Canada'," concluded the Bureau "was very demoralizing, the people being crowded into the smallest possible space, and the local board of health powerless to prevent the over-crowding, except in a case of an epidemic." A lack of appropriate oversight by the town allowed a prominent physician to maintain his slums. As in Brunswick, throughout the region, local governments were neutralized by the influence of prominent citizens.

Journalist William Bayard Hale visited Fall River in 1894.[50] He describes a town divided between two classes: factory operatives on one side, and mill owners and managers on the other. These groups each tried to take advantage of the other, but, writes Hale, "it is not difficult to guess which is more successful at this." Hale also visited the tenements, entered them and spoke to their inhabitants. At the Borden mill tenements, he found 16 blocks with a central courtyard "littered with refuse." "One threads one's way among unsavory heaps," writes Hale. Beneath the roof of every block he saw piles of potato-peels, eggshells, and other garbage. "This description must pause," continues Bayard, "...for it dare not tell how the centre of the court – which is the playground of children and the thoroughfare for all – is occupied....In certain details of filth, hideous indecency, and indescribable shame, this place is probably not matched outside of Fall River anywhere in what we call civilization. And in the centre of all stands a pump."

Hale says, however, that Fall River's Little Canada was in even worse condition than the Borden tenements. "It would be an abuse to house a dog in such a place," Hale observes. He claims that the Globe mill tenements were deserted because rats had driven the human beings out of their homes. Another clutch of tenement dwellings, says Hale, "do not compare favorably with old-time slave-quarters" those dwellings a memory of a not-so-distant past in 1894.

Elin Anderson's ethnic study of Burlington, Vermont, published in 1937, discussed the housing woes of the Franco-American population of that city. This work shows that appalling standards of living in Franco-American neighborhoods continued in Burlington into the 1930s. As elsewhere, the influence of rich locals impeded the municipal agencies chartered to support more vulnerable citizens.

Anderson reports that the predominantly Franco-American tenements were an object of a study of housing in Burlington in 1919. The study's findings were "not given much publicity when it was discovered that some leading citizens in the community owned some of the shabbiest tenement houses." "Social workers," continued Anderson, "have pointed out that few cities have tenement houses comparable in shabbiness to a few of those in which some of Burlington's citizens live." To emphasize the point, Anderson includes in her book a photo of the North End Tenements that is the visual representation of the genre of squalor that novelist Bissonnette used words to depict.[51]

On occasion, Anderson notes, "leading citizens" were invited to inspect their dilapidated properties. "Although the stench at times has made them ill," Anderson writes, "it is felt that there is nothing that can be done about them." She also found that city health inspectors and fire chiefs were reluctant to condemn such buildings since they were the property of "influential" citizens, who could cause these officers "to lose their positions."[52]

Anderson's work elucidates the apathetic response to the squalor, even among people who were sickened by the stench of their own properties. She shows that the wealthier classes regarded poverty as a personal failing rather than a social ill.[53] Accordingly, the Yankees Anderson interviewed resented Burlington's Franco-Americans especially when they became "charity cases."[54]

In 1930s Burlington, systemic efforts to alleviate poverty were almost non-existent and aid to the poor relegated to badly organized, spot solutions.[55] Community mechanisms, such as health inspectors that could help to alleviate the symptoms of poverty, were dependent on "leading citizens," against whom they were loath to act. Franco-Americans had little stake in local governments because they perceived them as hostile or indifferent to the interests of low-income families. Anderson found that only one-half of the Franco-Americans eligible to vote did so regularly.[56] She also reports that the tenement areas that she does not hesitate to call "slums" also tended to produce the city's "juvenile delinquents."[57] Thus begins a cycle of poverty, political apathy, crime, and despair.

Not The Same Everywhere

Not all accounts of the Franco-Americans portray their conditions of life as miserable. An 1891 book by Fr. Edouard Hamon, S.J. describes tenement life among the Franco-Americans of Marlboro, Massachusetts. The author visited an apartment where he found the home well furnished, with a piano. A girl of the house reinforced the family's bourgeois *bona fides* by playing the musical instrument during the priest's house call. Hamon described a model of Victorian, domestic bliss. At Holyoke, the same author visited blocks of four and five story houses all occupied by Franco-Americans whom he depicts in a cheery passage. He noted groups of people walking and chatting, while men smoked their pipes. He heard laughter while folk songs rang through the quarter. In Burlington, the same writer found the Franco-Americans were building their own houses cooperatively. Carpenters donated free labor. He claims that poor Franco-American families relied on each other rather than on public charity.[58]

I believe that this author describes what he has seen. But the author also says that the priest at Marlboro guided him to select homes of his parishioners. It's not hard to imagine that the pastor selected homes that would make the best impression on a visiting Jesuit. Hamon's book also makes spectacular claims about the salaries Franco-Americans were earning in the U.S. in 1891 and the large savings they're able to accumulate.[59] His figures are demonstrably false.[60] The Jesuit wrote his work to counter negative views of Franco-Americans among the elites of Québec. It was politically motivated. However, the descriptions of conditions in Marlboro and Holyoke suggest that the mill towns were not all alike. Tenement life ran the gamut from a reasonably livable, working-class existence to disease-ridden squalor.

There were business owners who continued to show a type of paternalistic care worthy of Francis Cabot Lowell's generation. Thomas Goodall was splendidly successful, mainly in woolen textiles at Sanford, Maine. A native of England, Goodall came to Sanford in 1867 and founded a small empire in the town. He employed thousands and attracted a large Franco-American population to Sanford in the later 19th century. Goodall built houses for his workers that he sold to them at cost. The Goodall family also helped to bring a hospital, a local library, and a town hall to Sanford. The Goodalls supported recreational facilities including a ball field and a golf course. Students at both Sanford's public and Catholic schools received company-sponsored college scholarships, and executives even invited workers to their homes and summer cottages.[61] None of this *bonhomie* prevented Goodall from controlling fabulous wealth. He owned an opulent residence that rivaled, if it did not exceed, Benjamin Greene's Brunswick manor.

Paper magnate Hugh Chisholm, an English-Canadian by birth, provides another example of enlightened paternalism. In the first years of the 20th century, Chisholm built in Rumford, Maine a housing development known as Strathglass Park with clean, modern homes sporting the latest conveniences. The real estate company Chisholm formed for this purpose operated at a loss. He also built educational and recreational facilities for the workers who came from Québec and the former Acadia, as well as from Italy, Poland, Russia, and other countries.[62] Neither Goodall nor Chisholm were U.S.-born, and neither of them were cotton manufacturers. They both came to a small, rural village and built it into a company town that became like a fief overseen by a benevolent Duke.

The common denominator across the Franco-American mill town experience is *dependence*. The *Canadiens* arrived in the U.S. either in debt or having liquidated their assets to make the trip. In either case, they were vulnerable, and they had to make the States work for them. They were dependent on the company not only for wages but also for housing, for water, and, in some cases, for food provided through a company store. Their quality of life depended on the character of the bosses. Much depended on personality, on the generosity or the callousness of Management.

When the corporation controls a family's housing, their sustenance, and even where the input of the privy goes, it is intrusive and all-powerful. On a day-to-day basis, for the workers, the Corporation was far more puissant than any level of government. When private interests exercise an undue influence on local governments, then, in a federal system, only higher levels of government can intervene, as the State Board of Health attempted to do in Brunswick.

Is it too naïve to ask why the corporations of the Gilded Age could not have been more humane? Theorists argue that the inequalities of that age were necessary to create today's economy, while they minimize the damage done in places like Brunswick's French Quarter. It's a case of the end justifying the means, they explain. Some even have it that the Gilded Age was a Golden Age.

Cabot and Greene were not helpless pawns of implacable economic laws; they were agents who made their choices with eyes wide open. Besides, it is too convenient to ordain theoretical necessities, to wave away the consequences, when it is *the Others'* children who are living – and dying – in squalor. The arguments from necessity would garner credibility when one of the glib theorists would not only *accept* but *embrace* sending their child to work in a textile mill 66 hours per week while living in the typhoid and diphtheria infested tenements that claimed dozens of children in Brunswick's spring and summer of 1886. Few would wish that alleged necessity on *their own* child. That can only mean that the necessity is for *someone else's* child. This *someone else* raises the deeper implication of the case of the Cabot mill.

The very same summer of 1886 that diphtheria ransacked Brunswick's French Quarter, the philosopher Nietzsche published a book in which he wrote:

Every elevation of the type 'man' has hitherto been the work of an aristocratic society — and so it will always be: a society which believes in a long scale of orders of rank and differences of worth between man and man and needs slavery in some sense or other. Without the *pathos of distance* such as develops from the incarnate differences of classes, from the ruling caste's constant looking out and looking down on subjects and instruments...its holding down and holding at a distance, that other, more mysterious pathos could not have developed either, that longing for an ever-increasing widening of distance within the soul itself.[63]

It was the "pathos of distance" between one person and another, the "long scale of orders of rank and differences of worth between" one class of human beings and another, that made possible Brunswick's summer of 1886, and similar seasons in countless other times and places, then as now. The neglect evident in the French Quarter in that summer, a passive form of violence, is only possible where "the ruling caste" can "look down on subjects" as "instruments."

As Nietzsche went to press with his book, I can hear Mary Louisa Cabot having got wind of some trouble in the mill in Brunswick, asking her husband about it over coffee in their Victorian pile in Brookline. "Don't you mind about that, Louisa," Francis Cabot would reply, "those French-Canadian workers, they aren't like *us*." That *pathos of distance* between one person and another was a legacy of the likes of Thomas Perkins, passed down to son, to son-in-law, and to cousin, from one Cabot to another. It is what made Cabots, Cabots. Like the Liverpool slave-traders bound for Africa in an earlier generation, Cabot and Greene had to have *"ideas convenient to their business."*

No, it is not Adam Smith who is the lodestar of the Gilded Age, but Lord Acton, with his aphorism about absolute power. It is also the domain of Nietzsche who believed that the raising up of "the type 'man'" required an "order of rank" between human beings, with many gradations, in which there's a top and – far distant, a long way away – a bottom. Nietzsche with his rapier logic knew what it needed: "Slavery in some sense or other."

CHAPTER EIGHT

A Rich Uncle from the States?

Despite the poor housing conditions in the mill towns, *Canadiens* continued to come to New England seduced by tales of fabulous salaries. Relatives back in Québec seeing outward signs of wealth among New England cousins were inclined to draw hasty conclusions about Franco-American prosperity. They were unaware that an uncle from the States could flash a gold watch to impress the folks back home and still live in stiflingly overcrowded housing, with inadequate sewerage facilities, poisoned water, and high child mortality.

What the folks back in Québec may have misunderstood is that, in the U.S., two worlds can exist, at opposite poles of the economic spectrum, in some cases as close to one another as the next block over. Because wealth is pervasive in the U.S., it is possible for those who still struggle to acquire the necessities of life to possess a few high-status baubles. In the 19th century, these might include a third-hand watch with a chain, shiny factory-made shoes, or a single fine suit of stylish clothes. The workers in the textile mills often stitched those suits at home from cloth the mill had rejected.

Because the Franco-Americans had more cash flow in and out of their hands compared to their relatives in Québec, some Québécois observers conclude that Franco-Americans lived a life of ease in the United States. In the days when contacts between the two sides of the border were frequent, Franco-American relatives often came to Québec bearing gifts, and collective Québécois memory preserved these happy visits.[1] An *oncle des États* [uncle from the States] became an expression meaning a rich benefactor.

The misunderstanding about Franco-American prosperity found its way into Québécois scholarship. One scholar writes,

> [Franco-Americans] are found at all levels of success and enjoy, overall, a greater ease than most Québécois.
>
> A bourgeois class was formed even from the beginning...three or four individuals in each populous center are at the head of fortunes varying between $20,000 and $100,000. Of course, a few are poor. These are mostly located near the Canada-US border and in some parts of Vermont. They would be emigrants who, for lack of money, could not go any farther, but who have managed, without incurring debts, to shelter themselves from destitution. In general, *Canadiens* are living comfortably in the United States.[2]

This summary is baffling in almost every detail. It is striking that few Franco-American authors make the mistake of concluding that their forbears lived in comfort. Even into the second and third generation, few Franco-Americans ascended many steps up the economic ladder. And these low-income families were not confined to the immediate border regions as this author states but lived from Lake Champlain to the mills of Rhode Island. Until the end of our period, *poverty* was their salient feature in the eyes of the American mainstream, while their cousins in Québec believed Franco-Americans lived on easy street. Available data shows that by the standards of the working class of the U.S. North, Franco-Americans were relatively poor in the late 19th century and it was difficult for these families to save money to take back to Québec.

The 1875 Annual Report of the Massachusetts Bureau of Labor Statistics documents a study of the Commonwealth's working-class households in the earlier days of the Franco-American mass immigration movement.[3] The Bureau sent observers to gather data on 397 working-class families in various trades and occupations throughout the state. Twenty-nine of these families were Franco-American. Researchers gathered statistics on the yearly income and living expenses of each family and wrote brief observations of each household visited. Researchers also noted the ethnicity of each family, referring to native-born, English-speaking families as "American," while others are called "Irish," "German," "French-Canadian," etc.

The following description of a Franco-American family, called case No. 349, is typical.

LABORER, ON WHARF

F. Canadian

Condition – Family numbers 6, parents and 4 children from one to nine years of age. Have a tenement of 3 rooms in the third story of a twelve-tenement block; the rooms are small and out of repair; also poorly furnished. Family dresses miserable and looks haggard.[4]

Two of this family's three meals each day consisted of bread with butter or molasses, and a beverage. Meat or fish with potatoes and bread constituted their mid-day meal, the main meal of the day. The household's annual income was $510.00, but their cost of living was $555.38. The family was falling backward financially.

Another Franco-American family of five sends the father and an 11-year old son to work. Together they earn $510.00 per year, but their cost of living amounts to $539.00. They "occupy a tenement of 4 rooms, with fair surroundings. House is poorly furnished. Family dresses poorly." Two meals of the day consist of bread and butter with a beverage. A third meal consists of meat and potatoes. No fresh vegetables or fruit are served. And for this lifestyle, the family is sliding into debt.[5]

Other Franco-American families fared better. One family of seven had a father and two teenage children at work. They "occupy a tenement of 6 rooms, in a good locality, with pleasant surroundings. The house is well furnished, with one room carpeted. Family dresses well and attends church." They even have vegetables in their diet! Unfortunately, to maintain this reasonably comfortable lifestyle requires every cent earned by three wage earners.[6]

The highest income earned by an "American" family in this sample was $1,820 per year compared with $1,353 for the richest Franco-American family. The father of this Franco-American family is a carpenter, working perhaps on his own account, and the family also has two teenage sons at work.[7] This family earned roughly twice the annual income of the other Franco-American families. The family's earnings exceeded its annual cost of living by almost 17 percent. The wealthiest "American" family earned considerably more than their Yankee peers.[8] The head of this household was an Overseer in a mill. The gap between this "American" family and the next richest is smaller than that between the richest and second-richest Franco-American family.

A Yankee family that earned just $495.00 had the lowest yearly income in either group. But only three of the 125 Yankee families studied earned less than $600 per year, while eleven of the Franco-American families, over one-third of this small sample, earned less than that amount.

The following table summarizes the two groups' finances.[9]

TABLE 1

Home Finance of Working Class Families, Massachusetts 1875

	"Americans"	Franco-Americans
Median annual income	$768.50	$661.00
Median cost of living	$744.79	$653.50
Operating at a loss	5%	14%
Breaking even	34%	45%
Saving	62%	41%
Mean savings (% of annual income)	6%	3%

Ninety-two out of the 125 "American" families were single-income households while only two of the Franco-American families were. The Franco-Americans had more of the family working, for less income. While the "American" parents had the option of sending their children to school, Franco-American children worked along with the head of the household to put bread – and often little else – on the table.

Despite the often-repeated claim that *Canadien* families came to the U.S. to save money to bring back to Québec, most of these families are not saving a cent. Perhaps Franco-Americans were spendthrifts.

Some commentary from the period suggests as much.[10] But the American working-class families both earned more and spent more to sustain their standard of living.

Although the families studied were all working class, this research found that "the Americans and English have employed in branches of skilled work 85 + per cent of their whole number; while the French Canadians, Germans and Irish show 80 + per cent of their number engaged in unskilled labor."[11] English-speaking employees earned more because they worked at more highly skilled jobs.

The sample size of Franco-American families in this study is small, but we also have the qualitative descriptions of their diet, homes, and dress with which to compare them with the working-class Yankees. These descriptions reveal that the American workers are better fed, with a more varied diet, and more likely to live in a one-family home, in a more attractive environment. It is not surprising that an immigrant group is poorer than the established population. The immigrants began their climb near the bottom of the economic scale and had not yet time to ascend very far by 1875. It's clear, however, that Massachusetts Franco-Americans were relatively poor by contemporary standards in 1875.

Ten years after the 1875 study appeared, the Massachusetts Bureau of Labor Statistics researched food consumption among the working-class, publishing its findings in its 1886 report.[12] This research compared the quality and quantity of food between three groups: 1) miscellaneous working-class Massachusetts households; 2) Franco-American working-class families and boarding house dwellers of Holyoke, Lawrence, Lowell, Worcester, and Cambridge, Massachusetts; 3) comparable working-class households in Québec, in Montréal, Québec City, Saint-Jean, Sorel, Sherbrooke, Richmond, Saint-Hyacinthe, and Rivière du loup. The study found that the quantity and quality of food among the Franco-Americans was superior to their cousins in Québec. The greatest difference was in the fats consumed on the U.S. side of the border. The Franco-Americans consumed more protein, from a greater variety of sources, when compared with their confrères in Québec. The differences in vegetable consumption were small. The Franco-Americans spent more on food, a difference of 24 cents per day in Massachusetts versus 14 cents in Québec.

The researchers attempted to create a fair comparison by contrasting wage earners in the towns of Québec, many of whom lived in boarding houses, to their Franco-American counterparts. This approach, however, biases the Québec sample toward the workers in larger cities and towns such as Montréal and Québec City. Since most of the Franco-Americans came from small, rural parishes, a more meaningful comparison would contrast the Franco-American diet with its rural, 19th century counterpart. Descriptions of the 19th century rural diet include a greater variety of foods than appear in either the 1875 or 1886 descriptions of Franco-American regimens.

The rural Québec diet included fresh fruits and vegetables, in season, and a root cellar to provide for the winter, in addition to grains, legumes, and potatoes. Pork was the major source of protein. Protein sources were more varied in New England than in Québec. Bread was a staple on both sides of the border.[13] For the rural population of Québec, enjoying this varied fare depended upon having a functioning farm or sufficient income. New England offered an option to those who were not so favored. But the generalization that the rural Québec diet for most families was poorer than that in the mill towns cannot be taken for granted.

And not all of the studies from the period find answers to the food question as favorable to the Franco-Americans as the 1886 Massachusetts research. In July 1887, Maine's Bureau of Labor and Industrial Statistics conducted similar research.[14] The Maine study itemized sample budgets of "American," English, German and "Canadian French" families in Lewiston. The "Canadian French" family had the lowest paid head of household in this study and lowest overall family income. The family spent 56 percent of its budget on food alone, even though the prices for staple items such as sugar and flour had declined in Maine over the previous decade.

The report found that among the working class "great numbers of people can barely obtain their daily bread; their standard of living is far below that of the inmates of our charitable and reformatory institutions."[15] In the latter institutions, "the quality of food is very good, and the quantity supplied to the convicts limited only by their eating capacity."[16] To make the point, the researcher reproduced the menu at the Maine State Prison. It included vegetables, white and brown bread, various protein sources, coffee, milk, molasses, soups, corn, and oatmeal. The "Canadian French" factory operatives in 1887 Lewiston might have been better off pursuing a life of crime that ended in prison. They'd eat better at least.

Lifestyles in the Maine mill towns didn't seem to improve appreciably over the following decades. A depression struck the cotton industry in 1898.[17] A story in the *Boston Post*, reprinted in the January 29, 1898 edition of the *Labor Advocate* (Birmingham, Alabama), examined working-class life in Biddeford during this crisis when strikes led to hardship.[18] The article states that in the city of 16,000, "there are over 7,000 French Canadians and Irish, between 1,000 and 2,000 English and a good representation of Swedes and Norwegians." The article notes that almost everyone who is employed was dependent on the mills and that unemployment was high.

Among the employed, wages "are so small as to seem incredible." Wages paid in the Biddeford mills had decreased over the previous two decades. Some workers who had received $1.60 per day in earlier years were receiving just 90 cents in 1898. Other workers had seen a huge cut in wages from $1.08 to 40 cents per day. Children worked for 10 or 15 cents a day and, although a child labor law was on the books, it was ignored. The paper reports that there were two parochial schools, including a "French" school, as well as public schools. Out of a potential enrollment of five thousand, 3,600 children attended school. The others were in the mills.

Workers bore the brunt of the downturn. Bostonians held most of the stock in the mills and these stocks "paid upon par value dividends aggregating something like 25 per cent per annum." The reporter quotes the editor of a Biddeford newspaper who describes the political manipulations of the corporations resulting in "special favors, in the way of taxation concessions and privileges."

The newspaper summarizes conditions among the town's working class:

The destitution and want existing are great and volumes could be written relating instances of suffering that are saddening. The excess of French who speak only their own language makes it difficult to get at the true condition throughout their midst, but individual cases are plenty....Many families have to press their children into work in order to live. People go without butter on their bread, and meat is almost an unknown luxury. The interior of some of the homes shows an utter lack of even the common comforts. Soap boxes are used for seats, a board along the wall serving as a table, and in broken down stoves wood and chips picked up about the streets and along the river banks are burned as the only fuel.

This article describes the world of my maternal grandfather who was a three-year-old boy living with his family in the tenements in Biddeford-Saco in 1898.

Although the average wage was higher in New England than in Québec, what that income purchased was no life of ease.[19] For *Canadien* families with failing farms or inadequate income to support the family, the U.S. represented the bare minimum: *survival*. For others, the mill town represented a difference in potential between what they had in Québec and what they might grow to have in the United States. This *potential*, rather than a life of comfort, is a key to understanding the emigrants' world.

The 20th century vision of exotically attired, optimistic, determined immigrants, with American dreams dancing in their heads, waving their scarves as they salute the Statue of Liberty, does not portray these 19th century, cross-border émigrés. They weren't on their soapboxes proclaiming their American dreams to the world. They needed those soapboxes for furniture.

Drivers of the Emigration Movement

If life for the uncle from the States was austere, why did so many *Canadiens* emigrate to the New England mill towns? One of their number, Philippe Lemay, offers a succinct reply: "Because they had to make sure of a living for their family and themselves for a number of years, and because they greatly needed money. The wages paid by textile mills was the attraction."[20]

This terse account reveals that survival was at stake for the migrants from Québec. Wages paid "over a number of years" offered a modicum of financial stability to families on the economic margins and served as a magnet attracting the *Canadiens* into the textile mills. Lemay's statement also suggests that the *Canadien* immigrants were particularly cash-poor. What were the underlying economic conditions that put families in rural Québec in desperate straits?

There is a *standard theory*.[21] It begins by positing an agricultural crisis in Québec in the first half of the 19th century. This story says that the *Canadien* farmers resisted modern agricultural methods, such as the systematic rotation of crops. Their outmoded farming methods exhausted the land over generations, and agricultural productivity declined. This theory looks to cultural traits, to the "mentality" of the Québec farmers, to make its case.[22] The Québec farmers, says this account, were backward and hide-bound. They refused to adopt scientific methods and paid the price of their conservatism.

The standard theory also says that land pressure grew as farm families tried to establish numerous sons, each on his own farm. When the fertile land along the Saint Lawrence Valley became settled, the young farmers' search for land drove them into remote parts of Québec where, in many places, the terrain was unsuitable for agriculture. These families were distant from agricultural markets, as well as from the transportation infrastructures and other amenities long established in the more settled regions. Both the farmers in these settled regions, on their allegedly exhausted farms, and their sons trying to establish their own homesteads, found it difficult to make ends meet. Farmers were forced to borrow money and fell into debt. This version of events places the *indebted farmer* at the center of the emigration movement.

But, continues this tale, capital markets, which pool savings and channel them into investments, were immature in Québec. Unscrupulous lenders took advantage. Alphonse Desjardins, one of the architects of the Credit Union movement in North America, was inspired to undertake his work by a story he heard in the Canadian Federal Parliament of a man from Montréal who was made to pay $5,000 on a loan of $150.[23] When recruiters from the New England mills came to the Québec villages promising cash on payday, indebted farmers found hope for a way out of the financial hole. Per this account, most of the emigrants from Québec to New England owned land to which they expected to return. They did not intend to remain in the United States.

Historians who favor this standard theory also cite a sustained recession in Canada spanning from 1873 to 1896. Three consecutive bad harvests from 1888 to 1890 exacerbated the farmer's woes during a time of economic instability and swelled the ranks of the émigrés.[24]

Revisionists undermine several assumptions of this standard theory. They deny that there was an agricultural crisis in early 19th century Québec.[25] They insist that the lands under cultivation expanded and, overall, agricultural productivity per person increased during the first half of the century. They cite the rapid population growth, with declining mortality rates, as a reasonable metric of the success of Québec subsistence farms.

As for the view that the *Canadien* farmer's "mentality" was impeding their economic progress, analyses of the agricultural data from the 1831 and 1852 censuses of Canada found no significant difference in efficiency between farms in French-speaking and English-speaking areas.[26] However, another analysis of the 1852 data found that, in most regions, the French-speaking farmers had lower *incomes* from agriculture than their English-speaking counterparts.[27] English-speaking farmers may have had access to capital, resources, and infrastructures that enabled them to increase production, which could account for the income disparity. But, researchers found that the gap in *efficiency* between the French- and English-speaking farmers was small. Analyses of the agricultural data at mid-century reveal no simple relationship between speaking French and substandard agriculture.

The revisionist view also posits that it was not poor farm productivity that led farmers into debt but the need to respond to competition. Agriculture in Québec moved away from wheat, the traditional staple crop for market, not because farms were failing to produce but because of increased competition from further west.[28] As the West opened to settler agriculture, agile Québec farmers turned to other types of yields, dairy farming in one region, fodder crops or animal husbandry in another. The need to re-tool a farm from grain production to some other type of agriculture raises again the question of capital. Farmers needed to save large sums on their own to retool the farm absent a functional credit system.

This account, like the standard theory, foregrounds the indebted farmer. But it eliminates the hypothesis of an agricultural crisis as well as the judgments about the "backwardness" of Québec farmers.

Even if we posit an agricultural crisis, most sources agree that it was over by 1848 while the economic malaise of the later 19th century did not begin until 1873.[29] The end of the U.S. Civil War, that crucial turning point in the emigration movement, occurred during this interim period of relative prosperity. Fifty-thousand *Canadiens* per year departed the province beginning as early as 1866 and continued at about that rate until 1875.[30] By the time the depression began in 1873, the emigration movement was well underway. Economic woes after 1873 may have accelerated the movement. They were not its cause.

But rather than engage in the heated debates about Québec's economic history, let's pose the question from another angle: what underlying economic factors drive emigration across national frontiers, not only from Québec to New England but from *any* one country to *any* other?

Why Emigrate?

Economists Timothy Hatton and Jeffrey Williamson studied the economic levers of international immigration. They studied immigration to the U.S. in the period of open borders between 1850 and 1914, which overlaps with the period of the *Canadien* exodus to New England. Hatton and Williamson identified four main economic drivers of immigration.[31] They found that *the differential in wages* between the *source country* and the *destination country* was a major factor. When the gap between wages in the source and the destination countries widens, emigration increases. Emigrants also tend to go where their people have already gone. A sizeable number of people from the source country established already in the destination country is a predictor of emigration. They also found that a large *per capita* youth population tends to correlate with emigration.

On the other side of the ledger, if a current of emigration is to flow, the relocation costs cannot be prohibitive. Hatton and Williamson discuss the observation that "emigration from poor countries increases as economic development takes place in the source country."[32] Countries that produce steady waves of emigrants are not necessarily destitute lands in a state of economic stagnation, but ones that are growing economically, although they may be poor in comparison to countries that attract emigrants. The wave of emigration from poorer to richer countries tends to continue until living standards in the source country begin to rival those in the destination. A graph representing emigration from one country to another often resembles an upside-down "U" shape.[33] There's a sharp rise in the beginning, a leveling off, and then a rapid decline, as the wage gap between the source and destination countries closes.

Emigration costs are measured not only in dollars and cents. There are emotions and social pressures that also weigh on the cost side of the ledger. The family that departs its homeland leaves behind its extended kinship networks, its familiar terrains and haunts, and its customs and religious landmarks. Immigrants may have to learn to communicate in a language that is not their mother tongue. These considerations are further constraints on emigration.[34]

Does this Hatton/Williamson model apply to the Québec-to-New England case? First, was there a substantial gap between real wages in Québec and New England, as the Hatton and Williamson model holds?

Economic historians Green, MacKinnon, and Minns found that real wages for blue-collar, urban men among the *Canadiens* of Québec ranged from $289 to $431 per year by the first decade of the 20th century, depending on the worker's skill set. The same class and gender among the Franco-Americans in the Northern U.S. were earning from $425 to $538 per year in 1908-09.[35] The lower-paid end of the U.S. group earned just a few dollars less than the higher-paid group of *Canadien* workmen. There is a 32 percent gap between the lower end of the *Canadien* urban wage scale and their counterparts across the border in the United States. The wage gap between *rural* Québec and the mill towns of New England was probably larger than this data shows.

The Hatton/Williamson model also suggests that a critical mass of immigrants from the source country in the destination country encourages emigration from one to the other. Obviously, some person or group must be the first to make the move, the pioneers who form a nucleus for later arrivals. In the case of the Franco-Americans, these pioneers were the seasonal or migrant workers in New England before the Civil War. These earlier emigrants proved the concept of a move toward the New England mill towns and established the outposts of what became the *Canadien* communities in the region. They braved the social stigma attached to "abandoning" their homeland. The hundreds of thousands who followed these pioneers to New England, beginning immediately after the Civil War, created a critical mass, concentrated in one region of the U.S., attracting a steady flow of their compatriots.

The age composition of Québec and New England in the mid-century period is also consistent with the Hatton/Williamson model. The youth population in the rural portions of the St. Lawrence Valley grew as the same demographic in New England declined. Geographer Serge Courville and his associates divided the St. Lawrence Valley into 13 regions and tracked the percentages of youth, adults, and seniors in each region in 1831, 1851, and 1871.[36] In nine of the thirteen regions, there are more young people *per capita* in 1851 than there are in either 1831 or 1871. The population of young people outside of the larger towns grew in the mid-century period.[37] The youth of 1851 came of age in the 1860s and 1870s as the emigration movement began to gather a head of steam.

Across the border, the population of the Northeast U.S. under the age of 20 declined modestly but steadily between 1840 and 1870, from more than 51 percent to less than 45 percent of the population. In the Western U.S., the same age group grew more than 10 percent *per capita* between 1850 and 1870.[38] A 19th-century baby boom came of age in Québec as the Northeast sees a westward movement of the young. Although the youth population *per capita* in the two regions was not significantly different, New England's declines, while Québec's rises in mid-century.

The Hatton/Williamson model also suggests that the costs associated with the move must not be prohibitive. Philippe Lemay recalled his family's costly trip from Saint-Ephrem d'Upton, Québec to Lowell in 1864. The journey took five days and children were charged full fare on the train. From Saint-Ephrem to Sherbrooke, Québec was a day's trip. The next day, the family boarded a train at Sherbrooke that took them as far as the border town of Island Pond, Vermont. The following day took the family as far as Portland, Maine, where they stayed the night and the next day they took another railroad to Boston and stayed overnight there. Finally, on the fifth day, they reached Lowell.[39] And the large family had to find food and lodging along the way.

Since hundreds of thousands of *Canadien* workers moved to New England, it's evident that the costs were high but not prohibitive, and transportation improved over time. However, as Lemay states elsewhere in his oral history, families liquidated all of the possessions they could not carry to make the move. *Canadien* families had to be desperate or adventurous enough to risk all. But risking all was required.

The fact that, in good economic times, manufacturing jobs were readily available and that most families could find work immediately, mitigated the risks. If the family had had to support itself for the duration of a long job search, then that might have made the costs prohibitive. The rapid expansion of the textile industry meant a ready job, ensuring the emigrant families that the bet would pay – as long as the wage differential between Québec and New England remained high enough to justify the risk.

The development of the Little Canadas, and the institutional network associated with them, reduced the intangible costs of the move to New England. The development of enclaves where the emigrants could speak French and participate in the Catholic parish life they knew in Québec eased the anxieties associated with emigrating to the United States. It was common for Franco-American families already in the U.S. to offer temporary lodging to newcomers. Family, friends, or even Franco-American strangers were there to help the new arrivals to find work at the local mill.[40] These customs of the Little Canadas diminished both the financial and the emotional risks of the move.

As the Little Canadas developed, it became clear to the clerical elite that the move to the States did not entail losing one's language, one's name, and even one's very soul in the Protestant Yankee miasma.

A good *Canadien* family could be a good *Canadien* family even in a New England mill town – if they stayed within their enclave where they could remain French-speaking and Catholic. Many among the Québec elite still portrayed mass emigration as a national disaster. But at least with a *Canadien* priest in a national parish guiding the Franco-American flock, it became clear that a railway ticket to New England was not a one-way fare to the Inferno. Social pressure on the poorer classes to remain in Québec subsided as clerical condemnation of the emigrants eased, even if slightly. The softening of priestly censure further reduced the emotional costs of emigration.[41]

The Hatton and Williamson approach also suggests that countries that produce a stream of emigrants tend to have modest economic growth.[42] Vincent Geloso and Mathieu Bédard took an economic modeling approach to evaluating the performance of the Québec economy from 1815 to 1850. They found that prices were falling while the money supply was increasing faster than the population. Geloso and Bédard concluded that it would have been impossible for the growth in output per person to have been negative. Modest growth, less than one percent *per annum* on a *per capita* basis, is the worst possible scenario. They also point to other signs of economic growth in Lower Canada in the 1815-1850 period such as increased imports, the growth of urban areas and a decline in mortality rates.[43] A period of modest growth, followed by a wave of emigration, is consistent with the Hatton/Williamson model.

The movement from Québec to New England fits this model of international emigration. As emigration movements go, it was not unique. Québec-to-New England fits observable, general migration patterns.

Why Not Settle Elsewhere in Canada?

The current of emigration from Québec might have gone toward the Canadian West as the provinces of Manitoba (1870), British Columbia (1871), Saskatchewan (1905), and Alberta (1905) joined the Confederation. High transportation and set-up costs help explain why net emigration from Québec to the West was scanty.

The trip alone was expensive. A one-way ticket from Montréal to Boston in the 1890s ran about $4.25; the ticket to Portland, Maine cost $3.00. The Montréal to Winnipeg fare was $10.00 while a train from Montréal to Vancouver cost $25.00.[44] Tickets from Montréal to Winnipeg cost a family of six $60.00. Assuming an average yearly salary for a working-class, *Canadien* family was in the range of $350 per year in the 1890s, train tickets to Manitoba cost almost two months' salary.[45]

This sum does not include provisions for the journey, which was much longer than Philippe Lemay's trip from St-Ephrem to Lowell. Moving West to take up farming, other jobs being in short supply, also required the *Canadiens* to acquire land. To do so required paying a processing fee and improving the property in order to claim title. New arrivals from the East had to survive on their new property during the lengthy process of establishing a working farm. When the mills were hiring, the payback for the emigrants to New England arrived much more quickly than for the migrant West. All told, the risks of coming to New England were smaller than heading to the sparsely populated Prairies – and poor families of Québec had a low margin for risk. Remaining in Canada simply cost too much for many poorer Québec families.

Starting in the 1870s, the governments of Québec and Canada made efforts to convince the Franco-Americans to return home. Many of these *repatriation* efforts directed the Franco-Americans toward Manitoba. These schemes were largely unsuccessful because, like a move from Québec to the West, relocation expenses were too costly.[46] In 1886, an agent of the Canadian government claimed that it cost $1,000 to move from New England to Manitoba, which was on the order of two years' salary (or more) for the mill workers and beyond the means of most families.[47] At the same time, the Canadian government provided inducements to Europeans to settle the Canadian West. Franco-Americans were well aware that the Canadian government was courting immigrants from Europe while they toiled in a foreign country.[48]

In an April 1883 debate in the Canadian House of Commons, Joseph Tassé of Ottawa notes that in 1873 the Canadian government courted Mennonites from Germany to settle Manitoba. They were given a stipend for travel from Hamburg to Winnipeg, as well as free provisions during a portion of their journey. The Mennonites were also offered loans totaling $100,000. *Canadiens* of Québec were not offered such largess. Nor were Franco-Americans. The government, says Tassé, spent $2,713 on transportation for *Canadiens* in the U.S. wishing to return to Canada, while it spent $56,887 to transport European immigrants.[49]

Ethnic and political considerations also impeded the move West, from either Québec or New England. The suppression of the French-speaking Métis people in the two Northwest Rebellions (1869-1870 and 1885), and the execution of the revered leader of the Rebellions, Louis Riel in 1885, were well-known events and much discussed among New England Franco-Americans.[50] In 1890, the provincial government made English Manitoba's sole official language and funding was removed for parochial schools in favor of a public school system. French-speaking North Americans regarded these actions as a rebuff as well as a violation of the Manitoba Act that created that province, and which, many among them believed, had secured French-language rights there.[51] Whether they were intended to do so or not, these events did little to encourage French-speakers to move to Manitoba, especially during a time when Franco-Americans across the border were establishing French-speaking schools and other institutions. While supposedly encouraging repatriation from the U.S. to the province, the policy of both the Manitoban and Canadian Federal governments did the opposite. Political reasons, as well as financial ones, favored a current of emigration from North to South rather than from East to West.

If Manitoba was a non-starter, repatriation agents also offered to smooth a path for Franco-Americans from New England back to rural Québec. But, through at least portions of our period, there were competing offers of land from the U.S. government, through the Homestead Act. At the 13th Convention of the *Canadiens* of the U.S. held in Troy, New York in 1878, two delegates offered a resolution opposing repatriation in Québec or in Manitoba. The delegates pointed out that the U.S. government was offering farmers good land in Arkansas in the fertile Midwest.[52] For families that wished to go the rural route, claimed these delegates, free Arkansas land was a more viable option than returning to Québec.

However, the poor conditions in the mill towns continued to create an opening for repatriation rhetoric. A repatriation agent – himself a repatriated Franco-American – made the following pitch in Biddeford in 1910:

> You are tired of life in the mills. You have told me so. Many among you have written me to that effect and I have seen it with my own eyes. Your financial status is not what it should be. For a long time you have served masters without hearts. For too long you have built fortunes for rich Americans. It is time to think about yourself and your children. Your fifteen to twenty-year experience in the United States shows you that there is nothing but the life of a mercenary here. Do you want to be truly free?...Do you want your independence?[53]

But a successful transition from the mills to rural life in Québec required capital and the Franco-Americans' "financial status" was not what it should have been. By 1910 generations of Franco-Americans had been born in the U.S. and were unlikely to repatriate to a country in which they'd never lived. They had become industrial workers rather than farmers, many of them having labored in the mills from childhood.

Franco-Americans rejected repatriation not because they eschewed being *Canadien*. On the contrary, they attempted to bring Québec to New England. Repatriation foundered because it offered what these families had already rejected: rural poverty in a marginal area. For many families, repatriation would have meant a return to the same condition from which the agents of the New England mills had promised an escape. Franco-American mill workers may have been happy to return home if they could have sustained up North a level of economic security at least equal to the quite modest status they maintained in New England.

The Franco-Americans cherished an emotional connection to their homeland and desired to preserve its culture in their adopted home. But the continuing semi-colonial status of Canada was a hindrance to repatriation. For example, journalist Joseph Montmarquet of Lewiston rejected the idea of repatriation if it meant that the families returning to Canada would suffer hunger only "to allow England to count a few more settlers to exploit."[54]

One question remains: why weren't there enough economic opportunities in the cities and towns of Québec for the rural poor, struggling to make ends? Québec urbanized steadily throughout our period. The urban population rose from ten percent in 1831, to 28 percent in 1881, to 63 percent by 1931.[55] Urbanization and emigration were different responses to the same issues: rapid population growth coupled with structural changes in the rural economy. But Canada industrialized more slowly than did such countries as the U.S., the U.K., and Germany. In 1851, agricultural products along with the outputs of extraction industries – mining, fishing, trapping, and forestry products – accounted for almost one-half (47 percent) of Canadian Gross National Product. By 1900, this percentage had fallen to 37 percent, still better than one out of every three dollars produced.[56]

The actions of its colonial overload, Great Britain, over which the inhabitants of Canada had no control – least of all the impecunious farmer in Québec – also affected Canada's 19th-century economy. Colonial Canada's timber and wheat exports enjoyed a protected status in the trade with Great Britain, but London eliminated these preferences in 1846. The British North American colonies looked south to the U.S. as a natural outlet for their natural resource-based exports. Eventually, Canada and the U.S. agreed on a Reciprocity Treaty signed in 1854. The treaty opened U.S. markets to the products of Canada's abundant natural resources in exchange for U.S. fishing rights along the East Coast. The U.S. abrogated the treaty in 1866, due to Washington's grievances against the U.K. arising from the Civil War.[57] The colonial connection to Great Britain, once again, did Canada no favors. However, both British preferences before 1846 and the short-lived Reciprocity Treaty encouraged Canada to remain a colonial economy: exporting natural resources, while importing manufactured goods.[58] As a result, the demand for industrial jobs in the cities and towns of Québec grew more slowly than the supply of workers desiring to fill them.

There were also ideological impediments to Québec's industrialization. The clerical elite identified industrialism with what they regarded as Anglo-Saxon materialism.[59] Industrialization was for Protestants. *Canadien* Catholics were quintessentially rural, they believed. Rurality was a feature of national identity.[60] Therefore, to fill industrial jobs that would enrich Anglo-Saxons across the border was anathema. Their answer to the challenge from the New England mills was land schemes that opened new regions of Québec to agriculture. Repatriation was one facet of these internal colonization efforts.

But these colonization schemes often stranded the *Canadien* farmer in uncultivable, remote places.[61] In regions such as the Eastern Townships, found historian J. I. Little, the colonization movement pitted "French-speaking settlers" against "English-speaking capitalists." The *Canadiens* sought farmland, while English-speakers speculated in land or accumulated holdings for the lumber industry.[62] Many *Canadiens* in the remote regions worked in forests and mines owned by "the English," enriching Anglo-Saxon industrialists despite the rural ideals.[63] Neither the cleric-inspired colonization schemes, nor the federal government in Ottawa offered a viable alternative to the New England mill towns.[64]

At root, economic policies such as trade agreements, tariffs, and agricultural development strategy, inhibited Québec's industrialization. Canada was suspended between two giants: the British Empire, the 19th century's superpower, and the embryonic superpower to its south. The poorer classes of Québec, far from the centers of power in London or Washington, were at the effect of semi-colonial Canada's tentative economic policies. Despite all, Canada's Gross National Product grew by a factor of six during the second half of the 19th century. But this growth did not spawn opportunities that could compete with New England's until the 20th century.

In search of a livelihood, poorer farmers and laborers had the motive, the means, and the opportunity to emigrate. A significant differential in wages between Québec and New England provided a motive; the railroad system and the liquidation of existing assets provided the means; the abundance of manufacturing jobs, as well as the welcoming embrace of the burgeoning Little Canadas, created the opportunity.

CHAPTER NINE

WHO WERE THE IMMIGRANTS?

The standard theory claims that most of the *Canadien* immigrants to New England were farmers – deep in debt and sojourning only temporarily in the U.S. until they could save enough to return to Québec and set the family farm aright. But this is not the only important story about Franco-American origins in Québec. There were other patterns of migration to New England equally as important as the indebted farmer narrative. The story of the debt-strapped farmer might account for those who intended to return to Québec, but it does not account for those who came to New England to stay.

Meet my great-grandfather, Charles Vermette. When Charles was about two years old, his father Joseph and his mother Marie-Louise moved the family from the parish of Saint-Gervais in the St. Lawrence Valley to what was then known as the Eastern Townships region of Québec where Joseph eventually found work as one of the first generation of asbestos miners at Thetford-Mines. If Charles had stayed in Québec, he would probably have joined his father in the mines, as did several of his half-brothers. Charles would have been a wage-earner in Québec, like his father.

Instead, Charles came from Québec to Brunswick probably in early 1881, not yet 21 years old, and took a job at the Cabot mill. He made the trek with a brother named François, two years his senior, and they both came to join their eldest brother Joseph, who had preceded them to Brunswick by some eight years. Family oral history says, before they came to Maine, Charles and François worked in lumber camps.[1] Charles married Albina Ouellette at St. John's Church in Brunswick in 1887.[2] On September 5, 1888, exactly a year to the day after his wedding, he became a naturalized U.S. citizen. Charles threw in his lot with the U.S. and lived in Brunswick for the rest of his life.

Charles was not the only non-farmer among my forbears of Québec. Of my six *Canadien* great-grandparents (two were Acadians) only two appear to have grown up on family farms in Québec. My mother's grandfather was a teenager when he came with his family to Biddeford-Saco around 1887. His father from Sorel worked in transportation. He is listed in the Canadian Census of 1881 as a *navigateur*: a boatman. This great-grandfather's memory of Québec had nothing to do with farming. He remembered shipping lumber along the river with his father. Another great-grandfather, from Belle River, Ontario, was the son of a teamster and had been a horse-trader in his youth before his family came to Maine. Thomas Ouellette, Albina's father, worked in a tannery in Roxton Falls before coming to work in Brunswick's Cabot mill. Josephine Racine, Thomas's wife, was the daughter of a day-laborer in Roxton Falls.

These emigrants – day-laborers, operators of small vessels, workers in light industries – were *wage earners in Québec before they came to the United States*. Two of these families display a degree of mobility back and forth across the border but, on balance, these families came to the U.S. for good. Of my six *Canadien* great-grandparents, the three males became naturalized U.S. citizens. My forbears settled in the industrial towns of Maine and lived most of their lives in the Pine Tree State.

Many of my ancestors were not family farmers before they came to Maine and that piqued my curiosity about the Franco-American workers' backgrounds in Québec. Other data points raised doubts about the centrality of the indebted farmer narrative. For example, a parish census of the Franco-American church in Worcester in 1871 found that out of 2,805 parishioners, 562 families, only 57 were landowners in Québec.[3]

The Dillingham Immigration Commission (DIC) gathered the best available data regarding the occupations of Franco-Americans before they came to the United States. The DIC compiled forty-one dense, data-rich volumes, most of them devoted to a single industry. Volume Ten covers the cotton and woolen textile industries, recording conditions in 1908 or 1909. The researchers studied the textile workers in most of the New England states, as well as in New York and Pennsylvania. They performed a focused analysis of the classic textile towns of Lowell and Fall River.

The report studied two samples of cotton textile employees. The first is a general survey of the individuals employed in the textile industry, across the locations the researchers visited ("Study of Employees"). The commission also conducted a more detailed survey of select households ("Study of Households"). Let's look first at the study of households.

The researchers examined what they chose to call the respondents' "industrial condition" before coming to the United States. Researchers collected data from 143 "foreign-born" Franco-American cotton textile workers, men, at least 16 years old when they came Stateside. The study found that the largest cohort, 42 percent, were *working for wages before they came to the United States*. Only 17.5 percent were working for their own profit, a category that would include family farmers. The remaining individuals were "working without wages" or had no occupation.[4] The DIC report states that those who were working without wages "were usually at work with fathers or other near relatives."[5] The researchers counted payments in kind as "wages."

TABLE 2

Industrial Condition Before Arrival in the U.S.; Canadian French Males 16 or Older at Time of Emigration (*Study of Households*)

Without occupation	14.7%
Working for wages	42.0%
Working without wages	25.9%
Working for profit	17.5%

The researchers also recorded the respondents' occupations before they came to the United States. They divided those men who had been working in agriculture into three categories: 1) those working for wages; 2) men working on farms without wages; 3) farmers working for their own profit.[6]

It is safe to assume that the farmers working for their own profit were the heads of household and the main decision-makers on a family farm. If this assumption holds, then their relatively small numbers are not a surprise since one would expect there to be more family members than family heads in a survey of households. Nonetheless, in this sample, only about one-sixth of Franco-American men employed in cotton mills were heading their own farms back in Quebec.

When I tallied the percentage of foreign-born men across all nationalities surveyed (Irish, Greek, Portuguese, etc.), I found that 56 percent of cotton textile employees were working in agriculture before emigrating to the United States.[7] In percentage terms, before emigrating, *fewer* "Canadian, French" (45.5 percent) were working in agriculture than the foreign-born, male cotton workers taken together.

TABLE 3

Agricultural Workers Before Arrival in the U.S.; Canadian French Males 16 or Older at time of Emigration (*Study of Households*)

Farm laborers for wages	5.6%
Farm laborers without wages	24.5%
Farmers for profit	15.4%
All farmers/farm laborers	*45.5%*

Of the Franco-American men in the cotton industry who were not working in agriculture before their arrival in the U.S., nearly 40 percent (39.8%) were gainfully employed in other pursuits: general laborers, workers in hand trades, in light industries, or in other occupations.

The *Study of Employees*, the dataset of all of the cotton textile workers the DIC surveyed, includes 13,000 Franco-American workers, both men and women, although not all respondents answered every question.[8] Among 3,191 male Franco-American textile workers in this larger dataset, two-thirds of the respondents, precisely 2,100 of them, were farmers or farm laborers in Québec before emigrating. At first glance, this number would tend to confirm the theory that most Franco-American men worked in agriculture before they came to the mill towns.

TABLE 4

Occupations Before Arrival in the U.S.; Canadian French Males 16 or Older at time of Emigration
(*Study of Households*)

Farmers/Farm laborers	45.5%
All other occupations	39.8%
No occupation	14.7%

However, in the Study of Households, the researchers divided agricultural workers into three categories: farm laborers for wages, farm laborers without wages, and farmers for profit. I took the percentages for each of these three categories of farm employees from the Study of Households and supposed that they also held for the larger sample in the Study of Employees. Applying those percentages to the 2,100 agriculture workers in this sample yields the table of occupations below (Table 5).[9]

Better than one-tenth of the Franco-American men (12 percent) were employed as wage laborers either in textiles or some other manufacturing field before they came to the United States. Another 13 percent earned a wage as either farm laborers or "general" laborers. Adding these numbers together with the small number of domestic servants shows that more than one out of every four Franco-American men working in the cotton mills (26 percent) were wage-earners before they arrived in the United States.

Slightly more than one-fifth (22 percent) of the total sample were farmers working for their own profit, i.e., the heads of family farms. More of our sample were working for wages than were working for their own profit on farms before they came Stateside. Since the narrative of the indebted farmer cannot apply to all of the family farmers in the sample, that scenario depicts some subset of the 22 percent of male cotton workers who headed family farms in Québec. Indebted farmers account for at most one-fifth of the cotton workers surveyed, although a fair portion of the "farm laborers without wages" were likely to be family members of these men.

TABLE 5

Occupations of Canadian, French Males Before Coming to the United States (*Study of Employees*)

	Number of Respondents	Percentage of Respondents
Textile manufacturing	190	6%
Other manufacturing	194	6%
Farmers working for their own profit	*714*	*22%*
Farm laborers without wages	*1134*	*36%*
Farm laborers for wages	*252*	*8%*
General labor	170	5%
Hand trades	217	7%
Domestic service	24	1%
Trade	76	2%
Other	220	7%

Italicized numbers and percentages are calculated.

Farm laborers working without wages constituted the largest group among men involved in agriculture. I suspect many of these were young men, working on their family's farm who did not think it likely that they would establish themselves in Québec on their own farmsteads. A brother may have been slated to inherit the farm upon the death of the parents, and these young men, with their father's blessing, thought it a better deal to take their chances in the New England mills. These men were not likely to have any farm to return to in Québec. Some of them may have desired to come to the U.S. to earn money to establish a farm back home, but they probably did not own one in their homeland when they first came to the United States.

The wage laborers, the young men not yet established on their own farms, the small merchants ("Trade"), and tradesman ("Hand Trades") were probably not tied to a farm in Québec to which they intended to return, although some of them may have owned property there. Although many of these men may have returned to Québec, they would not fit the pattern of the indebted farmer mooted by the standard theory. Some large cohort of the 78 percent of respondents – those who were *not* farmers working for their own profit – probably intended to stay in the U.S. when they first arrived.

The DIC did not neglect women employed outside the home before coming to the United States. Among the 726 female cotton employee respondents, 22 percent worked in textile manufacturing before they crossed the border and took similar jobs. More than one-quarter of these women (26 percent) were working either in textiles or some other manufacturing industry in Québec. Another approximately one-tenth (9 percent) worked in sewing, embroidery, or lace-making, i.e., textile-related occupations. Forty-six percent worked on farms. Single-digit percentages of women were teachers, domestic servants, in trade, or in unspecified occupations. Forty percent of the women (those working in manufacturing, as teachers, and as servants) were wage-earners before they emigrated.[10]

More than 70 percent of Franco-American cotton workers surveyed by the DIC, both men and women, had been in the U.S. for ten years or more at the time of this study; more than 36 percent had been in the U.S. for 20 years or more at that time.[11] When these men and women report the occupations they had in Québec before their arrival in the U.S., their responses tend to reflect their situation north of the border in the 1890s, the 1880s, or even earlier. It may be that wage earners were represented disproportionately among the more recent arrivals to the U.S. but there's no data to support that assumption. The better conclusion is that the occupations respondents reported to the DIC represent a fair cross-section of the emigrants of the later 19th century, the period when the greatest numbers of them came to the mill towns.

TABLE 6

Occupations of Canadian French Females Before Coming
to the United States (*Study of Employees*)

	Number of Respondents	Percentage of Respondents
Textile manufacturing	160	22%
Other manufacturing	27	4%
Farming or farm labor	336	46%
Sewing, embroidering, lace-making	65	9%
Teaching	44	6%
Domestic service	61	8%
Trade	20	3%
Other	13	2%

These results suggest that my forbears who worked as day-laborers, in transportation, in lumber camps, or in light industries before their arrival in the States were not unusual. Many of the men and women who came to the New England mill towns were not employed primarily on family farms and were not intending to return to Québec.

The story of the indebted farmer coming to the mills to re-establish the family farm, often traveling back and forth from the farm to the factory, is not a fable. It is true for many families. But it is not the dominant story. The U.S. attracted men and women who were already working for wages in Québec, who were unemployed, or who came from farm families but neither inherited the farm nor established themselves on their own lands.

The Day-Laborers and the Move Away from Agriculture

The DIC data reveals that, among Franco-American cotton workers, about a quarter of the men and 40 percent of women were wage-earners in Québec before they came to the United States. About one-half of these male wage earners were day-laborers, those the DIC termed

"general laborers," as well as a large segment of the agricultural laborers for wages.[12] During our period, most employed people in rural
Québec were either farmers or day-laborers. No other occupation
comes close to the numbers of these two. The day-laborers formed
the lowest class in rural Québec in our period. They existed on the
margins both economically and socially. Day-laborer was not a career
but a lack of one. These workers had no fixed métier and most, though
not all, were landless.[13] Many Brunswick Franco-Americans came
from the day-laborer class, including my great-grandfather Charles
and my Racine forbears.

In the 1930s, anthropologist Horace Miner studied the parish of
Saint-Denis in Kamouraska, one of four counties that produced a significant emigration to Brunswick. Miner found that the day-laboring
families occupied the least desirable pews in church (a measure of
social status), were less observant Catholics, and were looked down
upon by their neighbors. They were never elected to parish council
or school board. Miner also observed that some of these families had
turned to prostitution and illegal liquor sales to make ends meet, and
such activities further alienated them from their neighbors. He judged
these families to be "more individualistic" and "less under paternal
dominance."[14] Miner also states that the socioeconomic status of this
day-laborer class had declined in the generation before his study.[15]

The day-laborers were good prospects for the recruitment efforts
of New England textile mill agents. Unlike the family farmer, the
day-laborers were already selling their labor for wages in Québec. They
were accustomed to working under supervision, in contrast to the
family farmers who worked on their own account. The day-laborers
were also highly mobile. They were accustomed to moving to where
they could find work. They also tended to live in the village, especially
those who did not perform farm work.[16] The village in rural Québec
in our period might have been no more than a crossroads with a
church and a few other buildings. Nonetheless, unlike the farmer, the
day-laborer was used to living on a small plot, in a town. Their indi-
vidualism and relative freedom from paternal and church influences
would also make them less susceptible to the clerical elite's agitation
against emigration.

However, only the more prosperous day-laborers could have borne the costs of emigration. The poorest of the poor were unable to move either to a city within Canada or to the U.S. industrial towns. If some day-laborers who were too poor to seek opportunities elsewhere, this could explain Miner's observation that this class was faring worse in his rural Québec parish of the 1930s than they had a generation prior. Those who could improve their lot, by moving to the U.S. or Canadian cities, did so. Those who were unable to move were left to fall even further behind their neighbors economically and socially.

To understand the 19th century day-laborers better, I analyzed the occupations of the residents of three parishes in the lower Saint Lawrence region in 1831 and 1861 using the manuscript Canadian Census.[17] I chose to study the town of L'Islet because it was an important source of emigrants to Brunswick. I also studied Saint-Gervais, my Vermette family's hometown, and Saint-Jean Port Joli, another parish in the county of L'Islet that I chose at random. I divided everyone whose occupations were listed in the census into three categories: *farmer proprietors (Fr: cultivateurs)*, *day-laborers (Fr: journaliers)*, and *all other occupations*. Per the standard theory, I expected to find the number of day-laborers increasing at the expense of the farmers, as arable land became scarce, forcing sons of farmers who were not inheriting land to sell their manual labor. I expected to find pools of landless labor accumulating in these parishes.

In each of the three parishes, however, the number of day-laborers was static or declined. Between about one-tenth to one-quarter of all employed individuals in 1831 were day-laborers in these parishes. By 1861 any surplus day-laborers may have already moved to other regions where they could earn a steady wage since the economy of these rural parishes could only absorb so many of these odd-jobbers. Some of the day-laborers may have taken up stable professions, or their children learned fixed trades. Whatever became of them, in *per capita* terms, they're not aggregating in these parishes.

The consistent trend in all three parishes is the growth in the percentage of employed individuals who were neither farmers nor laborers. The motion between 1831 and 1861 is not toward the bottom of the socioeconomic ladder, from farming to day-laboring, but away from the farmer-proprietor and day-laborer roles and toward a wider range of occupations. This motion suggests an economy that is diversifying and able to support this range. Competition in the agricultural sphere may have turned people who were formerly farmers to some other career. As farmers *per capita* decreased, there were fewer fences for day-laborers to mend and fewer harvests to help gather. Consequently, the diversification of occupations put pressure on the day-laborer class.

In L'Islet in 1861, the largest and most economically diverse of these parishes, the number of proprietary farmers decreased from nearly one-half to less than one-third of the employed population between 1831 and 1861. Many of the farmers seem to be trading their plows for boats or fishing equipment. Maritime métiers become more common in this parish as the century progressed. The number of small tradespeople running their own operations, such as cobbler shops, forges, and tanneries, also increased. L'Islet is even modern and sophisticated enough by 1861 to have a resident architect, mechanics, inventors, and other individuals with technical or professional training.

Following the trend, I continued the analysis by examining Saint-Jean Port Joli in 1871. I found that the trend away from farming

TABLE 7

Occupations in Three Lower Saint Lawrence Parishes (1831-1861)

		1831	1861
Saint-Gervais	Farmers	79%	67%
	Laborers	9%	9%
	All others	12%	24%
Saint-Jean Port Joli	Farmers	59%	65%
	Laborers	23%	13%
	All others	19%	22%
L'Islet	Farmers	49%	32%
	Laborers	25%	20%
	All others	26%	48%

and day-laboring and toward other occupations continued. Those who were neither farmers nor day-laborers increased from less than one-fifth (19 percent) in 1831 to more than one-third (35 percent) of employed individuals in 1871. The relative sophistication of these non-agricultural occupations in the parish increased steadily between 1831 and 1871. In the latter year, this parish supports not only the established professions of doctor, lawyer, and notary, but also teachers, a medical student, and a resident agent of the Grand Trunk Railroad. I do not see a parish dying on the vine, but a small community finding its way toward late 19th-century modernity.

This data tends to confirm the view that it was not economic *stagnation* but a measure of economic *dynamism* that put pressure on the poorer classes of Québec in the 19th century. As competition in the agricultural sector increased, farmers retooled their operations or moved to non-agricultural occupations. Some were able to make these transitions while others were not. The changes in agriculture and the growth in the Québec economy divided more sharply the fortunes of those who made this transition from those who did not. The exodus to the U.S. from this region of Québec was an extension of the move away from family farms and toward other occupations.

Emigration to New England also had a social dimension, especially for those from the day-laborer class. Consider Pierre Morin.[18] He was born in the town of L'Islet in 1847, the son of a day-laborer. He was educated in the local schools. His literacy, by no means a foregone conclusion in his generation, would serve him later in life. By 1870, Morin had moved to Brunswick apparently by himself. In the U.S. Federal Census of Brunswick in 1870 he is listed as "Peter Morin" living with three families in a single dwelling that housed 17 people.

Like the bulk of the *Canadien* immigrants in 1870, he worked for the Cabot mill. Morin labored there for many years before becoming a clerk in the grocery store of Noel Vandal, one of the town's Franco-American notables. Vandal also worked at the Cabot mill per the 1870 census, in the years before he established his store. He became President of the naturalization society the Franco-Americans founded in Brunswick in 1884.[19] Pierre Morin became a naturalized U.S. citizen in 1882. He was employed at Vandal's store for several years before establishing his own grocery store in about 1890. A brief biography penned in 1915 describes Morin's store as "one of the best conducted in this entire section of the State."[20] His store made him a prosperous merchant.

A Democrat, in 1912 Morin was elected to the board of Selectman, the highest office in a small New England town. Morin was the first Franco-American to hold the office of Selectman of Brunswick. He served several terms in that office. His biographer concludes, "During his long and honorable residence in the town, Mr. Morin has not only been regarded as a leading Franco-American, but as one of the most influential citizens."[21] Morin was one of the tiny Franco-American elite of the town, a mill worker made good. As the son of the lowest class in the stratified, hierarchical world of 19th century Québec, could Morin have risen as far had he stayed in L'Islet? Would he have been able to become a leader of L'Islet, as he became Selectman of Brunswick? Probably not.

When he came to the U.S., Pierre Morin joined others from a similar socioeconomic class. The trip across the border and into the mill town was a leveler, an equalizer. With rare exceptions, emigration placed people from various regions and occupations in Québec on an equal socioeconomic footing in the United States.

But it was not the "land of opportunity" at large that created this opening for Morin. It was the Franco-American enclave that enabled him to succeed as he did. Morin's obituary in the *Brunswick Record* notes, "In due course of time the French speaking citizens of the town desired to have a member of the board of Selectmen" and chose to elect Morin. His success in business and in politics depended on the "French-speaking citizens" and their desires. The French Quarter was a platform that allowed a son of a day-laborer to become a chief executive of his town.

Whether the *Canadien* immigrant came from the day-laborer class, like Pierre Morin and Charles Vermette, from struggling farms, or from the small shops and factories of Québec, no one would have tolerated the conditions of life in the mills unless it was necessary. *Canadien* families came to New England because changes in the Québec economy put their survival at stake. The families who came to the mill towns were desperately poor, but their poverty was not necessarily indicative of the general state of the Québec economy. We need not posit a Québec-wide crisis, at all times, and in all regions of the province during our period. It was a crisis for farmers and wage-earners on the economic margins.

No one higher in the social hierarchy was guarding the interests of these poor people. On the contrary, when circumstances forced them to sell their labor to *les Bostonnais* [the Bostonians] they were reviled as sell-outs or vagabonds and blamed for being poor.[22] The fact that a proportion of them came from the contemned day-laborer classes or the ranks of industrial workers made it easier for elites to condemn them. Elites lamented the exodus, but whether in Québec City, in Ottawa, or across the ocean in London, they did but little to stem the tide ebbing away from the *Canadien* homeland.

In 1936, some half-dozen years after the unofficial end of the emigration movement, a *Canadien* senator reflected on his government's inaction with tones of regret:

Canada was too indifferent to her sons' going away; we believed too easily that they might be profitably replaced by immigrants from overseas, either from the Orient or the Occident. Our government did not understand the problem; we failed to protect those who were in poverty, without employment, without bread. We should have established national industries, wisely protected, immediately after Confederation, not fifteen years afterwards.

In some ways the French Canadians protected the expatriates by supplying them, in foreign lands, with means of retaining their language and their religion, and thereby encouraged emigration to the United States. That proved to be one of the reasons for the failure of repatriation schemes....Too many schemes were made to establish a new Québec in New England. It was a beautiful thought inspired by love of race, but it did not prove profitable to Canada nor to the French Canadians who remained here.[23]

CHAPTER TEN

THEY CAME FROM L'ISLET

A large segment of Brunswick's Franco-Americans came from the town of L'Islet, and this movement began in earnest immediately after the Civil War. The Canadian Census of 1852 and 1861 discloses the economic life of this Québec town on the eve of the move of many of its poorer citizens to Brunswick.[1] A prefatory note, written in French in a studied, 19th-century hand, precedes the enumeration for L'Islet in 1852:

> The greater part of the farmers of this parish are quite comfortable and have leaning against their barns mills to grind grain, the motor power for which is wind. The price of these mills varies from £15 to £20 and even lower. These mills are of great benefit to them, saving them time, effort, fatigue and expense. Some people got them from the Nicoll factory at St Thomas [Montmagny, Québec]. These are small portable mills that two men can make work without getting too tired, using cranks. The Messieurs Nicoll have obtained a patent because the mills are their invention. All those who have them appear very satisfied.[2]

A general study of the agricultural data from the 1852 census corroborates the enumerator's observation that the L'Islet farmers were relatively prosperous. The county ranked high in farm surpluses.[3] L'Islet farmers were not congenitally averse to new agricultural technology. They used wind-powered, portable grist mills invented and patented by locals and manufactured in the region. One of the inventors, M. Nicoll, lived at L'Islet in 1852.

There was also a two-story, stone schoolhouse in L'Islet in 1852, built that very year. The census enumerator describes it as "a beautiful building" of "fairly large dimensions," capable of accommodating 160 pupils.[4] The local school board, claims the enumerator, hopes to attract the teaching order of the Christian Brothers to the school the following autumn. Most likely, future Brunswick Selectman Pierre Morin was educated at this school.

By 1861, the school board has expanded L'Islet's facilities. In addition to the stone structure, the board had built a wooden schoolhouse. The *fabrique* [parish council] at L'Islet also maintains in addition to the church, a two-story public hall, chapels, and a rectory. Together, the *fabrique* at L'Islet controls property worth $37,780. To calibrate this figure, just eight years prior, Frederick Cabot and his associates paid $42,000 for the textile mill complex in Brunswick (in 1861 $1US = $1CDN).

In 1852, the *Seigneur* of L'Islet, Eugene Casgrain, had recently built a small complex of mills contained in a three-story, wooden building. This facility included the traditional grist mill the *Seigneur* was expected to furnish for his tenants.[5] This water powered mill had three wheels to grind the grain, and there was also a machine on the premises to de-hull barley. These grain-processing operations employed three men.

In the same building in 1852, Casgrain operated a wool carding mill. The lower floor of the mill housed facilities for fulling fabrics the local farm families wove. It appears that the carding and fulling operations had one employee. On the same property, in a separate building, Casgrain had machines for dyeing and pressing fabrics. This textile operation supplied employment for another worker. The census enumerator notes that "M. Casgrain is presently occupied in having built in the same place a sawmill, which will have two scores, at a cost of £100 to £125. It is to be ready by the first of May next."

Nine years later, per the 1861 census, Casgrain has indeed expanded his operations. This census gives detailed information, in dollars, of the capital invested, the value of goods produced, and the revenues of industrial and commercial ventures. By 1861, Casgrain had his sawmill in operation, as planned, while still running his grist mill and his textile operations. Taken together, the Seigneur's various manufacturing activities in 1861 produced goods valued at $27,577, generating revenue in 1861 of $1,957. The capital employed totaled an estimated $16,000.

Together these mills employed ten people, eight men and two women. As the DIC's research demonstrates, women worked outside the home in industrial jobs in Québec in the 19th century. The designers of the census expected to find women employed outside the home since they provided a separate column on the form to count both male and female employees.

Casgrain's operation was small. It was no competition for the vast mills of New England. Nonetheless, textile manufacturing employed a small number of men and women in L'Islet. The concept of working in a factory setting was not unknown to the people who departed L'Islet for the textile mill in Brunswick.

It was not unusual for the *Seigneur* in a rural parish to make full use of water power as did Casgrain.[6] But he was not the only manufacturer in L'Islet in the 1850s and 1860s. In 1852, a certain Leonard Ennis, an engineer at L'Islet of Irish origin, "is currently occupied in constructing a manufacturing of an entirely new type....Already a building of three stories is constructed, and it contains a sawmill and some other apparatus." Here was another inventor in L'Islet in 1852. By 1861, Ennis operated a wheel manufacturing operation that employed four men, a flour mill that employed two men and one woman, and a sawmill that employed another man.

In addition to Casgrain and Ennis, several other small manufacturers were active in L'Islet in 1861. These plants included three sawmills, three potash manufacturing facilities, two tanneries, a grist mill, a wool carding operation, and a producer of lime. Together, these operations, including Casgrain's and Ennis's businesses, have capital invested in commerce and manufacturing of close to $95,000. In addition to these operations that employ at least one individual, there were many smaller, family-run hand trades such as shoemakers, carpenters, and blacksmiths. In some cases, entrepreneurs ran more than one business. For example, the Michaud brothers had a retail store as well as well as a potash manufacturing operation and a lime kiln. In 1861, however, two institutions, the church and the *seigneurie*, remain the richest in the parish.

Together, manufacturing employs only 36 people, both men and women, a small percentage of the population of L'Islet. Judging from the value of goods produced, these shops probably did not offer full-time employment. Small shops were the rule in Canada. As late as 1890, only 18 percent of Canadian manufacturers employed five or more individuals.[7]

Except for Ennis's mills, manufacturing in L'Islet is owned and operated by *Canadiens*. These small entrepreneurs of L'Islet were not unenterprising – they were undercapitalized. Unlike the Boston merchants, the entrepreneurs of L'Islet did not have access to large sources of capital from mercantile fortunes. Cut off from the sources of capital in Europe after the British conquest of Canada in 1760, the *Canadiens* were thrown back on their own ingenuity, their ability to scratch what they could out of the land and available resources. What they managed to create in the century following the Conquest compares favorably with other, relatively remote, rural regions of North America. Distinct as to language, history, and customs, Québec was economically and industrially of a piece with the rest of the continent. With its intense concentration of industry and large accumulations of capital in the form of joint stock corporations, it was 19th century New England that was the aberration.

The Stereotype of the Unenterprising, Stagnant Peasant

The decennial census takes only a snapshot of a single year, which can be deceptive. However, taken together, the available sources do not picture L'Islet as a depressed, stagnant place in the mid-19th century. On the contrary, between 1831 and 1861 there was a diversification of occupations. Schools were built. Small, *Canadien*-owned and operated industries grew. While most people in L'Islet remained family farmers, day-laborers, in maritime occupations or tradespeople in family shops, investments in commerce and industry amounted to substantial sums by their standards. Small numbers of L'Islet residents had industrial occupations. Invention and innovation were not unknown. There's no evidence that the people of L'Islet were allergic to modernity.

L'Islet was the chief town of its county. The back-country parishes were perhaps less progressive. And L'Islet is but one town in all of Québec. If we say that L'Islet was not typical because it was more progressive than other towns, then this raises the question of why a reasonably prosperous parish disgorged a measurable portion of its population into a Maine mill town. One reply to this question is that L'Islet corroborates the view that emigration tends to occur from places where there is a measure of economic growth rather than from among the poorest of the poor.

Wage differentials between L'Islet and Brunswick may also help to explain the exodus from the parish. One data point: the Canadian Census reveals that a woman employed in a carding mill at L'Islet earns $4.00 per month in 1861. Not many years before that, in 1853, Brunswick's Cabot mill was advertising positions for women doing the same or similar work, starting at $4.00-4.50 *per week*.[8] Faced with such differentials, many *Canadiens* at L'Islet responded by purchasing a railroad ticket south.

My investigation does not favor the image of 19th century Québec as a backward land of hide-bound farmers, mired in the past. These were stereotypes, and they were remarkably persistent. The *New York Times* recited the stereotype in 1889:

> [The French Canadian] is, in thousands of cases, where his ancestors were a century ago...living as he lived 100 years ago, working as he worked 100 years ago, entertaining the same beliefs he held 100 years ago....All the rest of the world may move: Quebec clings to the past. The farmer tills his fields according to the most approved methods of the days of the Grand Monarch [Louis XIV].[9]

The stereotype of the 19th century *Canadien* as unchanged since the 17th century served two ideological needs. First, the *Canadien* clerical elite in the second half of the 19th century wished to portray their people as a continuation of the old, Catholic France, prior to the Revolution of 1789. The vision of the unchanging *Canadien* differentiated the "French-Canadian race" from the Anglo-Protestants in Canada. Further, the *Canadien* clergy had concerns about industrialism and unfettered market economies, consistent with Catholic social teaching that emerged in the 19th century.[10] The fate of their compatriots in places like the French Quarter of Brunswick justified their concerns about industrialism. Seeing their flock in such straits reinforced their negative view of the alleged materialism and heartlessness of the Yankee Protestants and the capitalist, industrial system they came to represent.

For an educated class in the Northeast U.S., 19th century modernity was inseparable from industrial and economic "progress." In resisting these forces, *Canadiens* appeared hopelessly outmoded. English-speakers on both sides of the border perpetuated the stereotype of the unchanging French-Canadian peasant because it served their contrast between the allegedly forward-thinking, progressive Anglo-Protestant, and the supposedly backward, priest-ridden, medieval Catholic. It justified the *othering* of the Franco-American worker.

But there's a fact hiding in plain sight: if our ancestors were as priest-ridden as is claimed, the movement to the U.S. would never have occurred since the clerical elite was vehemently opposed to it. The fact that so many families bet on a risky move shows that they were able to make bold decisions, given their limited range of choices, within the systems imposed upon them by forces from outside their world.

When I examined primary sources absent preconceptions, the 19th century *Canadiens* do not appear as stagnant peasants but as physically mobile and economically adroit. Later generations of Franco-Americans, *Canadiens*, and *Québécois* internalized the stereotype of the unchanging French-Canadian peasant and tended to frame the story of our ancestors accordingly. We either idealize our "peasant" ancestors as quaint and picturesque remnants of ancient France, or we dismiss them as superstitious, ignorant dupes. The stereotypes pursued the *Canadiens* across the border. They contributed to Nativist apprehensions in Yankee America and spurred a backlash.

SECTION THREE

THE RECEPTION
OF FRANCO-AMERICANS

CHAPTER ELEVEN

FRANCO-AMERICANS AND AMERICANISM

"Unlike past immigrant groups, Mexicans and other Latinos have not assimilated into mainstream U.S. culture, forming instead their own political and linguistic enclaves...and rejecting the Anglo-Protestant values that built the American dream. The United States ignores this challenge at its peril."

Samuel P. Huntington, "The Hispanic Challenge," *Foreign Policy*, 2004.

For Huntington, Anglo-Protestant culture remains the "bedrock of U.S. identity." The nation's cohesion rests, he holds, on the inheritance of the 17th and 18th century British colonists. Huntington proposes that Spanish-speaking communities, forming a culture apart from the U.S. mainstream, are a threat to the English language and the alleged "Anglo-Protestant" culture that unite the United States. Paradoxically, he bemoans Hispanic separatism while he is also wary of Latin political and social influence on the U.S. mainstream. He even frets about a Spanish-American *"reconquista"* in the U.S. Southwest. The alleged "Hispanic challenge," he believes, is unprecedented in U.S. immigration history.

Huntington is unaware that the movement of *Canadiens* and Acadians across the U.S.'s northeastern border in the late 19th and early 20th centuries resembled in many respects emigration across the southwest border today. Mexican-Americans and Franco-Americans were both predominantly Roman Catholic groups that spoke a Romance language. Both groups had histories spanning many generations in North America, predating the founding of the United States. Their core homelands were contiguous to the U.S., and both groups had an historical presence in territory later incorporated into that republic. Both groups are – or were believed to be – "mixed" genetically with indigenous peoples.

In both cases, alarmists saw a threat to Anglo-Protestant culture understood as the cornerstone of United States identity. *In both cases*, English-language conformity and bilingual education attracted debate in the press, the legislatures and the courts. *In both cases,* there were concerns about the cultural cohesion and the geographical concentration of the immigrants. *In both cases,* there was an identified border region where the alleged threat concentrated. *In both cases*, there were fears of an attempted reconquest of U.S. territory by a neighboring country.

How Anglo-Protestant is the United States? Is it necessary to affirm an Anglo-Protestant cultural bedrock? Undoubtedly, the colonial enterprise led by London extended the English language and English institutions into North America. There were regions of the U.S. that were homogenously Anglo and Protestant before the industrial age. But on a national scale, the U.S. had ethnic and linguistic diversity from its origins. By 1776, the European-origin residents of the thirteen colonies were of German, Dutch, Swedish, Swiss, Danish, Finnish, French Huguenot, Jewish, Portuguese, Scots, Ulster Scots, Irish, as well as English descent.

For a period in the 18th century, European-descent Pennsylvanians were a third German and a third Ulster-Scots.[1] Nationwide, these two groups accounted for hundreds of thousands out of a population of approximately two million in 1776.[2] These were not tiny enclaves in an English mass but substantial minorities. That various European populations were allowed to settle the coast of North America under the British Crown was a strength of London's project as a colonialist enterprise.

Here also were the indigenous nations, the African slaves and other Africans who lived on territories the U.S. claimed, but the allegedly Anglo-Protestant political structures did not grant these peoples an equal stake in them. The U.S. was always racially, ethnically, and linguistically diverse. It was never an exclusively English-speaking, Anglo-Saxon ethnostate.

Although overwhelmingly Protestant, the citizens of the U.S. in 1776 also had religious differences that did not seem trivial at the time. The New England colony of Rhode Island was founded on these religious differences among Protestants. By the time of the American Revolution, some colonists were Deists, while adherents of Roman Catholicism and Judaism also inhabited the thirteen original states. A Roman Catholic signed the Declaration of Independence.

Attitudes toward the American Revolution divided along ethnic lines, with the Scots on side with the British King, the Ulster-Scots, Irish, and Huguenots (including the likes of Paul Revere) against the King, the Germans neutral, and the English bitterly divided.[3] The founding of the United States entailed a violent rejection of Great Britain's monarchy, in alliance with Britain's arch-enemy, France. Post-Revolution national myth-makers might have distanced the country from Anglo-Saxon roots, while emphasizing its diverse origins. And yet the Anglo-Saxon Protestant story became the dominant national *mythos* – *the* American story.

Through this *mythos*, the English-speakers in the U.S. indigenized their language and bound the Anglo-Protestant identity to the territory of the United States. The national myth extended the hegemony of the English language to the area Americans called *the frontier*. The presumed Manifest Destiny of the Anglo-Protestants became the U.S. counterpart to the "white man's burden" the British Empire assumed. By indigenizing the language and the Anglo-Protestant heritage, "American" became a race.

The national origin story included the ideology of an elect people informed by Puritan theology. The genealogies of families and the origins of institutions were traced, sometimes spuriously, to Anglo-Saxon origins. There was the insistence that the English language serve as the dominant or sole medium of communication, as the only language with a claim on the territory of the United States. Newcomers to the U.S. were expected to conform to allegedly Anglo-Protestant cultural norms.[4]

The yeoman farmer was the hero in this creation myth. Self-reliant, independent, and free, the origin story placed the American farmer in a Jeffersonian Golden Age. In this telling of the tale, the arrival of immigrants, especially those from Southern and Eastern Europe in the late 19th century, signaled the downfall of that mythic paradise. Subsequent U.S. history, in this reading, is characterized by the struggle to return to the Jeffersonian Eden. And if Paradise is lost, then at least the Anglo-Protestant stalwarts can fight against the encroachment of alien hordes.

Scholar Eric Kaufmann examined these origins of Anglo-Protestant identity in the United States.[5] For the inhabitants of the thirteen colonies, Kaufmann posits, the *Canadiens* and indigenous nations living to their North and West formed the primordial *Other*. The so-called French and Indian War was a catalytic event where the colonists began to construct an Anglo-Protestant identity in contrast to the *Other*: non-whites, those who did not speak English, and were either Catholic or pagan.[6] The genesis of the nascent U.S.'s Anglo-Protestant self-understanding was this contrast between themselves, and the *Canadiens* and their indigenous allies.

The Franco-Americans were among the first groups in the U.S. to challenge Anglo-conformity and the Anglo-Protestant *mythos*. They had their own national origin story including an account of their role in North America. Franco-Americans had a vision of who they were within the context of the U.S. and of what it meant to be a citizen and an American. Between 1880 and 1900, the Anglo-Protestant-identified mainstream engaged in an ideological duel with Franco-Americans around the meaning of U.S. citizenship.

A Different Idea of Citizenship

The 1891 book *Les Canadiens-français de la Nouvelle-Angleterre* [*The French-Canadians of New England*] by Father Edouard Hamon, S.J. was a seminal text in the debates of this period. Father Hamon was a Québec-based priest originally from France, well traveled among the Little Canadas of New England. He conducted interviews, visited communities, compiled lists, and crunched numbers to produce his book, one of the first detailed studies of Franco-Americans.

Concerning his chosen subject, Fr. Hamon declares himself to be *"ni un panégyriste ni un détracteur"* [neither a panegyrist nor a detractor].[7] The author spares neither Franco-American nor Yankee illusions. Writes the Jesuit,

> Here then are the true feelings of Americans towards the French-Canadians [in the U.S.]. They tolerate them, they do not like them, they see in them an element dangerous for the Republic, and if necessary they would not hesitate to resort to legal persecution to suppress or reduce a breed that shows itself resistant to Americanization....The goal [the Franco-Americans] propose is excellent: to keep their language and customs, and at the same time this will mean keeping their religion, but....in the United States they have no allies, and for support currently they can count only on each other. Their enemies or opponents are numerous, they have the strength in their hand, [and] it would be folly to provoke them by imprudent and unnecessary statements.[8]

Hamon's text relays three ideas. First, the *Canadiens* who came to New England in our period had no intention of assimilating to Anglo-Protestant culture. They intended to keep their language, religion, and traditions intact in their new home. Father Hamon writes that the *Canadien* émigrés "are in the process of forming in the eastern states bordering Canada an entire network of workers' colonies, which are rapidly expanding...[they are] tending to become a people distinct [in their] religion, race, and mores."[9]

Second, Hamon affirms that this Franco-American resistance to Americanization had aroused animosity and suspicion among the Yankees. Third, he warns the Franco-Americans against making "imprudent and unnecessary statements" that "provoke" their "opponents." Franco-American utterances were fueling Yankee suspicions.

The Franco-Americans' resistance to Americanization was not a mere gesture, a sentimental attachment to a beloved motherland. Its basis was an ideology called *la survivance*, i.e., *the survival* of the French-speaking, Catholic culture, with its distinctive traditions, as a transnational identity in North America. *La survivance* rested on three pillars: the French language, the Roman Catholic religion, and the customs and mores of rural Québec.[10] The Franco-American elite took every opportunity to reinforce these pillars, from the pulpit and in its French-language press.

The Little Canadas acclimatized immigrants to their adopted land, and in doing so were not appreciably different from the Little Italys or Little Tokyos elsewhere in the United States. For the Franco-American elite, however, these neighborhoods were not temporary enclaves where immigrants could feel at home while they paddled their way into the mainstream. They were to be permanent communities, replicas of Québec, where the Franco-Americans would preserve a distinct culture within the borders of the United States. The Little Canadas served as centers for promoting *la survivance*.

Their *Canadien* background prepared the Franco-Americans for the mission of cultural survival in a hostile environment. By the 1890s, the *Canadiens* had maintained their language and culture under British rule for nearly a century-and-a-half, the Acadians for even longer. In the 1760s, when *Canadien* Catholics swore allegiance to a Protestant King of England, they began to understand that their religious and linguistic identity was separable from their political allegiance. The *Canadiens* preserved their language, religion, and customs under several British North American constitutions. Franco-Americans had every expectation that they would be able to preserve that same culture under the Constitution of the United States. The Franco-Americans saw no difference between living surrounded by the dominant English-speakers in Canada or in a similar milieu in the United States. They retained *in the U.S.* the traditional *Canadien* posture of resistance to Anglo-Saxon Protestantism.

The Franco-American elites asserted the ideology of cultural survival, with its understanding of U.S. citizenship, in speech after lengthy speech at the series of General Conventions of the *Canadiens* of the United States held in cities from Chicago to Biddeford in our period. Franco-Americans held nineteen such conventions between 1865 and 1901.[11] In addition to these gatherings, local and state conventions were not infrequent. The nationwide conventions, held over several days, gathered delegates from the local branches of the Franco-American national societies. Most of the delegates were journalists, professionals, small businessmen, and priests. These conventions conveyed the messages the elite wanted to communicate to their fellow Franco-Americans in the Midwestern farms and forests, and in the factories of the Northeast.

A speaker at the 1901 General Convention in Springfield, Massachusetts suggests that the political structures of the U.S. were *better* suited to the preservation of the *Canadien* identity than the British Empire's:

> Since our nationality has no official status and since we do not really have a country we can call our own...it matters little to us that we be incorporated with the Anglo-Saxons of the British Empire or those of the United States. We will simply be exchanging our condition as subjects for that of citizens, and our new status would make us no less French than we could be under the tutelage of the English. Far from ceasing to be ourselves, by becoming voters in our adopted country we would acquire the means to exercise fully our natural rights as free men.[12]

Naturalization, in this view, was not a tool of cultural assimilation but a means to promote Franco-American interests within the borders of the United States. In this speaker's view, there was nothing essential to the *Canadien* identity in the English institutions imposed upon Canada. In the words of a Franco-American journalist writing in 1924, political ties to Canada were expendable, without sacrificing language, religion, or culture since the Confederation, as a political entity, was merely "an English colony in which we no longer wanted to live."[13]

The champions of *survivance* also found no contradiction between their continued resistance to cultural assimilation and full participation in U.S. civic life. Ferdinand Gagnon was one of the chief proponents of this view and *de facto* leader of New England's Franco-Americans in the late 19th century. A journalist and activist, Gagnon was born in Saint-Hyacinthe, Québec in 1849 and was a graduate of the seminary there. Rotund, eloquent by 19th century lights, in both French and English, Gagnon lived in Manchester before establishing himself in Worcester where he founded the French-language

newspaper *Le Travailleur* [The Worker].[14] An advocate of naturalization Gagnon wrote,

> Allegiance to a power does not change the origin of a subject or of a
> citizen; it only changes his political condition.
>
> In taking the oath of fidelity to the Constitution of the United States,
> nothing changes in my life....
>
> What does take place then?
>
> There goes into effect a political contract which obliges me to observe
> the laws of the different governments of my adopted country, to defend
> its flag and to work for the general prosperity of the nation....Nothing
> else passes between my conscience and my oath of allegiance.[15]

For Gagnon, U.S. citizenship establishes a narrow contract. Citizens,
of any origin, are obliged to observe the laws, defend the flag, and
contribute to the country's prosperity. Cultural expressions and traits
such as language, religion and customs are not bound by this contract.

Gagnon makes a distinction between one's *origin* and one's *pol-*
itical condition. He also writes of the allegiance "of a subject or of a
citizen." The term "subject" applies to Canada, and the term "citizen"
to the United States. Such terms describe one's political condition,
which is fluid, while one's origin is immutable. To formulate this
distinction, Gagnon coined the motto that circulated widely in New
England's Little Canadas: *Loyaux mais français* [Loyal but French]
sometimes modified as *Loyaux mais Canadien-français* [Loyal but
French-Canadian].[16] The motto intends to assert that there is no
contradiction between loyalty to the U.S. and the preservation of
Canadien identity.

When a banner at their conventions reading *"Notre langue, notre*
religion, et nos moeurs" ["Our language, our religion, our customs"]
flew next to another reading *"Loyaux mais Canadien-français"* ["Loyal
but French-Canadian"], Franco-Americans were not making threats.
These conventioneers saw no contradiction between the messages
on their banners and the earnest appeals to 19th century-style U.S.
patriotism that Franco-Americans delivered at these same events.
During our period, many Franco-American communities throughout New England celebrated the national holiday of the *Canadiens*,
Saint-Jean Baptiste Day, on June 24. The Stars and Stripes flew in

great flocks over the parades held on these occasions.[17] For Franco-Americans, the holiday had nothing to do with loyalty to the Canadian Confederation as a political entity. The loyalty expressed on June 24 was toward the *Canadien* "race" which could subsist in more than one political condition.[18]

Throughout the late 19th century, the speakers at the General Conventions promote Franco-American cultural survival under the U.S. Constitution. They argue for their status as co-founders of what became the United States and for their historical presence on its territory.[19] These appeals to history are intended to undercut the rationale for Anglo-conformity and to counter the myth of exclusive Anglo-Protestant priority on the territory of the United States.

Franco-American elites highlighted their ancestors' historical presence in North America, most notably in the Great Lakes region and the lands the Union acquired in the Louisiana Purchase. They also reminded whomever would listen that the French language was spoken in North America for as long if not longer than the English language. They applied the same historical argument to their religion and customs. As a distinctively North American community, the Franco-Americans made a claim for the peaceful co-existence of their culture and language in the U.S. side-by-side with the Anglo-Protestant American's.

At their General Conventions, the Franco-American elite presented their people not as foreigners in the U.S. but as Americans in the broad sense. Like the Anglo-Americans, the *Canadiens* had indigenized their identity within North America. They did not see themselves as immigrants to the United States from France who had had a sojourn of some generations in Canada. They no longer saw themselves as settlers from Europe but as a people whose identity was North American.

"The French-Canadian is as American as someone born in Boston. It is all the nationalities that emigrated here that truly constitutes the American people," said Civil War hero, Major Edmond Mallet, at the 1888 General Convention in Nashua. For Mallet, it was not necessary to conform to Anglo-Protestant ways to integrate into "the American people." For him, "American" is not an ethnicity but a collection,

FIGURE 13: Brunswick's French Quarter, June 24, 1894, Arch for Saint-Jean Baptiste day decorated with U.S. Flags. (Pejepscot Historical Society)

under the same flag, of "all the nationalities that emigrated here." [20]

Speaking at the 1901 Convention in Springfield, J. Camille Hogue, president of the Saint-Jean Baptiste Society of New York, supports Mallet's view. Said Hogue: "Here we are [in the U.S.], several different races living happily under the same starry flag, cherishing institutions full of liberty, conserving each one its distinctive character but all converging to the same end, all prepared to defend the great federation in time of danger." [21] For Hogue, the U.S. was less a melting pot than a bowl of fruit salad. Each element in the dish complements the other ingredients while maintaining its coherence and integrity.

Since they were already Americans, and a *peuple fondateur* [founding people] of the U.S., the Franco-American elite distanced their people from European immigrants. Says Hogue, "the immigration of French-Canadians ought not to be compared to the immigration of other peoples, Germans, Polish, Italians, etc." [22] He thinks that the Franco-Americans differ from European immigrants in the intensity with which his people concentrate in tight-knit neighborhoods and in the extent to which they have duplicated Québec institutions in these centers. He also believes that European immigrants are not as committed as the Franco-Americans to maintaining their distinctiveness within the United States. Doctor John Steele, speaking at that same convention agreed. He makes a distinction between Franco-Americans and the Irish, who were "descendants of the oppressed," while the Germans and Swedes in the U.S. were "irremediably separated" from their homelands. Steele also makes a distinction between Franco-Americans and *Canadiens*, in that the latter must "struggle against the covert but constant aggression" of the English-Canadians.[23]

Senator Henry Cabot Lodge of Massachusetts, a privileged member of the Anglo-Protestant elite, agreed with Hogue and Steele. Speaking just a few years after the 1901 Springfield convention, Senator Lodge stated, "[The Franco-Americans] are hardly to be classified as immigrants in the accepted sense. They represent one of the oldest settlements on this continent. They have been, in the broad sense, Americans for generations, and their coming to the United States is merely movement of Americans across an imaginary line from one part of America to another."[24]

Mallet, Hogue, Steele, and their colleagues might have been quite wrong as regards the differences between Franco-Americans and other immigrant groups in the United States. Right or wrong, Franco-Americans tended to see themselves as chronically unique.

But did the Anglo-Protestant majority perceive U.S. citizenship in terms of the narrow contract Ferdinand Gagnon describes? Didn't they demand more of the naturalized citizen, something beyond a mere "political contract"?

The Chinese of the Eastern States

The Franco-American vision of a United States composed of various religious and cultural groups arranged in a mosaic encountered immediate and vehement opposition from the U.S. mainstream. The 1881 encounter between Franco-American leaders and Carroll D. Wright, Director of the Massachusetts Bureau of Labor Statistics, epitomized this conflict.

Wright and his team were researchers commissioned by the state government to study issues related to the condition of the working class in Massachusetts. Beginning in 1869, the Bureau compiled annual reports that are invaluable, detailed sources for the state's labor history.

While investigating the merits of a law restricting the workday to ten hours, Wright claimed to have found a groundswell of opposition to a new class of laborer which had entered the state in large numbers during the decade and a half beforc 1881. In his Annual Report of the Bureau for that year, Wright took aim at these laborers whom he called "the Canadian French" of New England:

> With some exceptions the Canadian French are the Chinese of the Eastern States. They care nothing for our institutions, civil, political, or educational. They do not come to make a home among us, to dwell with us as citizens, and so become a part of us; but their purpose is merely to sojourn a few years as aliens, touching us only at a single point, that of work, and, when they have gathered out of us what will satisfy their ends, to get them away to whence they came, and bestow it there. They are a horde of industrial invaders, not a stream of stable settlers. Voting, with all that it implies, they care nothing about. Rarely does one of them become naturalized. They will not send their children to school if they can help it, but endeavor to crowd them into the mills at the earliest possible age. To do this they deceive about the age of their children with brazen effrontery. They deceive also about their schooling, declaring that they have been to school the legal time, when they know they have not, and do not intend that they shall....
>
> These people have one good trait. They are indefatigable workers, and docile. All they ask is to be set to work, and they care little who rules them or how they are ruled. To earn all they can by no matter how many hours of toil, to live in the most beggarly way so that out of their earnings they may spend as little for living as possible, and to carry out of the country what they can thus save: this is the aim of the Canadian French in our factory districts. Incidentally they must have some amusements; and, so far as the males are concerned, drinking and smoking and loun-ging constitute the sum of these.
>
> Now it is not strange that so sordid and low a people should awaken corresponding feelings in the managers, and that they should feel that, the longer the hours for such people, the better, and that to work them to the uttermost is about the only good use they can be put to.[25]

What Wright didn't imagine is that the "Canadian French" in New England would read what he had to say. Petitions protesting Wright's report came in haste to the Massachusetts State Legislature from Franco-American national societies in the towns of Lowell and Hudson. The resolutions in these petitions took issue with Wright's statements point-by-point.[26]

When called to account, Wright back-pedaled and shifted the blame onto his informants. Wright claimed that his statements in the 1881 report were made not "in malice, or through any prejudice against the French Canadians."[27]

What if not malice and prejudice could explain Wright's claim that hundreds of thousands of "Canadian French" in the region constituted a "sordid" and "low" people? That their "amusements" consisted of nothing but "drinking and smoking and lounging"? Or that they were a "horde of industrial invaders" with but "one good trait," and that their "only good use" was to be driven to work to exhaustion? How could he not have imagined that a large population in New England would regard these assessments as slanderous? If Wright merely repeated what his sources had told him, then he reiterated, in an official report, second-hand bile.

The statement calling the Franco-Americans the "Chinese of the Eastern States" was explosive in the unenlightened racial climate of the 1880s. And it had legs. Labor leader Frank K. Foster, a founder of the American Federation of Labor, read the salient portion of Wright's report at an 1883 U.S. Senate hearing on Labor issues. He added his color commentary, blaming the "domestic habits of the French Canadians" for poor conditions in the factory tenements.[28] Wright's "Chinese" comment was also repeated on the shop floor, intended as an insult to the Franco-Americans, a case of compound racism.[29] It was an attempt to cast the Franco-Americans as *ambiguously white*, despite Wright's denial that his statement had racial connotations. The comparison was politically significant because not long after Wright issued his report, Washington prohibited Chinese immigration to the United States.

To his credit, Wright dared to face those whom he had accused. In response to the petitions, a hearing was called at the Massachusetts

State House in Boston for 10:00 A.M. on October 25, 1881. About 60 Franco-American leaders and their witnesses testified, presenting evidence to rebut Wright's claims.[30] Wright had a full transcript of this hearing printed in the *Thirteenth Annual Report* of his Bureau in 1882.

The differences between Yankee and Franco-American interpretations of U.S. citizenship came to the surface at the hearing. Before the Franco-American representatives had a chance to present any evidence, Wright came directly to the point in an opening statement:

> While this land is open to all...the people of the United States will always look with disapprobation upon any attempt upon the part of settlers to be other than American citizens. Our laws protect the alien as well as the citizen, and all the benefits of our institutions are as free to you as to the native born; but you cannot be loyal Americans and loyal French Canadians at the same time.
>
> I am inclined to think that whatever prejudice there has been in the public mind against the French Canadians, and I am aware there has been such, has arisen from the seeming disposition of the French to insist upon preserving a distinct national existence within the Republic.[31]

Ferdinand Gagnon was the first witness called to answer Wright's charges. He began his testimony by repeating what was most inflammatory in Wright's 1881 report. Gagnon claimed that this was "the first time that such slanders of a national element find a place in an official document." "Moreover," continued Gagnon, "we say that malice, prejudice, and very probably individual interest, were the chief denunciators of our countrymen."[32]

Gagnon presented the view that the *Canadiens* were not immigrants in the usual sense. Through their long historical presence in the territory of the U.S. and through their involvement in the American Revolution, the Civil War and other defining events in U.S. history, the *Canadiens* were among the raw materials from which the U.S. was formed. Said Gagnon,

> We say that the French Canadian element ought to be respected as others, for they have rendered services in every manner to the United States; establishing cities, counties, States; fighting for the stars and stripes; pacifying Indian tribes; guiding explorers and United States armies.[33]

Gagnon then reminds the assembly of the history of the post-Civil War influx of *Canadiens* to New England. He states that it was the manufacturers themselves, for their benefit, who had recruited and transported to New England the Franco-American workers. He cites a letter from an agent of the Boston and Albany railroad in Worcester stating that at least one hundred managers of mills had applied for "French help." One mill requested up to fifty families at a time. And these workers, says Gagnon, "accept the wages fixed by the liberality, or sometimes the cupidity and avarice, of the manufacturers." Wright's informants were "the manufacturers themselves, who send agents to Canada to recruit factory help."[34] The manufacturers brought the *Canadiens* into their factories and then denounced them before Wright.

Gagnon then demolished each of Wright's claims. Refuting generations of histories that tend to portray the Franco-Americans as a transient population, Gagnon stated, "Canadians do not go back to their country in a large number, as is believed by many manufacturers."[35] The era of permanent Franco-American settlement in New England predated Wright's report by more than a decade. By 1881, Wright's image of the peripatetic Franco-Americans was passé. The rapid growth of the Franco-American institutional network, well underway by 1881, proved it. This network enabled the Franco-Americans to respond swiftly and effectively to Wright's charges. But officialdom's image of Franco-Americans was behind the times.

Wright claimed that the Franco-Americans had little interest in education and evaded compulsory school laws. As for children and their education, Gagnon put the onus on the manufacturers who hired them. Gagnon admitted that many of the Franco-American families, too poor to support themselves without sending their children into the mill, evaded the state's education law. But whose fault was that?

> Is it not the manufacturer who gives employment to young children of eight or nine years of age for merely nominal salary? These children, belonging to poor families, are submitted to a daily task of nine or ten hours, for thirty cents a day. Why does not the manufacturer cut the evil at its root, and refuse employment to these poor little ones, pay a little more to the adult members of these families, and give the children

a chance to have an education? But no! These manufacturers complain of the ignorance of the Canadian children, and they try to get them at their mills for a few cents a day. Yet, notwithstanding the opportunity offered by the cupidity of the manufacturer, few parents only evade the school law.[36]

Gagnon then refuted Wright's claims that Franco-Americans had no interest in U.S. political institutions. He cited the five-year residency requirement for naturalization implying that many newly-arrived Franco-Americans were not uninterested in citizenship but as yet ineligible for it. He also notes the barriers in the way of Franco-American naturalization in the New England states. Massachusetts required that a naturalized citizen must be able to read the Constitution in English. Rhode Island required that a voter must own real estate, while the New Hampshire Constitution debarred Catholics from holding office. Given these hurdles, Gagnon observed, "it is yet surprising to see so many Canadians who are citizens of the United States."[37]

Gagnon caps his testimony by summarizing the value that the Franco-Americans represent to the U.S. of the 1880s and throughout its history:

> Canadians have been great factors in the prosperity of manufacturing interests. Steady workers and skillfull [sic], the manufacturers have benefited by their condition of poverty to reduce wages, and compete favorably with the industries of the Old World.
>
> Americans who study but one history – their own – do not know enough of the services rendered to their country by Canadians. In fact, nearly all the large cities of the Western States have been established by Canadians. Consult the historical societies of Michigan, Illinois, Wisconsin, and Minnesota, and you will learn to respect and admire the French Canadian element.
>
> From Langlade, the father of Wisconsin; Juneau, the founder of Milwaukee; Joseph Robidon, the founder of St. Joe Mission; Vital Guerin, the founder of St. Paul, Minn.; Menard, first lieutenant governor of Illinois; to Jean Louis Légaré, the trader, who has persuaded Sitting Bull to surrender to the United States authorities, — the list is long of the Canadians who have rendered famous the name of our national element.[38]

Gagnon referred to Sitting Bull's surrender as elsewhere in his speech he spoke to the *Canadiens'* alleged ability to "pacify Indian tribes." He touts the supposed diplomatic skills of the *Canadiens* in their relations with indigenous peoples as a selling point. Gagnon is willing to vend these skills to promote the project of U.S. expansion. He does not support the interests of the indigenous peoples in alliance with the *Canadiens*, but, like an interviewee for a job, Gagnon pitches the skills he thinks the hiring manager needs.

The Franco-Americans who faced Wright at the hearing did not only wax eloquent. They came equipped with tables of statistics, letters, and testimonials. They examined witnesses and Wright cross-examined them. Franco-American advocates came from surrounding states to add their voices to the choir. Having had the chance to refute Wright's slanders, on the record, the hearing concluded amicably enough. In a later edition of his report, Wright added a conciliatory postscript, and nuanced his previous remarks. However, he regretted only the phrase "the Chinese of the Eastern States" and stood by the rest.

The Franco-American representatives at the hearing were eager to present their all-American *bona fides* when confronted by Wright's accusations. But they were not entirely forthcoming. They did not respond directly to Wright's statement that they could not "be loyal Americans and loyal French Canadians at the same time." Franco-American leaders' evasion of the question of dual identity did nothing to discourage a well-publicized conspiracy theory about the "Chinese of the Eastern States" that fermented in the press in the years following Wright's report.

CHAPTER TWELVE

FEARS OF FRANCO-AMERICAN CONSPIRACY

Twenty-first century Americans aren't accustomed to thinking of Canada as a threat. It is the country in all the world that is the most similar to the United States and a famously pacific neighbor. Many of their forbears of the 19th century, however, perceived the influx of hundreds of thousands of *Canadien* Catholics into New England as a threat to the territorial integrity of the United States.

As strange as it sounds to modern ears, in the twenty years before 1900, a segment of the U.S. press presented the view that the Québec Roman Catholic hierarchy conspired to conquer New England. The Franco-American workers, this theory posed, had been sent by their clergy as the advance-guard of an attempt to annex New England to a newly independent country, a resurgent New France. Along with Québec and New England, the new country was to include pieces of New York, Ontario, and the Canadian Maritimes. This theory held that the Franco-Americans planned to seize political control of the mill towns. Slowly, Franco-Americans would displace the Anglo-Protestants, and New England, with its wealth and resources, would become part of a newly independent, French-speaking country in North America.

The allegedly benighted Franco-American workers were cast as robotic foot soldiers in a "popish plot," a sinister, international conspiracy. The Franco-Americans were radicalized, said the pundits, by a religious ideology called ultramontanism that advocated the papacy's role in political affairs. In the context of Québec, ultramontanism was an ultra-Catholic, ultra-conservative ideology. Anglo-Protestants in the U.S. made it stand for everything they imagined to be objectionable among the French-Canadian "papists." Alarmists mooted ominous "secret societies," under Jesuit influence, fomenting dark designs. Press reports presented as indisputable fact the notion that all Franco-American Catholics were complicit, and that the revival of New France represented a "tradition" known to them all.

A Boston paper epitomized the chief features of this theme:

> Romanism is already a terrible power in our country....To this...must be added the French ultramontane power....The French Jesuits have conceived the project of forming a Catholic nation out of the province of Québec and New England, and this project of making New England French Catholic has already taken proportions capable of alarming the most optimistic. The French number more than a million in the United States....The number of their children is unimaginable for Americans.... They are kept a distinct alien race, subject to the Pope in matters of religion and of politics. Soon, with the Irish, they will govern you, Americans.[1]

The *New York Times* followed the story of the alleged Franco-American conspiracy closely, featuring it in both news stories and editorials. The May 1, 1881 edition of the *Times* cited Wright's "Chinese of the East" contentions, and adds a gloss to his accusations:

> [The French-Canadians] are, indeed, a peculiar class of people, bearing little resemblance to the intelligent and thrifty laboring population of France, and still less to that of any other nationality on this continent. They are the descendants of the early French settlers of Canada, and under a century and a quarter of British rule have preserved a distinctive character, which shows little sign of progress or improvement. They are, for the most part, ignorant and unenterprising, subservient to the most bigoted class of Catholic priests in the world, and constitute a peasantry belonging more to the eighteenth than the nineteenth century. In recent years they have been seeking employment...in the manufacturing towns of New-England....They care nothing for our free institutions, have no desire for civil or religious liberty or the benefits of education....[T]he feeling which they excite...is not fear or jealousy, but a sort of contempt.

Here the *Times* is not yet imagining Franco-Americans as sub-versives, but several of the conspiracy theory's features are present in embryo. The *Times* portrays Franco-Americans as "a peasantry," with "little sign of progress" and as "ignorant and unenterprising." This stereotype of the Franco-American as ossified and medieval was a chief feature of the conspiracy theory as it developed. As the *Canadien* emigration into New England reached a peak in the 1880s, the *Times*'s contempt mutated into fear.

The *Times*'s coverage of Franco-Americans on its news pages contradicts the allegations in its 1881 editorial. For example, in 1884, the *Times* covered the General Convention of Franco-Americans at Albany, New York:

> ALBANY, Aug. 5. — The third National Convention of French Canadians assembled this morning, about 200 delegates being present, principally from the Eastern States and Canada[2]....The object of the meeting...is to discuss subjects of universal importance and in which the French Canadians have a special interest. "Not the least among them [a delegate] said, "is the education of the growing generation. We also desire to impress upon our people the necessity of becoming citizens of this great Republic and to utilize the advantages and benefits to be derived from such citizenship; to remind the great family of French people of the United States not to forget their mother country by allowing the use of her beautiful language to be neglected; to inspire our people to have a sacred respect for our religion"....During its sessions the following topics will be discussed: "Establishment of French Catholic schools," "The French Canadian Press," "Naturalization," "Emigration"...The last discussion of the convention will be, "Would it be to our interest to take part in the political affairs of this country?"[3]

The editorialist of 1881 complains about the Franco-Americans' alleged lack of interest in education. But schools are at the top of the agenda in Albany in 1884. The reporter's quotation from a spokes-person for the convention cites "the education of the growing gen-eration" among the gathering's chief concerns. Franco-Americans failed to take any interest in the U.S.'s "free institutions" suggests the *Times*'s 1881 editorial. On the contrary, the 1884 convention cites "the necessity of becoming citizens of this great Republic." Its agenda also engages the question of "tak[ing] part in the political affairs" of the United States.

The *Times* reports on the convention with reasonable accuracy in 1884 but the facts do not impede its editorial agenda. In 1885, under the headline "Canadians in New England," the *Times* repeated its allegations against the Franco-Americans, with greater urgency than in its 1881 piece:

> In such towns as Fall River and Holyoke the French Canadians have nearly shouldered out the native American [sic] operatives, who a generation ago impressed foreign observers by their superiority to any persons engaged in similar occupations elsewhere. They have crowded the Irish very hard, and they form a much more intractable element in the social problem. Where they constitute an appreciable part they constitute much the most physically degraded part of the "tenement house population." Their dwellings are the despair of sanitarians and themselves the despair of social philosophers. Nor is there any prospect of an improvement. They are the Chinese of New-England inasmuch as they seem rarely to strike root in our soil. Whatever may be the fate of the Irish immigrant, there is always the hope that his children and his grandchildren may be assimilated with the native population. He himself has at least come with the intention of remaining. His interest in the land of his birth is chiefly sentimental....But even if the French Canadian leaves his bones here his thoughts all lie beyond the Canadian border, and he cannot be brought to take any interest in the life around him of a community in which he regards himself as merely a sojourner. He maintains his own churches and no schools. Add to this feeling of alienism that he is absolutely unenterprising, and it becomes evident that he must be a troublesome element in the population.[4]

This piece contrasts the Irish, the alleged *good immigrant* of the past, with the "intractable" newcomer. A few decades before this article's publication, Irish immigrants met anti-Catholic riots, and torches were put to their houses of worship.[5] But after the Nativists turned their attention to a new target, in this case the newcomers from Québec, they reevaluated the earlier wave of immigrants in a brighter light.

Within a generation, the Franco-Americans themselves were transmuted, by Nativism's sleight-of-hand, into the *good immigrant*, as newcomers from Southern and Eastern Europe were cast in the role of the "troublesome element." The DIC recorded the following comments on the Franco-Americans of Lowell circa 1908: "A prominent educator in the community has pronounced the French population thrifty, law-abiding, progressive, and inclined to acquire the English language."[6] Chinese of the Eastern States no longer.

Each wave of immigration became re-imagined as the *good immigrant*. The descendants of each wave tend to see their ancestors as this good immigrant who assimilated easily to U.S. culture, while they recast more recent comers as a "troublesome element." Over time, each immigrant group is grafted into the narrative of the "good immigrant" of the past in contrast to newcomers, who resist assimilation.

But the *New York Times* wasn't ready to christen the Franco-Americans as good immigrants in the 1880s. Two months after its September 1885 editorial appeared, the *Times* reprinted a piece it credits to a publication called *The Contemporary Review*. The alarm bells of conspiracy begin to sound:

> The French Canadian race now numbers perhaps 2,000,000, half of whom live in Quebec....They hold frequent continental race reunions.... By reason of its phenomenal fecundity, [it] is fast gaining ground, not only in [Québec], but in all the surrounding States and Provinces....This people, in its romantic hours at least, idolizes its language, and holds sacred every severing characteristic, and now distinctly aspires to form a new France occupying the whole northeast corner of the continent.[7]

By the decade's end, the *Times* began to perceive a conspiracy behind this influx:

> There is no evidence that the habitant or his [ecclesiastical] leader has thrown overboard a tradition that in the last few years has evoked something more serious than a smile from the average Anglo-Saxon. The tradition is that within a period not included within the present century there will be a country in North America called New France. It is to be constituted of Quebec, Ontario as far west as Hamilton, such portions of the maritime provinces as may be deemed worth taking, the New-England States, and a slice of New-York. No effort is to be made to realize this tradition until the French race in America reach a certain number.[8]

The *Times* returned to the story more than once in 1889. In its August 13 edition, the paper published a piece under the headline "A Franco-American State, The High Ambition of the French-Canadians," endorsing the view that the *Canadiens* were in New England for the purpose of founding a French-speaking, Catholic state. The editorial predicts that the Franco-Americans will become an element the U.S. "will one day have to wrestle with as with any other foreign conspiracy."

> The French Canadians are here [in Canada] as a foreign element and it is their aim and boast that they are to remain foreign. Even into the United States they are importing, besides their language and religion, their traditions and aggressive aims....Their ideal is the formation here, in this corner of the world...of a nation which shall perform on this continent the part France has played so long in Europe. They confess openly that their ideal is to found a nation which shall profess the Catholic faith and speak the French language....To insist upon British principles in the face of this race ambition is an impossible pretense. The problem that is before Americans as well as Canadians is to assimilate the foreign material that is cast among them....The French in the United States have no intention of becoming citizens themselves, and their priests are taking care that the children of the French shall not aspire after that right.... They point with secret pride to the New-England factory towns, really French villages transported from Québec.

This article regards *Canadiens in Canada*, as a "foreign element," as "foreign material cast among" the other "races" of Canada. The French founded Montréal and their descendants had been in that city for two and a half centuries by the 1880s. Yet this writer regards them as just one among other "foreign" elements. This is inconsistent with the theory that the *Canadiens* were among the "founding peoples" of the Canadian Confederation.

Where the article discusses the *Canadien* element in the "New-England factory towns," it errs in stating that the priests were discouraging naturalization. By this date, the Franco-American elites were begging the rank and file to become naturalized and boasting of the numbers who did so. Although the figures were feeble, Ferdinand Gagnon bragged about the numbers of naturalized Franco-Americans at the October 1881 hearing in Boston.[9] In 1884, the

Times reported that Naturalization was on the agenda at the Albany General Convention as it was a topic at almost every Franco-American convention between 1865 and 1901.

By 1892, the *Times* is ringing the alarm bells of conspiracy with gusto:

> It is said that there are more French-Canadians in New-England than there are in Canada. There are 400,000 in round numbers...and in five of its principal cities they hold the balance of power to-day....Quebec is transferred bodily to Manchester and Fall River and Lowell. Not only does the French curé follow the French peasantry...he also perpetuates the French ideas and aspirations...and places all the obstacles possible in the way of the assimilation of these people to our American life and thought....These people are in New-England as an organized body, whose motto is *Notre religion, notre langue, et nos moeurs*. This body is ruled by a principle directly opposite to that which has made New-England what it is. It depresses to the lowest point possible the idea of personal responsibility and limits the freedom which it permits. It is next to impossible to penetrate this mass of protected and secluded humanity with modern ideas or to induce them to interest themselves in democratic institutions and methods of government...[The] migration of these people is part of a priestly scheme now fervently fostered in Canada for the purpose of bringing New-England under the control of the Roman Catholic faith.... This is the avowed purpose of the secret society to which every adult French Canadian belongs, and....the earnest efforts of these people are to turn the tables in New-England by the aid of the silent forces which they control.[10]

This 1892 editorial contradicts itself. The *Times* accuses Franco-Americans of taking no interest in American civic institutions and yet they are said to hold a balance of political power in their communities. In 1881, Wright groused that Franco-Americans were a transient population who would take their savings and go home without contributing to the United States. A decade later, when the U.S. mainstream began to notice that Franco-Americans were settling permanently in New England, the newcomers were accused of participating in a demographic maneuver to conquer New England.

In this 1892 piece, the *Times* cites and paraphrases an October 1891 article called *The French-Canadians in New England* by Egbert C.

Smyth published in the journal of the American Antiquarian Society. Smyth's article does not sound the newspaper's note of paranoia. Smyth's piece is a summary of the history of Québec intended to help a U.S. audience understand the Franco-Americans better. Smyth is concerned about the rapid growth of the Franco-American population and about their intention to retain their transnational identity within the United States, but he concludes his piece on only a mildly cautionary note.[11]

The *Times* mentioned "the secret society to which every adult French Canadian belongs." There was a tradition of *Canadien* secret societies in Québec as well as in New England. The *Frères Chasseurs*, a secret paramilitary society appeared during the Rebellion of 1838. Later, in the 1920s a secret society called the *Croisés* took hold in Woonsocket.[12] In that same decade, *Canadiens* in Québec formed a secret society known as *l'Ordre de Jacques-Cartier* [the Order of Jacques Cartier] on the pattern of the Knights of Columbus.[13] There were many others. But subversion of the United States was not their aim and the *Times*'s charge that "every adult French Canadian" belonged to such a group was false.

Large numbers of Franco-American adults *did* belong to church-related societies, and these are the groups Smyth mentions. He cites the *Dames de la Bonne Sainte Anne* [Ladies of Good Saint Anne] for married women and the *Ligue du Coeur de Jesus* [Sacred Heart of Jesus League] for men.[14] These were not unlike the Holy Name or St. Vincent de Paul societies, which still exist today. Those familiar with them will attest that they tend to pursue such dangerously subversive pursuits as charity bake sales or whist drives. Smyth also mentions the Saint-Jean Baptiste Society, which he construes as primarily oriented around *la survivance*. In the U.S., this group was a mutual aid association providing insurance and other benefits, although its aims included the preservation of Franco-American language and culture.[15] Such groups were not unique to Franco-Americans. Ethnic mutual aid societies were ubiquitous at the time. These parish and mutual benefit societies are the groups that the *Times*, in citing Smyth, seems to have construed as nefarious "secret societies."

The Case for the Defense

Other voices counseled moderation and rejected the conspiracy theories. The Norwich (Connecticut) *Courier* ran a piece reprinted in the *New York Times* defending the Franco-Americans. Under the headline *French Canadians as Citizens*, the *Courier* states,

> There is a prejudice in the Northern part of New-England against the French-Canadians, who are regarded, from their love for their native land and their disinclination to become citizens, as inimical to the interests of this country — as residents who would unite the New-England States to Canada — who are without an impulse of love or of patriotism for the country in which they find employment and the comforts of home. This view is so far from the truth that in this part of the country, where the French-Canadians and their descendants are among our most intelligent and thrifty citizens, it seems like fiction....They can be counted as among the most active and most loyal of our adopted citizens.[16]

William MacDonald, a professor at Bowdoin College, also countered the conspiracy rhetoric. In a piece published in *The Nation*, under the dateline "Brunswick, Me., September 1896," MacDonald gives a frank assessment of the Franco-Americans of the state. He quotes the "Chinese of the Eastern States" language but rebuts Wright's assertions. He confirms, however, that Wright's adverse views of the Franco-Americans were prevalent in New England:[17]

> Useful and indispensable as they [Franco-Americans] have become, they are nowhere received with cordiality, or commonly referred to save as an inferior class; even their religion is denounced as un-American, and the influence of the Church little regarded or else misconstrued....As a class, they are treated considerately in public because of their votes, disparaged in private because of general dislike and sought by all for the work they do and the money they spend.[18]

Other voices confirm MacDonald's observation regarding the "general dislike" of Franco-Americans. In 1888, investigator Flora Haines visited working women in the Maine towns of Lewiston, Waterville, Biddeford, and Saco and reported her findings to the Maine State Bureau of Labor and Industrial Statistics. Writes Haines, "The strong race feeling, especially against the French girls, is much to be regretted."[19] She found that the Franco-American women were "often hated by their co-workers" although "their ancestors were on this continent before ours."[20] Was this last comment a tepid defense of the Franco-American women or a reason why they were despised?

To minimize their alleged demographic threat, in his piece in *The Nation* MacDonald downplays the numbers of Franco-Americans. He quotes impressive statistics regarding Franco-American real estate ownership in Maine and concludes that such numbers were not likely to be "found among an alien people who care nothing for American institutions and hold themselves obstinately aloof from American life." He regrets that the Franco-Americans remain isolated, living apart within their own neighborhoods and that they "seem content to be thought a distinct class in the community."[21] The college professor concludes that the Franco-Americans in Maine, despite these obstacles, "are a permanent element within the population," who "are making rapid progress in the direction of useful citizenship."

After publishing his article in *The Nation*, MacDonald produced a more lengthy, scholarly paper titled *The French Canadians in New England*. This April 1898 piece in the *Quarterly Journal of Economics* is data dense. MacDonald analyzes relevant portions of the 1890 U.S. census, and also relies upon the writings of Fr. Hamon and Ferdinand Gagnon.

MacDonald addresses the causes of the suspicion and conspiracy mongering around Franco-Americans: their desire to preserve their transnational identity, and their theory of U.S. citizenship as a contract between a loose aggregation of "races." MacDonald holds that the Franco-American elite's efforts to conserve the "distinctive characteristics and the language of their race in this country, justly exposes them...to criticism and suspicion." He also believes that Franco-American "protestations of loyalty and patriotism," while sincere, "ring hollow" and appear "un-American" to the U.S. mainstream. He states that neither the "spirit" nor the "conditions" of American life favor the "maintenance of distinct groups of population, bounded by lines of race," language, and religion. Even if Franco-Americans declare their loyalty to the U.S., hold property, and vote, the U.S. mainstream will still see them as aliens, as long as they continue to maintain a distinct identity within the United States. MacDonald believes that the policy of Franco-American cultural survival in the U.S. is doomed:

> That policy rests upon the theory that a distinct national type, formed in one country during generations of undisturbed growth, can be made to persist in another country where nearly every essential condition of life is wholly different, and where every economic and political consideration demands readjustment and change. For such a theory there is no sufficient justification in experience.[22]

As in his earlier piece in *The Nation*, MacDonald intends his sober, quantitative analysis of the Franco-Americans as a counterweight to the fear mongering of the *New York Times* and other outlets. More than once he eschews any suggestion of conspiracy and emphasizes that the Franco-Americans pose no danger. Quoting a phrase from the Wright report, MacDonald concludes, "The time for apprehension, if such there ever was, lest our institutions should be overborne by this 'horde of industrial invaders,' is past. The dangers of the future are for the French Canadians, not for us."[23]

The Protestant Crusade

The agitation around the alleged Franco-American menace was no mere creature of the Press. Despite MacDonald's assurances, clergymen from several Protestant denominations perceived a Franco-American Roman Catholic threat to New England. Hundreds of Protestant missionaries made it their vocation to convert the Franco-Americans. These clergymen believed that they had a mission, both religious and patriotic, to evangelize the Franco-Americans as well as their cousins North of the border. Protestant groups gathered funds and trained missionaries for the task. Fervent believers wrote books and periodicals; at least one seminary established a department dedicated to this work. And a contraption called a Gospel Wagon wheeled down the road to preach to the poor Franco-American masses the Protestant way to salvation.

Reverend Calvin Elijah Amaron was one of these dedicated missionaries who made the conversion of Franco-Americans his life's work.

Amaron was born in North America, but his roots were in European Calvinism. Missionaries recruiting in Geneva enlisted Amaron's father to cross the ocean to help convert the Roman Catholics of Québec.[24] Like his father, Calvin Amaron became a missionary. He was also an author, a journalist, and founder and president of a college dedicated to missionary work among Franco-Americans. Founded as the French Protestant College, today it is known as the American International College in Springfield, Massachusetts. Amaron promoted non-denominational efforts to convert the "Romish" Franco-Americans, but his support came from the Congregationalists of Massachusetts, successors to the Puritans of old.[25]

In 1885, Amaron published a pamphlet titled *The Evangelization of the French-Canadians of New England.* Its purpose was promotional, to help raise funds to establish the French Protestant College. In this publication, Amaron recounts the history of Protestant proselytism among the *Canadiens*, beginning with a mission at Grande-Ligne, near Montréal established in 1835. A half-century later, Amaron claims "100 French Protestant preaching stations with about 4000 members and 11,000 adherents; 65 Sabbath schools and 25 mission schools with an attendance of 3000 children; 110 missionaries, colporteurs and teachers diffusing Gospel light" among the *Canadiens* of Québec.[26] In the United States, Amaron claims between 50 and 70 preaching stations. Amaron boasts that the Protestant evangelization of the Franco-Americans "is gradually becoming one of the important missions of the churches of Massachusetts."[27]

Amaron claims that "some aggressive work has been done in that part of Lowell known as Little Canada" including meetings held in Roman Catholic homes.[28] In Lowell, Rev. T. G. A. Côté founded the French Protestant church in 1877, and Amaron became its pastor seven years later. Amaron cites similar, but less successful, missionary work among the Franco-Americans of Fall River, Springfield, Lawrence, and Holyoke.[29]

Reverend Amaron then makes his case for a French Protestant College that will provide education for Franco-Americans and train some of them as missionaries to their people. He calls for $50 donations to support scholarships for students.[30] Before his final pitch,

Rev. Amaron builds in his readers a sense of urgency around what he perceives as the Roman Catholic threat to the United States:

> Too long already has the mistake been made of regarding Romanism as simply one among the Christian denominations of this land. A Protestant Christian nation readily grants such a position, but Rome knows well that in this position she cannot hold her own. Therefore she must take measures to overthrow your free institutions because she cannot stand their influence....She is building herself up, she is taking successful means to withdraw the mass of her people from those influences which are inimical to the spirit that has always governed her.[31]

His appeal bore fruit since Amaron founded his French Protestant College at Lowell in 1885, moving it to Springfield three years later.[32]

Reverend Amaron's 1891 book, *Your Heritage; or New England Threatened* extends the themes in his earlier pamphlet. It is a long-form treatment of the theory of Franco-American conspiracy. The text speaks of the Franco-American workers as an "invading force" to be "conquered" and lays out "the engines of war" the contenders possessed.[33] It extends this martial metaphor throughout, while it fulminates against the evils of the "Romish" religion of the Franco-Americans. Amaron inveighs against ultramontanism as the ideology that is radicalizing the Roman Catholics.[34]

For Rev. Amaron, U.S. political institutions and Protestantism are inseparable. He holds that the "Romish Church" is both a religious and a political system in which the Catholic's first loyalty is to the Pope.[35] A "Romanist" cannot be *both* a devout Catholic *and* a loyal U.S. citizen he insists. Led by the radical ideology of ultramontanism, the "Romish clergy" imposes on its devotees a "moral and intellectual bondage" that is "worse than southern slavery," writes Amaron.[36] There can be no compromise with Catholicism since "there is a conflict between the Christian civilization of this country and Romanism."[37] Faced with this clash of civilizations there is only one choice: to convert the Roman Catholics. This work, he holds, is not only a God-given duty but also a patriotic one.[38]

Amaron repeats, in outline, the conspiracy theory as it appeared in the *New York Times*. He cites influential *Canadien* bishop Louis Laflèche of "Three Rivers" as his source for the alleged Franco-

American conspiracy to undermine New England.[39] *Canadien* clergy, Amaron alleges, have a long-standing tradition that one day they will establish an independent French-Catholic state, and they're conspiring to annex New England to it.[40] He portrays the Franco-American workers as a homogeneous mass carrying out an international conspiracy on behalf of the Church to which they offer undeviating obedience.[41] Marching together in conspiratorial unanimity, every Franco-American is complicit. Reverend Amaron states all of this as proven, long-settled fact.

Amaron views the Franco-American churches, schools, national societies, and press as so many agents of a foreign power bent on the subversion of the United States. The secular press, he holds, cannot be trusted to report the news accurately since it is owned by "Romanism."[42] He rejects out of hand the Franco-American notion of citizenship based on the duality of "origin" and "political condition." He abhors the Franco-American motto "our language, our religion, and our laws."[43] Immigrants must conform to the language and customs of their adoptive country.

In service of his evangelizing mission, Rev. Amaron cites the statistics on the numbers of churches founded and missionaries in the field under the aegis of Congregationalists, Methodists, Episcopalians, Baptists, and Presbyterians. Many of the pastors and missionaries he cites bear *Canadien* surnames. As of 1891, Rev. Amaron claims 10,000 Protestant converts in New England and 40,000 nationwide. That same year, the French Protestant College in Springfield had 72 students with four faculty members and four assistants.[44]

The Gospel Wagon Hits the Dusty Trail

In his book, Rev. Amaron acknowledges the Baptists' efforts to convert Franco-American Catholics. In 1893, the American Baptist Home Mission Society discussed this work in its monthly publication. This piece titled *The French Canadian in Québec and New England* by Henry Lyman Morehouse, begins by contrasting New England with Québec:

[New England is] a magnet attracting the world to itself...[Québec is] repellant and shunned by the world's best blood; the one a mighty current that has nourished the noblest characters, that has been as the water of life to the civilized world — the other, a sluggish, slimy stream, that has fructified nothing and given to mankind nothing noteworthy; the one a civilization where Protestant principles are regnant — the other, a civilization where mediaeval Romanism is rampant; the one helper — the other, a hindrance to Gospel truth....Against the abhorrent forces of this Romish civilization we are contending, especially in New England.[45]

Morehouse finds the people of Québec base, superstitious, disloyal to their sovereign, and plagued with political corruption and simony. Thus, an Anglo-Protestant stereotypes Québec and its inhabitants. Consider how the Catholic priest, Fr. Hamon, stereotyped Anglo-Protestants: "The French character is diametrically opposed to the Anglo-Saxon-American character. As one is cheerful, expansive, care-free, compassionate towards the miseries of others, ready for the most generous sacrifices, while the other is cold, concentrated, calculating and selfish."[46] At the threshold of the 20th century, New England and New France remained locked in spiritual combat, conjuring ghosts of 17th-century European religious wars.

Morehouse recounts the history of the relationship between the United States and Québec, and contrasts the two. He then delivers a not inaccurate report of the *Canadien* movement from Québec into New England. Morehouse also discusses the possibility of U.S. annexation of Canada. He claims that before the Civil War, the South had opposed annexation because it would have given the North a "preponderating influence in Congress for the destruction of slavery." "Slavery in the United States has gone," writes Morehouse. "The next great act of emancipation is that which shall free from mental and religious servitude the people of Quebec, and so open to them a new and nobler future. Then nobody will object to union."[47] For Morehouse, as for Amaron, the crusade to convert the *Canadiens* and Franco-Americans is parallel to the abolitionist movement.

Morehouse furthers the conspiracy theory in the press, citing Fr. Hamon's book. He portrays Hamon as having "the vision of independent Quebec or 'New France' still floating before his mind." Hamon cherishes the hope, believes Morehouse, that one day "these unassimilated French-Canadians in New England may become allies in the furtherance of a great Church-and-State scheme on the continent of North America."[48]

In response, Morehouse, like Amaron, calls for nothing less than a missionary crusade. He holds that "for a generation at least" the mission to convert the Franco-Americans "will continue to be a great and needy field for Christian effort." And like Amaron, for Morehouse, the assimilation of New England's Franco-Americans assumed the character of a duty both pious and patriotic.

Morehouse claims that the Baptists were the first to field an effort to evangelize the Franco-Americans. As early as 1853, the American Baptist Home Mission Society appointed a missionary to the Franco-Americans in Clinton County, New York. Baptists then dispatched apostles to the Franco-Americans of Illinois in 1859 and 1860, and of Detroit in 1863. The Congregationalists and Methodists then joined their efforts. But "the principal work" among the Franco-Americans, writes Morehouse, has been in New England, beginning in 1870.[49]

Morehouse claims that, as of his writing, 14 Baptist missionaries operated in five of the six New England states "with gratifying results." Some of these missionaries had several preaching stations. Morehouse states that the Home Mission Society had received 769 Franco-American converts to the Baptists. Converts made among the Baptist churches brought the total to about one thousand. By 1893, small congregations of Franco-American Baptists had taken hold especially in Worcester, Massachusetts and Waterville, Maine.[50]

He also reports that Newton Theological Institution of Massachusetts opened a "French department" to train missionaries to work among the *Canadiens* and Franco-Americans. The first year saw six students in this course. A missionary dedicated three days each week to teaching homiletics and missionary tactics. As of Morehouse's writing, 14 students had taken the course since 1889, and two returned to Canada to evangelize Sorel and Maskinongé, Québec. Morehouse calls for "some benevolent Baptist" to donate $30,000 to create an endowed professorship in the French department at Newton.[51]

To bring the Protestant religion out of the seminaries and into the streets of the Little Canadas, Morehouse describes an elaborate contrivance called a "Gospel wagon," a mobile preaching station:

> To reach the multitude who will not come to a Protestant meeting, the 'Gospel wagon' or 'Bonne Nouvelle' has been devised and adopted with success. Bro. LeClaire, of Lowell, procured about five hundred dollars for the outfit, consisting of a good, strong horse and the wagon...with seats along both sides for about twelve persons, and entered from the rear by two or three iron steps, on which the preacher stands as he addresses the people. There is also an adjustable stand for the Bible. A small cabinet organ occupies the front end of the aisle. The wagon is covered at the top and open on the sides, and for use at night a lantern is attached to each of the four standards at the corners. When he began preaching from the wagon, in the midst of a dense French population in Lowell, there were many ugly demonstrations against him. But he got the ear of thousands who never would have heard him otherwise.[52]

Morehouse recounts a nighttime meeting conducted from the Gospel wagon, attracting a crowd of over one thousand Franco-American mill workers of Lowell. Missionaries deployed the wagon at Lynn, Massachusetts and Great Falls, New Hampshire. It "has proved very effective," judges Morehouse.[53]

In a call to action at the end of his piece, Morehouse demands more missionaries, more copies of the Bible in French, and more and better tracts in that language. He would also have a French-language Protestant "religious periodical." He notes that the Congregationalists had such a publication supported by the Massachusetts Board by an annual appropriation.[54]

Morehouse concludes his review of these Baptist missionary activities with this peroration:

> The greatest need is a deeper conviction of our duty at this hour to this peculiar people, who have been sent among us....Unless New England arouses itself to the gravity of the situation it will incur the penalties of neglect, as the deepening shadows of error that in Quebec have eclipsed Gospel truth, shall envelop the land of the Pilgrim and the Puritan, and its lustre shall become only a memory. We owe it to God, to our land, and especially to the people themselves to give them the truth that shall make them free indeed.[55]

Like Amaron, Morehouse identifies Protestantism with Americanism. The Catholics cannot remain as they are. Missionaries must alter them so that, from Protestantism, they will absorb the American spirit.

Howard Grose's 1906 book *Aliens or Americans?* confirms the scale of the Baptists' missionary efforts among the Franco-Americans that continued into the 20th century. Grose records the number of "mission fields" and missionaries working among 19 different nationalities in the U.S. in 1906. The numbers of mission fields (29) and missionaries (650) among the Franco-Americans are larger than those for any other nationality except Germans, Norwegians, and Swedes, three groups with large numbers of Protestants. The Baptists invested more resources in converting the Franco-Americans than in any other predominantly Catholic groups listed, including Italians, Poles, and "Mexicans in U.S."[56]

Grose was a Baptist minister, a former lecturer in history and former President of the University of South Dakota. He also served as editor of the *Home Mission Monthly*, the periodical that had published Morehouse's lengthy article.[57] Grose, writing in the first years of the 20th century, is more anxious about Asian and Eastern European immigrants than Franco-American ones. But he is not unaware of emigration from North of the border and several passages in his book continue to weigh the alleged Franco-American threat.

Grose's work has humanitarian concerns absent from Amaron and Morehouse. Grose holds the bosses and slumlords responsible for what he regarded as the degraded conditions of the immigrants in the tenements.[58] The author suggested that the immigrant, living in tenements and slums, had little cause to admire U.S. Protestantism.[59] He also alleged that the "exclusiveness" of Anglo-Protestant Christianity was a barrier to assimilation.[60]

New England had symbolic significance for Grose. It was the quintessence of the alleged Anglo-Protestant spirit of the United States. For Grose, the "social morality of the Puritan settlers of New England" was among the chief characteristics of "American state and social life."[61] But this prototypical Anglo-Protestant region was in danger of falling into enemy, "Romish" hands. "New England is no longer Puritan but foreign," writes Grose. "The farms sanctified by many a Puritan prayer are occupied to-day by French-Canadian and Italian aliens."[62] Grose cites as a bad omen that "in New England conventions are held to which only French-Canadian Roman Catholics are admitted. At such a convention in Nashua, New Hampshire, attended by eighty priests, the following mottoes were displayed: 'Our tongue, our nationality, our religion.' 'Before everything else, let us remain French!'."[63]

For Grose, the Protestant faith "formed the basis of our colonial and national life." "Whatever would make this country less distinctively Protestant in religion tends to destroy all the other social and civil characteristics."[64] Grose, Morehouse, and Amaron held in common the belief that Protestant Christianity and U.S. political institutions were indivisible. None of these men could foresee that a religiously pluralistic U.S. could retain its political culture.

Less Than Obedient Servants of the Hierarchy

The conspiracy theories in the pulpit and the press depended upon the notion that the Franco-American Catholics marched in lockstep with their clergy. To their chagrin, the Roman Catholic hierarchy of New England could only wish that its flock were as obedient as Rev. Amaron thought it was. If the Protestant pastors had been aware of events in the Little Canadas, they would have known that Franco-Americans clashed with the Irish-American hierarchy throughout the region. In the eyes of New England's Catholic bishops, Franco-Americans were anything but uncritical, obedient servants. They were often fractious, bitterly divided among themselves, and jealous to protect their perceived rights within the Church.

From the 1880s through the 1920s, Franco-Americans in such towns as Fall River, Ware, and North Brookfield, Massachusetts; Danielson, Connecticut; and Woonsocket, Rhode Island battled the Irish-American hierarchy.[65] These conflicts erupted over Franco-American assertions of a right to have pastors of their own "race" as well as over local control of parish property and finances. Parishes in Québec had an elected, lay council known as the *fabrique*, which managed church property and other temporal affairs.[66] The Irish-Catholic church in New England did not share this practice, and this difference in parish management was at the root of many of the conflicts.

In our period, Franco-American parishioners peppered Rome with petitions, complaining of ill-treatment at the hands of "Irish" clergy. During these intra-Catholic skirmishes, parishioners became divided into factions, and sometimes churches were shuttered. Pastors resigned from their positions unable to control their flocks. Lay parish leaders filed lawsuits. Leaders of groups regarded as "schismatics" by the Church fomented division among disgruntled parishioners and attempted to lure Franco-Americans away from the Catholic faith.[67]

The most well-documented of these donnybrooks was known as the Sentinelle Crisis, named for a newspaper called *La Sentinelle* [*The Sentinel*]. This lengthy conflict between Franco-American parishioners and the Irish-Catholic hierarchy over diocesan control of parish funds broke out in Woonsocket in the 1920s. During this battle, Rome even resorted to excommunicating leaders of the Franco-American resistance. The Sentinelle Crisis had repercussions throughout the region. It reached across the border and invited comment in Québec. This case of lay disobedience and conflict with the church hierarchy occupies more pages in the general histories of Franco-Americans than any other event.[68]

Brunswick also had its conflict between Franco-American parishioners and the Catholic hierarchy. The first pastor at Brunswick's St. John's church was Fr. Joseph Noiseux, a Franco-American priest who resigned due to harassment from some of his parishioners.[69] In 1881, Fr. James Gorman, a fluently bilingual Irish-American priest, replaced Fr. Noiseux. Eight years later, St. John's parishioners filed a complaint with the ranking Bishop, James Augustine Healy of Portland. They accused Fr. Gorman of drunkenness as well as financial and sexual impropriety. According to the 1891 deposition of Alexis Sainte-Marie, whose family had lost two children in the 1886 diphtheria outbreak, locals referred to Fr. Gorman as "old man Trudeau's son-in-law." Brunswick's Franco-Americans eventually appealed their case all the way to Rome.[70]

Bishop Healy denied the allegations against Fr. Gorman and claimed that the parishioners were aggrieved because the pastor had

had three Franco-Americans discharged from the choir. "Old man" Trudeau's adult daughter, Olivine Trudeau, was a music director at the church, adding weight to the theory that a shake-up in the choir triggered the allegations against the priest.[71] In 1890, one of Fr. Gorman's accusers recanted and retracted his statement. This reversal vindicated the priest in the eyes of the hierarchy and Fr. Gorman remained Pastor of St. John's.[72]

A Monseigneur Williams, writing to Rome about these events in Brunswick, suggested that ethnic conflict was the cause of the discontent at St. John's: "The Canadians wanted a Canadian priest and, as they are wont to do, tried to force the hand of the church."[73] This statement suggests that Franco-Americans in Brunswick as elsewhere were anything but mindlessly subservient to church authority.

Brunswick was also a center of the fight against a Maine law known as the *Corporation Sole*. This 1887 legislation made the Bishop of Portland sole owner of all church property in the state. The stated purpose of the law was to clarify relationships between the Church and lending institutions. It also provided a single, identifiable plaintiff in any lawsuits over Church property. Franco-Americans, with their custom of lay administration of parish finances, opposed the law, while the Bishops supported it. On October 4 and 5, 1909, Franco-Americans from across the state met in Brunswick and appointed a Standing Committee to oppose the Corporation Sole legislation. To force the Bishop's hand, Franco-American leadership in the state called for a boycott of the collection plate under the slogan "close your wallet." When Bishop Louis Walsh of Portland came to Brunswick, not long after the October Convention, an angry Franco-American mob greeted him. The bishop had to have the doors of the rectory barred against the crowd attempting to press its way in.[74]

In 1913, after having failed two years earlier, Franco-Americans achieved a compromise, and the legislature amended the Corporation Sole law. But not before Bishop Walsh placed under interdict a half-dozen members of the Standing Committee, as well as the editors of two prominent French-language newspapers, *Le Messager* of Lewiston and *La Justice* of Biddeford. Editorializing against the Corporation Sole law, Alfred Bonneau, editor of the latter newspaper, and his colleague of Lewiston Jean-Baptiste Couture called Bishop Walsh a "Francophobe," and a "barbarous assimilator" who was intending to "saxonize" Franco-American children.[75] These are hardly the words of spokesmen for compliant Catholics offering unquestioned obedience to the commands of their hierarchy.

Although they sometimes reacted explosively, Franco-Americans were rarely the aggressors in these conflicts. The Irish-American clergy often took a supercilious attitude toward them. For example, one "Irish" priest drew the ire of Franco-Americans when he said they were "good for nothing more than making babies."[76] Another asked his parishioners why they wished to have French-speaking priests since they'd all be speaking English in ten years anyway.[77] More autocratic than diplomatic, clerics were frequently oblivious to Franco-American sensibilities.

Although the hierarchy had granted Franco-Americans their national parishes, an act of apparent magnanimity, the Church tended to view these grants as a stopgap, a concession to an immigrant community. Throughout our period, the Church in New England exerted a slow and steady pressure on Franco-Americans to anglicize and to assimilate to American Catholic — i.e., Irish Catholic — ways.[78] With their North American, continental perspective, the Franco-Americans viewed the Irish Catholics as late-comers to the U.S., with no right to dictate terms to them. Their *Canadien* ancestors had been Catholic pioneers on the continent and their priests were among the North American martyrs.

The Sentinelle Crisis and the Corporation Sole controversy occurred in the early 20th century after the *New York Times*'s editorializing and after the publication of Amaron's book. However, intra-Catholic conflicts involving Franco-Americans in Fall River and Ware pre-dated both. There was ample evidence in the 1880s and 1890s that New England's Franco-Americans were not so many worker bees in a vast Roman Catholic hive. Catholic unanimity was a Protestant misconception.

The Providential Mission: A Conspiracy Theory Refuted

The conspiracy theories around the Franco-Americans in the 1880s and 1890s were elaborate growths germinating from a withered seed of truth. An element among the Québec elite and its extensions across the border promoted a messianic vision, a "Providential mission" for the *Canadien* people in North America. This messianic strain in Québec religious ideology posited that the "French race" in North America had a duty ordained by divine Providence to serve as a civilizing, Catholic bulwark on the continent. The *Canadiens*, it was imagined, would continue the missionary work undertaken by France prior to the Revolution of 1789.[79] A small number of extremists who held such views *did* imagine a future that included a French-speaking Catholic state in the Northeastern portion of the continent.

The Providential mission was a tenet of the ultramontane faction among the Québec elite. With the blessings of the British authorities, the ultramontanes' influence in Québec grew after the failure of the Rebellions of 1837-38.[80] Ultramontanes did not have a monopoly on the minds of Québec, but they represented an influential coterie. The remnants of the liberal, moderately anti-clerical viewpoint represented by the *Patriotes* of 1837-38 continued to stir beneath the surface, especially in Montréal among members of a literary society known as the *Institut Canadien*.[81] Influenced by the Enlightenment *Philosophes*, and the French and American revolutions, the descendants of this faction would not triumph politically in Québec until 1960. Meanwhile, the ultramontanes controlled many of the pulpits and printing presses of the Province. The utterances of this staunchly conservative faction of the elite provided ample fodder for fantasists south of the border.

One of the most notorious ultramontane firebrands, journalist Jules-Paul Tardivel, expressed the messianic message: "God planted in the heart of all French-Canadian patriots to continue in the soil of America the work of Christian civilization that old France pursued with such glory for so many centuries."[82] The *Canadien* priest and historian Henri-Raymond Casgrain defined the aims of the Providential mission. He believed that the Catholics would execute a pincer move, bearing down on the U.S. "empire of Protestantism" from both the

Gulf of Mexico and the St. Lawrence. "The children of the truth hastening from the North and the Middle," the priest believed, would "embrace on the banks of the Mississippi" and "establish the reign of Catholicism."[83]

As early as 1869, Fr. Louis Joseph de Goësbriand, who labored among the Franco-Americans of Vermont, saw the finger of the Almighty in the *Canadien* diaspora. In an influential article, the priest wrote, "In this astonishing immigration, Divine Providence, which rules the world, has designs which are hidden from us. Let it do its work....We believe that these immigrants are called by God to cooperate in the conversion of America, just as their ancestors were called to implant the faith on the banks of the St. Lawrence."

Historian Yves Roby found that the "vocabulary employed" by the messianic ideologues conveyed "the concepts of conquest and reconquest" of New England.[84] For example, a Franco-American priest intoned, "We are in the process of *restoring* to the former New France the immense domain seized by our forefathers, then dedicated by them to the church."[85] Invoking Napoleonic images, even an opponent of the ultramontane faction asserted that, "The French-Canadian immigrant in the United States...is the advance-guard, a scout of the grand army of invasion."[86] However, the majority of the Franco-American elite did not share these ambitions. They advocated the more modest goal of cultural survival in their new milieu across the border.[87]

The talk of reconquest gave rise to understandable concerns in Yankeedom. These expansionist pronouncements were among the "imprudent" statements Fr. Hamon censured as provoking the Anglosphere unnecessarily. The U.S. press was within its rights to take a closer look at such ambitions. A cursory investigation, however, would have discovered the flaws in the conspiracy narrative.

First, the conspiracy theory misunderstood the Franco-American notion of transnational identity. Hogue's speech at the 1901 General Convention of Franco-Americans in Springfield showed that a transnational identity may embrace *both* the Providential mission *and* loyalty to the United States. Hogue observes that nothing could stop the emigration movement from Québec, neither family ties, nor attachment to the home parish, nor apprehensions and fears on the part of the emigrant. Hogue sees in this unstoppable force the evidence of "the action of God," a fact "of a providential order."[88] For Hogue, the *Canadien* movement into New England is "a slow and measured invasion."[89]

Hogue's talk of "invasion" would tend to confirm the concerns of U.S. alarmists. But the remainder of his speech might have allayed their fears:

> There is nothing less anti-patriotic than the position that we wish to take! In vain would one look to find that which is detrimental to American institutions in this refusal to merge ourselves in any fashion. In wishing to remain who we are, we do not expect to forfeit our traditions. Our duties toward our adopted country we will fulfill wholeheartedly and generously.
>
> For ultimately not one of us, gentlemen, will refute my assertions; we love our new country. We admire its powerful democratic institutions, and if need be we know how to offer the tribute of blood and tears; Cuba and the Philippines prove it, the country can count on the valor and the fidelity of our arms.
>
> But the American has a heart and a head expansive enough to understand that we do not give up the respect and sacred love of our old mother country in accepting the constitution of [this] country with all its duties.
>
> The two loves can only help one another.[90]

Despite Hogue's generous assertion, Anglo-Americans had a great deal of difficulty appreciating the notion of dual loyalties. Dual identity was an outgrowth of the *Canadien* context for Hogue, but it threatened elements in the U.S. which attributed nefarious motives even to people who persisted in asserting their loyalty.

The conspiracy theory also assumes that the Québec and Franco-American elites had one — and only one — political future in mind for their homeland: an independent state of New France. In fact, the period's *Canadiens* and Franco-Americans entertained different scenarios for Québec's political future.

For example, at the General Convention of *Canadiens* of the United States held in Worcester in September of 1870, three eminent Franco-American leaders engaged in a debate about the political future of their homeland. Ferdinand Gagnon, his fellow journalist and sometime partner Fréderic Houde, and the professor George Batchelor envisaged three different scenarios for Québec's future. Batchelor favored U.S. annexation of Canada, while Gagnon supported Canadian independence vis-à-vis Great Britain. Houde preferred that Québec remain a part of the Canadian Confederation, but if a change came, he preferred annexation to the U.S. to Canadian independence.[91] Had there been a long-established tradition regarding an independent New France cobbled out of bits of Canada and the U.S., these three didn't seem to know about it. And if anyone knew about some such tradition, it would be these men, especially Gagnon who studied at the Seminary of Saint-Hyacinthe, an ultramontane bastion.

In 1870, George Batchelor was the Secretary of a New York-based group called the *Club Unioniste Canadien* [Canadian Unionist Club] advocating the annexation of Canada to the United States. At a meeting that year, this club received a communication from none other than Louis-Joseph Papineau, leader of the Rebellions of 1837 and 19th century *Canadien* national hero. Papineau, then at the very end of his days, expressed his support for U.S. annexation of Canada. Dissatisfied with the post-Confederation government, in a communiqué to the Club in New York, Papineau "drew a forcible picture of the haughtiness, pride, and impotence of the 'valets of Downing-street['] in their misgovernment of Canada."[92] Rather than plotting to annex bits of the U.S. to Canada, these New York Franco-Americans were agitating for Canada's annexation to the United States.

Batchelor was a key figure in the General Conventions and one of the chief Franco-American activists of his generation. He was a representative of the liberal, *Patriote* strain among *Canadiens*, evincing ideological diversity among Franco-American leaders. Before he left Canada in 1847, Batchelor co-founded a newspaper called *L'Avenir* [*The Future*]. Originating with a small group of young radicals, associated with Montréal's *Institut Canadien*, this paper continued to promote the legacy of the *Patriotes* of 1837 and their leader, the aging Papineau. *L'Avenir*'s supporters were among a small faction of *Canadiens* who, making strange bedfellows, joined a number of English-Canadian Tories in support of U.S. annexation of Canada in the mid-19th century.

Although his influence had waned in Québec long before his demise, *annexation* was Papineau's final political destination.[93]

Papineau and Batchelor were not alone in advocating annexation. One of the first General Conventions of *Canadiens* of the United States in October 1868 condemned the then-recently created Dominion of Canada. It censured what the convention saw as undue pressure on Nova Scotia to enter the Confederation. The Convention called for U.S. annexation of Canada or a republican form of government for the latter.[94] Some Franco-Americans resisted assimilation to Yankee ways because many of them expected the imminent union of Canada and the U.S. under the Stars and Stripes. When annexation came, Franco-Americans would reunite politically with a million *Canadiens* across the border. Then they would have the numbers to maintain their distinctiveness within this vastly expanded American Republic.[95]

For U.S. advocates of the conspiracy theory, Father Hamon's 1891 book on Franco-Americans was the instruction manual for the alleged "Romish" conspiracy to subvert New England. But Fr. Hamon's book also proposes not one but two possible futures for Québec: "Either the province of Québec will one day have its autonomy, and will become an independent people; Or it will be annexed to the United States. Independence or annexation: here are the two possible hypotheses."[96]

What Fr. Hamon does *not* imagine is that Québec will remain a part of the Canadian Confederation; nor does he picture that Québec will maintain a connection with Great Britain. The Jesuit speculates that in a century after his time the U.S. will have a population of "over 100 million" people. This huge country, Fr. Hamon ventures, might split into several republics. He posits that one of these fragments might become incorporated with Québec into an independent French-speaking, Catholic state. Hamon recognizes, however, that all such scenarios are notional.[97]

Father Hamon also imagines a day when Franco-Americans will populate the land between the mill towns of New England and the Québec border. At that moment, Hamon dreams, the *Canadiens* of Québec and New England will join hands with one another and become one people.[98] He does not say under which government this people will live. He implies that it might be under the Stars and

Stripes or within an independent Québec. Nowhere in his book is there any indication that there is a universally-known tradition among the *Canadien* people that an independent, French-speaking state is inevitable. On the contrary, Fr. Hamon expects his prediction of an eventual cross-border reunion to surprise his readers.[99] Nor does the author define the borders of this putative state. On the topic of the long-term future of Québec, Hamon presents no blueprint, only dreams and airy conjectures.

Hamon is clear that all such matters fall under the watchful eye of divine Providence. The Faithful must leave them to the Deity's timeline.[100] The Yankee alarmists didn't comprehend this fatalistic streak in Québec Catholic spirituality. In this spiritual world, the ideal was submission to God's will — if not always to an Irish hierarchy. One did not impose one's will on the world.[101] One waited for divine Providence to work. The hoped for Catholicizing of the U.S. was God's work. It only required that the *Canadiens* in New England remain faithful to what they were. In the minds of the *Canadien* Catholics, the Providential mission did not require plots hatched in darkened, smoke-filled rooms. Its workings were more celestial than mundane.

This quietist, fatalist aspect of the *Canadien* Catholic faith mitigates the apparently aggressive talk about a "slow invasion" and "reconquest." This subtlety in cross-cultural understanding was easy to miss. However, U.S. alarmists might have caught a clue from the contradiction in their portrayals of the *Canadiens* as inert and unadventurous, but at the same time involved in bold, elaborate, international subterfuge.

I have come across no evidence of organized attempts by Franco-Americans to convert U.S. Protestants to Catholicism through missionary activities parallel to those of Amaron and Morehouse. The Protestants of the Eastern U.S., believed Fr. Hamon, were "dechristianizing" themselves. "Entrenched in his pride, disdain, and skepticism, the American, as a rule, is not converted" by the example of Franco-American Catholics, wrote Fr. Hamon.[102] Casgrain held similar views. He believed that in the U.S. "as in Europe, and even more quickly than in Europe, Protestantism is dying. Divided into a thousand sects, it falls into the dust and it is going to lose itself in rationalism."[103] Protestantism would dissolve, these men believed, without any aggressive moves on the part of the Catholics.

Rather than converting the Protestants, Father Hamon thought that the Catholics would out-reproduce them.[104] The job of the Catholic rank and file was to keep the faith and to continue propagating while Providence worked out the rest. Implicitly, Hamon extends to U.S. soil the traditional strategy of the "revenge of the cradles" as executed in Québec. This demographic maneuver against the English conquerors imagined that the *Canadiens* would eventually regain the country by out-numbering them.

The revenge of the cradles, on both sides of the border, put the onus on women. There are many instances where *Canadien* and Franco-American women were pregnant for most of their lives between ages 20 and 40. Many died in childbirth, which appears to be the case with my great-great-grandmother Marie-Louise Pouliot who died in her 30s after bearing ten children. Her husband, Joseph Vermette, then 38 years old, married his next-door neighbor's 17-year-old daughter, Rebecca Turgeon, who bore 13 children, bringing the total of Joseph's offspring to 23. The custom of maximizing reproduction put different pressures on the patriarch of the family whose role it was to find some way to feed this crowd of hungry mouths and to establish his children in some occupation.[105] Providential missions were easier for celibate clergy to formulate than for their parishioners to execute.

Further, the Québec and Franco-American elites had multiple, contradictory responses to the emigration movement. A single-minded conspiracy requires a measure of discipline around the core messages. Elites, lay and clerical, had no such coherence. For example, Tardivel spoke more clearly than anyone in his day about his dreams of an independent French-Catholic state in North America. Yet he was a life-long opponent of emigration to New England. Had he been single-minded about expansionist plans, would he not have encouraged emigration? The most articulate account of Tardivel's vision of a revived New France appeared in his *Pour la Patrie* — a science-fiction novel set in the distant mid-20th century. He also believed that the French-Catholic state he envisaged would be impossible absent divine intervention. None of this resembles a practical political platform.[106]

Besides, Tardivel was all alone, inhabiting an ideological desert island. His views did not reflect those of much of the elite, let alone the working class of Québec.[107]

Like Tardivel, Bishop Louis Laflèche, a prominent member of the ultramontane faction, also spoke in seemingly contradictory ways about the allegedly Providential nature of the *Canadien* emigration to New England. While he appeared to support the messianic interpretation of the Franco-American movement, elsewhere the Bishop condemned the emigrants and excoriated the *Canadiens* who recruited their compatriots for the New England mills.[108] His message for the rural poor of Québec was not to sally forth as missionaries into New England. It was to stay put and garner spiritual benefits from the salutary sufferings of poverty.[109] In a conversation with a priest in Springfield, Bishop Laflèche had supposedly spoken of Québec annexing parts of New England, but it was unclear to his interlocutor whether he meant that Québec would annex or be annexed.[110]

The equivocation of Tardivel and Laflèche bedeviled Québec messianism at large. While some voices spoke of Providential missions, others among the elite were involved in the efforts to repatriate Franco-Americans in the Québec hinterlands. If conspirators were planting *Canadiens* in New England as part of a plot to seize political power, why spend a cent to bring them back across the border? If the Québec and Franco-American elite, with a phalanx of "secret societies," had been co-conspirators in a plot to take over New England, wouldn't they have been unequivocal and united in encouraging emigration while discouraging repatriation?

It is tempting to frame events sequentially, as if the clerical elites condemned the *Canadien* emigration movement at first, later lauding it for contributing to the Providential mission. Although it is true that the invective toward the emigrants softened over time, responses to the emigration movement were fluid. The opinions of members of the clerical elite varied depending on when and to whom they were speaking. The one certainty that emerges from their utterances is that the clerical elite and its lay supporters did not have a stable platform on which to foment international subterfuge.

While the ultramontanes were casting about, proposing various responses to the emigration movement, U.S. alarmists imagined a consensus among them. They did not understand that the Québec clerical elite was not driving events. They were reacting to them. The talk of a Providential mission was the elite's attempt to make sense of what they could not control — that their efforts to discourage the rural poor from pursuing a living wage south of the border had failed.

The economic realities of eastern North America, as well as the policies of the British Empire and its colonial government in Canada, were in the cockpit. This combination of markets and policies created conditions that drove a substantial portion of Québec and the former Acadia out of the country. Since elites saw poverty as a personal failing, rather than a consequence of systemic economic conditions, they could not offer solutions that addressed the causes of the poor families' flight. Without a framework to take corrective action, the ultramontanes annexed the emigrants ideologically to their messianic illusions. They dabbed ideological perfume upon malodorous facts.

Those of us who knew Franco-American working people born in the 1880-1900 period might be amused at the alternately exalted or sinister interpretation given to their mill town existence. Although loud discussion of political events was on the agenda of amusements, in their spare time they enjoyed their music, sports, card games, storytelling, or family gatherings. They were hardly the stuff of international conspiracies. The hyperbolic ideological quantum ascribed to these poor laborers in small industrial cities is incongruent with the atmosphere in the mill town blocks. The ideological interpretations surrounding the Franco-Americans reveal more about the interpreters than they do about the workers.

The revealing fallacy of the *New York Times* and other conspiracy theorists was to assume that the most strident utterances of a portion of a remote elite were the uncontested views of the population at large. They then construed the rationalizations of pipe-dreamers as a coherent religio-political agenda. The Yankee press also failed to comprehend the difference between the concerns of the working-class Franco-Americans and the tiny elite.

The conspiracy theorists erred not only because they did not understand the political and religious discourse among *Canadiens* and Franco-Americans, but they did not think there was anything to be understood. *In fine*, there was no plot to annex New England. No secret societies were meeting on alternate Tuesdays to plan their next anti-American gambit. There were merely the fever dreams of a faction of extremists who couldn't agree even amongst one another.

CHAPTER THIRTEEN

Eugenics and the Alien in Our Midst

Emigration from Québec to New England slowed to a trickle after 1900. Some observers declared the movement finished. Mentions of the alleged Franco-American plot to subvert New England dwindled in the first years of the 20th century as New Englanders, with the rest of the U.S., became distracted by more urgent concerns. There was the war with Spain and its long and bloody aftermath in the Philippines; the assassination of President McKinley; and waves of emigration from southern and eastern Europe. There was the movement for reform known as the Progressive Era, followed by a World War.

In the 1920s, the current of emigration from Québec to New England surged again as a post-war recession struck the *Canadien* homeland.[1] Poorer Québec workers began once more to arrive in the Little Canadas of New England, energizing efforts to conserve the traditional *Canadien* culture. In response, defenders of the alleged Anglo-Protestant character of the U.S. inaugurated a new phase of activities to either Americanize or suppress what they regarded as potentially dangerous aliens in their midst.

The renewed backlash against Franco-Americans in the era following the First World War was part of a nationwide trend targeting "hyphenated Americans," U.S. residents who spoke a language other than English. Several streams converged to enflame pre-existing racial and ethnic tensions. The fear of German-American sympathizers and fifth-columnists during the First World War spread like a contagion to other "foreigners" deemed potentially disloyal.[2] The Russian Revolution of 1917 led to concerns about Bolshevik infiltration of the United States. Foreign-born Americans became suspected of political radicalism.[3] The war also spurred a *Great Migration* of African-Americans from the South in search of industrial jobs in the urban North. The decline in European emigration to the U.S., following restrictions on immigration enacted by the Federal government in the first half of the 1920s, encouraged the African-American migration northward.

The resurgence of Nativism fueled two early-20th century currents: the eugenics movement and the revived, new-look Ku Klux Klan. These movements had earlier antecedents, but each flexed its muscles in the 1920s and influenced legislation locally and nationally. Both movements threatened New England Franco-American *survivance*. If nothing else, the published statements of both eugenics and Klan supporters reveal much about Yankee perceptions of Franco-Americans in the early 20th century.

Patricians and academics were at the center of the eugenics movement. Franco-American mill workers, well beneath their rarified social *stratum*, were little aware that an influential coterie of intellectuals was engaged in conversation about them. By contrast, the resurgent KKK was a popular movement in the 1920s that Franco-Americans opposed in their French language press and in the streets.

The British scientist Sir Francis Galton coined the term *eugenics* in 1883.[4] Galton was a cousin of Charles Darwin and eugenics was a disfigured outgrowth of the increasing acceptance of Darwin's theory of natural selection.[5] In the perennial undergraduate philosophical debate over whether nature or nurture plays the dominant role in forming our character, the eugenicist comes down squarely on the side of nature. Eugenics theory posited that mental capacity and character traits, as well as physical ones, are transmitted from parent to offspring through a biological system they called "germ plasm."[6] Not all eugenicists were diehards. Some admitted the role of social forces in the development of psychological traits and cognitive abilities. But the true believers, who held that our biology is our destiny, tended to define the movement.

Since genes were all-important, eugenicists reasoned, one could breed physically and intellectually superior human beings like so many racehorses, show dogs, or prize pumpkins. *Positive eugenics* is the term used for this strategy of selective breeding. In the early 20th century, as eugenics took hold in several countries, advocates turned to the question of *negative eugenics*, that is preventing so-called inferior human specimens from breeding and thus perpetuating their alleged defects.[7]

Negative eugenics became increasingly ominous when allied with a scheme that divided humanity into discrete races arranged in a hierarchy. In 1916, a New Yorker named Madison Grant published an influential treatise of the eugenics movement, *The Passing of The Great Race; Or, the Racial Basis of European History*. His biographer Jonathan Spiro found that it was Grant who promoted the notion of a master race, composed of blond, blue-eyed Nordics. Grant insisted that the state had an interest in protecting its racial hygiene by sterilizing or otherwise eliminating from its gene pool allegedly inferior races.

Grant's book creates a taxonomy of racial groups. From blue-blooded New England roots, Grant places his self-identified racial type (surprise!) at the top of the hierarchy. After all, there's little sense in creating racial hierarchies unless one places oneself at the apex. For Grant, Africans and Europeans are not merely different races but distinct species. He sub-divides the so-called white species of Europe into three races he calls the Nordic race, mainly in the North of Europe, the Mediterranean race, along the southern fringes of the continent, and the Alpine race, roughly in the middle.[8] With some nuances and concessions, Grant arranges these European races hierarchically. The Nordics are on top, the Mediterraneans in the middle, and the Alpines at the bottom of the heap. Only the Nordic is the genuine European type, asserts Grant, "the white man par excellence."[9] Writes Grant, "The Nordics are...a race of soldiers, sailors, adventurers, and explorers but, above all, rulers, organizers, and aristocrats in sharp contrast to the essentially peasant character of the Alpines."[10] The Alpines are "servile," Grant held. They "have the mentality of serfs."[11]

Grant believed that the U.S., founded on a particularly pure, Anglo-Saxon branch of the Nordic race, must prevent an infusion of so-called inferior breeding stock to maintain its racial purity. He argued that the immigration of inferior Mediterraneans and Alpines, not to mention the other "species" from Asia, endangered the U.S. at a genetic level. Grant's book was only modestly popular Stateside. It gained more enthusiastic and thoroughgoing devotees when it appeared in German in 1925.[12] Adolph Hitler wrote Grant a letter referring to *The Passing of the Great Race* as his "bible."[13]

Although Grant's training was in law, many of the most prominent eugenicists were degreed and even eminent scientists from fields such as evolutionary biology, paleontology, and zoology. Many made noteworthy contributions to their specialties in addition to their work in eugenics. Eugenics founder Galton made enduring advances in biometrics, meteorology, and geography.[14] Grant was a forerunner of the environmental movement, helping to save the bison, the bald eagle, and the California redwood.[15] Paleontologist Harry Osborn, Grant's longtime associate and author of an introduction to *The Passing of the Great Race*, gave the name Tyrannosaurus to that prehistoric predator.[16]

Eugenics supporters regarded themselves as progressives.[17] They represented modernism, ideas based on the latest science. Implicit in the promise of eugenics was a belief in the perfectibility of humanity through technological means. They were also willing to bring to bear the coercive power of the State to regulate the matter of human reproduction. The eugenics movement came to embrace birth control as well as sterilization measures, both of which were opposed by religious traditionalists. Indeed, Grant was contemptuous of religious scruples. He disdained "sentimental" notions about the sanctity of human life.[18] For Grant, the mass, the great number, captured in abstractions like "society" or "the race," mattered more than the individual.

Grant was no mere theorist. Possessed of unstoppable energy, like his friend Theodore Roosevelt, he organized, planned, and put his ideas into practice. Grant's program included birth control to reduce the number of "undesirables," anti-miscegenation laws and strict racial segregation, and the sterilization of "defectives."[19] Through a network of organizations they founded, Grant and his colleagues had a direct influence on legislation in two areas: state sterilization laws and federal immigration policy.

Harry H. Laughlin was the man Grant needed to help make public policy out of scientific racism.[20] Laughlin was a protégé of Charles Benedict Davenport. Formerly a professor of evolutionary biology at Harvard, Davenport persuaded the widow of a railroad magnate to bankroll his activities to the tune of a half-million dollars, and he founded the Eugenics Record Office (ERO) in 1910, at Cold Spring Harbor Laboratory in Long Island, New York.[21] Davenport also drew financial support from John D. Rockefeller, Jr. and the Carnegie Institution.[22]

Davenport appointed Laughlin to serve as Superintendent of the ERO and Laughlin became a public face of the eugenics movement. Laughlin wrote model legislation for sterilizing those deemed "unfit" to reproduce. The "socially inadequate classes" who were liable for sterilization according to Laughlin's model law included alcoholics, drug addicts, the mentally ill, people convicted of crimes, and "the dependent," a class that included orphans and the homeless.[23] The Supreme Court upheld a Virginia sterilization law modeled on Laughlin's draft in the case of *Buck v. Bell* (1927).[24] By 1931, 30 of the 48 states had sterilization laws.[25] More than 60,000 Americans deemed "unfit" were sterilized under such legislation.[26] The U.S. was not alone. Several other countries and a few Canadian provinces passed similar legislation in this period, and eugenic sterilizations continued in some regions into the 1970s.[27]

Laughlin was also instrumental in the legislative efforts to restrict the immigration of allegedly inferior races into the United States. Grant befriended Congressman Albert Johnson, a Republican of Washington, chairman of the U.S. House of Representatives Committee on Immigration and Naturalization, and a member of the Ku Klux Klan.[28] Laughlin gave testimony before Johnson's committee over two days in April 1920. He provided "scientific support" for a policy restricting immigration. Laughlin informed the Committee about "the bad breeding stock that was entering the country and spoiling its inborn natural qualities."[29] Johnson's committee appointed Laughlin to serve as its "Expert Eugenics Agent," a position he maintained for eleven years.[30]

Grant and Laughlin advocated a quota system that would restrict emigration of so-called undesirable Alpines and Mediterraneans from Europe. In May 1921, Congress passed the Emergency Quota Act, which restricted the number of immigrants allowed from any European country to three percent of the total population from that country in the U.S. as indicated by the 1910 census.[31] This Act decreased emigration from Europe from about 805,000 in the year before the law was signed to less than 310,000 a year after it came into effect.[32]

But this measure was only temporary. Grant and his supporters wanted permanent restrictions on immigration, a measure that would place an invisible wall around the U.S. and debar "inferior races" from "polluting" the Nordic gene pool. With the help of eugenics supporters, the Johnson-Reed Act of 1924 made the quota system the law of the land.

The Johnson-Reed Act passed with large majorities in both houses of Congress. The Act took the 1921 law further by reducing the quota of legal immigrants to two percent of the U.S. population from any given European country as per the 1890 census. Since there were fewer southern and eastern European immigrants in the U.S. in 1890 than in 1910, the Act of 1924 placed greater barriers in the path of these immigrants than had the 1921 legislation. The Johnson-Reed Act also debarred emigration from most of Asia. Grant and the eugenicists got what they wanted. Emigration to the U.S. declined precipitately. Emigration from Europe fell from circa 2.5 million in the 1920s to about 348,000 in the following decade.[33] With some modifications, the quota system would remain in place until 1965.

According to Laughlin, "Madison Grant was *the* instrumental force in the framing" of the Johnson-Reed Act.[34] During the debates over the 1924 Act, Grant and Johnson were in daily contact.[35] Grant supplied statistics to Congress that enabled the legislators to establish the quota system. Congressman Johnson endorsed Grant's major work telling his colleagues that Grant's *The Passing of The Great Race* was an "important book." The lawmaker recommended the book "to all those interested in the racial and political aspects of the [immigration] question."[36] Senator Ellison DuRant Smith of South Carolina recommended Grant's book from the floor during the debates on the bill. The Senator signaled his embrace of eugenics doctrine when he said,

Thank God we have in America perhaps the largest percentage of any country in the world of the pure, unadulterated Anglo-Saxon stock; certainly the greatest of any nation in the Nordic breed. It is for the preservation of that splendid stock that has characterized us that I would make this not an asylum for the oppressed of all countries, but a country to assimilate and perfect that splendid type of manhood that has made America the foremost Nation in her progress and in her power.[37]

President Calvin Coolidge, a New Englander, signed the 1924 bill into law. Coolidge's rhetoric demonstrates the penetration of eugenics ideas into the highest levels of government. "America must be kept American," declared the President. "Biological laws show...that Nordics deteriorate when mixed with other races."[38]

The impetus behind the Johnson-Reed Act was the desire to restrict the emigration of Europeans, and especially European Jews, to the United States.[39] Emigration from Canada, Mexico, and other parts of the Americas was not subject to the quota system. As emigration from Europe declined, the emigration of *Canadiens* increased. Between 1920 and 1930, the proportion of Franco-Americans born in Québec rose across the U.S. and in every New England state.[40] Grant and his associates were not unaware of the renewed influx from Québec. Into the 1930s, their writings reflected continuing Anglo-Protestant anxieties regarding New England's Franco-Americans.

Franco-Americans in Eugenics Literature

Before Grant discovered eugenics, the Franco-Americans already chafed under Anglo-Saxon perceptions that they were, in so many words, an "inferior race." A speaker at the 1901 Springfield Convention cites "the opinion of the Anglo-Saxons who do not hesitate to award us [Franco-Americans] the title of an inferior race."[41] Several other speakers make similar allusions using the phrase "inferior race" verbatim.[42] Evidently, the notion of Franco-American "inferiority" was in the air among the Anglo-Saxons.

Grant's writings provide a foundation, by his own lights, for the assessment of *Canadiens* and Franco-Americans as racially inferior. In *The Passing of the Great Race*, Grant writes,

The Dominion [of Canada] is, of course, handicapped by the presence of an indigestible mass of French-Canadians, largely from Brittany and of Alpine origin although the habitant patois is an archaic Norman of the time of Louis XIV. These Frenchmen were granted freedom of language and religion by their conquerors, and are now using these privileges to form separatist groups in antagonism to the English population. The Quebec Frenchmen will succeed in seriously impeding the progress of Canada and will succeed even better in keeping themselves a poor and ignorant community of little more importance to the world at large than are the Negroes in the South.[43]

Thus spoke Hitler's Bible. But Grant's statement is factually incorrect in many respects. Although there was a Breton influence among the *Canadiens*, it is inaccurate to claim that they were "largely from Brittany." From the standpoint of eugenics, this claim justifies Grant in classifying the *Canadiens* as Alpines, i.e., the lowest form of whiteness in his racial scheme.

Nor did the large-scale immigration of this "indigestible" *Canadien* community into New England escape Grant's notice. In a revised edition of his work, he added the following comment to his very first chapter:

During the last century the New England manufacturer imported the Irish and French Canadians and the resultant fall in the New England birthrate at once became ominous. The refusal of the native American [sic] to work with his hands when he can hire or import serfs to do manual labor for him is the prelude to his extinction and the immigrant laborers are now breeding out their masters and killing by filth and by crowding as effectively as by the sword.

Thus the American sold his birthright in a continent to solve a labor problem. Instead of retaining political control and making citizenship an honorable and valued privilege, he intrusted the government of his country and the maintenance of his ideals to races who have never yet succeeded in governing themselves, much less any one else.[44]

Elsewhere in his *meisterwerke*, Grant gives yet more reasons to think of the *Canadiens* and Franco-Americans as occupying an inferior place in his racial hierarchy:

In the Catholic colonies...of New France and New Spain, if the half-breed were a good Catholic he was regarded as a Frenchman or a Spaniard, as the case might be. This fact alone gives the clew [sic] to many of our Colonial wars where the Indians, other than the Iroquois, were persuaded to join the French against the Americans by *half-breeds who considered themselves Frenchmen.*[45]

Grant did not regard these "French-Canadian-Indians" as "Frenchmen," due to a principle of eugenics known as "reversion." According to this doctrine, the cross between members of what eugenicists regarded as a superior and an inferior race produces a specimen of the inferior kind. In Grant's scheme, "superior" blood does not elevate "inferior" blood; the "inferior" admixture lowers the level of the "superior." By the principle of reversion, writes Grant, "The cross between a white man and an Indian is an Indian."[46]

For Grant, not only were *Canadiens* allegedly inferior Alpines, but they were also mixed genetically with a non-Caucasian "species," the native North Americans. For Grant, the *Canadiens* represented inferiority mixed with inferiority to produce, by his principle of reversion, a decidedly inferior mix.

Here Grant is trading on the commonly held assumption that the *Canadiens* were a mixed-race people. Genealogists today remain divided on the extent of inter-marriage between *Canadiens* and indigenous peoples. However, that *Canadiens* were a mixed-race people was a very common belief among Americans throughout our period. So general was the assumption that the *Canadiens* had "Indian blood," that many references to that belief are comments tossed off casually under the assumption that it was common knowledge. The repeated denials of extensive "mixing" between *Canadiens* and indigenous peoples, from many quarters, also suggest that the belief was widely held.

An item in the *New York Times* from 1878 noted that it is "beyond dispute that there is hardly a French Canadian family...that does not inherit strongly-marked traces of Indian blood."[47] Flora Haines, observing women working in the textile mills in predominantly Franco-American Biddeford in the 1880s commented, "Occasionally, I remark one [worker] who shows very plainly her Indian blood."[48] Elin Anderson's work on ethnicity in Burlington quotes a banker who held a jaundiced view of Franco-Americans on the grounds that "they intermarried with Indians in early days and so became irresponsible."[49]

Denials of the biological *métissage* between *Canadiens* and indigenous peoples also reveal the persistence of the belief in the mixed-race origins of Franco-Americans. Egbert Smyth's 1891 article on the Franco-Americans states,

> Some authors have contended that there is in this [*Canadien*] race a large percentage of Indian blood. This admixture is credited to the time of the earlier settlers, and traces of it are claimed with great confidence to be apparent in the features of many Canadians of the present day. Such a representation appears to be insufficiently grounded in what is known of the early history, and to involve a great exaggeration of what is now observable, or insecure inference from it.[50]

The Dillingham Commission's *Dictionary of Races and Peoples* states that the French-Canadian "race...is not widely intermingled with Indian blood, as some misinformed people think."[51]

Despite these denials, the cadre of eugenicists tended to believe that the *Canadiens* were mixed-race. A paper by Davenport titled "Race Crossing in Man," asserts that the *Canadiens* "hybridized extensively with the Amerindians." Davenport's paper does not support the notion of "reversion." He tags "the French-Canadian-Indian" as exhibiting "hybrid vigor."[52] Charles M. Goethe, another prominent eugenicist, agreed. A millionaire banker, Goethe founded the Eugenics Society of Northern California. He also established the Immigration Study Commission that lobbied for the extension of the quotas in the Johnson-Reed Act to Latin America.[53] In a 1935 letter to the press, arguing for the restriction of Mexican immigration, Goethe mentions the "Canadian [Dionne] quintuplets" an instance of multiple birth in 1934 that caused a media sensation. Goethe writes, "it is well known... that the very high birthrate of Quebec is due, in a great degree at least, to the Indian strain."[54]

Accepting the principle of reversion, the notion that *Canadiens* were a mixed-race people was all Grant needed to tar Franco-Americans and their *Canadien* cousins in Québec with the brush of racial inferiority, the possessors of degenerate "germ plasm."

In 1930, Grant and Charles Stewart Davison co-edited a volume of essays on the theme of immigration entitled *The Alien in Our Midst or Selling Our Birthright For a Mess of Industrial Pottage*. Sandwiched between stirring quotations from the Founding Fathers, these essays bear such titles as "The Control of Trends in the Racial Composition of the American People" and "The Howl for Cheap Mexican Labor." Among these offerings appears an essay called "The French-Canadian Invasion" by Robert Cloutman Dexter. Dexter addresses the alleged Franco-American problem much more extensively than did Grant in his earlier book.

Dexter was a protégé of Grant who made something of a career out of anti-Franco-American agitation. In 1923, Dexter submitted his doctoral thesis at Clark University (Worcester, Massachusetts) entitled *The Habitant Transplanted: A Study of French-Canadians in New England*.[55] Dexter wrote a piece for *The Nation* in August of that year called "The Gallic War in Rhode Island" in which he criticized Franco-Americans who had objected to laws intending to make English the only approved language of instruction in private schools. He charged them with stoking "the fires of hate and racial ambition."[56]

He then published a piece in 1924 in the magazine *The World's Work* entitled "Fifty-Fifty Americans" in which he revives the anti-Franco-American conspiracy rhetoric of the late 19th century.[57] "At no distant date," warns Dexter, Franco-Americans "may have a practical dominance in political and social affairs" in New England since they comprise one-seventh of the population of the region.[58] He admits that their presence is necessary to contain labor costs. They're beneficial, claims Dexter, to industrialists and to militarists in search of cannon fodder, but he sees little of value in them beyond these utilities. He repeats "the Chinese of the Eastern States" allegations from the 1880s, already out of date when Wright issued them more than 40 years before Dexter's piece.

Dexter then attacks the Franco-American institutional network, including the French-language press under the usual pretext that it keeps Franco-Americans superstitious, ignorant, and priest-ridden. Franco-Americans have the effrontery, sniffs Dexter, "to embrace such of our traditions as they desire, not American traditions *in toto*."[59] To the stock charges, Dexter adds one innovation inspired by the era of Prohibition: he accuses the Franco-Americans of smuggling illegal liquor from across the border. Dexter concludes with the warning that the Franco-Americans "hope ultimately to occupy and dominate the United States East of the Mississippi."[60]

Dexter's essay in Grant's and Davison's 1930 collection is among the book's milder chapters tucked amid eugenicist screeds. Despite his measured tone, Dexter declares that the New England Franco-Americans of his day, "have certain peculiar characteristics which tend to make them far more difficult of assimilation" than other immigrant groups.[61] In his discussion of these characteristics, Dexter sounds familiar themes such as the proximity of the Franco-American's Québec homeland and the famed "fecundity of the race." He also presents a moderate form of the then familiar image of a French-Canadian horde poised to dominate the northeastern States.

His prescription for turning back the "French-Canadian invasion" of New England is forced assimilation of the generations born in the U.S. by means of the public schools. Dexter prefers that children be required to attend public school where English will be the obligatory language of instruction. He would also require, contrary to the traditions of New England, regulation of schools at the state level as a means of circumventing Franco-American control of school boards in municipalities where they constitute a majority. He also mulled the suggestion that emigration from Canada should be restricted only to those whose mother tongue is English.[62]

The last of Grant's major works, *The Conquest of a Continent*, appeared in 1933. In a dedicated chapter in this book discussing Canada, Grant again identifies *Canadiens* as Alpines. Although here he confers on them the title of "White" (with a capital "W") he also states that French-Canadians "must be put in a class by themselves" claiming that they are less like the French than New Englanders are like the English.[63] He suggests, as did Dexter, that perhaps only English-speaking Canadians should be allowed to emigrate to the United States. Effectively, he would have the border closed shut to *Canadiens*.[64]

In the same book Grant discussed immigrants to the West Coast:

California is determined that the white man there shall not be replaced by the Chinese, the Japanese, the Mexican, or the Filipino. The Eastern States should face this problem understandingly, and recognize the simple fact that the white men on the Pacific Coast of the United States and Canada are determined to maintain a white ownership of the country, even though the East has been willing to see New England swamped by French-Canadians and Polaks, and the industrial centers of the North filled to overflowing with southern and eastern Europeans.[65]

Grant includes the French-Canadians of New England among a list of what he regarded as inferior races who were threatening the "white ownership of the country."

Franco-Americans and the Vermont Eugenics Project

Davenport, like Grant and Dexter, also took an interest in Franco-Americans. On February 20, 1923, he penned a letter to a kindred spirit, Dr. Henry F. Perkins of Vermont. Wrote Davenport to Perkins,

> Did you know, that in the study of defects found in drafted men, Vermont stood at or near the top of the list as having precisely or nearly the highest defect rate for quite a series of defects? This result I ascribe to the French Canadian constituents of the population which, I had other reasons for believing, to contain an undue proportion of defectives. I wrote to a friend in St. Johnsbury about this and she made some inquiries and concluded that, indeed, there is a large number of gross physical defects among the French Canadians at that place.[66]

Henry Perkins was a Professor of Zoology at the University of Vermont, Director of the Vermont Eugenics Survey, and Vermont's point man on eugenics. One-time President of the American Eugenics Society, Perkins was a staunch advocate for the preservation of the Anglo-Protestant character of his state. Describing "Harry" Perkins's background, Nancy Gallagher writes, "All dimensions of Harry's life conspired to reinforce the traditions, values and obligations of the Protestant Yankee elite culture and erected formidable boundaries to understanding or appreciating people who lived outside this world."[67]

Spiro shows that the main men of the eugenics movement, including Grant and Davenport, shared this blue-blooded, New England Anglo-Protestant heritage even if they weren't native to the region.[68] They identified the "Yankee Protestant Elite" with "America," and the interests of the United States with their own ethnic and class interests.

They used science as a means of reinforcing the foregone conclusion of their "natural" superiority. Their elite position was not, in their minds, because their families had been well-off, educated, and influential for generations. It must have been the Nordic "germ plasm."

In 1928, Perkins proposed to Davenport a systematic study of Vermont's Franco-Americans, the largest foreign-born population in the state.[69] The study would allow Perkins to explore the high "defect rate" among Vermont draftees. Perkins was in collaboration with an anthropologist at Columbia University to develop a series of tests that he would correlate with the degree of French-Canadian ancestry among his subjects.

"My reason for being particularly interested in the French-Canadians," Perkins informed Davenport, "is that they are so characteristically and so important a part of the population. They have been studied less than have European nationals. The problem is not unlike that of the Amerind invasion along the Mexican border."[70] Davenport did not support Perkins in these efforts, but the Vermonter found other means to further his studies of the Franco-American population.

Harriet Abbott assisted Perkins with his fieldwork on "degenerate" lines for his Vermont Eugenics Survey. From a background in social work, Abbott studied at Davenport's ERO.[71] In the documentation of her research, allegedly "degenerate" Vermont families were pseudonymized pejoratively as "the Pirates" or "the Gypsies." The "Gypsies" were not Roma but a family line that Abbott traced back to an ancestor from Québec. The research concluded that this "Gypsy Family" was "of mixed ancestry with apparently very strong doses of Indian and Negro."[72] The "Pirate" family's ancestry was also traced back to *Canadiens*.[73]

Perkins's eugenics interests made him a proponent of legislation that allowed the State of Vermont to sterilize "voluntarily" persons deemed "idiot(s), imbecile(s), feeble-minded or insane." In 1931, after more than one attempt, Vermont enacted such legislation.[74] Lutz Kaelber researched eugenic sterilizations throughout the United States. He found that 253 persons were sterilized under the Vermont legislation most of them in the period between 1931 and 1941.

Relying on Gallagher's work, Kaelber found that "Poor and socially ostracized families were targeted for investigation of the three D's (delinquency, dependency, and mental defect)." He claims that targeted families included those who lived outside of "accepted moral or social convention," such as families that had illegitimate children, were illiterate, were suspected of incest, or that had members who were institutionalized. He also found that the "poor, the disabled, French Canadians, and Native Americans" were targeted, and more women than men.[75]

The targeting of these groups by 20th century eugenicists reflected prejudices in the region that predated them. For example, historian Rowland E. Robinson, in his 1892 book *Vermont: A Study of Independence* gives an account of the earlier, temporary *Canadien* settlers in the state in the pre-Civil War period as honest, simple peasants. More recent imports from Québec, Robinson calls an "inferior class" and "an abominable crew of vagabonds, robust, lazy men and boys, slatternly women with litters of filthy brats, and all as detestable as they were uninteresting." Although he claims this wave of "vagabonds" had passed, he concludes that "the character of these [*Canadien*] people is not such as to inspire the highest hope for the future of Vermont."[76]

Robinson saw the *Canadiens* and their Native American allies as the primeval enemies of colonial Vermonters, as representing an "insidious and continuous invasion."[77] Robinson's views inform the elaborate exercise in confirmation bias that was the Vermont Eugenics Survey. The Survey's research produced a 20th century, modernist variation of 19th century nationalist prejudices.

In the 1930s, Elin Anderson, a social worker from Winnipeg, Manitoba, conducted a more measured piece of research under the auspices of Perkins's Vermont Eugenics Survey. Anderson's work included a detailed study of ethnic groups in Burlington as well as a study of three rural towns in the state.[78] As an outsider to New England, Anderson had no stake in defending the Anglo-Protestant character of the region. Sociology rather than eugenics formed the theoretical framework for her studies.[79] Her research on rural communities found that the Vermont Yankee farmers respected their

Franco-American peers, especially when the latter participated in non-sectarian organizations such as The Grange. The Yankee farm families regretted the exodus of their own from the Vermont country-side but had no animus towards the Franco-Americans who had taken over farms from those who had left the region.[80]

Anderson's field research contradicted Perkins's biases about the situation in rural Vermont. Interviewed by Anderson in 1932, Perkins gave the following assessment of Vermont's Franco-American popu-lation and its place in town and country:

General Yankee attitude to [the] French is that of humerous [sic] disdain and derision....Also that they are a neighborly folk but many have a pretty low I. Q. They came as longshoremen and lumberjacks and since then have graduated to filling stations and are the better mechanics in all our garages as well as doing trucking, etc, etc....

The farm population of Vermont is pretty sore at the French Canadians because they took the farms from the Yankees which the Yankees couldn't make pay and have made a go of them, living at a lower standard but at the same time have been able to present a fairly good appearance, send their children to school, well-dressed, etc. One of the chief hopes of the VCCL [Vermont Committee on Country Life], was that the French Canadian would be given his proper due, that is, his proper place in society; the Commission felt that he was considered a much lower person on the social scale than he really is and that a greater appreciation of him was necessary because he deserved a higher place socially.

When Dr. Perkins asked Paul Moody of Middlebury College if he had had any students of French Canadian descent who had made a name for themselves in any type of endeavor Mr. Moody immediately said no, and even on consideration said he thought a lot about it and checked up that not one Canadian had risen to a place of responsibility. When asked if they hadn't contributed much to the community of Middlebury itself, Mr. Moody added another vehement no, stating that the whole French Canadian population could be wiped out of Middlebury and no one would miss it....

Usually the Frenchman is treated superciliously by the Yankee. The Frenchman begins to feel inferior and he fails because he lacks the characteristics of drive to overcome that handicap. The French are a complacent people; it would be impossible to have a French Mussolini for instance. That kind of drive is lacking.

The French are undoubtedly an oppressed race in eastern Canada. As a people they have a daintiness, a delicacy and liveliness that is not to be found in the older Yankee or Irish. Their poetry has an unusual charm and humor. Many of the traits of the French are superior to that of at least the Irish. They are always more friendly and genial and kindly and make better neighbors than do the Irish. There is of course another class of French who is the voyageur and lumberjack who is roistering and rough and callous but is nevertheless full of song.

Yet with all this appreciation of the French race and of their very fine qualities, Dr. P. admits that socially of course they will never be recognized. There is and probably always will be a wall there. They are nice people – at a distance.[81]

When Anderson published her findings, some of her general remarks about Burlington's Franco-Americans are paraphrases of Perkins's views.[82] For instance, Anderson states that the attitude of Yankees toward Franco-Americans is like "the attitude of an adult to a child, [with] an appreciation of their warm, earthy simplicity and a delight in the 'quaint' aspects of their behavior....But this attitude is accompanied by a rejection of some of the very qualities that make them charming."[83] She also calls the Franco-Americans "unassertive" and states that it was the general opinion among the Yankees that the Franco-Americans' forbears "had been held back in Canada as a conquered people."[84] These statements have close parallels in the Perkins interview. Either Perkins influenced Anderson's views, or his assessment of Franco-Americans was indicative of what Anderson heard in her interviews with other Vermonters.

Whatever their source, Perkins and Anderson leave the impression that the general attitude of Yankee Vermont toward Franco-Americans is one of derision and condescension, of contempt more than hatred. As individuals, they are perhaps merely risible; only in the mass, as an allegedly defective gene pool, were they regarded as formidable.

The Eugenics Legacy

Eugenics was an international phenomenon. Numerous countries had eugenics societies and true believers in the early 20th century.

The initial impetus came from the Briton Sir Francis Galton. Another Englishman, Houston Stewart Chamberlain and the Frenchmen Gobineau and La Pouge were forerunners of the movement.[85] It was the German eugenicists, however, who put the management of gene pools at the front of their agenda in the 1930s and 1940s. Laws inspired and promoted by U.S. eugenicists had a direct influence on Nazi German policy.

Harry Laughlin's draft sterilization law became the model for Nazi legislation of 1933.[86] In *Mein Kampf* and in his unpublished "Second Book" Hitler cited and praised the restrictions on immigration enshrined in the Johnson-Reed Act.[87] Nazi "protégé" and "race anthropologist" Hans F. K. Günther recognized Grant as one of the "spiritual fathers" of this legislation and recommended the law as a model for Germany.[88]

A list of Nazi-recommended books "in the field of human heredity" in 1936 included Grant's *The Passing of the Great Race*, one of only two non-German works to make the cut.[89] When a German-language edition of Grant's *Conquest of a Continent* was published in 1937, Nazi eugenicist Eugen Fischer wrote an introduction, and Grant made sure that Nazi chief ideologist Alfred Rosenberg received a copy. In his introduction to the German edition published in 1937, Fischer wrote that, "no one today should pay more careful attention to Grant's work than the people of Germany where racialist thinking has become the chief foundation of the population policies of the National Socialist State."[90] Grant had been in contact with Fischer and Günther through the 1920s and into the 1930s.[91]

At the Nuremberg trials, Dr. Karl Brandt was accused of carrying out the infamous Nazi medical experiments among other crimes. Brandt entered into evidence for the defense passages from Grant's book.[92] He and other defendants cited the Johnson-Reed Act and U.S. sterilization laws. They also cited anti-miscegenation legislation and the Supreme Court decision in *Buck v. Bell* to show that eugenics was not an exclusively Teutonic preoccupation.[93]

Collaboration between U.S. eugenics supporters and the Nazis was no secret at the time. In May 1935, respected paleontologist William K. Gregory resigned from the Galton Society, one of Grant's eugenics associations, because U.S. eugenics supporters were "aiding agents of the German government by advice, correspondence and personal contact."[94] The *Eugenic News*, the "official organ" of three major eugenics associations, with Davenport and Laughlin among its editors, covered Nazi German eugenics in a favorable light as late as 1939, and Gregory registered his objections to the publication's positive coverage of the regime.[95]

These connections are no surprise since there was little daylight between the beliefs of Grant and associates, and those of the Nazi Party. In a 1911 book, Davenport foreshadowed the "final solution" when he called for the execution of individuals with "defective germ plasm."[96] Laughlin penned an article for a German journal based on a talk he had given in Munich declaring that sterilization was "necessary for the well being of the state" and commending the "prohibition of procreation for certain members of degenerate tribes."[97] Laughlin began to collect newspaper clippings about the Nazis even before their rise to power in Germany. In the margin of one of the clippings is a handwritten note: "Hitler should be made honorary member of the ERA," i.e., the Eugenics Research Association, a U.S.-based group.[98] Through the ERO, Laughlin acquired a Nazi film called *Hereditary Defective*. Laughlin raised funds to market the film to "churches, clubs, colleges and high schools" and an edited version of the film, under the title *Eugenics in Germany*, was screened in the U.S. in 1937-38.[99]

For his part, Grant dreamed of the day when the "true" racial hierarchy would emerge, with the Nordic Anglo-Saxons at the summit, untrammeled by democratic scruples.[100] Grant's dreams were realizable since eugenics enjoyed the favor of a cadre of elites that included scientists, intellectuals, state legislators, Congressmen, Senators, and U.S. Presidents Coolidge and Harding.[101] Only the WWII, and the discredit it threw upon eugenics impeded U.S. eugenicists from realizing even more of the items on their agenda.

For Grant and most of his associates Franco-Americans were but a small part of a larger set of conversations about race, while Henry Perkins and Robert Dexter were eugenicists who were specialists on the topic. It is clear where Franco-Americans would have ranked in the racial caste system of a Grantian eugenics dystopia. To Grant and his associates, Franco-Americans were "defectives," inferior "Alpines," and "hybrids" carrying a substandard variety of "germ-plasm."

Today, we would think it far-fetched to suggest that Franco-Americans, a mostly forgotten, white-identified ethnic enclave in New England, might have fallen afoul of anything like a "final solution" had these proto-Nazis gained the upper hand. But the long history of racially-inspired barbarity does not inspire confidence.

CHAPTER FOURTEEN

A KLAN FOR NEW ENGLAND

Most Americans tend to think of the Ku Klux Klan as a Southern insti-tution, targeting mainly African-Americans. However, in the years following the First World War, the Ku Klux Klan enjoyed nationwide support. It wielded considerable influence in the Northeast, Midwest, and Northwest, as well as the South. This so-called Second Klan of the 1920s set its sights not only on African-Americans, but also on Catholics, Jews, and organized Labor.

African-American community leaders recognized that this 20th century Klan was a different animal from its 19th century predecessor. In a 1922 report, the National Association for the Advancement of Colored People (NAACP) noted that the Klan had broadened its targets since the 19th century. The NAACP circu-lated a pamphlet entitled "What the Ku Klux Klan Stands For and How to Oppose It." The pamphlet "emphasized the fact that the revived organization is anti-Catholic, anti-Jewish, anti-Labor and anti-Negro."[1] The *New York World*, in a lengthy 1921 exposé of the Klan, came to the same conclusion: "When it was organized, it was against the Negro...Today it is primarily anti-Jew, anti-Catholic, anti-alien and it is spreading more than twice as fast through the North and West as it is growing in the South."[2]

The Ku Klux Klan originated in Tennessee in the immediate aftermath of the Civil War. The name derives from the Greek word *kuklos* meaning circle. The Klan began as a satirical social circle tar-geting the hated Northern occupation of the South that followed the war, but it soon developed into a potent terrorist group. During the Reconstruction period, the Klan's aim was to maintain the supremacy of the white-identified population in the region following the emancipation of the African-American slaves. The Federal government passed anti-Klan legislation in 1870 and 1871, and some thousand Klansmen were arrested. Despite the crackdown, assorted Klannish orders survived under various monikers.[3]

Thomas Dixon's novel *The Clansman*, published in 1905, brought the Reconstruction-era Klan to the attention of a wider, latter-day public. Dixon, whose father was a slaveholder and a Reconstruction-era Klan member, wrote the book as part of a trilogy presenting his revisionist view of Southern history. Dixon's work glorified the Ku Klux Klan as the protector of "white womanhood" in particular.

Dixon later brought *The Clansman* to the stage. The novel's more popular adaptation was for the silver screen under the title *Birth of a Nation* (1915), the work of film innovator D. W. Griffith. The film carried forward the theme of the Reconstruction-era Klan as the allegedly heroic defenders of morality and justice. Griffith, too, was a Southerner and the son of a Confederate officer.

Birth of A Nation was among the longest and most technically ambitious films of its day. It was a hit at the box office and screened at the White House where it garnered the approval of President Woodrow Wilson. Griffith was among the earlier directors to craft films that were not merely photographed plays. Film, Griffith realized, was a medium in its own right with the ability to evoke powerful emotions with the stories it conveyed through the juxtaposition of images. The protests, threats, and occasional violence that followed screenings of *Birth of a Nation* spoke to the power, for good or ill, of the new art. *Birth of a Nation* was among the first instances where Hollywood's art influenced life beyond celluloid as the film led to a Klan revival.[4]

The lynching of Jewish factory boss Leo Frank in Georgia in 1915 was another catalytic event in the Klan resurgence.[5] Frank was convicted, on slim evidence, of the rape and murder of a teenage girl who worked in the factory he managed. Georgia's governor commuted Frank's sentence, but a mob kidnapped the convict from prison in August 1915 and hanged him.[6]

A former Methodist preacher named William Joseph Simmons revived the Ku Klux Klan just months after the lynching of Frank. Simmons had been a salesman of memberships to a fraternal organization called the Woodmen of the World.[7] He was a member of more than a dozen such lodges. In October 1915, Simmons led a party of 34 men to the top of Stone Mountain, Georgia, 16 miles from Atlanta. Among the group were three elderly former members of the Reconstruction-era Klan.[8] Reportedly, members of Leo Frank's lynching party were on hand as well.[9]

On Stone Mountain, Simmons placed on a makeshift altar a sword, the Bible, an American flag, and a canteen of river water. Simmons declared himself the Imperial Wizard of the Invisible Empire of the Ku Klux Klan and inducted the other men present into the order. The assembly also burned a cross, a ritual derived from Dixon's novel.[10] Cross-burning was not a part of 19th century Klan liturgics.

The Ku Klux Corporation was organized on October 26, 1915, headquartered in Atlanta. The charter named twelve incorporators, Simmons topping the list. The charter authorized the company to "own and control the sale of all paraphernalia, regalia, stationery, jewelry and other materials needed by the subordinate branches of the order for the conduct of their business." It also authorized the Klan to publish, and to "buy, hold and sell real estate."[11] The power to sell Klan-related "regalia," along with the purchase and sale of real estate became revenue generators for Klan Inc. as it expanded.

The Second Klan grew slowly in its first years. At most, a few thousand Georgians and Alabamans signed on but then growth slowed.[12] In 1920, Simmons engaged a public relations firm called the Southern Publicity Association. The principals in this firm were an unmarried couple, Edward Young Clarke and Elizabeth Tyler. The pair had success in fundraising for the war effort during WWI and for such causes as the Salvation Army and the Anti-Saloon League.[13] They then brought their PR savvy into the Klan's service.

Simmons placed the management of Klan Inc. in the hands of Clarke and Tyler. Clarke became President of the Gate City Manufacturing Company that produced the Klan outfits. Tyler became the major stockholder of the *Searchlight*, a Klan-oriented newspaper, as well as serving as Klan Inc.'s press agent.[14] Together, the pair also ran a Klan-linked real estate company.[15] The *World's* September 1921 series on the Klan referred to Simmons, Clarke, and Tyler as the "Big Three" of the Klan revival.[16] The papers pegged Elizabeth Tyler as "the brains of the secret order."[17]

If the Klan was to grow beyond its base in the South, it needed to speak to the concerns of other regions of the country where the demographics were unlike Georgia. The Klan had to respond to the changes that had occurred in the U.S.'s social and demographic landscape in the half-century between Reconstruction and the post-WWI era. The unease in Yankee America caused by the massive immigration to the U.S. from all over the world, especially the emigration of Jewish and non-Protestant Christians from southern and eastern Europe, created an opportunity for a nationwide Klan movement. Under the tutelage of Clarke and Tyler, the Klan broadened its appeal by invoking the anxieties of the U.S.-born, white-identified population faced with the social consequences of immigration and urbanization.

The Klan portrayed itself as engaged in a religious crusade to defend what it regarded as traditional, Protestant Christian morality. This explicitly religious bent had been missing in the Reconstruction-era Klan. The original Klan was sectional. It had no ambitions outside the South. The Second Klan was a bastion nationwide of the view that the U.S. was fundamentally and inescapably a White, Anglo-Saxon, and Protestant country. Simmons's successor as Imperial Wizard claimed that Protestantism and Americanism "spring from the same racial qualities."[18] In Klan ideology, U.S. political institutions were nothing but "Protestantism translated into government."[19] A minister in Fort Worth, addressing a Klan audience, declared that only Protestants were "the real white folks."[20]

In his 1923 book, *The Klan Unmasked*, Simmons affirms Pan-Saxonism as Klan ideology. For Simmons, U.S. society was not only white-led but specifically Anglo-Saxon in character. The Klan's 20th century mission, according to Simmons, was to "maintain Anglo-Saxon civilization on the American continent from submergence due to the encroachment and invasion of alien people *of whatever clime or color*."[21] Simmons speaks of the Reconstruction-era Klan as "intrepid men who preserved Anglo-Saxon supremacy in the South." [22] The Klan's struggle, Simmons claims, was for "Anglo-Saxon democracy, refinement and civilization."[23] Simmons speaks of "Anglo-Saxon methods of free speech, free press, democratic methods and popular respect for the law."[24] He labels the Bill of Rights itself as "Anglo-Saxon."[25] Simmons takes Pan-Saxonism to its logical conclusion, calling for the English-speaking peoples to lead the world, with the U.S. in alliance with the British Empire.[26]

The Klan saw itself as the enforcer of Anglo-Protestant norms. It depicted its aggression as a defensive stand on behalf of "the principles where America will stand or fall, the love of race and country, and a belief in the broad Protestantism upon which our Nation was founded...these things being the ancient landmarks of our Anglo-Saxon civilization in American Institutions."[27] Using language derived from eugenics, Simmons boasts that the U.S.'s "peculiar Nordic civilization, the creation, par excellence of the whitest of the white European races" is destined to dominate North America and become "the greater Nordic Europe."[28] Klan promoters encapsulated this Anglo-Protestant supremacist ideology in the slogan "100 *percent Americanism.*"

In contrast to the "100 percent American," Klan rhetoric depicted Roman Catholics as terrorists and Jews as political radicals. For example, the *Searchlight* in February 1921 published "15 facts" portraying Catholicism as a terrorist religion. Among these "facts" the *Searchlight* claims that the assassins of Presidents Lincoln, Garfield, and McKinley, as well as the man who shot Theodore Roosevelt, were Catholics. The piece holds that "the plot that took the life of Lincoln emanated from Roman Catholic influence in the house of a Roman Catholic." Notorious terrorists of the day, including "bridge dynamiters" and "bomb throwers," were also Roman Catholics, alleged the Klan publication. "More than 65 per cent of prison convicts of all grades and of all kinds of prisoners are Roman Catholics," claimed the Klan source.[29]

The Klan was concerned that allegedly terrorist Catholics were establishing a parallel, countercultural legal system in the United States. Klan publicists printed a series of cards with propagandistic messages beginning with the phrase *"Do You Know?"* One of these messages read,

> Do you know that the Pope is a political autocrat, with 115 princes of his Government installed in our cities, where he has courts enforcing the canon law? That he controls the daily and magazine press? That he denounces popular Government as inherently vicious and condemns the public schools and forbids children to attend them? That popery enthroned in great cities controls politics? That our war industries were placed exclusively in Roman Catholic hands?[30]

As for Jewish-Americans, Klan propaganda claimed they were plotting the overthrow of the U.S. government and intended to foment a war between factions of the white-identified population.[31] Through the Moscow-based Third International, Klan sources alleged, Jews were infiltrating all Gentile governments. While Klan messaging associated Catholics with crime and terrorism, it connected Jewish-Americans with subversion and political radicalism.

This anti-Catholic and anti-Semitic branding opened a coast-to-coast market for Klan Inc. Led by seasoned PR professionals, the Second Klan deployed sophisticated sales and marketing tactics. The Klan corporation enrolled a small army of recruiters. Clarke led this troupe of traveling salesmen called *Kleagles*. In 1921 there were 1,100 Klan Inc. salesmen, working in eight territories in 45 of the then 48 U.S. states.[32] Kleagles reported to a King Kleagle (District Sales Manager), who reported to a Grand Goblin (Regional Sales Manager).[33] James Weldon Johnson of the NAACP described Klan's Inc.'s business as "commercializing race hatred," and its sales staff enabled the KKK to seize the hate market.[34]

Kleagles followed the standard procedure of the era's traveling salesmen. Each Kleagle covered a region and received a sales kit including a prospect list.[35] When a Kleagle came to town, he would first attempt to win over to the Klan's cause Protestant pastors, police, and local officials.[36] Kleagles and local Klan officials often arranged public events open to all comers, including field days, parades, and dances as well as public talks on Klan ideology in a town or a church hall.[37] The Kleagle, and sometimes a local pastor, would address the crowd at public lectures and present the Klan's version of *100 percent Americanism*. A recruiting drive followed the meeting.[38]

Klan salesmanship also included special promotions. Protestant ministers could join for free. The Klan targeted members of other fraternal organizations and canvassed at their lodges.[39] It placed advertising in newspapers that included a membership application form.[40] In addition to a direct sales strategy, the Klan also had an advertising budget and a national PR campaign that included telegraphed press releases and propaganda films.[41] The hooded order even purchased two colleges.[42]

Each new inductee to the order paid a membership fee of $10 called a Klecktoken. The Klan Inc. salesforce formed a pyramid, with Clarke at its apex. The Sales staff divided the $10 fee according to this pyramid structure, but accounts of the split differ, and the architecture of the pyramid changed over time. One version says that the Kleagle pocketed $4 out of the $10, forwarding the remaining $6. The King Kleagle took a dollar and handed the remaining five dollars to the Grand Goblin who took $0.50 leaving $4.50 to Klan Central. If a King Kleagle made a direct sale, he pocketed $5 of the $10. A Grand Goblin collected $5.50 from a direct sale. Should the Imperial Wizard himself make the sale, he kept the entire $10. Another account of the pyramid scheme alleges that Clarke received $2.50 out of every $10 "donation."[43] Members also paid a $5 annual membership fee and an "Imperial tax" of $1.80.[44]

New members also had to have the robes, the hood, and other regalia. The Klan sold the outfits for $6.50 apiece. They cost $1.25 to manufacture, providing a hefty profit for the Clarke-led corporation that made them.[45] Clarke's kleagling was lucrative. His income was an estimated $360,000 in 1921.[46]

With a motivated sales force, working on commission, the Klan grew exponentially. Klan Inc. expanded outside the South and moved into the North and West. There were large Klan chapters that exercised political influence in such states as Colorado and Oregon, with Indiana emerging as a Klan bastion.[47] By May 1923, there were 2.5 million Klansmen, and estimates range as high as 4 to 5 million members at the Klan's zenith.[48] For a period in the early 1920s, the

Invisible Empire was adding 3,500 members per day.[49] Approximately $50,000 came into the KKK coffers each week in 1921.[50]

The Klan attempted to enhance its prestige by recruiting members of influential and powerful professions such as prosecutors, judges, officials at all levels of government, and members of the Armed Forces.[51] Women were another growth market for the Klan. Women won the right to vote in 1920 and were poised to play a broader role in public affairs. With the women's vote an untested proposition, the Klan moved to exploit this new electorate. Elizabeth Tyler led the movement to form a Women's Ku Klux Klan (WKKK) and held the title of "grand chief" of the group.[52] The WKKK insisted that it was not an auxiliary of the men's Klan but a parallel order with similar principles.[53] Klan Inc. reasoned that its focus on issues around education and "public morality" would prove attractive to women. There were approximately half-a-million Klanswomen throughout the U.S. by the mid-1920s, a quarter of a million in Indiana alone.[54]

The rise of the KKK was not without opposition. The exposé in the *New York World* in 1921 spanned a series of articles that ran daily for more than two weeks. The *World* investigated the Klan's history, its finances, and what the journalists viewed as the hypocrisies of its leaders. The *World* recorded the denunciations of the Klan by church and civic leaders. The newspaper painted a picture of a noose tightening around Klan Inc.'s neck as it faced government scrutiny. Reprinted in papers nationwide, the series won a Pulitzer Prize.

The *World*'s revelations included the information that in 1919, not long before they had signed a contract with the Klan, Clarke and Tyler were arrested for disorderly conduct and possession of alcohol. They were found together "in their bedclothes" in a place described by the press as "a notorious underworld resort" apparently operated by Mrs. Tyler in Atlanta. Clarke's wife May Cartledge Clarke tipped off the police as to Clarke's whereabouts. She claimed that Clarke had abandoned her in 1915. The authorities dropped the liquor charge, but Clarke and Tyler were found guilty of disorderly conduct and paid a fine of $5 apiece.[55] Since the Klan were proponents of Prohibition, this scandal dented the armor of the self-proclaimed knights.

It also came to light that a former client had accused Clarke of embezzling and had filed a civil suit. Further, Clarke had been expelled from his Methodist church, charged with selling bogus stock, extortion, misuse of funds, and other financial improprieties when he was treasurer of a church-linked publishing house.[56]

After the revelations about the duo's past, Clarke and Tyler tendered their resignations to the Imperial Wizard, while denying any wrongdoing. Simmons refused to accept them. The passion play continued as Tyler vowed to continue her work on the Klan's behalf while Clarke pressed his resignation. A tiff between Clarke and Tyler followed. Tyler accused Clarke of being "weak-kneed" in persisting in his desire to resign.[57] Clarke and Tyler may have choreographed these moves to keep the story in the papers. In the end, the pair stayed with the Klan for the time being.

The series in the *World* also covered incidents of alleged Klan-related intimidation and violence. Newspapers tallied such incidents – so many killings, floggings, tar and featherings, threats, and other outrages – tabulated them and kept the count up to date. Most of the targets of alleged Klan violence in the incidents reported in the *World's* series were white-identified people accused of some moral infraction in the eyes of the Klan, such as a doctor who performed abortions or a woman suspected of bigamy. The papers reported that a white-identified Episcopalian Archdeacon was seized, beaten, and tarred and feathered for preaching "racial equality" and "intermarriage" to "Negro audiences." Klansmen targeted an Irish-Australian living in the U.S. because the knights confused *Australians* with wartime enemy the *Austrians*.[58]

But the authors of the series own that many attacks went unreported which made it difficult to track Klan targets. An article in the *World's* series cites a letter from a former resident of Jacksonville, Florida. Among other violent acts, the correspondent mentions the case of a Jewish business owner who was seized, attacked, and driven out of town. He also holds the Klan responsible for the burning of an entire African-American section of a nearby town after a resident tried to defend his right to vote. The letter reiterates that many atrocities, including murders, are committed with impunity.[59]

The Klan became the focus of Congressional hearings in October 1921. Imperial Wizard Simmons testified, fainting in the chamber following the hearing, while calling for forgiveness for the "persecutors" of the Klan – drama sure to make the papers.[60] Klan Inc. also faced investigations by the FBI, the Postmaster General, the Treasury Department and the Prohibition Commission (the latter for allegedly intimidating law enforcement officers).[61]

But all press proved to be good press for the Klan in the early 1920s. The publicity generated by the *World's* series increased its reach and popularity.[62] The press also stoked the fires of opposition. During the Congressional hearings, a would-be assassin fired several shots at Tyler, through a window of her home.[63] She was unhurt but shaken. Simmons also received death threats.

The Klan Comes to New England

In 1921, a tumultuous year for the order, Klan Inc. brought its traveling salesmen to the quintessential land of Yankeedom: New England. The "commercializing of race hatred" in the Northeast meant that Klan Inc. had to market to the demographics of the region.[64] The corporation succeeded in honing its messaging since *per capita* Klan membership in New England, in its 1920s salad days, was enormous.

Franco-American historian Mark Paul Richard has performed the definitive research to date on the New England Klan. Richard found that, at its 1920s height, Maine had 150,141 KKK members, Massachusetts had 130,780, Vermont, 80,301, New Hampshire some 75,000, while there were 65,590 Klansmen in Connecticut and 21,321 in Rhode Island.[65] That totals more than half-a-million hooded followers of the Georgia-based movement in the northeastern border region. Richard calculates that in the three northern New England states of Maine, New Hampshire, and Vermont, about one-third of the white-identified, U.S.-born population were Klan members at the Invisible Empire's zenith. Between ten and fifteen percent of the same demographic joined the Klan in the other three New England states.[66]

The Klan and its opponents inflated the order's membership figures, and members tended to come and go, which renders estimates such as these dubitable. Nonetheless, photographic evidence from the period shows vast rallies with crowds of hooded Klansmen and lengthy Klan parades across New England. In Portland, Maine, the Klan built a headquarters dedicated in 1924 that included an auditorium seating 4,000 and a banquet hall of comparable proportions.[67] In Connecticut in 1927, the Klan had sufficient numbers and breadth of support to set crosses blazing in thirty different locations across the Nutmeg State on the same day.[68] The intensity of opposition to the Klan, from fair-minded Protestants, and targeted Catholics and Jews alike, also argues in favor of the visibility of KKK activities in the region. Such evidence, along with contemporary estimates of the sizes of crowds at Klan events, tends to confirm Richard's figures at least to an order of magnitude.

New England could have been a tough market for the Klan. In 1920s New England, the African-American and Jewish populations were quite small, where they existed at all. The African-American population of Maine and Vermont did not exceed 0.2 percent per the 1920 Federal Census. In the six-state region, Rhode Island had the largest African-American population in 1920 comprising but 1.7 percent of the total.[69]

We cannot assume that the small numbers of African-Americans indicate that they were not a target of the New England Klan's ire. It is not the case that relatively homogeneous regions harbor fewer prejudices against those who do not happen to live among them. However, the Klan's utterances and contemporary reports reveal that the region's Roman Catholics were the primary targets of the order. A 1924 piece in the *Bethel Courier* of Vermont stated, "In this part of the country...the K.K.K. has only one strong appeal to prejudice, and that is the disfavor in which the Catholic Church, priesthood and people are held by a portion of the non-Catholics."[70] Both anti-foreign and anti-Catholic appeals had potential resonance in New England. Nationwide, Massachusetts and Rhode Island were two of the three states with the largest foreign-born populations *per capita* by 1900.[71] U.S. Census Bureau data shows that one-quarter of New Englanders were identified as "foreign-born whites" in 1920.[72] Reinforcing the supremacy of Anglo-Saxon Protestantism, in the face of an influx of Catholic "foreigners," was the New England KKK's *raison d'être*.

The statements of the leading New England Klansman of the era, F. Eugene Farnsworth, confirm it. "America was built upon the foundations laid out by the Protestant Bible," asserted Farnsworth. "The Ku Klux Klan intends that this country shall be continued in the control of Protestant mentality."[73] "Keep Protestant Americans in the lead," Farnsworth exhorted Mainers, "not only in numbers, but in fact."[74] In his speeches throughout the region, Farnsworth claimed to stand for nothing but "the old-fashioned Protestant principles of our fathers."[75]

In a speech at Portland, Farnsworth made it clear that the Klan's *100 percent Americanism* entailed not only native birth but also Anglo-Saxon ethnicity: "This country was not built by native born Americans, but by Anglo-Saxon races and blood."[76] The powerful WKKK spoke out against "undesirable aliens who are unable to demonstrate their ability and willingness to speak the English language, absorb the Anglo-Saxon ideals upon which our government is founded, and live according to the standards of the White race."[77] Although the "White race" is held up as a standard, a light complexion was not sufficient for *100 percent Americanism*. The immigrant must also be willing to speak English and embrace Anglo-Saxon "ideals," whatever they made be.

As non-Protestant, non-Anglos, Franco-Americans became natural targets of regional Klan agitation. A supporter and former New Hampshire legislator identified them as targets of New England's Klan in unambiguous terms: "New Hampshire is going to oust from power the Irish, and Canucks, and Catholics through but one agency – the Ku Klux Klan."[78] In Rhode Island, the Klan eyed Woonsocket, the largest Franco-American center in the state, as a "citadel of Romanism." "Let's go to that city and Americanize it," a Klan spokesman exhorted his followers. "Put their schools and French daily newspapers out of business and the victory is ours."[79] The spokesman targets schools and newspapers, two components of the network of institutions established to support the Franco-American project of *survivance*.

Southern Klansmen who came North noted the difference in emphasis between the sections. A Tennessean Grand Goblin in the

KKK named Padon, secretly a Catholic, and who later left the Klan due to its anti-Catholic stance, met a dim reception when he came to New England. He tried to reorient the Northeastern Klan around "white supremacy," rather than religious prejudice. "Why spend your time knocking [Catholic] white men?" asked Padon. His question was not at all well received by the Northerners.[80]

The cognitive dissonance between Padon and his northern Klan brethren is a product of the stark demographic differences between the sections. For instance, New Englanders' fears about Franco-Americans dominating local governments and imposing their "Romanism" were nearly incomprehensible in the South, where there were practically no Franco-Americans. In much of the Old South in the early 20th century, most people, whatever their skin tone, were also English-speaking, Protestant, and U.S.-born. Skin color differences were more than sufficient to define the *Other*. In 1920s New England, where almost everyone was white-identified, but many were neither English-speaking nor Protestant, religion and language were differentiators between Klan members and Klan targets. Since, in most cases, New Englanders had little occasion to interact with non-whites, distinctions of language and faith served as the practical basis for *othering* minorities. Bigotry requires local targets to sustain its passion.

Thus, Richard folds the New England Klan into the history of prior anti-Catholic movements including the Know Nothings (1840s-1860s) and the American Protective Association (1880s-1890s).[81] In the northeastern border region, the 1920s KKK's appropriation of symbols and costumes from the Reconstruction-era Klan was a convenient support for a continuation of the region's anti-Catholic Nativism.

In the U.S./Canada border region, Anti-Catholic and Anglo-Saxon supremacist notions easily crossed the border and reinforced one another. They trumped U.S. and Canadian nationalism as Anglo-Protestants were bound together across the border by Francophobia and Anti-Catholicism.[82] The Klan established chapters in several Canadian provinces from New Brunswick to Saskatchewan. Richard found that the Klan had contacts with the Orange Order, a group of Irish Protestant origin with a strong presence in Canada that was rabidly Francophobic and anti-Catholic.[83] A Klan newspaper reported that the Orangemen and Klansmen held a joint meeting and parade in Lincoln, Maine in 1924.[84] English-Canadians living in the U.S. also supported the Klan's anti-Franco-American, anti-Catholic aims.[85]

Padon was perhaps not the only Klan member who questioned the wisdom of "knocking white men" who were also Catholics. The *Chicago Herald* reported that Edward Young Clarke suggested that the Klan modify its anti-Catholic stance. According to the *Herald*, Clarke had proposed an "extension of Klan membership to all Caucasian races" and advocated repealing the provision "which debars members of the Catholic faith from membership." The alleged intention of this change was to make "white supremacy the principal object of the order."[86]

Clarke denied making any such overtures toward Catholics reiterating that "it is impossible for Catholic, Jew, negro or foreign born to ever become members of our organization." He did, however, approve of plans to expand the Klan outside of the U.S. but only to "the Protestant white men of the world," in order to uphold "the supremacy of the white race throughout the world."

The story that Clarke had gone soft on Catholics was a prelude to his departure from the Klan. One month after the *Herald* article appeared, Clarke resigned, this time for good. The statement announcing Clarke's departure referred to fiscal matters noting that Clarke "no longer derives one cent of revenue from the order."[87]

Clarke's ouster was one gambit in an internal power struggle that saw Simmons paid off, and Clarke and Tyler pushed aside, as a Texan dentist called Hiram Wesley Evans seized control of the Klan. But the Klan knew how to ease Clarke's way out the door by spreading the claim that he favored opening the order to Catholics. It was a Klan newspaper that reprinted the story from the *Chicago Herald* reporting Clarke's alleged attempts to court Catholics, leaving Clarke to deny it. Clarke and Tyler had taught the Klan their PR tactics. But the students had become the masters.

Just Because They Were Catholics?

Some observers claim that the New England Klan did not target Franco-Americans as such but that they were merely incidental targets of the Klan's anti-Catholicism.[88] Franco-Americans were targets not only as Catholics but also because of the perceived dangers posed by the proximity of their Québec homeland. Klan sources also denounced Franco-Americans for alleged disloyalty to the Stars and Stripes during the First World War.

In 1927, a "Klan-sympathetic" newspaper based in Washington, D.C. noted the "hundreds of thousands of French Canadians" in the New England mill towns "separated from their compatriots on the St. Lawrence by a belt of Protestants." The paper feared that if Catholics were to overrun this Protestant "belt," the "French Romanists in Canada and the United States" would unite across the border because they were more loyal to the Pope than "to the governments under which they reside."[89] The article revives late 19th century concerns about alleged efforts to unite the French-speakers across the border.

Klan sources also alleged that Catholic immigration officials were conspiring to bring illegal immigrants across the Québec/New England border. They portray this border region as a vulnerable underbelly, easily exploited by allegedly criminal or subversive Roman Catholics. "Rome is controlling immigration on this continent wherever it can," a Klan newspaper declared. "Especially is it trying to govern the flow of aliens into the United States."[90] Allegations of the smuggling of illegal, Catholic immigrants gave the Klan a motive to hold in suspicion anyone entering New England from Québec.

Klan leader Simmons suggested another reason why Franco-Americans drew fire from the order: he believes they were pro-German during the World War. The French-Canadians in the U.S. joined German-Americans, "Jewish Bolsheviks" and "Sinn-Feiners" on Simmons's list of groups he says were disloyal to the U.S. cause during the war.[91] In *The Klan Unmasked*, Simmons writes,

> The French-Canadian immigrants among us number, with their children, nearly half a million. During the war they were, strange as it may seem, anti-French. The French Canadian population is completely dominated,

politically, socially and intellectually, by their clergy. These clericals still hate France and the French Government because the French Revolution over-threw the power of the Roman Church in France. They still belong to the ancient regime. So they naturally took the side of the ancient regime, the German side. Among us, they were largely passive. In Canada they actively opposed every war activity of their government from start to finish of the war.[92]

Simmons believed that Franco-Americans were neither more nor less loyal than other "foreigners." The phenomenon of dual loyalties is thought by Simmons to infect all "foreigners" at least potentially. But he accuses only four nationalities with actual and not merely potential disloyalty during the war and Franco-Americans were among those four.

The founder of the Second Klan's comments about Franco-American conduct during the war combine well-worn tropes with misunderstandings. Simmons confused *Canadien* attitudes toward the war with those of the Franco-Americans. The two French-speaking groups had different responses to the World War. Québec's opposition was not to the war itself but to the draft. Many *Canadiens* objected to being forced by law to fight in what they regarded as a war for the British Empire. Their sentiment was not anti-French but, if anything, anti-British.[93]

Far from remaining "largely passive" on the U.S. side of the border, as Simmons alleges, the Franco-Americans served in the war with enthusiasm and supported the war effort at home. Franco-Americans looked upon the war as a way to prove themselves true to their motto: *"Loyal But French."* Some scholars see the differing attitudes toward the war as the beginning of the end of the transnational unity of French-speakers across the border, and the emergence of a uniquely Franco-American identity.[94] Anecdotally, both of my grandfathers volunteered during the First World War and two of my great-uncles served overseas in that conflict. A 1927 book celebrating the 50th anniversary of Brunswick's Saint John's parish contains a page lauding Franco-American parishioners who served in the Great War.[95]

Franco-Americans were also part of an urban working class that Simmons had written off. For Simmons, the rural American was the true American while urbanism was like a virus infecting the United States.[96] Simmons divides the urban working class into skilled and unskilled workers. The skilled group, he believes, consists mainly of northern Europeans: British, Irish, Germans, and Scandinavians. The unskilled group consists of "Italians, Negroes, Slavs, Jews, French-Canadians, and thirty-odd other elements from the south and east of Europe and from Asia," writes Simmons.[97] Here, Simmons groups the French-Canadians in the U.S. with non-whites and the immigrants from eastern and southern Europe, a decidedly inferior crop, in Klan ideology.

Simmons also makes much in his book of the falling birthrate among the Anglo-Protestant population in contrast to the Catholic foreigners. "Fourteen children," Simmons notes, "is not an uncommon number at all for an Italian or French-Canadian couple to add to the citizenship of our country."[98] Speaking in Oklahoma, Simmons used New England's Franco-Americans as an exemplar of the "problem" posed by immigration. Franco-Americans, said Simmons, "speak the French language, support parochial schools and breed like rabbits."[99]

If the New England Klansmen paid attention to the statements of their order's founder, then they had reason to single out Franco-Americans for acts of terrorism not only because of their Catholicism but for other reasons as well.

Klan-related Violence in New England

The New England Klan did not confine itself to occasional denunciations. The Klan took direct action against Franco-Americans. It aimed its fury against what we now call soft targets. Historian C. Stewart Doty summarized the Klan's anti-Franco-American activities in the region:

> Throughout New England, rallies with thousands of hooded participants and cross-burnings were common in cities and towns, big and small. In Maine, Franco-American loggers of the Industrial Workers of the World (IWW) turned back forty hooded Klansmen from Greenville in zero temperatures of February 1924. In Fairfield, Maine, on 1 July 1924, Ku Klux Klan forces and Franco-Americans battled each other with

rocks and clubs before a fiery cross was torn down. In September 1924 Franco-Americans defended Biddeford from the Ku Klux Klan storming the bridge from Saco....In September 1924 nearly one hundred people were injured by stones and buckshot in Klan versus anti-Klan clashes in Lancaster, Spencer, and Haverhill, Massachusetts....In October 1924 stoning and destruction of cars ended a Klan rally in nearby Worcester. The year 1925 saw similar outbreaks at Northbridge and Dedham. In Rhode Island, Lucien Sansouci, a reporter for La Tribune of Woonsocket, claimed to be branded by Klansmen after he was caught observing one of their rallies in 1924. Large Rhode Island Klan rallies in such towns as Rhodes-on-Pawtuxet, Greenville, and East Greenwich caused the Providence News to warn – in French: "Le Ku Klux Klan declare la guerre aux candidats catholiques. Il se ligue avec le parti républicain. Ce qu'il importe de faire." ["The Ku Klux Klan declares war on Catholic candidates. It is in league with the Republican Party. It knows what it has to do."] Southeastern New Hampshire had a similarly large Klan movement, strong enough to make believable a hoax that the Klan had captured and branded a Rochester man....Older Franco-Americans...remember, as children, being hidden under beds and in closets and behind locked doors in the darkened houses of the petits Canadas of the Northeast.[100]

Doty's account is somewhat dramatized. For example, the Klan did not "storm" the bridge at Saco. The Klan had a permit to march in Saco and threatened to parade into predominantly Franco-American Biddeford as well, crossing the bridge that separates the two towns. Speaking through the press, the Franco-American mayor of Biddeford warned the Klan against crossing the bridge into his city. Expecting that the Klansmen would attempt to march into Biddeford without permission, the mayor installed his police and fire departments at the bridge to block the Klan's egress. A crowd gathered, and a tense stand-off occurred. A policeman drew his weapon, but no shots were fired, and no one was injured. The Klan did not cross the bridge but fighting broke out here and there throughout the night. The Klan's threat to march into Biddeford was a deliberate provocation, but, as elsewhere in New England, Franco-Americans refused to be intimidated.[101]

There were other incidents that Doty's summary omits. The Klan detonated a bomb in 1924 in the heavily Franco-American town of Lewiston to celebrate the order's perceived victory in the Republican gubernatorial primaries. The Klan detonated the bomb by night to draw attention to a burning cross on a high point overlooking the town. When the Klan-supported candidate won the general election, "at least a dozen bombs exploded" in surrounding towns.[102]

Tensions in the small town of Dexter, Maine originated in an incident involving a bank clerk who had attended a KKK meeting. The confrontation between Klan and anti-Klan residents drew the attention of the *New York World*, which defended the town's "French citizens." The paper claimed that Dexter's Franco-Americans formed "one armed camp; the members of the Klan another." This was not journalistic hyperbole. Klan members had drawn their guns on hecklers who had harassed and thrown rocks at them.[103]

Klan and counter-Klan violence flared especially in Massachusetts. In the town of Leominster, the KKK burned the Franco-American parish school at Saint Cecilia Church. Receiving a note that the Klan had targeted Saint Bernard's Church in nearby Fitchburg, the Franco-American parishioners formed a "human shield" around the church by night to prevent a Klan attack.[104] The Klan were suspects in church fires in the Massachusetts community of Shirley and the Dorchester section of Boston.[105]

As Doty notes, Massachusetts was the scene of riots where anti-Klan forces closed ranks to battle the Kluxers with *ad hoc* weapons. In some cases, the Klansmen were armed with more than sticks and rocks, and gunshot wounds were inflicted, with the Klansmen as victims in some cases. Belying their reputation for docility, the Franco-American newspaper *Le Citoyen* editorialized, "[The Klan] may be able to thrive in the South where colored folks are afraid of the whites, but in this section of the country they are going to have casualties....These fanatics...should first arrange with the undertaker for a decent burial, for, believe us, they are going to get all that's coming to them."[106]

Richard discovered that anti-Klan resistance in the Bay State included a Franco-American counter-Klan group called *Les Vigilants*, the aim of which was to ensure that *Le Citoyen's* admonitions were not idle talk. Formed in Haverhill, Massachusetts in the strongly Franco-American Merrimack Valley region, the group also called itself the P.P.P.: *Progrès, Protestation, Punition* [Progress, Protest, Punishment]. Richard found that Catholics of any ethnicity, Jews, and African-

Americans were encouraged to join this counter-Klan. The P.P.P. wore robes and hoods in mockery of Klan regalia.[107]

Not all opposition to the Klan was in the streets. Despite close ties between Klan chapters and Protestant clergy, some men of the cloth denounced the Klan including Episcopalian, Baptist, and Methodist clergy, while the Boston City Council passed an anti-Klan resolution.[108] The Klan's bigotry offended the independent spirit of Vermonters in particular, and the Green Mountain State's newspapers battered the Klan in their columns.[109] Calls for boycotts against the businesses of known Klan members was a common, non-violent anti-Klan activity.

Samuel Gompers, head of the AFL, added his voice to the anti-Klan chorus. The AFL, meeting in Denver in June 1921, passed a resolution condemning the Klan for its "outrageous crimes" and its tendency to "create discord among the working people of the country." The resolution labeled the Klan as "un-American" and as opposed to the Constitution. A Franco-American named James Legassie [Lagacé] from strongly Franco-American Berlin, New Hampshire, offered this resolution to the AFL.[110]

Despite opposition, the Klan battled in the halls of the legislatures as well as in the streets. In Maine, a Klan-supported measure changed the city charter of Portland to diminish the political power of Irish-Catholic and Jewish neighborhoods.[111] The Klan also clashed with the state's Catholic Church over a measure to enforce the reading of the King James Bible in schools.[112]

The Klan claimed a political victory when Republican Ralph Owen Brewster won Maine's gubernatorial election in 1924. Although Brewster denied he was a Klan member, the hooded order believed that the Governor was a sympathizer. Franco-Americans were sure of it. The French-language newspaper *La Justice* of Biddeford, urging newly-enfranchised Franco-American women to vote in the election, described Brewster as "the man the K.K.K. has chosen."[113] The Indianapolis Klan newspaper, the *Fiery Cross*, applauded Brewster's victory with a banner headline across its front page with the sub-heading "Candidate Who is Backed By Klansmen Wins." The paper portrayed the election as "a fight between the foreign element...and those who stood four-square for American principles and ideals." Brewster's

Democratic opponent was said to have wooed Maine's "foreigners and Roman Catholics."[114]

In the then solid South, reliably Democrat in the 1920s, the Klan tended to work through the Democratic Party. In Northeastern cities where large contingents of Democrats were working-class Catholics, Republicans became natural allies of the Klan. In States such as Indiana, Nebraska, and Oregon, the KKK was often associated with the GOP and the New England Klan leaned Republican.[115] But the Klan was happy to exploit either major political party. Intolerance was bipartisan.[116]

Where it held political influence, enforcing English as the only language of instruction in schools was a signature legislative issue for the Klan. Nationwide, bilingual schools came under attack during the post-World War I Nativist surge. Several states passed legislation to prohibit instruction in any language other than English. A 1919 Nebraska law called the Simian Act banned any language other than English as the language of instruction in any school public or private.[117] Foreign-language classes were allowed only to students who had passed the 8th grade. A 1922 Oregon statute compelled children from age eight to sixteen to attend public school where English was the language of instruction.[118] The U.S. Supreme Court overturned both state laws.

Maine passed legislation imposing English as the sole language of instruction in public schools in April 1919. The Maine law was not dependent on Klan support, despite Franco-American lore to that effect. The Klan had not yet come to New England in early 1919. At that point, it was a small band barely visible outside the South. The Maine law did not go to the extremes the Supreme Court later over-ruled. It neither compelled students to attend public school nor barred non-English languages in private schools. French/English bilingual parochial schools in the Franco-American mill towns were untouched by the law. However, in the Acadian-identified regions in the Northern parts of the state, in communities where French was the language of the majority of the population, French-speaking nuns often served as teachers in public schools.[119]

The Maine law forbidding instruction in French in public schools caused considerable suffering for schoolchildren. Children were punished and humiliated for speaking so much as a few words of French even on the playground. The image of "the silent playground," the title of an essay by Ross and Judy Paradis, refers to schoolchildren who played games in complete silence. They did not know the words associated with their games in English and would be punished if they used the French terms. Ross and Judy Paradis show that prior to the 1919 legislation, the schools had done an effective job of teaching English to French-speaking children. Bilingual education had worked.[120]

The 1919 English-only legislation had an effect diametrically opposed to its intention. Since children were forced to speak English, they resisted the language and spoke it as little as possible. Children who were bewildered by classes in school taught in an incomprehensible tongue were discouraged from taking an interest in education. Rather than "Americanizing" schoolchildren, it discouraged them from speaking English and from pursuing formal education.

The law was not enforced strictly in all schools. But when I have spoken to older Franco-American Mainers who remembered the English-only law, the bitterness remains. At a Franco-American conference, a woman told the story of a schoolgirl who was severely ill. She did not know how to ask for help in English and didn't dare request it in French. A bilingual teacher took the girl into the bathroom, then into a stall, and shut the door and only with difficulty coaxed the sick girl, in a whisper, to reveal her symptoms in French. Teachers, as well as students, faced censure if they were caught speaking French on school grounds. The symbolism couldn't be clearer: French in Maine was to be whispered, behind closed doors. The State repealed the legislation in 1969, long after the damage was done.

In Rhode Island a law with a similar intent, the Peck Act (1922), named for Providence Republican Frederick Peck, placed parochial schools under state rather than local control. This law aimed to impose statewide standards on parochial schools that would effectively mandate English as the language of instruction.[121] But by 1922, the Klan was a force in the region. Three Franco-American Rhode Island legislators who tried to amend the law received threatening missives signed "KKK."[122]

The Klan in Brunswick

As it brought its message to other New England communities, Klan Inc. also marketed its wares in Brunswick. The Klan established itself in nearby Orr's Island by November 1923. An item that month in the *Brunswick Record* reports, "The Ku Klux Klan have changed their lodge night meetings from Saturday to Friday night. No one knows how many have joined the order here but from the attendance at the meetings it would seem that sixty-five percent of the adult residents are affiliated with the Klan."[123] The 65 percent figure, and the fact that there were weekly Klan meetings, indicates that the order was well-ensconced in the area. The Brunswick newspaper covered the 1920s Klan on the page where it reported the activities of fraternal and civic organizations.

The following month, the same newspaper covered a large meeting held at Brunswick Town Hall featuring the region's chief Klan spokesman. "Ku Klux Klan Holds Meeting in Brunswick" read the headline, "Town Hall Comfortably Filled to Hear F. Eugene Farnsworth Wednesday Night."

> A large audience of both men and women, estimated at about 800 all told, attended the meeting held in Town Hall last evening in the interests of the Ku Klux Klan to hear F. Eugene Farnsworth speak on relations of Americanism and the Klan. Mr. Farnsworth, who is one of the leading Klansmen of the state proved to be a very fine speaker and impressed his audience greatly with some of his arguments. He gave an outline of the reasons for the Klan and what had already been accomplished and told of plans for the future....The meeting was very orderly and everyone was admitted.[124]

The population of Brunswick was 7,261 in 1920. If the estimate of 800 attendees at Farnsworth's talk is reasonably accurate, then a sizeable proportion of the town's adults were at least open to considering Farnsworth's "Americanism," although it is unknown how many in the audience came from surrounding areas.

Events of the decade before Farnsworth's appearance in Brunswick prepared fertile soil for the Klan leader's message. When the town elected Pierre Morin Selectman in 1912, a foreign-born, Franco-American Catholic exercised executive political power over

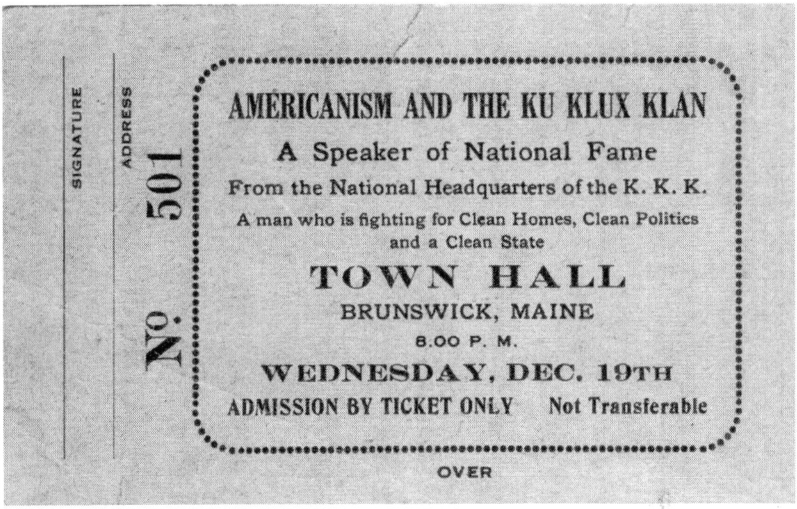

SIGNATURE

ADDRESS

Nᵒ 501

AMERICANISM AND THE KU KLUX KLAN

A Speaker of National Fame

From the National Headquarters of the K. K. K.

A man who is fighting for Clean Homes, Clean Politics and a Clean State

TOWN HALL

BRUNSWICK, MAINE

8.00 P. M.

WEDNESDAY, DEC. 19TH

ADMISSION BY TICKET ONLY   Not Transferable

OVER

FIGURE 14: Ticket for Klan meeting at Town Hall, Brunswick, December 19, 1923. (Pejepscot Historical Society)

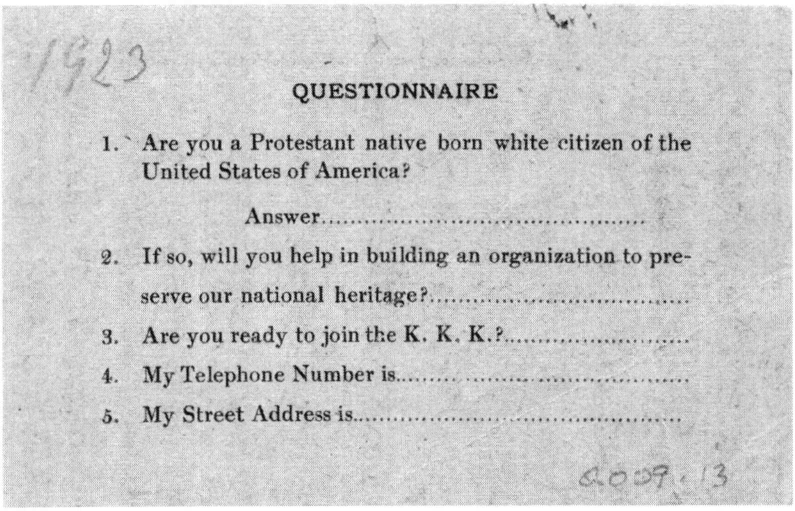

1923

QUESTIONNAIRE

1. Are you a Protestant native born white citizen of the United States of America?

   Answer...

2. If so, will you help in building an organization to preserve our national heritage?...........................

3. Are you ready to join the K. K. K.?.......................

4. My Telephone Number is..................................

5. My Street Address is.....................................

2009.13

FIGURE 15: Promotional copy on back of Klan ticket (December 1923). (Pejepscot Historical Society)

"100 percent Americans" for the first time in Brunswick's history. This was an alarming notion to anyone inclined toward Klannish views. In 1915, Franco-American Catholic Israel Racine, son of Civil War veteran Philibert, was elected Selectman by "one of the largest votes ever received" for the office to that date.[125] This election proved that Morin was no fluke. French-speaking Catholics had arrived as a political force in the town. When Farnsworth came to Brunswick in the early 1920s, assailing Catholic political power, the message resonated with a segment of the area's Protestants.

Two months after Farnsworth's speech in Brunswick, the *Record* reports again on the active Klan chapter in Orr's Island. This notice shows that the classic Klan activity – cross-burning – was on the agenda in the Brunswick area as in other parts of New England:

> The Ladies' Circle of the M. E. [Methodist Episcopal] church held a sociable and supper at the vestry, Friday night, which was well patronized by island people. The Ku Klux Klan attended the supper in a body. After the supper was served the ladies carried a large pot of coffee and dozens of doughnuts to the Klux lodge room and donated them to the Klan for a late Lunch.
>
> The Ku Klux Klan had an illuminated cross burning near the Red Men's hall last Friday night which could be seen from almost any point on the island. Several of the clansmen stood at the foot of the cross while it was burning and sang "Onward, Christian Soldiers," accompanied by a cornet which was being played in the hall. The music was loudly applauded by a large number of people who were in attendance at the supper at the M. E. vestry.[126]

The Methodist Episcopal church on Orr's Island still stands. When I visited the site of these events in 2014, an Orr's Island resident informed me that the Klan burned a cross directly opposite the home of one of the island's only Catholic families.

An item in the September 24, 1925 edition of the *Brunswick Record* reveals the scope of Klan activities in the Brunswick area. "Ku Klux Klan Holds Field Day At Bath," reads the headline, "Has Big Attendance – Many Visitors Present From Various Parts of Maine And Massachusetts." The Paper notes that "sentries" wearing their Klan robes and masks guided "motoring Klansmen and Klanswomen to the field." While clams, corn, and frankfurters were served, "interesting talks were delivered," notes the *Record*. At night, the Klansmen and Klanswomen marched through "the central business district" of Bath. While most of the marchers wore their hoods, men carrying "an immense American flag" went unmasked. Reverend Eugene V. Allen of Rockland, "a former chaplain of the Maine state prison," spoke at the event. After a fireworks display, the "closing ceremony" of the event including a cross-burning. The cross blazed for more than an hour.

The article states that the local Klan took its marching orders from "general headquarters in Atlanta, Ga." Would the forbears of the 1920s New England Klansmen, who fought a war with the South that destroyed Atlanta, be surprised to find their sons and grandsons taking orders from the Georgia capital?

A month before the Klan field day in Bath, an estimated 35,000 Klansmen marched in Washington, D.C.[127] It was the largest KKK rally ever held and the crest of the wave of the Second Klan. Not long after the rally in the U.S. capital, the Klan began to unravel from self-inflicted wounds. In 1922, the FBI began to investigate the Klan in earnest at the behest of Louisiana Governor John Parker. The Bureau found that the Klan all but controlled the state. The FBI's efforts would lead to the arrest of Edward Young Clarke in 1924 for violation of the Mann Act, an anti-Prostitution measure.[128]

In 1925, the Grand Dragon of the powerful Indiana KKK, David C. Stephenson, was convicted in the kidnapping, brutal assault, and rape of 29-year-old Madge Oberholtzer, who ran a state literacy program. Oberholtzer later died from ingesting poison after naming Stephenson as her assailant. The Grand Dragon was sentenced to life in prison. Stephenson thought that the Klan-controlled governor, Republican Ed Jackson, would pardon him. When the governor did no such thing, Stephenson turned state's evidence, opened his books, and told all. There followed the prosecution of Klan-backed politicians and officials on corruption charges.[129]

These scandals, exposing the brutality, cynicism, and hypocrisy of Klan leaders, discouraged the Klansmen and Klanswomen in the field and dampened recruiting efforts. Nationwide, Klan numbers declined from millions to just 37,000 by the end of the 1920s.[130] In Maine, the Klan still claimed 61,136 members in 1926; membership fell to 226 by

1930.[131] The Klan limped along, trying on an anti-Communist message. In 1944, the Internal Revenue Service came calling in search of nearly $700,000 in back taxes from the Klan Inc.'s heyday. As a corporation, the Second Klan folded quietly.[132]

How much of a chilling effect the Klan had on Brunswick's Franco-American community during its 1920s prime is open to question. The Klan does not seem to have had much of an effect on its public activities. For instance, in 1930, after the rise and fall of the Klan in Maine, the *Brunswick Record* reported on a large parade for Saint-Jean Baptiste Day celebrated with much fanfare by the town's Franco-Americans.[133] Large and very public Franco-American weddings and other events seem to have continued as they had before the Klan's coming and going. Whether the Brunswick-area Klan ever went beyond singing songs and eating doughnuts is unclear.

The era of the New England Klan left its scars nonetheless. According to Richard, Josephine La Brecque, a Franco-American from Westbrook, Maine remembered that, "her mother would keep her indoors when she learned the Klan planned to parade in their community." Richard also writes,

> The Ursuline sisters recorded their fear of being burned out of their Waterville convent by the KKK. Candide Desrosiers recalled seeing Klan members riding on horseback, dressed in their white robes, when she was a young child in Patten. Her mother, aware of the Klan's dislike of Catholics, feared they had come to burn down their home; Desrosiers's mother would draw the shades, bless the windows with holy water, and pray the rosary with her five young children, all of whom she kept indoors while the Klan paraded.[134]

Frances Emmons Carver witnessed Vermont Klansmen burning a cross in the cemetery of Saint Augustine Catholic Church in Montpelier, Vermont as a ten-year-old girl. Many years later she wrote,

> One night I reached to draw the curtain before retiring and was terrorized by a massive cross in raging flames and hooded maniacs prancing around it....It was many years before the nightmares ceased; I was a Catholic and in my childish mind I relived the horror and felt sure they were coming after me....Fifty five years have not erased the agony of that night nor its aftermath.[135]

According to some interpretations, the 1920s Klan was little more than a fraternal organization comparable to the Rotary, the Elks, and other lodges that were popular in the 20th century.[136] As regards the New England Klan, the comparison would be apt if the Rotary Club were burning schools and churches, detonating bombs, engaging in street brawls, lobbying for ethnocentric laws, and proclaiming a message of Nativism and Anglo-Protestant supremacism. The Second Klan borrowed the methods of fraternal orders, familiar to Simmons, just as it borrowed the symbolism of the 19th century Klan. But in New England, it was a Nativist hate group, albeit a short-lived and inept one.

The ongoing debate about the legacy of the Confederacy in the South; the continuing, racially-charged discussions about the U.S.'s long Southwestern border; the internment of Japanese-Americans during World War II; these are well-known, vetted regional narratives. New Englanders might see themselves as immune to such conflicts or even as morally superior to regions such as the Deep South with long and well-known histories of racial conflict.

Referencing the work of Matthew Fry Jacobson, historian Thomas Pegram holds that "the behavior and associations of immigrants in America sometimes influenced racial status in such a way as to establish local variations of racial categorization."[137] He cites Italians in Louisiana who worked and associated with African-Americans and therefore occupied a social position, in the eyes of the white-identified native-born, closer to black than white. Although European immigrants, as well as Franco-Americans, had legal status as "free born whites," local, popular perceptions of race did not necessarily adhere to these strictures. Franco-Americans in New England are a classic example of these "local variations of racial categorization." As Roman Catholics who spoke a foreign language, who were perceived widely as a mixed-race people, they were not classed among the Klan's "real white folks."

The history of bigotry against white-identified minorities is eclipsed by more egregious racial injustices with more immediate implications in contemporary political discourse. Today, some descendants of yesterday's white-identified KKK targets incline toward

Klannish views themselves. But the fact that New England's Franco-Americans were white-identified, did not make the fear experienced by the families of Josephine La Brecque and Candide Desrosiers any less real.

SECTION FOUR

TENACITY
AND MODERNITY

CHAPTER FIFTEEN

TEXTILES GO SOUTH

Father Hamon imagined a world of the late 20th century, one hundred years after his day, in which the *Canadiens* of New England and Québec would meet at the border. He reasoned that New Englanders would not close their border to Québec because they would always need laborers from across the frontier. The Franco-American population would continue to increase, thought Fr. Hamon, until it filled New England. Hamon's scenario implies that the textile industry, and the other industries that employed Franco-Americans, would continue to thrive in the region.[1]

However, by the mid-20th century the textile mills that attracted workers from Québec to the region, and that once led the nation's manufacturing, were no longer there. Today, defunct mills, gigantic brick hulks, mark the U.S.'s northeastern landscape. Some mills are repurposed as retail space, as condos, or as offices. Others are empty and silent. They're like the fossils of dinosaurs, the remnants of a mass extinction event. Without the manufacturing jobs, the Little Canadas lost their economic *raison d'être*. The network of institutions that developed to support these French Quarters began to contract. The Little Canadas slowly shriveled.

The textile industry had a gradual decline in the region as the U.S. South became a center not only of cotton agriculture but of cotton manufacturing as well. In 1850, Southern mills consumed one bale of cotton for every five shipped to New England.[2] By the 1880s, the South was competing with New England in earnest and by the first years of the 20th century Northern mills felt the heat.[3] Records from the Whitin Machine Works, of Whitinsville, Rhode Island, one of the leading suppliers of machinery for textile mills, demonstrate the rapid tooling of the Southern mills in the first years of the 20th century. The Whitin company registered 60 sales of machinery of $50,000 or more to Southern mills between 1888 and 1906 and all but three of these orders came from North Carolina, South Carolina, and Georgia. These sales peaked during the years between 1903 and 1905. In 1903, the Whitin company made nine sales of machinery to southern mills, five of which exceeded $100,000, while one sale exceeded $150,000.[4]

By the end of the first decade of the 20th century, the U.S. South was the third largest cotton textile producing region in the world, topped only by the U.K. and the Northern United States.[5] In 1923, the number of spindles nationwide began to decline.[6] Two years later, the South had more spindles turning than the North. By 1965, spindles in Southern mills outnumbered those of the North twenty-four to one.[7]

The center of gravity of the textile industry moved south because of labor costs.[8] As wages rose in New England, and working conditions improved, the region's textile workers became victims of their success. They were priced out of the market. But progress for the workers came at a price that they continued to pay even as the mills went south. The Lawrence textile strike in 1912 and a general strike in 1934 battered the New England mills, Labor and Management alike.[9] In Woonsocket, the 1934 strike saw 10,000 workers battling the National Guard resulting in at least one fatality and fifteen wounded.[10] A 1922 strike in the Amoskeag mills devastated Manchester, built around the textile industry. An increase in working hours, coupled with a massive 20 percent cut in wages, precipitated the strike. Median annual earnings of Amoskeag employees fell from $805 per year in 1923 to $577 by 1934.[11]

Organized Labor was less entrenched in the South, and there were fewer local government regulations. While Massachusetts had laws limiting the hours of labor, at least for women and children, dating back to the 1870s the South promised less of such government "inter-ference" with fewer labor agitations.[12] Besides, boasted the promoters of Spartanburg, South Carolina, the South's labor was "of purest Anglo-Saxon stock."[13]

Technological changes contributed to the move southward. First came the steam mill, adopted in New England after 1850. Then came the electric mill in the late 19th century. These innovations meant that no Charles, or Merrimack, or Androscoggin River was required to power a mill.[14] Mills became portable and down they went, below the Mason-Dixon line. Increased automation and the standardization of technology meant that mills became off-the-shelf facilities that could appear anywhere, with little skilled labor required. Inside the mills, the new Southern shops used the latest machinery.[15]

The move of the textile industry to the South was not Dixie's revenge for Appomattox. Many of the same New England firms based in Nashua, New Hampshire or Lawrence or Lowell, Massachusetts, owned and operated southern mills.[16] Other shrewd northern invest-ors leaped on the southern bandwagon.[17] The move south allowed these Northerners to turn the calendar back to industry labor stan-dards of a previous era, including extensive use of child labor.[18]

Between 1922 and 1933, ninety-three Massachusetts cotton mills were shuttered.[19] Seventeen of these failed mills were in the Connecticut Valley region and closed in the few years between 1929 and 1933. These operations employed nearly 58 percent of the area's industrial workers. By 1933, a quarter of the population of the Connecticut Valley town of Chicopee was on relief.[20] In Maine, Lewiston's Franco-American population declined by 8.6 percent between January 1927 and January 1929.[21] Manchester's population declined by more than 13 percent during the 1920s.[22] In 1930, Thomas McMahon, President of the United Textile Workers, said, "There is perhaps more destitution and misery and degradation in the mill towns of New England today...than anywhere else in the United States."[23]

When the great Amoskeag, once known as the largest textile mill in the world, closed its doors in 1934, the closing credits began to roll for the New England cotton industry. In old Lowell, once the standard bearer of mill towns, the Boott and Merrimack mills sputtered along, after a brief resurgence of the textile industry during and immediately following the Second World War. But these hold-outs expired in the 1950s.[24] The early 1950s represented a "peak of mill closings" and by 1954 one-half of the jobs in the New England textile mills had evaporated.[25] In Fall River, the vaunted "third largest French speaking city in America," the last of the cotton mills closed in 1965.[26]

The Decline and Fall of the Cabot Mill

The latter-day history of Brunswick's Cabot mill followed the pattern of the decline of the industry elsewhere in the region. Francis Cabot and Benjamin Greene, the two-headed beast that had turned the mill into a profitable business, departed the stage in the 1890s. Several local managers and more than one ownership group would succeed them.

In 1890, Benjamin Greene retired as Agent, passing away in 1904.[27] Francis Cabot went blind as of Thanksgiving Day 1897 and retired thereafter. He survived Greene by one year. The 1900 U.S. Federal Census, the last to record his whereabouts, finds Cabot and family in the (now) upscale community of Cohasset, to the south of Boston, where the blind man could enjoy the cool sea breezes in the coastal town.[28] Cohasset was most likely a summer residence since his address on his death certificate reads "Heath Street, Brookline," his long-time abode.[29] Cabot genealogist Briggs suggests that the passages from Shakespeare, the Bible, the philosophers, and the poets that Cabot had committed to memory aboard a New Bedford whaler in his youth fed his intellect in his final, sightless years.[30]

Francis Cabot's son, Frederick Pickering Cabot, sat on the Board of Directors of Brunswick's Cabot Manufacturing Company following his father's retirement. He represented the third generation of Cabots to do so. Frederick lent his name and the prestige of his family to the Board, but this Cabot's game was not textiles but the Law. After a career as a corporate attorney, he was appointed a judge and became a reformer in the field of juvenile justice.[31]

FIGURE 16: Francis Cabot (1825-1905) c. 1900.

Russell W. Eaton took over from Greene as resident Agent of the Cabot Company. Unlike Greene, Eaton was a Mainer by birth. Born in Readfield on November 24, 1855, he studied engineering at Maine State College, later called the University of Maine, Orono. He served as a mill engineer in Hyde Park, Massachusetts and Providence, Rhode Island. He then held the position of assistant engineer for the Ponema Mills of Taftville, Connecticut. In 1885, he moved to Montréal where he managed the Merchants' Manufacturing Company before returning to Maine to take the position at the Cabot mill. Like Greene before him, he was a director as well as Agent of the Cabot Company.[32]

Eaton's regime inaugurated major changes in Brunswick. The Cabot Company built a new, four-story brick mill completed in 1892.[33] This building still stands. A land development company established a new neighborhood across the river in the town of Topsham, called Topsham Heights, providing housing for the Franco-American workers.[34] The John A. Roebling's Sons Company, the same firm that constructed New York's Brooklyn Bridge, built a pedestrian walkway across the river enabling the workers living in Topsham to reach their jobs at the mill.[35] The Topsham Franco-Americans formed a social and economic unit with those across the bridge in Brunswick.

Eaton also led a project to bring a proper sewer system to Brunswick. The town's Pejepscot Historical Society preserves a handbill advertising a "Sewer Meeting" on July 3, 1893, enumerating "a dozen facts about sewers in Brunswick." This advertisement states that the proposed sewer project would cost less than $90,000 and that the Cabot Company would pay one-sixth of the costs. Fact number 11 declares "sewers are cheaper than typhoid fever." At the bottom of the handbill is a note written in pencil by an anonymous hand recording that the sewer proposal met defeat by six votes, "French Canadians voting against it."[36]

Why would they vote against it? The Maine Bureau of Labor and Industrial Statistics reports that in 1893 the Cabot Company spent $625 on "sanitary improvements" relating to "water-closets, sinks and drainage."[37] These improvements were most likely in the mill itself rather than in the tenements, but the Cabot Company appears to have moved on its own to make its property more livable. An 1895 article in the local paper states that Eaton had indeed taken the initiative "to sewer" at least some of his tenements on the company's dime.[38] If the Cabot Company were making these improvements at its own expense, why should the workers vote to pay for them out of their tax dollars?

On a subsequent attempt, in April 1894, the town approved a general plan to build a modern sewerage infrastructure.[39] Advocates apparently convinced enough of the Franco-American voters to support the plan. The local newspaper notes that during at least one debate on the sewer, an interpreter was on hand at the town meeting to translate the proceedings into French for voters who required it. The paper notes that there was "quite a French vote."[40] By 1896, contractors brought the new sewer system to the downtown area, including the French Quarter with a growing number of privately-owned

Franco-American residences. Eaton was on the town committee that oversaw the construction of the new infrastructure.[41]

In 1897, Manley Uriel Adams, a resident of Newton, Massachusetts, took over as Treasurer of the Cabot Company after Francis Cabot's retirement. Adams had a name worthy of a Boston Brahmin, but he was a self-made man. Adams was born in Spencer, Massachusetts on September 9, 1845, the son of a farmer, Francis, and his wife, Almeria. He left home before age 14 and found his way to Smithfield, Rhode Island. He served as a Private in the 9th Regiment, Rhode Island Infantry, Company D in the Civil War. After his military service, in 1864 he became a machinist in Lewiston, Maine, very likely working for one of the textile mills in that town.[42]

Adams worked for the mothership of the New England textile industry, the Boston Manufacturing Company at Waltham. He also worked at the Potomska Mills of New Bedford. When Francis Cabot went blind, Adams took over his position as Treasurer not only for the Brunswick operation but for Cabot's entire portfolio of mills, including the Fisher and the Winthrop Mills companies. Adams continued to do business out of offices at 70 Kilby Street, Boston where the Cabot Manufacturing Company had been headquartered for almost twenty years.[43] Adams was also a director of the Dundee Mills of Hooksett, New Hampshire and of the Merchant's National Bank of Boston.[44]

Under the regime of Adams and Eaton, company directors organized a new firm. A real estate transaction filed on March 25, 1911, shows that the Cabot Manufacturing Company sold the mill and all its property to a new firm of the same name incorporated in Boston with its legal address at Devonshire Street.[45] This was the company's third iteration and the successor to the previous incarnations of 1853 and 1858. Frederick Pickering Cabot witnessed the sale as Justice of the Peace. The mill remained in Brunswick, but the corporate entity had moved from Maine to Massachusetts. The management and ownership did not change.

Adams died suddenly of a heart attack on February 10, 1920, and Eaton followed him into the hereafter on March 5, 1921.[46] On New Year's Day 1920, just a month before Adams's demise, the regime of Eaton and Adams ended abruptly when the uncle/nephew team of John Farwell and Nathaniel Farwell Ayer bought up the stock of the company and acquired a controlling interest. The same team operated the Nyanza Mills, Woonsocket; Farwell Mills, Lisbon, Maine; and the Farwell Bleachery of Lawrence, Massachusetts. At the time of the sale, the Cabot mill had about 70,000 spindles, and 1,600 looms.[47] Ayer took the title of Treasurer, while Farwell became President of the Company.[48]

John W. Farwell was born at Waltham, Massachusetts on April 17, 1843, the son of Nathaniel Farwell and the former Eliza Fletcher. He was an eighth generation American. His English ancestor came from Boston, England to Chelmsford, Massachusetts in 1636. Nathaniel rose from a position as a watchman at the Boston Manufacturing Company to become an owner or director of several businesses in more than one industry in Lewiston. The elder Farwell served as mayor of Lewiston as well as in the Maine state legislature. Nathaniel played his part in Maine Franco-American history as a promoter of the railroad link between Lewiston and Canada's Grand Trunk. Lewiston became one of the major Franco-American centers in the state via this railroad line.[49]

John Farwell attended Tufts College, class of 1866, but failed to graduate. He then began his career in his father's bleachery in Lewiston. He also worked in the same industry at Somersworth, New Hampshire, and in Lisbon and Lawrence. After Nathaniel Farwell's death, John took over his father's interests in the various family textile operations and was also involved in banking and insurance. And like his father, he served in local political offices, as well as in the Maine and Massachusetts legislatures. When he died on October 7, 1929, he was living in Boston.[50]

Farwell's nephew and close business associate, Nathaniel Farwell Ayer was born in Boston on June 24, 1879, the son of a physician Dr. James Bourne Ayer and Mary Eliza Farwell. Ayer attended Harvard, graduating in 1900. Immediately upon his graduation, he entered his uncle's textile-related businesses, working in the Boston offices of the Farwell cotton mills and the bleachery at Lowell. He later became President of these companies as well as Treasurer of the Nyanza Mills of Woonsocket and the Cynthia Mills of Boston. Ayer was a Director of the Boston Safe Deposit and Trust Company, the National Shawmut Bank, and the New York Life Insurance Company.

During the First World War, Ayer served as Commanding Officer of the U. S. Naval Radio School at Harvard attaining the rank of Commander. Ayer was a keen yachtsman and a member of numerous yacht clubs. He was also a member of the Harvard and University Clubs of New York City.[51]

Immediately after taking control of the Cabot mill in 1920, Farwell and Ayer brought in their man, William Worsnop, to serve as resident Agent. Before coming to Brunswick, Worsnop had worked for the Farwell Mills in nearby Lisbon and managed both mills, at least for a time.[52] Born in England on November 1, 1874, the son of Allan and Ann (Saville), Worsnop came to the U.S. as a boy. He worked in the textile mills of Woonsocket and Brattleboro, Vermont before coming to Lisbon in 1914. A biography of Worsnop published in 1928 describes him as "one of the most expert technicians in the textile industry of New England." By that year, Worsnop, Farwell, and Ayer had expanded the Cabot mill to run 90,000 spindles with 2,080 looms. It employed 850 workers.[53]

Within its first year, the new regime at the Cabot mill faced opposition from the ranks. In August 1920, Cabot mill workers, now unionized under the American Federation of Textile Operatives, went on strike. "We have not received many good things from this new company as of yet," complained the local union leader to the *Brunswick Record*.[54] The union representative also said that the employees would not return to work under Worsnop's management. Evidently, the union did not receive satisfaction on this demand since Worsnop stayed with the company until 1937, first with the title of Agent in charge of operations and then as General Manager.[55]

By 1928, the mill was dabbling in the manufacture of silk and rayon fabrics. In the early 1930s, faced with competition from the South, the Cabot mill abandoned cotton manufacturing for rayon. But Southern and Japanese competitors crowded the rayon market.[56] In the 1930s, amid the global economic crisis, the Cabot mill contracted the malaise infecting the entire New England textile industry.

In a three-part series printed in January and February of 1938, the *Brunswick Record* recounted the Cabot Company's woes.[57] The Cabot mill remained the largest employer and taxpayer in the town as it had been since the 19th century. But the mill was unprofitable as of late 1937, and the newspaper names southern competition as the cause. A new General Manager, Willard F. Staples, replaced Worsnop that year. The Cabot mill's wages were lower than elsewhere, but overhead remained high. The paper cites Fred Steele of the National Cotton Manufacturers legislative committee who claims that, on average, the differential in wages between the northern and southern mills was $6.56 per week, per employee.

Multiply that differential by the approximately 1,200 employees on the Cabot Company's payroll in 1938, each working fifty weeks per year, and the Cabot mill was spending over $393,000 more per year in payroll costs than a comparable operation in the South. Northern textile mills sought federal legislation to equalize wages across the industry to give them a chance to compete. But the hour was late for the Cabot Company. The mill cut back to 50 percent capacity in the second half of 1937. When asked what the company could do to help the workers who were laid off, an executive replied: "Nothing. They should have saved money while they were working."[58]

Sometime in the late 1930s, Ayer and his associates brought in Jacob Ziskind, a liquidator of textile mills. Ziskind's game was to assume control of languishing mills, refurbish the machinery, and sell it to textile operations in the South or overseas. He would then sell the premises of the defunct mills to a non-textile company, preserving manufacturing under a new guise in the former textile towns. Some of his successes in this line included the sale of a textile machinery/machine tool shop in Pawtucket to Pratt & Whitney. He also brought Firestone Tire & Rubber to Fall River.

Born in Lowell, Massachusetts on September 11, 1899, Ziskind was the son of David and Rose (Elkind) Ziskind. Like Francis Cabot and John Farwell before him, Ziskind didn't finish college. Leaving Boston University after his freshman year, he returned to Lowell to engage in the family scrap metal business. In 1928, he moved to Fall River where, in 1933, he formed the Crescent Corporation and began to recondition and resell textile equipment. He later opened offices in New York and Spartanburg. Ziskind also bought and operated textile mills that he succeeded in bringing back to profitability.

Although Ziskind was the grim reaper of New England textiles, he was popular with his employees. To the line workers, Ayer, with his Harvard degree, yacht, and Beacon Hill address, may have seemed a man apart. Ziskind was accessible to his employees and came down to the shop floor to speak with them. He insisted on decent wages and healthy working conditions.[59] His liquidation scheme also extended the life of the mills for a time, and that meant jobs rather than layoffs. Ziskind was a philanthropist. Upon his death in Boston on October 18, 1950, he left one-half of his substantial fortune to charity, most of it to medical research.[60]

Ziskind's appearance was not the only indication of the Cabot Company's demission. Starting in 1938 and into the early 1940s, the company began to sell its property.[61] Franco-Americans bought from the company the tenements they occupied. A November 1940 article in the *Brunswick Record* reported that these sales amounted to about $125,000. The article claims that the sales were the buyers', not the seller's idea. But county real estate records reveal that a meeting of the Cabot Company of November 1940 authorized the company to sell "parcels of land and the buildings thereon" not used for manufacturing.[62] The end was nigh.

In a deed of December 21, 1942, the Cabot Manufacturing Company sold the mill and its remaining property to Gilbert Verney of Manchester.[63] Verney operated mills in Manchester and Peterboro, New Hampshire at the time of the sale. A new firm called the Verney Mills of Brunswick came to town.[64] The Cabot Company maintained its office in Boston and its name but detached itself from the property in Brunswick after the better part of a century. Ayer remained among the major stockholders in the Cabot Company at the time of the sale. He died while vacationing in Canada on July 26, 1948 and Ziskind came into possession of the Cabot Company name and trademark.[65] After Ziskind's death the Cabot Manufacturing Company faded from history.

When the Verney Company assumed control of rayon production in Brunswick, the new owners planned to add a third shift, putting many new workers on the payroll.[66] The new owners modernized the mill's equipment and its management style, but the Verney mill's tenure in Brunswick was short-lived. At its height, in 1945, during the brief wartime resurgence of the industry, the Verney mill produced 660,000 yards of synthetic cloth per week.[67] By May of 1955, however, the mill ran into trouble from overproduction. Two hundred workers were laid off, and more pink slips were expected. The union held its breath expecting an unwelcome announcement from Management. The Verney company had endured three years of losses and the *Brunswick Record* cited a familiar cause: "wage differentials between northern and southern mills."[68]

"Many of the Verney employes [sic] have been employed at the mill for most of their working lives," observed the *Record*. "These people, on the whole, know no other occupations and would find difficulty in adapting themselves to a different kind of work. It is expected that some of these people may be absorbed by Lewiston textile mills, to which they could commute without disrupting their homes. Others may seek textile employment in other manufacturing centers of New England, or even in the south."[69]

The same article notes that by mid-century, the textile mill at Brunswick was no longer the town's largest employer. The Brunswick Naval Air Station had taken the lead in that category. The Naval Air base opened during World War II. It closed after the war but reopened in 1951 and provided employment for both military and civilian personnel.[70] It remained in town for a half-century. The Bath Iron Works, a shipyard in a neighboring town, also offered manufacturing jobs.

Brunswick was unlike towns such as Lowell and Manchester, built to serve the textile industry. It had other large institutions such as the Naval base and Bowdoin College. It had had an economy before the textile industry became a success there in the 1850s and it would continue to have one after that industry's departure a century later.

The *Brunswick Record* noted that commuting to a nearby town, in this case Lewiston, was an option for former Verney mill employees.[71] The advent of the automobile meant that workers did not need to both live and work in the same community. Research on the geography of Franco-American Maine found that, after Biddeford's mills closed, the Franco-American population did not depart immediately. Cars made it possible for the Franco-Americans to live in the old neighborhood and work at a nearby site such as the Portsmouth Naval Shipyard in Kittery, Maine.[72]

In June 1955, the Verney mill closed its doors for good.[73] The last piece of factory-made textile fabric came off the line in Brunswick and an era came to an end. Per a deed filed on November 11, 1955, the Gera Corporation of New Jersey bought the remaining real estate owned by the Verney Corporation.[74] The heap of brick Eaton built in the 1890s was repurposed in numerous ways. It served as an indoor poultry farm and as retail space.[75] Today, it houses antique stores.

The decline of the town's textile industry from the late 1930s until 1955 did not lead to a decline in Brunswick's population. On the contrary, the population of the town nearly doubled between 1940 and 1960. Its population rose steadily in each decennial census until 2010, where the town saw a slight decrease. Since Franco-Americans remained a large slice of the population of the town until mid-century, these numbers do not argue for their sudden exodus. But the neighborhood known in the late 19th century as the French Quarter slowly lost its cohesion. The downtown portion of Brunswick, which included the former French Quarter, lost population in the late 20th century.[76]

CHAPTER SIXTEEN

DRIFTING AWAY FROM LITTLE CANADA IN BODY AND MIND

Franco-Americans began to move out of the Little Canadas even before the mills fell silent. They were searching for a better education and better jobs for their children, and a higher socioeconomic status than the mills could offer. And as they moved away from the enclaves, they had fewer opportunities to speak French. Their children and grandchildren ceased to hear it at school, on the streets, in church, and then, finally, in the home. As early as the 1880s, Ferdinand Gagnon complained about girls at a Franco-American picnic who spoke to each other only in English.[1] Starting in the second third of the 20th century, the Franco-American elite's concerns about anglicization, mentioned in passing at first, became a chorus condemning those who had assimilated.[2]

The ideal of *la survivance*, of a new Québec in New England, became difficult to justify as each passing generation, born in the States, came of age. The more families began to speak English, the more the militants of *survivance* vilified them. And the more they were vilified, the more the Franco-American rank and file became desensitized to their ostensible leaders' cries.

The radicals among the Franco-American elites heaped upon "deserters" from the Little Canadas the same calumnies the *Canadien* elites had hurled at their forbears who had departed Québec. The militants branded as traitors, sell-outs, and rabble Franco-Americans whose children no longer spoke French, and did not attend a bilingual parish school.[3] These recriminations had as negligible an effect as the Québec elite's similar excoriations in a previous generation.

In the 19th century, elites could not browbeat *Canadien* parents in Québec, who needed to feed their growing families, into forgoing economic opportunities in the mill towns. In the 20th century, Franco-American elites could not dragoon their compatriots, who needed to speak English after leaving the Franco-American enclaves, into preserving their language and institutions. The militants never learned the lesson that people cannot be bullied into preserving the forms of a culture that are no longer congruent with their circumstances. A minority cannot preserve a language based on habit or on an angry rejection of the dominant culture. At least not for long. If a minority is to preserve its language, the mother tongue must be not a burden but a precious heirloom. The project of *la survivance* had to be a labor of love and not a grim duty.

Franco-American workers tired of the endless harangues of ultra-conservative priests and newspaper editors inveighing against modernity itself. Everywhere and in every way, the 20th century U.S. brought change, mobility, and ferment. The automobile and the airplane brought people to the world, while radio and television brought the world to people. One of the best-known Franco-Americans of the 20th century, author Jean-Louis (Jack) Kerouac, celebrated this mobility in his most famous work, *On The Road*. His seminal work was utterly out of sync with the messages the conservative elite in the French-language newspapers were still preaching to Kerouac's generation. His books celebrating Franco-American Lowell, such as *Visions of Gerard* and *Vanity of Duluoz*, better works than *On The Road*, were misunderstood. The U.S. mainstream, least of all university-educated critics, had no context for the Franco-American mill town culture that inspired Kerouac's rhapsodies. Similar books written from an Hispanic or a New York City Italian perspective might have had a hearing. The mainstream, English-speaking U.S. had at least a hook on which to hang such a work. Kerouac's references to Franco-American Lowell were too esoteric.

Other literary Franco-Americans of the 20th century were equally transgressive. The first fifty pages of Franco-American author Grace (de Repentigny) Metalious's best-known work, *Peyton Place*, which suffered from melodramatic movie and television adaptations, exposes the hypocrisy of the New England mill town. Her frank portrayal of women's sexuality shocked a 1950s suburban United States. She also wrote lesser-known works with frankly Franco-American content but from a more distanced, less affectionate standpoint than Kerouac's. Her book *No Adam in Eden* (1963) "presents powerfully drawn female characters in complete revolt against traditional Franco-American values."[4]

Non-fiction author Will Durant was a generation older than Kerouac and Metalious. From the factory town of North Adams, Massachusetts, Durant co-authored with his wife Ariel a series of histories called *The Story of Civilization*. These were on the shelf of almost every family in the U.S. that had a collection of books in the mid-20th century. The couple won a Pulitzer Prize in 1968 and the Presidential Medal of Freedom in 1977. Durant ran in politically radical circles and was an avowed socialist, who had married a Jewish woman, contraventions of the dictates of Franco-American traditionalists.[5] Kerouac, Metalious, and Durant, the three most celebrated literary Franco-Americans of the mid-20th century, were outsiders, to both the Anglo mainstream and their working-class, Catholic roots.

As more Franco-Americans began to question the orthodoxy, and as they began to write and speak in English, these English-speaking Francos began to insist that the English language had its place at church, in school, and in the national societies. It was, in many cases, the Franco-American parents themselves who demanded that their families who no longer spoke French had a right to send their children to the parish school.[6] Their parents, too, had created these institutions and their children deserved to be there, even if they no longer understood classes in French. Franco-American National parishes began to have one Mass on the weekend calendar with a sermon preached in English. And then another such Mass. Finally, the "French Mass" became the exception, a single service on the schedule. Today, St. Joseph's in Biddeford, and the Basilica of Saints Peter and Paul in Lewiston are among the few New England parishes that still serve a French Mass.

Another Exodus

A double move toward the larger cities and toward the suburbs contributed to the erosion of the Franco-American enclaves. Before 1920, my mother's family departed the majority Franco-American mill town of Biddeford for Maine's largest city, Portland.[7] My mother grew up in Portland in a working class, multi-ethnic neighborhood where the common-denominator language was English. After the move to Portland, my grandfather faced ridicule because of his accent, as well as demands that he "speak white!" The "white" language was, of course, English. My grandfather wanted his children to speak English without a "French-Canadian" accent. Fluency in French died in my mother's line with the move to Portland. My mother's cousins who remained in Biddeford retained their French.

Both of my paternal grandparents in Brunswick worked for the Cabot mill as young people. My grandfather left the mill for employment in shipyards, among several other trades. His work brought him to the Quincy shipyard on the outskirts of Boston by 1920. The family moved several times between Boston and Brunswick over the next two decades, eventually settling in Portland in the early 1940s. They then moved permanently to the inner-city Boston neighborhood of Dorchester after World War II. Again, the common denominator language there was English. The next generation, the Baby Boomers growing up in the 1950s-1970s in Boston and vicinity, were not expected to know any French, although their grandparents' generation continued to speak it among themselves. My father's cousins who remained in Brunswick were bilingual.

My immediate family then joined the exodus of ethnic, white-identified families from the inner city to the suburbs in the early 1960s. In these outlying suburbs south of Boston lived families with classic *Canadien* and Acadian names such as Cloutier, Levesque, Bergeron, Beauregard, Tetrault, and Chiasson. But the pronunciations of these names and their spelling was anglicized, and French was not heard. Only two older women in my neighborhood could speak French to my grandmother. There was no Franco-American consciousness, and I never heard the term used.

Some of these suburban families, although they had a French surname, were of mixed heritage by the third or fourth generation. Part Irish or part Italian were common mixes. A family with a name like Surette might identify more strongly with an Irish maternal line than with their Franco-American heritage. The move from the mill towns, to the cities, to the suburbs acted as a process of filtration. The precipitate from the mill towns settled, forming a new chemical solution, some (not all) of their ethnic characteristics boiled off.

In my family, with two parents of *Canadien* and (on my mother's mother's side) Acadian origins, Franco-American identity did not disappear. My family continued to enact customs from rural Québec and Acadia, but without any context for them. For example, the traditional Christmas celebration known as *réveillon*, with the foods and visits associated with it, continued in my childhood but I didn't know the word for it or that it was an ethnic custom.

The slow drift away from New England's mill towns also included moves to other parts of the United States. After the Second World War, Franco-American easterners joined the trail of Americans heading west. Some 150,000 to 200,000 Franco-Americans departed the region, many for California and Florida in the two decades before 1950.[8] The Golden State had a particular allure for these natives of snowy climes. By 1942, there were 72,000 Franco-Americans in California, more than their numbers in Vermont.[9] Today, Southern California has an active French-Canadian Heritage Society based in Burbank.

Along with the drift westward, Franco-Americans of the mid-20th century became swept up in the currents of U.S. demographic trends. Military service in the World Wars, in Korea and Vietnam, as well as attendance at universities, were forces of homogenization for Franco-Americans, as for the other working-class white-identified "ethnics" throughout the country.[10]

Despite the departure of many families toward sun-splashed regions, in New England today, the numbers of families with *Canadien* and Acadian names is immense. It goes unnoticed because most observers don't have a frame of reference labeled "Franco-American" and without that conceptual scheme, the phenomenon goes unrecognized. But to those who know their regional history or Franco-American genealogy, New England remains as Franco-American as parts of the Southwest are Mexican in origin. On local television news in the Boston market, it is not uncommon for a reporter named *Jolicoeur* to interview a witness named *Laviolette*, to a crime against a victim whose name is *Arsenault*.

Franco-Americans are everywhere in New England, but especially in certain regions, such as the Blackstone Valley, including the major Franco-American center of Woonsocket; the South Coast region and Worcester County, Massachusetts; the southern portions of the Connecticut River Valley in the western parts of the Bay State; the Maine counties of York, Androscoggin, Kennebec and Cumberland, as well as the Acadian-identified regions in the St. John Valley that borders Canada; the Merrimack Valley from Suncook through Manchester and Nashua, New Hampshire and across the Massachusetts border into Lowell, Lawrence and Haverhill; in New Hampshire there's also Berlin, Claremont, the area around Laconia, and the area in the east that includes Somersworth and Rochester among others; in Connecticut, Franco-Americans congregate in Windham County in the East, as well as in the communities of Bristol, Waterbury, and Hartford. In Vermont, the region around Lake Champlain remains strongly Franco-American with pockets around Burlington and other areas.

Absent markers, such as the French language or accented English, Franco-Americans became identified as "ethnic Catholics" or "working-class whites." Or, in the language of a recent U.S. Federal Census, we are now identified as "non-Hispanic White." And nothing else. The ghost empire has become spectral indeed. Outside of the region, one hears hardly a whisper of our existence. Among Franco-Americans, our very invisibility is a common topic.

In Québec, historians and history buffs know the story of the exiles, but, in general, north of the border there is little awareness of Franco-Americans. But the exodus of 1865-1930 touched so many families that when the topic arises many Québécois(es) will make a family connection. "My aunt worked in a factory in Nashua." "My grandparents lived in Lowell but came back to Québec because their children were losing their French." "My great-aunt was born in Chicopee but sent back to Québec by her parents." "My grandparents were married in Central Falls, Rhode Island." Individual families have preserved a fragment of the story, each its own tiny, jagged piece.

Some Québécois(es) see Franco-Americans as a cautionary tale about cultural assimilation. Occasional reports in the French-language press in Québec portray the Franco-Americans as a sad remnant of the past, or as a dire warning regarding Québec's possible future.[11] As in the late 19th century, journalists and historians tend to use the Franco-Americans as a stick to beat various ideological drums. A 1998 piece in the English-language newspaper the *Montreal Gazette*, titled "Welcome to the Town of Ghosts," profiled Lewiston. "For Québécois nationalists, [it's] the nightmare come true," opines the journalist. "Ethnically, the city is overwhelmingly 'Franco-American' but hardly anyone under the age of 50 speaks French."[12]

Neither Lewiston's nor other Franco-Americans are "nightmares." Franco-Americans reject the scare quotes the English-language journalist chooses to place around their ethnonym. In potential, Franco-Americans are a sweet dream for "Québécois nationalists" since they represent a large, untapped natural resource across the border. This potential pool of friendship and support numbers in the millions. The Franco-Americans who are aware of their history and identity – a subset of the total – are proud of their historical connections to Québec and welcome deeper cross-border links.

The Enclave That Refused to Die

The negative press fails to recognize that assimilation is more complex than the discussions about it would maintain. It is not an event but a process that may take several generations.[13] And the process may be reversed. There is no single moment of transubstantiation where a *Canadien* is transformed mystically into an American. When would that moment be? When one speaks one's first word of English? When one speaks English on a daily basis? When one prefers baseball to hockey? When one celebrates July Fourth rather than June 24? Such transformations happen slowly and imperceptibly. Today, most

Franco-Americans are more American than anything else. Their politics and attitudes tend to follow those of the various regions of the U.S. they inhabit. Virtually all speak English although many more than is generally acknowledged have at least some facility with French, since knowledge of a language is something that admits degrees. Total assimilation would mean that our origins would have become invisible even to ourselves, that none of us would feel any connection to a Franco-American identity. But this is not the case.

For the generations born after World War II, the English language became the language of the future; the French language was identified with the past. And the past was not always so happy. Speaking to many Franco-Americans, now middle-aged, I find that most did not hear much about their family's story growing up. For many families, a dark cloud emanated from the mill town and followed them to the larger cities or to the suburbs. The cloud was distant, it hovered far above our heads, it obscured a less-than-pleasant past, but let in little light. To many of the Baby Boomer and subsequent generations preserving a past characterized by poverty, and what many regarded as obscurantism and ultra-conservatism, was unattractive and ran counter to the spirit of the mid-century United States. There was no way to be modern *and* Franco-American. Many Baby Boomers felt that they had to choose one or the other. And when they made their choice, they also made it for their children and grandchildren.

Beyond the Acadian regions in Northern Maine, which have a separate history from the Québec diaspora in New England, French is rarely heard in the streets of New England. In towns such as Lewiston, Manchester, and Woonsocket, French survives. But one has to know where to find the French-speakers and how to approach the matter. No longer required for communication, the French language has become symbolic, a sign of identity and continuity with the past.[14] Québécois cousins of today, including journalists, travel to the mill towns, walk down the street and hear no French and conclude that there is no more Franco-America in New England. The inaudibility of the French language in public does not indicate that Franco-Americans no longer exist there. It means that *what it is to be* a Franco-American has changed. Whether one wishes to identify as

Franco-American or not is now a matter of choice. My grandparents had no such luxury.

For many observers, the Franco-American story is about cultural loss. There's an alternative to this glass-half-empty approach. There is another interpretation in which Franco-Americans provide eloquent testimony to the resilience of the *Canadien* people. In light of the story I have uncovered, it is a miracle that anyone in New England speaks French, that there is a single French Mass on the schedule in any parish there, that anyone remembers (and with pride) the name of the home parish of his or her ancestor in Québec, as many Franco-Americans do today. Given their historically low socioeconomic status, their modest average level of education, their invisibility in the annals of U.S. history, and the length of their tenure in the U.S., Franco-Americans should be as extinct as the pterodactyl. There should be as many self-identified Sumerians as Franco-Americans.

Today ours is a story of *cultural* survival despite *language* loss. If our heritage is reduced to *speaking a language*, which anyone of any background can learn in school if they start early enough, then it follows that there is no identity without the language. If language *is* culture, then we have nothing. But Franco-Americans know better. They could teach what they know about this matter of *language* and *culture* to the world if anyone would listen.

With the cultural traits that they preserve – *joie de vivre*, combined with a keen sense of irony, a fierce love of family, and strong identification with their communities – it is difficult for them to admit today that they were an underclass in the mill towns. The stoicism and fatalism in the culture, its aversion to "complaining," shaped the collective memory. Dyke Hendrickson's interviews with Franco-Americans conducted in the 1970s, with a generation past middle-age at that time, reflect these attitudes. "Our family never believed in complaining... we've taken life as it was dealt to us. That's been our attitude," says one interviewee. "I accepted everything that was offered to me. Many a time I didn't like it. But I said I have to do it, and that's all there is to it," said another. "What was to be was to be. There are no regrets," says another voice. "The way people thought was 'this is the way it's going to be,'" says another speaker. "They didn't expect more – they didn't get it."[15]

For the remnant of this older generation, this book will appear as a species of "complaining." "Don't try to turn us into victims!" some will say. It is distasteful, disempowering, and, for the men, emasculating to point out what is evident in the historical record: that the *Canadiens* and Franco-Americans of the 19th and 20th centuries were a subaltern people. In the U.S., their pigmentation allowed them to blend in with the dominant culture – as long as they surrendered a great deal of what made them what they were. But this very ability to blend into whiteness disguises their history, not so very far in the past, as an allegedly "inferior" people, as a distinct, alien race.

CHAPTER SEVENTEEN

A Distinct Alien Race
No Longer

The assumption of Franco-Americans into non-Hispanic whiteness was simultaneous with a new social context that altered the meaning of the word "race." As the term lost its double meaning, by about 1940, Franco-Americans were a distinct alien race no longer.

That the double meaning of the word "race" was still operative well into the 20th century is evident in Elin Anderson's 1937 study of ethnic groups in Burlington. She writes, "Instead of the more common word 'race,' the term 'ethnic group' is used [in this book] wherever possible, to distinguish groups of common cultural heritage and character."[1] Anderson here implies that "race" is a "common word" used in the 1930s for populations that share a "common cultural heritage." Anderson's text demonstrates that the word "race" was also used for categorizations based on phenotype, of course, as it had been used long before her time. But the parallel usage of the word "race," where it was indistinguishable from our term "ethnicity," continued into the late 1930s.

Throughout the remainder of her book, however, Anderson does not adhere to her stated convention of substituting "ethnic group" for the latter definition of the word "race." For example, she comments on the Burlington Jewish community's "strict adherence to lines of race," the word "race" here meaning Jewish cultural identity.[2] Elsewhere she explains how the Franco-Americans of Burlington listen to Québec radio to "maintain their identification with their own race."[3] She maintains that "French-Canadians have been noted for their strong consciousness of race" which refers here not to the so-called white race but to their cultural identity. She also speaks of the "traditional feeling of racial superiority" among the "Anglo-Saxons," meaning not white superiority, but alleged Anglo-Protestant superiority vis-à-vis the other white-identified ethnic groups in the city.[4]

Elsewhere in her work, however, her usage of the word "race" is closer to our contemporary discourse. For example, she refers to "the white race" and gathers under this category all of the European-descent groups. The peoples she calls "Negroes" and "Chinese" she clearly does not regard as a part of "the white race."[5]

Anderson notes that the Anglo-Protestant and Franco-American populations fall at the opposite ends of the socioeconomic scale in Burlington.[6] Among the Yankees, all is self-confidence and certainty of their worth. For them, it was English-speaking Protestantism that created the U.S.'s "free institutions." The other groups in the city were expected to conform to their cultural norms. Mixing with the non-Yankee groups in the town was acceptable, avowed one Burlington Yankee, but not too intimately. Otherwise the others might "forget their place."[7]

By contrast, according to Anderson, Franco-Americans suffered more than any other group from feelings of inferiority.[8] They were the underclass of the town, many of them living in decrepit tenements, while they constituted 85 to 90 percent of the blue-collar mill work-ers.[9] Some Franco-Americans in the city were embarrassed by their nationality and tried to hide it.[10] In a city that was overwhelmingly "white" by our modern lights, there was a stratification of castes, with the Yankee at the top and the Franco-American at the bottom, and several other white-identified "races" in between.

Anderson is clear that all of the white-identified groups in Burlington in the 1930s, including the Franco-Americans, did not want to have "Negroes" or "Chinese" as neighbors and most would not approve of intermarriage with these groups.[11] The hierarchy of races, in the sense of skin color, still prevails, but in 1930s Burlington it has little opportunity for practical application. The *effective* racial caste system finds Anglo-Saxon Protestants at the top and Franco-American Catholics at the bottom.

In the four decades between the imposition of the eugenics-inspired immigration quota system and its abolition in 1965, emerged *whiteness* as we know it today – as a designation encompassing all people of European descent in the United States. As the European-descent elements in the population became anglicized and began to live together, side-by-side in the same neighborhoods, their most important identifier became "white" rather than Italian, Irish, Polish, Franco-American, etc. Tactics such as red-lining and other urban planning policies discouraged people of color from living in neighborhoods where ethnic whites were tolerated.[12] The "real white folks" – U.S.-born, Anglo-Protestants – accepted these "ethnics" as long as they "spoke white" and, in the words of the Klan's Elizabeth Tyler, lived up to "the standards of the white race." The breakdown of the ethnic neighborhoods and suburbanization facilitated the construction of whiteness.

This construction had a long history, to be sure. But it is clear that a change in the meaning of the word "race" occurred in the second third of the 20th century and this change in usage marked a stage in an historical process. The sense of the word "race" as a designator for a cultural or linguistic group became passé sometime around World War II, while the category of "whiteness" congealed in the era between the immigration legislation of 1924 and the changes in immigration law in 1965.

After the Franco-Americans had learned to "speak white," there was no barrier to their entry into unmitigated whiteness. As Franco-Americans became subsumed into whiteness, their past as a distinct alien race was forgotten. Today, to even suggest that Franco-Americans form a distinct "race" sounds ludicrous. But as recently as my parents' lifetimes, observers like Anderson still described them as such. Anglicization and the breakdown of the Little Canadas were local stages in a nationwide transformation where "the white races" became "the white race."

You can take the family out of the tenements and move them to a suburb, but it's far more difficult to take the tenements out of the families. Many who were accustomed to thinking of themselves as a subaltern group in their mill towns experienced cognitive dissonance when they moved out of the enclaves. Their identification as "white" became solidified as they moved to places where there was a greater diversity of phenotypes, and more recent, non-white immigrant communities. To those outside of their group, unaware of the history, Franco-Americans were simply white people, top dogs in the U.S. racial hierarchy. And yet, in their internal dialog, many Franco-Americans retained the psychology of an underclass, of the tenement-house dwellers.

Available studies show as much. The loss of their status as a subaltern "race" did not automatically raise the socioeconomic status of Franco-Americans in New England. On average, that status remained low for several generations. And in some places, this remains the case to this day.

Leon Bouvier examined socioeconomic differences between Franco-Americans and other white-identified, predominantly Roman Catholic ethnic groups as of 1950.[13] He found that across the country, Franco-Americans whether born in Québec or the U.S., had lower median incomes than Irish-, Italian-, or Polish-Americans. They also had a smaller median income than the foreign-born, white-identified population of any religion.

Bouvier calculated the difference in income between the foreign-born and U.S.-born generations for each ethnic group he studied. We would expect to see an increase in income between the immigrant generation and their children, the first-generation Americans. For the Franco-Americans, the differential in income between these two generations was smaller than that of the white-identified, foreign-born population as a whole. It was much smaller than that of the Irish-American or Polish-American groups.

Bouvier also examined educational attainment among Franco-Americans at mid-century. Canadian-born Franco-Americans had more years of schooling than the immigrant generation from Italy or Poland. The "French-Canadian, born abroad" group in his study had a median of 8.2 years of schooling, about equal to that of the white-identified, foreign-born population at large. However, other ethnic groups raced ahead of the Franco-Americans in the following generation. Italian-Americans and Polish-Americans born in the U.S. had more schooling than their U.S.-born Franco-American counterparts by about one year.

A more recent study looked at educational attainment among Franco-Americans in the later 20th century.[14] This research found that Franco-Americans spent less time in school by a full year in comparison to white, English-speaking New Englanders, although the gap had closed by the year 2000 for Grades 1-12. By the beginning of the 21st century, rates of post-secondary education among Franco-American men remained lower than average, although women had caught up to other New Englanders. This same study compared Franco-Americans with Italian-Americans as of 1970, using mother-tongue data from the U.S. Federal Census. The study found that Italian-Americans in 1970 had as many years at school as New Englanders at large while Franco-Americans lagged behind. The research also concluded that Franco-Americans had retained their French to a greater degree than Italian-Americans had conserved their Italian.

It is unclear why there should be differences in income or education between Franco-Americans and other white-identified, ethnic Catholics. Conditions of life and work were no better for Irish, Italian, and Polish immigrants than for Franco-Americans. In general, these immigrants came from conditions of poverty at least as dire as that of the rural poor of Québec. And yet, with respect to social status markers such as income and education, Franco-Americans remained behind the curve in the 20th century.

In 2012, the Maine legislature appointed a task force to gather demographic data on Franco-Americans and to "evaluate the current economic and educational circumstances of this population group." The task force engaged a professional polling outfit which administered a 55-question survey to 600 self-identified Maine Franco-Americans. This is the most complete, scientific study of Franco-Americans in the 21st century.[15]

The sample had about equal numbers of men and women. Fifty-six percent of the respondents were between 18 and 45 years old. The study found that 28.5 percent of the sample claimed fluency in French.

More than three-quarters (77.8 percent) responded that they were able to speak the language to some degree ranging from an ability to "understand and speak a little French" to fluency. A comparable number (77 percent) indicated that someone in their household or family was fluent in the language. This represents an unexpectedly high degree of linguistic survival.

Just over 61 percent claimed that they were "somewhat" or "extremely" proud of their Franco-American heritage. About one out of every five Franco-Americans surveyed claimed that either they or a family member "had been discriminated against because of [their] Franco American heritage/culture." About 30 percent said that they felt that "non-Francos" think "somewhat less highly" or "look down on" the Franco-American heritage, although the largest percentage (36.8 percent) claimed that they did not know how to answer this question.

The survey found that rates of post-secondary education among Maine's Franco-Americans remained comparatively low. Nearly 77 percent of respondents said that neither of their parents had graduated from college. About 21 percent of respondents were college graduates compared with 28 percent of the state's general population.[16]

The study also examined how Franco-Americans self-identify. The research found that various percentages of those surveyed identified with labels such as "Acadian," "French Canadian," "Franco," etc. One-tenth of respondents identified as "Québécois." This Québécois-identified cohort had distinct characteristics. The researchers found that 68 percent of this "Québécois" sub-group claimed fluency in French, a much higher percentage than the sample as a whole. Fully 86 percent of the "Québécois" sub-group said that they believed in "most" or "virtually all" Roman Catholic doctrine. More than one-half of the "Québécois" sub-group (56 percent) said that "Franco American heritage" was "a factor to be taken into consideration" when voting for a political candidate as compared with about a third of those who identified with other labels. Members of the Québécois sub-group were more likely to own a "large" business and to have graduated from college.

Maine Franco-Americans identifying as "Québécois" would puzzle our cousins north of the border. They would not recognize Franco-

Americans as such. And the identification with the Catholic religion among the "Québécois" group in the study is a surprise, given the secularism of modern Québec. Nonetheless, the existence of this more affluent and educated subgroup identifying with the label "Québécois," representing perhaps one-tenth of Maine's Franco-Americans, raises the question of the relationship between Franco-Americans and today's Québec.

CHAPTER EIGHTEEN

Franco-Americans and Québécois

In the mid-1980s, the Boston Public Library had a photo exhibit about Franco-Americans. One photo showed a woman standing beside her machine in one of the region's few remaining textile mills. A quotation from the woman appeared next to her photo: "We Franco-Americans are different from the French-Canadians. We're more democratic." In the same exhibit was a photo of an older man with a weary face. The text accompanying the photo spoke of his childhood in Salem, Massachusetts where he remembered being repeatedly pursued and beaten up by Yankee children on his way home from school because he was "French-Canadian." "When Québec gets its independence," this man declared, "then we'll get some respect."[1]

The textile worker wished to distinguish Franco-Americans from their relatives across the border, appealing to the U.S. secular religion's main tenet of "democracy." The man from Salem, abused because of his identity, ties Franco-American respectability to the status of Québec. And in the mid-1980s, he saw Québec independence as an inevitability, a matter of *when* and not *if*. These two contrasting views exemplify the differing attitudes of Franco-Americans toward Québec. One side emphasizes Franco-American autonomy from Québec; the other binds the fate of Franco-Americans to that of the mother country.

Québec today is not the land our ancestors exited. In the early 20th century, Québec industrialized rapidly. Living standards and literacy improved. Today, there is little difference in material culture between the U.S. and Québec. The descendants of the *Canadiens* on both sides of the border struggled with the question of modernity in the 20th century. In Québec, the *Canadiens* resolved the matter by casting themselves in a new role.

Between 1960 and 1980, Québec underwent a social revolution known as *"la Révolution tranquille"* – the Quiet Revolution. The 1960s and 1970s were a time of social change throughout the western world, but perhaps nowhere else were the changes as rapid or as profound as in Québec. From one of the most Catholic regions of North America, Québec transformed itself into one of the most secular parts of the continent. Until the 1960s, the Catholic Church had controlled education, and dominated medicine and social services. The Quiet Revolution changed that. This period and its aftermath recast the older French-Canadian tradition. The revolution retained certain aspects of the older identity while rejecting others. Of the three pillars of the 19th century ideology of *la survivance* – language, religion, and customs – *language* became the defining element, the *sine qua non* of identity.

With this Quiet Revolution came a new national label: *Québécois*. This label affirmed the secularized, forward-looking stance adopted by the new Québec. It rejected the former, hyphenated identity "French-Canadian," a hybrid something-or-other, some part French and some part Canadian. Québec embraced the new label with astonishing rapidity. It was a brilliant piece of what we would now call rebranding.

One of the innovations of the term *Québécois* is that, unlike the terms *Canadien* or *Canadien-français* [French-Canadian], the new designation ties itself to a specific geography, that of Québec. The label "French-Canadian" crossed geographies. French-Canadians were French-Canadians whether they lived in Montréal, Michigan, Manitoba, or Maine. *French-Canadians* were a nation without a state. The intention of those who transformed the *French-Canadians* of Québec into *Québécois*, was to reinforce the viability of the latter as a nation with its own territory as a prelude to establishing an independent republic. In 1968, the *Parti Québécois* (PQ) emerged as a political party advocating the secession of Québec from the Canadian Confederation, to stand on its own as an independent nation-state.[2]

The rebranding was formidable within Québec but it had consequences keenly felt among the French-speakers who lived in the other provinces of today's Canada. In the main, and increasingly over time, these minorities opposed the ambitions of Québec to national independence. Attached to a *Canadian* identity and to the Ottawa government, which they tend to believe had secured their rights, the French-speaking minorities in the provinces west of Québec continued to describe themselves as "French-Canadian," or to identify with their province (Franco-Ontarian, Franco-Manitoban, etc.).

The PQ gained power in the Québec provincial government in 1976 under the leadership of René Lévesque. A signal event of the PQ's mandate was the passage in 1977 of Bill 101 also known as the Charter of the French Language. This law made French the official language of Québec and the "normal language of work, education, communications, and business."[3] In 1980, the PQ held a referendum to garner the assent of the people to its efforts to establish Québec as a sovereign state. Voters rejected the PQ's bid for Québec sovereignty by almost 20 percentage points. In the 1990s, after Lévesque's death, the PQ came to power in the province once again. In 1995, it held another referendum on the question of Québec independence, which was defeated by the thinnest of margins: 50.6 to 49.4 percent.[4]

Today, many Québécois tend to see the independence movement as a thing of the past. However, a vocal minority persists in its support for national independence. The struggle between those in Québec who continue to support a separate nation-state (called *Sovereignists*) and those who think Québec's interests are better served from within the Canadian Confederation (called *Federalists*) continues into the 21st century.

In assenting to a Québécois-American identity, one-tenth of the respondents in the 2012 Maine legislature's survey signal their identification with this assertive, post-Quiet Revolution Québec. This engaged sector of the Franco-American population appears to identify with *today's* Québec and not the land our ancestors left. Two contrasting Franco-American leaders of the 20th century demonstrate continuing

328 A DISTINCT ALIEN RACE

connections between a transformed Québec and the diaspora in New England.

Journalist and newspaper editor Wilfred Beaulieu represented one of the last of the old guard Franco-American militants. He remained determined to champion the fading cause of *la survivance* in the U.S. into the later 20th century. For the viewpoint Beaulieu represented, the French language, the bilingual parochial schools, and the national parish continued to be the pillars of Franco-American identity. In the view of this old guard, any deviation from this cultural inheritance imagined as a complete, unalterable package delivered from the past to the present, was a betrayal of it in its entirety. Since this package was formed in the distant past, in response to the needs of earlier generations, this vision of Franco-American identity precluded modernity.[5]

Yvon Labbé was Wilfred Beaulieu's opposite number. In the early 1970s, Labbé, Claire Bolduc, and others led a group of young Franco-Americans at the University of Maine at Orono. For the group's name, they appropriated the ethnic slur "frog" and transformed it into the acronym FAROG: *Franco-American Resource and Opportunity Group*. This group advocated for Franco-American students on campus, many of whom were first-generation college students who felt ill at ease at the University. Later, FAROG evolved into the Franco-American Center at the University, which continues today under the leadership of Susan Pinette and Lisa Desjardins Michaud. The FAROG founded a bilingual newspaper under the title *FAROG Forum* published today as *Le Forum*.[6]

Combative, often sarcastic, the *FAROG Forum* was a gadfly on the Franco-American elites, exposing what a younger generation in the 1970s saw as the hypocrisies of the old guard. It represented Baby Boomers determined to assert a modern Franco-American identity. This group was inspired by the spirit of Québec's Quiet Revolution, as well as by the movements for civil rights in the U.S. in the 1950s-1970s including the struggles of African-Americans and Hispanics, and the Feminist movement. For the faction led by Labbé, there were no linguistic or religious litmus tests for Franco-American identity. Membership in the Franco-American group was a matter of self-identification.

Although Beaulieu and Labbé were supposed to represent opposing factions, they had one thing in common: support for René Lévesque, the PQ, and Québec independence. Beaulieu's *Le Travailleur* became "the most Québec-oriented" among the Franco-American newspapers, and Beaulieu was "an ardent supporter of Québec independence."[7] For his part, interviewed in the late 1970s, Labbé stated,

> I support the direction of [René] Levesque's government. We support the people of Quebec....We have a need to know Quebec, and we have a need to be closer. If Levesque is successful in his efforts to create some kind of separate entity [i.e., an independent Québec], he will be looking this way. They will need friends, and I think there will be a greater connection between the French-Canadians and the Franco-Americans.[8]

Indeed, Lévesque did look toward Franco-Americans. In the aftermath of the failed 1980 referendum, the Premier of Québec visited the Franco-American Center in Orono and shook Labbé's hand. Lévesque expressed his support for Franco-Americans and his recognition of their role in providing a link between a potentially independent Québec and Washington. However, an eyewitness to these events described Lévesque at this stage as "a defeated man."[9]

Lévesque's government did more than just talk about renewed links across the border. His government invited Franco-American leaders to Québec to establish an umbrella organization to act as a center of communication with the northeastern states. A Québec government organ known as the Permanent Secretariat of the Francophone Peoples also offered to smooth the path for Franco-Americans wishing to do business in Québec.[10] In 1981, the Québec government played a role in establishing Action pour les Franco-Américains de Nord-Est [Action for Franco-Americans of the Northeast], known as ActFANE, under the direction of Paul Paré. This group coordinated activities in New England and New York, acted as an information source, and as a proxy for Franco-Americans to international Francophonie.[11] No other Québec government of any party had done so much to reach out to Franco-Americans in at least half-a-century. However, when the Liberal Party returned to power in Québec, ousting the PQ, it pulled the plug on initiatives to reconnect Franco-Americans with Québec.[12]

If they knew of them, Beaulieu's and Labbé's expressions of support for the PQ and its Québec independence plank would have been anathema to many among the French-Canadian minorities living in Canada outside of the province of Québec. My contacts among French-Canadians living outside of Québec have expressed the view that Americans have no right to an opinion on Québec independence proposals that, in their view, have threatened the survival of Canada as they know it. The secession of Québec would represent a loss for these minorities because the departure of the only province with a French-speaking majority would erode the support of English-speakers for an officially bilingual Canada.

By contrast, for Beaulieu's newspaper, "the Franco-Americans are living proof of the inefficacy of the Canadian Confederation. From 1870 to 1930, Canada was welcoming millions of immigrants while, at the same time, hundreds of thousands of Francophone Quebecers were heading towards New England." Le Travailleur suggested that "an independent Québec would have directed her energies toward preserving her human resources."[13]

Le Travailleur's remarks show how Franco-American perspectives may differ from those of French-Canadians outside of Québec. Franco-Americans, as a rule, have neither loyalty nor enmity toward Ottawa. This indifference is no surprise. The ink was hardly dry on the British North America Act that created the Dominion of Canada in 1867 when our ancestors began to depart Québec. The Canadian Confederation and the post-Civil War exodus of the Canadiens to New England were approximately simultaneous events. With a few exceptions, where the Franco-Americans have preserved their language and culture it was through their own efforts, with no help from the government in Ottawa and with little support from anywhere else. Engaged Franco-Americans in New England tend to look to Québec as their homeland. A province such as Saskatchewan is a part of a foreign country in which the Franco-Americans of New England have neither more nor less stake than any other U.S. citizen.

The Franco-Americans remain an untapped natural resource for Québec whatever its future holds. As Yvon Labbé suggested forty years ago, Québec needs friends. The key to any future friendship is for the Québécois to be able to engage Franco-Americans *as they are today* and not as they wished or hoped they were. If Québec views Franco-Americans as nothing more than an admonition about assimilation, then there is no basis for friendship. But if the two sides can accept each other as they are, then friendship is not only possible but likely. The Québécois(e), whatever his or her views on Québec's political future, will have no faster friend than the New England Franco-American.

The documentary film *Réveil – Waking Up French* (2002) by filmmaker Ben Levine has helped to prepare younger generations to continue to engage with questions of Franco-American identity and its connections north of the border. When Levine, a New Yorker of Jewish heritage, moved to Maine he noticed the ubiquity of French names but was puzzled that he heard very little French. He began to research the question and produced two films on the subject. Levine and his partner Julia Schulz have screened the 2002 film all over New England, as well as in Québec, Louisiana, and France. Following screenings of the film, Levine leads a discussion and often films these encounters.

I attended three such screenings. Woonsocket received the film warmly, with the crowd bursting into song in French on more than one occasion. In the discussion after the film, one viewer proclaimed that five generations of his family had lived in Woonsocket and his grandchildren could still speak to him in French. In Manchester, the film met a cooler reception. Some viewers wondered if Levine had overemphasized the negative aspects of the reception of Franco-Americans in the U.S., such as the activities of the 1920s Ku Klux Klan. At M.I.T. in Cambridge, Massachusetts, the film met academic and ideological critiques. Despite the criticisms, the film has had an undeniable catalytic effect on the post-Baby Boomer generations of Franco-Americans.

In 2015, the Mayor of Québec City formed *Le réseau des villes francophones et francophiles d'Amérique* [The Network of Francophone and Francophile cities of America]. Québec City along with the Acadian city of Moncton, New Brunswick and the self-identified *Cadien* ("Cajun") bastion, Lafayette, Louisiana, led the loose association of communities all over the Americas with historic ties to New

France. New England cities participating in this initiative include Woonsocket, Biddeford, Lewiston-Auburn, and the New Hampshire communities of Manchester, Nashua, Rochester, and Somersworth.

Over the past decade, the state of Connecticut has had a Franco-American Day on June 24 with the Québec flag flying over the State House in Hartford. As the flag rises over the state capital, a large crowd joins in singing *Gens du Pays* by Québécois singer-songwriter Gilles Vigneault, the unofficial national anthem of Québec. This song and its composer are associated with the 1960s and the Québec independence movement. Neither the flag nor the song existed when our ancestors left Québec for the mills of New England between 1865 and 1930. Franco-American Day in Hartford celebrates ties with 21st century Québec, not with the Lower Canada of the 19th century, nor the confederated Canada of today.

Numbers and Characteristics of 21st Century Franco-Americans

If Franco-Americans represent an untapped resource, how large is the pool? Per the 2010 U.S. Federal Census, some 11.5 million residents of the 50 states identified as having either "French-Canadian" or "French" ancestry. It is a safe bet that the majority of the people who reported having "French" ancestry in the 2010 census are the descendants of *Nouvelle-France* rather than the French of the European continent.

It will surprise many North Americans to learn that the majority of people who have spoken French in the U.S. are of *Canadien* or Acadian roots rather than imports from directly across the Atlantic. France never produced a large out-migration to the U.S. despite the upheavals that wracked her between 1789 and 1945. During the great era of emigration from Europe in the 19th century, French immigrants to the U.S. never numbered more than 3,000 per year. Most immigrants from France to the U.S. were urban dwellers, from the professional or skilled worker classes.[14] They tended to settle in three states: New York, California, and Pennsylvania.[15]

Census data from the period before 1924, shows the relative weakness of emigration from France to the United States. Per the 1910 U.S.

Federal Census, Canada was the place of birth of almost 73 percent of all "foreign-born white" French-speakers in the U.S., while France accounted for 21 percent. Immigrants from Belgium, Switzerland, and Germany made up the bulk of the remaining six percent.[16] The foreign-born population from France declined by 11.4 percent between 1920 and 1930 after the imposition of quotas on European immigrants, while the number of foreign-born French-Canadians in the U.S. grew by 20.5 percent.[17]

The figure of 11.5 million "French" or "French-Canadian" descendants today does not include those who identify as Creole or Cadien. And since the census does not have searchable numbers for those who identify as Acadian, the figure does not count these individuals. We can assume that many Acadian descendants identified their ancestry as "French" but the data is unclear. The figure of 11.5 million includes only self-reported ancestry. It does not include those who have *Canadien* or Acadian ancestry but choose not to report it. Nor does it include those who do not know their ancestry or are of mixed ancestry and did not specify their French/French-Canadian heritage. I believe that 10 million is a conservative estimate of the Franco-American population of the U.S. today. Of this population, over two million remain concentrated in New England.

I would divide this 10 million into the following groups:

1. Those who identify their heritage as "French" or "French-Canadian" but know nothing more about it. This group is vast.
2. Those who are aware of their heritage and origins but for whom this is primarily a genealogical or historical reality with, they believe, little relevance today.
3. A small group of ardent Franco-Americans who not only know their history but continue to identify today with Québec or Acadia. As a rule, they are either French-speaking, have some French language ability, or wish they did.

Some of the first and second group are sometimes converted to the third as they learn more about their heritage. Today, as yesterday, the ten million Franco-Americans represent many different orientations and attitudes, from those who are contemptuous of their roots, to those who are apathetic about them, to those who follow events in Québec as if it were a second home.

Where does all this leave the two million Franco-Americans in New England today? After 150 years, it is still too early to tell. A flame still smolders on the outskirts of the former mill towns all over craggy New England. Every now and again there's a crackle from below and a brief puff of smoke rises. Will the last embers blow away in the wind? Or is there a gust just gentle enough to nourish a spark and ignite a fire among the two million? Or among the ten million?

BACK TO THE CEMETERY

Route 1 South in Maine is a hilly, coastal road, much of it lined by pine trees. It was April 2016 and I was driving away from the annual gathering of Franco-American writers and artists under the auspices of the Department of Franco-American Studies at the University of Maine. This conference had just wrapped, but I had another place to be. A filmmaker had requested an on-camera interview for her film about Israel Shevenell, the first Franco-American of Biddeford.

The gathering at the University that year was unusually tumultuous. I had opened my mouth to express my belief that Franco-Americans should speak for themselves. I felt that if there were public events or newspaper columns about Franco-American life, Franco-Americans should take the leading role. Since there are so few such opportunities, shouldn't Franco-American voices be heard? It seemed a simple, common sense affirmation. Were it any other ethnic or racial group in the U.S. such a statement would be entirely uncontroversial. Not so for Franco-Americans apparently.

Franco-Americans will allow non-Franco-American people to speak for them, to tell their stories, to advocate for them, and even to dominate the discussion at events that are supposedly about them. Some of these allies are also friends and many of them do excellent work. One does not have to be Franco-American to write about Franco-Americans. But Franco-Americans, a people so marginalized that they're virtually invisible, need to find their voice. At events supposedly for them, with impeccable *politesse*, the Franco-Americans will sit on their hands waiting for their turn, never interrupting their "betters." I had pointed this out at the conference making the *faux pas* of saying openly what several Franco-Americans present had grumbled about privately.

Like the boy in the tale of the Emperor's New Clothes, who makes himself a pariah by speaking an impolitic truth, no one present seemed to have liked what I had said. More than one non-Franco-American person present took umbrage at my truth-telling and I received an earful. In the parking lot, as I loaded my bag into my car to depart, I heard another earful from one such person. I said nothing. I put my bag in the trunk of my car and drove away, sick at heart.

There was no time to lick my wounds. There was work to be done. I, as a Franco-American, had to be about the business of telling our story to a filmmaker. Besides, we're not complainers. On my suggestion, the filmmaker conducted the interview in Brunswick. Into the town I drove, past the former Cabot mill, past one of the only remaining tenement buildings, speeding through what was once the French Quarter of Brunswick. With time to kill before the interview, I visited St. John's Cemetery in the town, the ground where generations of Franco-American mill workers and their families sleep eternally.

I found my way past the gravestones, with their French inscriptions, bearing the names of the descendants of Québec: *Desjardins, Tardif, Fournier, Caron,* until I found the familiar monument on which was engraved my own surname. Here was the final resting place of sons of Saint-Gervais-de-Bellechasse, Charles Vermette and his brother François, whose grave bears his American moniker "Frank." Here was also my great-grandmother, Albina Ouellette, who was working full shifts in the mill by age 12, who had born nine children and died from complications of a hysterectomy at age 50. Here also was my great-uncle Ludger, veteran of the U.S. Army in the First World War, a talented musician who never married, and who died at the age of 43. In the family plot, there is also a small stone marked "Joseph – Père." This stone commemorates my great-great grandfather of Saint-Gervais and later of Thetford-Mines, the father of 23 children.

Old Joseph lived all but the last few months of his 83 years in Québec, dying in Brunswick in May 1912. Per the 1911 Census of

Canada, he is still living in Thetford-Mines with the eldest daughter of his second wife and her Dubois family. The same census finds Joseph's wife living elsewhere in Thetford-Mines. Her marital status in the census reads *Separée* [Separated]. His marriage over, Joseph came in the final months of his life to die and to be buried in a foreign country, with the sons of his first marriage. His second wife, Rebecca Turgeon, died in 1923 in the Beauport Mental Asylum in Québec.

As I pulled grass and weeds away from the stones, reading the names and dates I knew so well, still smarting from the morning's events, I spoke to the ancestors with my thoughts as if they could hear them: "I did this for you. See! I've gone to these lengths just for you, because of your life in the mills, because of your lives that are remembered by only a few."

And I received a reply. No, I didn't see a ghost. I didn't hear a voice. But the reply came. "*Non*," said the ancestors, "*pas du tout*. We do not need anything where we are. You need not do anything for us. We did it all for you. Now, it is up to you."

ACKNOWLEDGEMENTS

First, I would like to thank on-line correspondents including Jeannine Ouellet, David Jacques, Laurent Desbois, James LaForest, James Scott, Réjean Beaulieu, Michel Bouchard, Seb Malette, Denis Tardif, Linda Bouthillier, Don Levesque, Ken Theriault, Christophe Landry, Michael Guignard, Michael Gilleland, Janine LaFleur Penfield, Lucie Leblanc Consentino, and the late Arin Aucoin Gaudet. Thanks to everyone who supported my crowdfunding campaign.

I would also like to thank all participants in the annual gathering of Franco-American creatives under the auspices of the Franco-American Studies Department and the Franco-American Center at the University of Maine, Orono.

Thanks to Larissa Vigue Picard and Stephanie Ruddock of the Pejepscot Historical Society of Brunswick, Maine for their assistance and their kind permission to print images from their collection. Thanks to Laura Amalsi of Brunswick for her help. Thanks to the Curtis Library in Brunswick, the New England Historic and Genealogical Society in Boston, St. John's College library, Annapolis, Maryland, and the Library of Congress. Thanks also to the Franco-American Center in Manchester, New Hampshire.

My thanks to scholars, artists, and activists who encouraged me and informed my perspective: Lise Pelletier, Rhea Côté Robbins, Ben Levine and Julia Schulz, Gregoire Chabot, Susan Pinette, and Patrick Lacroix. Special thanks to Yvon Labbé.

Abby Paige, Dr. Vincent Geloso, and Dr. Mark Paul Richard read parts of the manuscript and made corrections and useful suggestions. Gratitude to Kerri Arsenault, James Myall, and Juliet Burch who read the draft and provided invaluable feedback. I'd also like to thank Jon Tremblay who compared my translations from the French with the original texts and made insightful suggestions. All translations from the French are my own unless otherwise noted.

I acknowledge friends whose conversation challenged me: Roger Burton, Dr. J. Gary Elliott, Dr. Joel Benington, Felice Lopez, Steve Thomas, Steve Thorson, and Dr. Seymour Simmons. Special thanks to Josh Cole for his partnership throughout. Thanks also to Chris Stokes and Alessandra Ferzoco for their generous support.

I would like to thank teachers: Jim Farrow, the late Chaninah Maschler, the guitar craft with Robert Fripp, Cecil McBee, Ran Blake, Fr. Antony Hughes, and Robin Amis. Thanks to Robin Philpot for his faith in the project.

Thanks to the Vermette family for its support especially to Ida Lorraine Vermette McDonald for information and to Erica Vermette who prepared original maps for this book. Thanks to my sister Joan Vermette for her partnership and collaboration. For her support, a special acknowledgment to Juliet Burch. To all my forbears who here and elsewhere lie asleep, this book is dedicated.

My views and my mistakes are all my own. No one else is responsible for them.

NOTES

For a list of works cited see:
www.barakabooks.com/
catalogue/a-distinct-alien-race/

INTRODUCTION

1. Mark Paul Richard, *Loyal But French* (East Lansing: Michigan State University Press, 2008), 155.

2. U.S. Congress, Senate, Reports of the Immigration Commission, *Immigrants in Industries (In Twenty-Five Parts), Part 3: Cotton Goods Manufacturing in the North Atlantic States*, vol. 10, 61st Cong., 2nd sess., 1911, S. Doc. 633, 35-36. (*This volume of the Dillingham Immigration Commission reports I will refer to hereafter as DIC.*) Data derived from the 1900 U.S. Federal Census. DIC includes figures for Maine, Massachusetts, New Hampshire, Rhode Island and Connecticut. The figures for Vermont derive from U.S. Department of Commerce and Labor, Bureau of the Census, Special Reports, Occupations and the Twelfth Census, 1904, 400-403 (Table 41).

3. Yves Roby, *The Franco-Americans of New England: Dreams and Realities* (Sillery, QC: Septentrion, 2004), 1. Roby is quoting Albert Faucher.

4. François Weil, *Les Franco-Américains 1860-1980* (Paris: Belin, 1989), 26.

5. Félix Gatineau, *Historique des Conventions Générales des Canadiens-Français aux Etats-Unis 1865-1901* (Woonsocket: L'Union Saint-Jean Baptiste d'Amerique, 1927), 356-57. Before 1900, Franco-Americans tended to call themselves "*Canadiens* des États-Unis"

[*Canadiens* of the United States]. Beginning with the 1901 Convention in Springfield, Massachusetts, delegates began to use the term "Franco-American" as a way of designating both the *Canadien* and Acadian elements in the United States. The consistency with which the term was used at that convention, and its sudden adoption at that event, suggests that the delegates were coached by their leaders to use it.

6. Roby 2004, 344-49. This dispute came to the fore particularly in the 1930s.

7. "Statement on race, Paris, July 1950," in *Four Statements on the Race Question*, United Nations Educational, Scientific, and Cultural Organization, 1969, 33, http://unesdoc. unesco.org/images/0012/001229/122962eo. pdf (accessed October 24, 2017).

8. *Reports of the Immigration Commission: Dictionary of Races or Peoples*, 61st Cong., 3d sess., 1911, S. Doc. 662, 54.

9. "Race Prejudices in Canada," *New York Times*, September 26, 1885.

10. See *Dictionary of Races or Peoples*, 3. The commission accepts here five "races of mankind" based on morphology.

11. *Dictionary of Races or Peoples*, 63.

12. See DIC, 179 for one example of the use of "American" to designate a "race." "American," "English" and "Irish" are described as "racial groups."

13. Edward Alsworth Ross, *The Old World in the New* (New York: Century, 1914), 291.

14. Elin L. Anderson, *We Americans: A Study of Cleavage in an American City* (New York: Russell & Russell, 1967), 63.

15. John G Bitzes, "The Anti-Greek Riot of 1909 – South Omaha," *Nebraska History* 51 (1970): 199-224.

16. U.S. Department of Commerce, Bureau of the Census, *Historical Statistics of the United States 1789-1945*, 1949, 27. See note on "Series B 48-71, Population – Race by Regions: 1790-1940."

17. Ian Haney-López, "State of race: The Hispanic question on the US census," 10 *Insights on L. & Soc'y* 8 (2009-2010): 9.

PROLOGUE: A Sprint Through 250 Years of History

1. Gilles Havard and Cécile Vidal, *Histoire de l'Amérique Française* (Paris: Flammarion, 2003), 403-04.

2. Havard and Vidal, 403-09.

3. Daniel Paul, "Mi'kmaq, Acadian Relationship Built on Respect," *Halifax Herald*, July 25, 1997. http://www.danielnpaul.com/Col/1997/Mi'kmaqAcadianRelationship-Respectful.html (accessed September 11, 2017).

4. "Spanish civilization crushed the Indian; English civilization scorned and neglected him; French civilization embraced and cherished him." Francis Parkman, *The Jesuits in North America in the Seventeenth Century*, pt. 2, France and England in North America (Boston: Little, Brown, 1897), 131.

5. Adam Gaudry and Darryl Leroux, "White Settler Revisionism and Making Métis Everywhere: The Evocation of Métissage in Quebec and Nova Scotia," *Critical Ethnic Studies* 3, no. 1 (Spring 2017): 116-142. Cf. esp. 121-23.

6. For the size of Wolfe's invading force see John Dickinson and Brian Young, *A Short History of Québec*, 4th ed. (Montréal & Kingston: McGill-Queen's University Press, 2008), 47.

7. "For abolishing the free System of English Laws in a neighbouring Province, establishing therein an Arbitrary government, and enlarging its Boundaries so as to render it at once an example and fit instru-ment for introducing the same absolute rule into these Colonies."

8. Charles H. Metzger, S.J., *The Quebec Act: A Primary Cause of the American Revolution* (New York: United States Catholic Historical Society, 1936), *passim*.

9. Metzger, 24.

10. For a translation of a primary source on *Canadien* attitudes toward the war see Michael P. Gabriel, ed., *Quebec During the American Invasion 1775-1776*, translated by S. Pascale Vergereau-Dewy (East Lansing: Michigan State University Press, 2005).

11. Earl of Durham (John George Lambton), *Report on the Affairs of British North America* (Toronto: Printed by Robert Stanton, 1839), 127.

12. Earl of Durham, *Report on the Affairs of British North America*, 131.

13. Some sources say that Lower Canada had debt, but a much smaller sum than Upper Canada's.

14. Earl of Durham, *Report on the Affairs of British North America*, 117.

15. For a readable, general history of Québec from an English-speaking perspective see Dickinson and Young, *A Short History of Quebec*, 4th ed. (Montréal & Kingston: McGill-Queen's University Press, 2008). For a French-speaking approach see Jacques Lacoursière and Robin Philpot, *A People's History of Quebec* (Montréal: Baraka Books, 2009). For the period of *Nouvelle-France* the best synthesis is Gilles Havard and Cécile Vidal, *Histoire de l'Amérique française* (Paris: Flammarion, 2003). For the founding of *Nouvelle-France* see David Hackett Fischer, *Champlain's Dream* (New York: Simon and Schuster, 2008). For the story of the Acadians and the Deportation see John Mack Farragher, *A Great and Noble Scheme* (New York: Norton, 2005). For the 200 years following the English Conquest see Mason Wade, *The French Canadians 1760-1967*, 2 vols. (Toronto: MacMillan, 1968). Wade is dated but remains a valuable synthesis in English.

CHAPTER ONE: "Head of the Mercantile Community of Boston"

1. *Boston Directory* 1849-1850, 7. See the digitized collection of directories at the Boston Athenaeum Digital Collections online, http://cdm.bostonathenaeum.org/cdm/search/collection/p16057coll32 (accessed October 24, 2017). All citations of the *Boston Directory* refer to the documents in this collection.

2. *Remarks Made by the Hon. T. H. Perkins* (Boston: Samuel Dickinson, 1841), Introduction. Emphasis in the original document.

3. Quoted in Rachel Tamar Van, "Free Trade & Family Values: Kinship Networks and the Culture of Early American Capitalism" (PhD Dissertation, Columbia University, 2011), 410.

4. Lloyd Vernon Briggs, *History and Genealogy of the Cabot Family, 1475-1927* (Boston, C.E. Goodspeed, 1927), xvi.

5. Robert F. Dalzell, Jr., *Enterprising Elite: The Boston Associates and the World They Made* (New York: Norton, 1987), 58.

6. Briggs, 589.

7. Carl Seaburg and Stanley Paterson, *Merchant Prince of Boston: Colonel T. H. Perkins, 1764-1854* (Cambridge: Harvard University Press, 1971), 418.

8. Seaburg and Paterson, 19. For many of the details of Perkins's life I have relied on this often-cited biography.

9. Seaburg and Paterson, 22.

10. Seaburg and Paterson, 62.

11. Orlando Patterson, *Slavery and Social Death: A Comparative Study* (Cambridge: Harvard University Press, 1982), 162.

12. Briggs, 470.

13. Hugh Thomas, *The Slave Trade: The Story of the Atlantic Slave Trade 1440-1870* (New York: Simon & Schuster, 1997), 534.

14. Seaburg and Paterson, 40-41.

15. Samuel and Joseph Cabot, 1814-1821, 1 Volume, Records of Boston Merchants Engaged in Foreign Trade, 1739-1887, Baker Library Historical Collections, Harvard Business School, Harvard University, Cambridge, MA. http://oasis.lib.harvard.edu/oasis/deliver/~bak00238 (accessed October 24, 2017).

16. Mary Cable, *Black Odyssey: The Case of the Slave Ship Amistad* (Middlesex, England: Penguin Books, 1977), 7-8.

17. Van, 69.

18. Briggs, 390.

19. Voyage 37262, Katy (1794), The Trans-Atlantic Slave Trade Database, Voyages, http://www.slavevoyages.org/voyage/37262/variables (accessed September 26, 2017); Seaburg and Paterson, 145. The online database has the ship still afloat in 1794 and apparently lost that year, while the letter in Briggs indicates that the Brig *Katy* went down by 1793. Another voyage of the *Katy* in this database lists Daniel McNeill among the owners in 1793.

20. Briggs, 505.

21. Briggs, 391. Emphasis in the original document.

22. Briggs, 391.

23. Howard Zinn, *A People's History of the United States* (New York: HarperCollins, 2003), 29.

24. Seaburg and Paterson, 61.

25. *Acts and Resolves of Massachusetts* (1786-1787), Boston: Adams and Nourse, 1787 (reprinted 1893, Wright and Potter), 1787, Ch. 48, 615-617, https://archive.org/stream/actsresolvespass178687mass (accessed October 24, 2017).

26. Van, 69.

27. Van, 80.

28. Samuel Eliot Morison, *The Maritime History of Massachusetts, 1783-1860* (Boston: Houghton Mifflin, 1941), 167.

29. M. A. De Wolfe Howe, *The Children's Judge: Frederick Pickering Cabot* (Boston: Houghton Mifflin, 1932), 8.

30. For Jefferson's phrase "execrable commerce" see his original draft of the Declaration of Independence in Merrill D. Peterson, ed., *The Portable Thomas Jefferson* (New York: Viking Press, 1975), 238.

31. Susan M. Harvey, "Slavery in Massachusetts: A descendant of early settlers investigates the connections in Newburyport,

Massachusetts" (Master's thesis, Fitchburg State University, 2011), 47-50.

32. Bernard Bailyn, "Slavery and Population Growth in Colonial New England," in Peter Temin, ed., *Engines of Enterprise: An Economic History of New England.* (Cambridge: Harvard University Press, 2000).

33. Van, 41; Seaburg and Paterson, 41.

34. For the general acceptance of smuggling and bribery among colonial era merchants see Bailyn in Temin, ed., *Engines of Enterprise*, 255.

35. Morison, 168.

36. Seaburg and Paterson, 43-44.

37. Seaburg and Paterson, 267-68.

38. For a brief account of the economics of the U.S. opium trade see Jonathan Lewy, "The American Opium Trade," http://www.jonathanlewy.com/american_opium_trade/ (accessed January 11, 2017).

39. Van, 360.

40. Jacques M. Downs, "American Merchants and the China Opium Trade, 1800-1840," *Business History Review* 42, no. 4 (Winter, 1968): 421.

41. Lewy, "America enters the Chinese Trade." For the phrase "opium rushes" see Downs, 422.

42. Seaburg and Paterson, 265.

43. Seaburg and Paterson, 298n.

44. Seaburg and Paterson, 263-64.

45. Van, 358 citing Charles Stelle.

46. Van, 363, 359; Downs, 429-430, 431n45, 432.

47. Dalzell, 62.

48. E.g. cf. Morison, 277.

49. Lewy, "America enters the Chinese Trade," "Conclusion."

50. Lewy, "The Second Phase of the American Trade."

51. For the Perkins Co.'s profits and Cushing's return see Seaburg and Paterson, 372.

52. Dalzell, 61.

53. For the China Trade as "an important source of investment capital" see Peter Temin, "The Industrialization of New England," in Temin, ed. *Engines of Enterprise*, 147. For the importance of the larger slave economy to the early industrialization of New England, see Bailyn, also in *Engines of Enterprise*, 259. Bailyn also credits New England's rapid population growth as contributing to the region's extraordinary economic development in the early industrial period.

54. Cf. Dalzell 64-67. A major theme of Dalzell's book is that industrialization was a risk mitigation strategy for the Boston merchants.

CHAPTER TWO: A Textile Industry for New England

1. *An Act laying an Embargo on all ships and vessels in the ports and harbors of the United States*, 10th Cong., 1st sess. (December 22, 1807), 5, 451-53.

2. Before the Embargo Act was passed Congress enacted a law to prevent the importation of certain goods from Britain. Maryland Congressman Joseph Nicholson's list of items that the U.S. should refuse to import from Great Britain, that the U.S. could presumably produce itself or acquire elsewhere, did not include cotton goods. *Annals of Congress*, House of Representatives, 9th Congress, 1st Session (1806), 450-451.

3. Peter Dobkin Hall, *The Organization of American Culture 1700-1900* (New York: New York University Press, 1984), 82. Statistics derived from Figure 3.

4. William Moran, *The Belles of New England* (New York: Thomas Dunne Books, 2002), 48-9.

5. Sven Beckert, *Empire of Cotton* (New York: Alfred A. Knopf, 2015), 74.

6. Beckert, 72-74.

7. Moran, 49.

8. Dalzell, 5-6; Moran, 51-52.

9. Thomas, 487-488; Robert H. Patton, *Patriot Pirates: The Privateer War for Freedom and Fortune* (New York: Vintage Books, 2009), 12.

10. For the whipping rooms see Moran, 52. The source for this information is unclear, however there are credible sources for

the corporal punishment of children in factories. The Massachusetts Bureau of Statistics of Labor, *First Annual Report* (Boston, 1870), 107, mentions the practice and in a footnote gives an eyewitness account of the strap used in a Rhode Island mill. The Mass. BSL *Second Annual Report* (Boston, 1871), 489 gives another account of children beaten in mills claiming that such abuses had been prosecuted, a verifiable fact. Cf. also Edith Abbott, *Women in Industry* (New York: Appleton, 1910), 347 and the notes on that page.

11. This and subsequent quotations from the papers of the Boston Manufacturing Company are from the following collection: Boston Manufacturing Company records, 1813-1930 (inclusive), volume 1 & 2. Mss:442 1813-1930, Baker Library Historical Collections, Harvard Business School, Harvard University, Cambridge, MA. https://iiif.lib.harvard.edu/manifests/view/drs:8353623$1i (accessed January 14, 2017).

12. Eric Hilt, "Democratizing Incorporation: Law and the Industrial Enterprise in Massachusetts" (Cambridge, MA: National Bureau of Economic Research, May 2008), 6. Cf. also Dalzell, 49.

13. Moran, 54; Chaim M. Rosenberg, *The Life and Times of Francis Cabot Lowell, 1775–1817* (Lanham, MD: Lexington Books, 2011), 248. Rosenberg claims that sales in 1815 were a mere $412 in 1815, rising to $51,203 two years later.

14. Moran, 54; Rosenberg, 248; Dalzell, 51. Moran claims that dividends ranged from 12 to 28 percent. Rosenberg's figure is 8 to 13 percent in the first decade, while Dalzell reports a high of 27.5 percent in 1821.

15. Winifred Barr Rothenberg, "The Invention of American Capitalism: The Economy of New England in the Federal Period" in Temin, ed., *Engines of Enterprise*, 98.

16. For India Wharf see Dalzell, 9; Rosenberg, 145-50.

17. This Moses Brown is not the man who financed Samuel Slater. For this Moses Brown, partner of Israel Thorndike, see

Duane Hamilton Hurd, ed., *History of Essex County, Massachusetts*, vol. 1 (Philadelphia: J.W. Lewis, 1888), 755-757.

18. For a sketch of Israel Thorndike see Hurd 1888, 754. For the business activities of Brown & Thorndike see Octavius Thorndike Howe, M.D., *Beverly Privateers in the American Revolution* (Cambridge: John Wilson and Son, 1922), 321.

19. Dalzell, 134.

20. For Jackson see John A. Lowell, *Memoir of Patrick Tracy Jackson* (New York: Hunt's Merchants' Magazine, 1848). For Appleton see Robert C. Winthrop, *Memoir of the Hon. Nathan Appleton* (Boston: John Wilson and Son, 1861).

21. Charles C.P. Moody, *Biographical Sketches of the Moody Family* (Boston: Samuel G. Drake, 1847), 145-157.

22. Rosenberg, 260.

23. Rosenberg, 261-62; Dalzell, 36.

24. F. W. Taussig, *The Tariff History of the United States* (New York: G. P. Putnam's Sons, 1892), 30-35; cf. also Rothenberg in Temin, ed. *Engines of Enterprise*, 101-103.

25. Rosenberg, 7.

26. Dalzell, 37.

27. Dalzell, 48-49.

28. Lowell, *Memoir of Patrick Tracy Jackson*, 8.

29. Lowell, *Memoir of Patrick Tracy Jackson*, 8.

30. Edith Abbott, "History of the Employment of Women in the American Cotton Mills, Part 1," *Journal of Political Economy* 16 (1908): 605. See the table at the bottom of this page.

31. The best description of the mill girls is by one of their own: Harriet H. Robinson, *Loom and Spindle or Life Among the Early Mill Girls* (New York: Thomas Y. Crowell, 1898), 60-96. Cf. also Abbott 1908, 689; Rosenberg, 249-251; Moran, 11-46.

32. Robinson, 76-77; Moran, 8.

33. Henry A. Miles, *Lowell, As It Was and As It Is* (Lowell: Powers and Bagley and N.L. Dayon: 1845), 129-30. Emphasis in the original.

34. *Report on Condition of Woman and Child Wage-Earners in the United States*, 61st Cong., 2d sess., 1910, S. Doc. 645, vol. 9, 85.

35. Moran, 17.

36. Moran, 26, 45-46.

37. Robinson, 82.

38. Dalzell, 45-46; Moran, 26-27.

39. Robinson, 81.

40. Robinson, 74-75.

41. See Beckert, 57. He makes a comparison between Lancashire and Silicon Valley.

42. Dalzell, 47.

43. After 1842, the China market for U.S. textiles amounted to more than a million dollars annually. Cf. Dalzell, 51.

44. Beckert, 140.

45. François Weil, "Capitalism and Industrialization in New England, 1815-1845," *Journal of American History* 84 (March 1998): 1353.

46. Rothenberg in Temin, ed., *Engines of Enterprise*, 93.

47. Beckert, 140.

48. John S. Hekman, "The Product Cycle and New England Textiles," *The Quarterly Journal of Economics* 94, no. 4 (June 1980): 697–717.

49. Elizabeth A. De Wolfe, *The Murder of Mary Bean and Other Stories* (Kent, OH: Kent State University Press, 2007), 10.

50. Robinson, 68-69.

51. My account of the causes of New England's early industrialization is indebted to Peter Temin, "The Industrialization of New England," in Temin, ed. *Engines of Enterprise*. Cf. esp. 113-116.

52. Robinson, 72.

53. Carl E. Prince and Seth Taylor, "Daniel Webster, the Boston Associates, and the U.S. Government's Role in the Industrializing Process, 1815-1830," *Journal of the Early Republic* 2, no. 3 (1982): 283-99.

54. Colonel Perkins and Others to Mr. Webster, October 18, 1822, in *The Writings and Speeches of Daniel Webster, Private Correspondence* 1, Fletcher Webster, ed. (Boston: Little, Brown, 1903), 17:321.

55. For Webster's "recklessness in pecuniary matters" and the Boston Associates' aid in the matter see Dalzell, 191-92.

56. Thomas A. Bailey, *A Diplomatic History of the American People*, 8th ed. (New York: Appleton-Century-Crofts, 1969), 172-75 (Spanish Claims) and 195-98 (French Claims). Another grievance against Spain was its refusal in 1802 to allow U.S. ships a right of deposit in the port of New Orleans, then under Spanish control.

57. Prince and Taylor, 296-98; Merritt Roe Smith, "New England Industry and the Federal Government," in Temin, ed., *Engines of Enterprise*, 264-66.

58. Beckert, 76-80.

CHAPTER THREE: Enter the Cabots

1. Hall, 64.

2. Hall, 64.

3. Thomas, 271.

4. Briggs, 66.

5. Hall, 64.

6. Edgar Stanton Maclay, *A History of American Privateers* (New York: Appleton, 1899), 7.

7. Patton, 27.

8. Some of the 13 states had their own navies.

9. Patton, 114.

10. Briggs, 100-101.

11. Briggs, 73.

12. Briggs, 84, 74.

13. Maclay, 165.

14. Patton, 111.

15. Patton, 131-33.

16. Briggs, 75; Hall, 65.

17. Briggs, 99.

18. Briggs, 99. Emphasis in the original document.

19. Briggs, 100.

20. Robert W. Lovett, "The Beverly Cotton Manufactory: Or Some New Light on an Early Cotton Mill," *Bulletin of the Business Historical Society* 26, no. 4 (1952): 221.

21. John C. Fitzpatrick, ed., *The Diaries of George Washington 1748-1799*, vol. 4, 1789-1799 (Boston: Houghton Mifflin 1925), 41.

22. Lovett, 231.

23. For Cabot's letter to Hamilton and his attempt to gain the support of Federal and State governments see Lovett, 231-32.

24. Lovett, 234.

25. Howe, *Beverly Privateers in the American Revolution*, 349; Briggs, 195.

26. For Francis Cabot see Briggs, 194-96.

27. Rosenberg, 203.

28. To George Washington from Benjamin Lincoln, 10 June 1791, in *The Papers of George Washington, Presidential Series, vol. 8, 22 March 1791–22 September 1791*, Mark A. Mastromarino, ed. (Charlottesville: University Press of Virginia, 1999), 259n1.

29. Mastromarino, ed., 259.

30. Beckert, 114; Jane Thompson-Stahr, *The Burling Books: Ancestors and Descendants of Edward and Grace Burling, Quakers (1600-2000)*, vol. 1 (Baltimore: Gateway Press, 2001), 322.

31. *Boston Directory* 1813, 82.

32. *Boston Directory* 1816, 77.

33. *Boston Directory* 1818, 56.

34. *Boston Directory* 1820, 57.

35. Michael C. Jensen, "The Cabots of Boston," *New York Times*, March 12, 1972. The article quotes Francis H. Cabot: "The Cabots over the years have been interested in two things – one is marrying rich women and the other is group singing." The article also quotes Thomas Cabot: "The Cabots got their money the hard way. Samuel [his great grandfather] went to work for T. H. Perkins...He [Cabot] married the boss's daughter."

36. For the "intensive and extensive" patterns of marriage alliances among the Cabots and related families see Hall, 65-68.

37. Dalzell, 59; Hall, 68.

38. *Boston Directory* 1820, 57.

39. Dalzell, 65. Perkins delayed his retirement to support his sons-in-law Samuel Cabot and T.B. Gary.

40. Seaburg and Paterson, 362.

41. An Act to Incorporate the Elliot Manufacturing Company, *Laws of the Commonwealth of Massachusetts Passed by the General Court*, ch. 11, 219 (1823). Approved June 12, 1823.

42. Richard Clarke Cabot appears as Frederick Cabot's partner in the *Boston Directory* 1823, 57; Whitney then becomes a partner of Frederick and Richard Cabot per the *Boston Directory* 1827, 56.

43. Seaburg and Paterson, 238, 241.

44. For Pettee see William Bond Wheelwright, *A Chronicle of Textile Machinery 1824-1924* (Boston: Saco-Lowell Shops, 1923), 35-41; Duane Hamilton Hurd, ed., *History of Middlesex County Massachusetts*, vol. 3 (Philadelphia: J. W. Lewis, 1890), 92-97.

45. An Act to incorporate the Upper-Falls Religious Society, and the Proprietors of the Upper-Falls Meeting-House in Newton, *Laws of the Commonwealth of Massachusetts Passed at the Several Sessions of the General Court Beginning May, 1825, and Ending March 1828*, ch. 100, 758-760 (1828). Act approved March 28, 1828.

46. Hurd, ed. 1890, 3:92.

47. Kenneth W. Newcomb, *The Makers of the Mold: A History of Newton Upper Falls, Massachusetts*, Rev. ed. (2006), Chapter 2 "Industry"; Hurd, ed. 1890, 3:91-97; Seaburg and Paterson, 311-313.

48. An Act to incorporate the Lowell Manufacturing Company, *Laws of the Commonwealth of Massachusetts Passed at the Several Sessions of the General Court Beginning May, 1825, and Ending March, 1828*, Chap. 47, 655 (1828). Act approved February 8, 1828.

49. *Laws of the Commonwealth of Massachusetts Passed at the Several Sessions of the General Court Beginning May, 1831, and Ending March, 1833*, ch. 89, 320, approved March 5, 1832; *Acts and Resolves passed by the General Court*, ch. 13, 8 (1846), approved February 5, 1846; and *Acts and Resolves passed by the General Court* (1850), ch. 77, 326-27, approved March 16, 1850.

50. John Higginson Cabot, son of Frederick and Marianne Cabot, was born on February 11, 1831 at Dracut, Massachusetts (Briggs, 280).

51. For the dimensions of the mill, the phrases "Negro cloth" and "plantation wear" cf. Hurd, ed., 1890, 2:75. For the Lowell Manufacturing Company as producers of "coarse goods commonly called Negro cloths" see also *Lowell Directory*, 1833, 7 https://archive.org/details/lowellmassa-chuse1833livo (accessed October 25, 2017).

52. Beckert, 147.

53. Hurd, ed., 1890, 2:75-76; cf. also *Contributions of the Old Residents' Historical Association*, vol. 6 (Lowell, MA: Old Residents' Historical Association, 1904), 72-74; Frederick W. Coburn, *History of Lowell And Its People*, vol. 2 (New York: Lewis Historical Publishing, 1920), 131-133; Alexander N. Cook ed., *A Century of Carpet and Rug Making in America* (New York: Bigelow-Hartford Carpet Company, 1925), 11-15.

54. William Furness Cabot, son of Frederick and Marianne Cabot, was born on January 17, 1835 at Philadelphia (Briggs, 280). In her will, Marianne Cabot leaves to this son some silverware "made when we first lived in Philadelphia in 1831." Last will of Marianne Cabot, January 20, 1887, *Massachusetts, Wills and Probate Records, 1635-1991* [database on-line]. Provo, UT, USA: Ancestry.com Operations, Inc., 2015.

55. *Boston Directory* 1839, 110.

56. Holmes Ammidown, "Hon. Alexander De Witt," in *Historical Collections*, 2nd. ed. (New York, 1877), 1:250-53.

57. Briggs, 280. Briggs mistakenly locates the Norway Plains Company in Maine. The *Boston Directory* for 1848-49 (87), 1849-50 (89) and 1850-51 (107) lists Frederick Cabot as the Treasurer of the Kennebec and Norway Plains companies.

58. John A. Poor, *Memoir of Reuel Williams* (Maine Historical Society, 1864).

59. An Act to incorporate the Kennebec Company, *Private and Special Acts of the State of Maine Passed by the Eighteenth Legislature, January Session, 1838* (1838), ch. 419, 522-23. Act approved February 28, 1838.

60. James W. North, *The History of Augusta* (Augusta, ME: Clapp and North, 1870), 639.

61. For my comparison of the stockholders in 1845 and 1848 see: "An Abstract of the Returns of Corporations, Made to the Office of Secretary of State, in January, 1845 for the Year 1845," 23-24 in *Documents Printed by Order of the Legislature of the State of Maine During Its Session, A.D. 1846* (Augusta: Wm. T. Johnson, 1847); "An Abstract of the Returns of Corporations, Made to the Office of Secretary of State in January, 1849 for the Year 1848," 7-9 in *Documents Printed by Order of the Legislature of the State of Maine During Its Session, A.D. 1849* (Augusta: Smith & Robinson, 1850).

62. *Boston Directory* 1848-49, 87.

63. *Boston Directory* 1848-49, 87.

64. New Hampshire, *Journal of the Honorable Senate of the State of New Hampshire at Their Session held at the Capitol in Concord, June 1846* (Concord NH: Asa McFarland, 1846), 113, 115, 129, 194; New Hampshire, *Journal of the House of Representatives of the State of New Hampshire at Their Session held at the Capitol in Concord, June 1846* (Concord NH: Asa McFarland, 1846), 75, 241, 245, 282, 350, 417.

65. Duane Hamilton Hurd, ed., *History of Rockingham and Strafford Counties, New Hampshire* (Philadelphia: J.W. Lewis, 1882), 748-50; Franklin McDuffee, *History of the Town of Rochester* (Manchester, NH: John B. Clarke, 1892), 477-78.

66. *New-England Mercantile Union Business Directory 1849* (New York: Pratt & Co., 1849), 107, 207.

67. Manuscript United States Federal Census of 1860, Brookline, Norfolk County, Massachusetts, 127.

68. George Augustus Wheeler and Henry Warren Wheeler, *History of Brunswick, Topsham, and Harpswell, Maine* (Boston: Alfred Mudge & Son, 1878), 575-77. The authors list banks in 19th century Brunswick. None of the ten banks listed had a capital stock worth more than

$100,000 and only one bank listed had total deposits in excess of Cabot's worth.

69. Massachusetts, Death Records, 1841-1915 [database on-line]. Provo, UT, USA: Ancestry.com Operations, Inc., 2013.

70. Last Will of Frederick Cabot, November 7, 1867, Massachusetts, Wills and Probate Records, 1635-1991 [database on-line]. Provo, UT, USA: Ancestry.com Operations, Inc., 2015. The will leaves to his widow $75,000 as well as his house, out-buildings and everything in them, and bequeaths $12,000 to his daughter, with an unspecified remainder to be divided between his sons.

CHAPTER FOUR: Textiles in Brunswick – The First Half-Century

1. Wheeler and Wheeler, 564.

2. For Ezra Smith see Wheeler and Wheeler, 603, 614.

3. Parker McRobb Reed, *History of Bath and Environs, Sagadahoc County, Maine 1607-1894* (Portland, Maine: Lakeside Press, 1894), 328-336; for his involvement in the cotton carrying trade cf. Reed, 151; cf. also Wheeler and Wheeler, 758-59.

4. Wheeler and Wheeler, 787-88. That Smith, King and Porter were the leading forces behind the 1809 cotton mill see Wheeler and Wheeler, 564.

5. Wheeler and Wheeler, 560, 569, 571 (Eastman), 578 (Jones).

6. Wheeler and Wheeler, 565.

7. Wheeler and Wheeler, 259, 565.

8. Wheeler and Wheeler, 565; Cumberland Real Property Records, Cumberland County (Maine) Registry of Deeds, Volume 137, Page 136, filed June 3, 1834.

9. Cumberland County Registry of Deeds, Volume 118, Page 116, filed July 31, 1829.

10. Cumberland County Registry of Deeds, Volume 137, Page 136, filed June 3, 1834.

11. Cumberland County Registry of Deeds, Volume 143, Page 207.

12. Cumberland County Registry of Deeds, Volume 143, Page 195, filed September 16, 1835.

13. For William Appleton's membership in the Perkins clique see Van, 468; that he was a cousin of Nathan Appleton see Mary Caroline Crawford, "The Appleton Family," *Famous Families of Massachusetts* (Boston, Little, Brown, 1930), 2:170; for mention of his political career cf. Crawford, 172. For his investment in Merrimack Manufacturing Company see Dalzell, 48. For Appleton's involvement in banking see Dalzell, 95, 233.

14. Cumberland County Registry of Deeds, Volume 143, Page 198, filed September 16, 1835; Volume 143, Page 202, filed September 16, 1835.

15. Cumberland County Registry of Deeds, Volume 144, Page 236, filed January 19, 1836.

16. Wheeler and Wheeler, 566. For Deering see George Derby and James Terry White, eds., *The National Cyclopedia of American Biography*, rev. ed. (New York: James T. White, 1909), 10:250. For Beard as a newspaper editor see Wheeler and Wheeler, 309.

17. Cumberland County Registry of Deeds, Volume 166, Page 290, filed November 13, 1839.

18. Cumberland County Registry of Deeds, Volume 173, Page 119, filed May 13, 1841; the date of the agreement is October 1, 1840.

19. Cumberland County Registry of Deeds, Volume 169, Page 567, filed March 2, 1841; Volume 173, Page 6, filed March 2, 1841.

20. Wheeler and Wheeler, 566.

21. Cumberland County Registry of Deeds, Volume 179, Page 292, filed on April 13, 1843.

22. Cumberland County Registry of Deeds, Volume 179, Page 294, filed on April 13, 1843.

23. Cumberland County Registry of Deeds, Volume 179, Page 352, filed on June 8, 1843.

24. Cumberland County Registry of Deeds, Volume 189, Page 545, filed on October 29, 1845.

25. Cumberland County Registry of Deeds, Volume 203, Page 293, filed on May 14, 1847. For Thompson see Wheeler and Wheeler, 269, 615, 616, 917.

26. An act to incorporate the Warumbo Manufacturing Company, *Acts and Resolves Passed by the Twenty-Seventh Legislature of the State of Maine* (1847), ch. 26, 28. Approved July 3, 1847.

27. John Dunning Coburn is buried in Range 4, grave 79 at Pine Grove Cemetery in Brunswick. See Donald and Mark Cheetham, Pine Grove Cemetery, Bath Road, Brunswick, Maine, vol. 1 of 2, Range 1 thru 8, 2005, http://www.curtislibrary.com/wp-content/uploads/2013/08/Pine-Grove-Cemetery-searchable.pdf (accessed October 9, 2017). Cf. also Wheeler and Wheeler, 726.

28. Cumberland County Registry of Deeds, Volume 238, Page 274, filed on June 24, 1852.

29. Cumberland County Registry of Deeds, Volume 245, Page 55, filed on February 19, 1853.

30. An act to incorporate the Cabot Company, *Acts and Resolves as Passed by the Thirty-Second Legislature of the State of Maine Legislature* (1853), ch. 34, 33-34. Approved March 4, 1853. Cumberland County Registry of Deeds, Volume 282, Page 500. The document records that the sale transpired on Sept. 16, 1853 although the document was filed on February 4, 1858.

31. For Shepley see George Derby and James Terry White, eds., *The National Cyclopedia of American Biography*, rev. ed. (New York: James T. White, 1909), 10:78.

32. *Brunswick Telegraph*, May 28, 1853, 2; "Enlarging," *Brunswick Telegraph*, January 7, 1854, 2; and "The Cabot Mill," *Brunswick Telegraph*, July 21, 1855, 2.

33. *Brunswick Telegraph*, November 3, 1855, 2; Joel W. Eastman, "Embryonic Metropolis: Brunswick, Maine and the Urbanization of America 1800-1900," Pejepscot Historical Society Collection, Brunswick, Maine, 1984, 6.

34. Meeting of the Cabot Company, November 21, 1855, Charter, By Laws and Records: Cabot Co. 1853-1858, Pejepscot Historical Society Collection, Brunswick, Maine.

35. Meetings of the Cabot Company, July 23, 1856 and November 10, 1857, Charter, By Laws and Records: Cabot Co. 1853-1858, Pejepscot Historical Society Collection, Brunswick, Maine.

36. Cumberland County Registry of Deeds, Volume 286, Page 35, filed on February 19, 1858. The sale took place on December 15, 1857 per January 27, 1858 meeting of the Cabot Company. See Charter, By Laws and Records: Cabot Co. 1853-1858, Pejepscot Historical Society Collection, Brunswick, Maine. For Nickerson as fish merchant (as a partner in Ebenezer Nickerson & Co.) see *Boston Directory* 1858, 273. For his Masonic activities see William Richard Cutter and William Frederick Adams, eds. *Genealogical and Personal Memoirs Relating to the Families of the State of Massachusetts*, (New York: Lewis Historical Publishing, 1910), 2:749-50.

37. An Act to incorporate the Cabot Manufacturing Company, *Acts and Resolves Passed by the 37th Legislature of the State of Maine* (1858), ch. 130, 125. Approved January 18, 1858.

38. Cumberland County Registry of Deeds, Volume 286, Page 38, filed on February 19, 1858.

39. For Greene as Agent of the mill see "The Cabot Mill," *Brunswick Telegraph*, July 21, 1855, 2.

40. The Cabot Manufacturing Company won an award for cotton fabrics at the Centennial International Exhibition in Philadelphia in 1876. See *The Awards and Claims of Exhibitors at the International Exhibition, 1876*, National Association of Wool Manufacturers, Boston (Cambridge: John Wilson & Son, 1877), 98.

41. For Francis Cabot see Briggs, 652-53. Cf. also Obituary of Francis Cabot, *New York Times*, April 13, 1905, 11; Howe, *The Children's Judge*, 10-12.

42. Howe *The Children's Judge*, 11. For the phrase "rakish conduct" and for his brief account of the life of Francis Cabot see George Prochnik, *Putnam Camp: Sigmund Freud, James Jackson Putnam, and the*

Purpose of American Psychology (New York: Other Press, 2006), 217. Prochnik is Cabot's great-great-grandson.

43. Howe, *The Children's Judge*, 11.

44. For the "bookish streak" cf. Howe, *The Children's Judge*, 7, 24-25.

45. Prochnik, 217.

46. A Francis Cabot, age 22, appears on a "list of passengers on board the ship Cortez of New Bedford...bound from the Sandwich Islands to New Bedford," dated January 15, 1849. We would expect Francis Cabot to be 23 years old in January 1849.

47. *Boston Directory* 1851, 43. Francis works out of the same address as his father at 25 Doane.

48. *Boston Directory* 1856, 58.

49. *Boston Directory* 1857, 60.

50. John Eliot Parkman and the historian Francis Parkman were sons of Rev. Francis and Caroline (Hall) Parkman. Howard Doughty, *Francis Parkman* (Cambridge: Harvard University Press, 1983), 4, 7.

51. Briggs, 652. Briggs mentions that Francis Cabot was involved in the "East India trade" at this time. For the detail that the firm of Francis Cabot & Co. was trading in Calcutta see the Harvard alumni publication, *Class of 1850* (Cambridge: John Wilson and Sons, 1895), 8.

52. Tirthankar Roy, "Trading Firms in Colonial India," *Business History Review* 88 (Spring 2014): 16.

53. *Boston Directory* 1858, 61, 419.

54. *Boston Directory* 1859, 70, 464, 525.

55. *Boston Directory* 1889, 211.

56. See An act to incorporate the Winthrop Mills Company (Winthrop, Maine), *Acts and Resolves Passed by the Forty-Fifth Legislature of the State of Maine* (1866), ch. 13, 9-10. Approved February 1, 1866. The Obituary of Francis Cabot, *New York Times*, April 13, 1905, 11 and his biography in Briggs (652) mention Cabot's role in the Fisher Manufacturing Company of Grafton, Massachusetts.

57. *The Boston Directory* 1890, 1522-23 cites "F. Cabot" as Treasurer of the Cabot, Clinton, Fisher, Norway Plains, Waumbeck, and Winthrop companies as well as the Norwich Woolen Company. He runs these firms from 70 Kilby Street.

58. Obituary of Francis Cabot, *New York Times*, April 13, 1905, 11.

59. Prochnik, 217.

60. For Sturtevant's interest in these mills see Hurd, ed. 1882, 749. For Amasa Clark's involvement in this same portfolio see his obituary in the *Bulletin of the National Association of Wool Manufacturers*, vol. 37 (Boston, 1907), 402-03. Clarke was a Cabot relative and Sturtevant's son-in-law. See also *Directory of Directors in the City of Boston and Vicinity*, 7th ed. (Boston: Ernest S. Woodaman, 1911), 70. This directory lists Francis Cabot's son Frederick P. Cabot as a Director of the Fisher, Winthrop, and Clinton Mills as well as of the Cabot Manufacturing Company.

61. "Death of Benjamin Greene," *Brunswick Record*, March 18, 1904; *Wool and Cotton Reporter*, March 17, 1904, 7.

62. For Greene's place of birth, the names of his parents, and his father's occupation see Record of a Death: Benjamin Greene, Maine State Archives, Vital Records 1892-1907, Roll Number: 23, record number 484.

63. That Greene was an owner of the Adams brothers' store see *Brunswick, Bath, Richmond Directory 1867-68*, 90, https://catalog.hathitrust.org/Record/100487213 (accessed November 18, 2017). For the general opinion that this was the company store for the Cabot Manufacturing Company and Greene's denial of the same, see "Strike," *Brunswick Telegraph*, August 12, 1881, 2: "The grocery store commonly known as the factory store (though it is fair to say that the proprietors of the factory deny all connection with the grocery store) kept by the Messrs. Adams Bros. was closed." The same article indicates that employees at the mill were sometimes paid in orders from the store.

64. U.S. Department of the Interior, *Benjamin Greene House*, Historic American

Buildings Survey, National Park Service, Washington, DC, HABS No. ME-226.

65. Letter of Eben Everett, June 16, 1835 (addressee unrecorded), Papers of Kimball & Coburn, Pejepscot Historical Society Collection, Brunswick, Maine.

66. For evidence that women were the bulk of Cabot Mill employees in the 1850s see *Brunswick Telegraph* May 28, 1853, 2 (the mill "stood ready to employ from 75 to 100 female operatives"); Advertisement, *Brunswick Telegraph*, June 11, 1853, 3 and June 25, 1853, 3 ("weavers and girls wanted"); "Enlarging," *Brunswick Telegraph*, January 17, 1854, 2 ("'Women's Rights' to work for good pay are beginning to be extensively recognized here"). The payroll books for Kimball & Coburn from October 1844 through March 1847 (Pejepscot Historical Society Collection, Brunswick, Maine) show that almost all of the employees were women.

67. David Gilman, "Something About Cotton Manufacturing: Brunswick's Greatest Industry," *Board of Trade Journal* 17, no. 7 (1904): 41.

CHAPTER FIVE: Franco-Americans Rescue King Cotton

1. *Boston Directory* 1861, 585.

2. Manuscript 1861 Census of Canada East, Saint Gervais, Bellechasse, 140/42, Drouin Institute (microfilm), at New England Historic Genealogical Society Library, Boston.

3. Pierre Poulin, "Les Journaliers Dans La Vallée Laurentienne: L'Example de la Paroisse de Saint-Jean Chrysostôme Entre 1831 et 1842" (Masters diss., Université Laval, 1995).

4. Manuscript 1940 U.S. Federal Census, New York, Kings County, New York City, 12-1963; Theodore lives at 154 Madison Street. Ancestry.com. 1940 United States Federal Census [database on-line]. Provo, UT, USA: Ancestry.com Operations, Inc., 2012.

5. Robert Rumilly, *Histoire des Franco-Américains* (Montréal, 1958), 17-25; Armand Chartier, *The Franco-Americans of New England: A History*, (Manchester, NH: ACA Assurance and Worcester: Institut Français, 2000), 4-6.

6. Yves Roby, *Les Franco-Américains de la Nouvelle-Angleterre 1776-1930* (Sillery, QC: Septentrion, 1990, 25); Chartier, 5; Rumilly, 23-25.

7. Yolande, Lavoie, *L'émigration des Québécois aux États-Unis de 1840 à 1930*, Documentations du Conseil de la Langue Française, 1981, "Les régions touches." See also Roby, 2004, 10.

8. Roby 1990, 53; Roby 2004, 10.

9. Gerard J Brault, *The French-Canadian Heritage in New England* (Hanover, NH: University Press of New England, 1986), 56; Roby 1990, 53.

10. Colonial Department, Downing Street, *Copy of the Report of the Commissioners appointed in Lower Canada*, under an Ordinance of 1 Vict. c. 7, to inquire into the Losses sustained during the late Rebellion; also, of the Names of Persons who claimed Compensation before the said Commissioners, and the Amount of their Claims, 11 June 1839, 29. Prudent Racine was a *journalier* who lived in the first *rang* of Saint-Charles per the manuscript 1831 Census of Canada. I have traced him and his family from his birth via the parish registers at Saint-Marc, Saint-Charles, Saint-Damase, St-Pie, and St-Jean Baptiste (Roxton Falls).

11. For a grisly, eyewitness account of the Battle of Saint-Charles, from a source unsympathetic to the rebels, see George Bell, *Rough Notes By an Old Soldier* (London: Day and Son, 1867), 2:48-54.

12. Weil 1989, 26 (Table 1.3); Roby 1990, 18 (Table 1), 22. Weil's and Roby's numbers are based on Ralph Vicero, "Immigration of French Canadians to New England, 1840-1900: A Geographical Analysis" (PhD Thesis, University of Wisconsin, 1968).

13. Geographer Barry Rodrigue, with Alaric Faulkner, has done the definitive work to date on the Old Canada Road.

See Canada Road, Historic Roadways, Maine's French Communities, http://www.francomaine.org/English/Histo/Canada/Canada_intro.html (accessed September 4, 2017); cf. also Richard 2008, 11-12; Roby 1990, 14, 52.

14. Roby 1990, 19.

15. For this "agroforest" economy see Dickinson and Young, 138. Not all regions of Québec participated in this economy.

16. As late as 1907, seasonal movements, from factory to farm and back again, continued. See "French Canadians Return," *Fibre and Fabric*, September 7, 1907, 3.

17. Edouard Hamon, S.J., *Les Canadiens-Français de la Nouvelle-Angleterre* (Québec: N.S. Hardy, 1891), 7-10.

18. For the exodus from Lower Canada to the U.S. Midwest see Rumilly, 17. For Chiniquy and the French-Canadians of Central Illinois, see Caroline B. Brettell, "From Catholics to Presbyterians: French-Canadian Immigrants in Central Illinois," *American Presbyterians* 63, no. 3 (1985): 285-98. The detail about Chiniquy and Lincoln is on page 288. For Michigan see Jean Lamarre, *The French Canadians of Michigan* (Detroit: Wayne State University Press, 2003). The French-Canadian presence in what is now the U.S. Midwest, from the French Regime until today, awaits a comprehensive historical study.

19. Norma Meir, "Once Upon a Time: French Canadians Sought Their Fortunes in Kansas," *Clifton Illinois Advocate*, November 13, 1980, 9.

20. Thanks to writer James LaForest for the insight that there were *two waves of immigration* toward the Great Lakes, one in the days of New France and another in the 19th century.

21. The term "ghost empire" is author Philip Marchand's. Cf. Marchand's *Ghost Empire: How the French Almost Conquered North America* (Toronto: McClelland & Stewart, 2006).

22. Albert A. Belanger, *Guide Officiel des Franco-Americain*, 11th ed. (Providence,

RI: Albert A. Belanger, 1935), 7. The Long Beach community may have been the product of a secondary migration of New England Franco-Americans westward.

23. Roby 1990, 22.

24. For the population statistics of the various New England states and the region as a whole in 1860 see Weil 1989, 26. Statistics derived from Table 1.3.

25. Weil 1989, 42.

26. Brault, 54.

27. Roby 1990, 46-47.

28. Franco-American General Conventions met in Troy in 1867, Glens Falls in 1875, and Cohoes in 1882 (Gatineau, 6). See also the location of New York Franco-American newspapers in 1860-1880 in Weil 1889, 99 (Table 3.3). The subject of the Franco-Americans of the state of New York needs a dedicated study.

29. Robert Forant and Christopher Strobel, Ethnicity in Lowell, U.S. Department of the Interior, National Park Service, Northeast Region Ethnography Program (Boston, 2011), 42-48; Moran, 75.

30. Dalzell, 163.

31. Massachusetts Bureau of Statistics of Labor, *Comparative Wages, Prices, And Cost of Living* (from the *Sixteenth Annual Report of the Massachusetts Bureau of Statistics of Labor*, for 1885), reprint ed. (Boston, 1889), 34-5. *I will refer to this series of reports of the Massachusetts Bureau of Statistics of Labor as "Mass. BSL."*

32. *Report on Condition of Woman and Child Wage-Earners in the United States*, 61st Cong., 2d sess., 1910, S. Doc. 645, vol. 9, 82.

33. There's a widely held theory that successive waves of immigrants displaced ethnic groups already ensconced in the textile mills, with Franco-Americans giving way to southern and eastern Europeans in the early 20th century. I challenge this theory. Manchester's Amoskeag Company, for one, kept records on the ethnic composition of its workforce in the 20th century. Between 1912 and 1928, the Franco-American contingent averaged 41 percent of the workers,

354 A DISTINCT ALIEN RACE

in contrast to 14 percent Irish, 13 percent "American," 11 percent Polish, 8 percent Greek and 14 percent all others. Franco-Americans, Irish and "Americans," the three nationalities that were in the mills by about 1870, still comprise 68 percent of the employees on average over this period. If the Franco-Americans were not "displaced" by 1928, then they never were.

34. Mass. BSL, *Fourth Annual Report* (Boston, 1873), 281-82. Also cited by Frances H. Early, "The Settling-In Process: The Beginnings of the Little Canada in Lowell Massachusetts, in the Late Nineteenth Century," in *Steeples and Smokestacks*, Claire Quintal ed. (Worcester: Institut Français, 1996), 94.

35. Richard 2008, 19.

36. DIC, 177-78.

37. For these explanations for the termination of the era of the "mill girls" see DIC, 289.

38. Dalzell, 217.

39. Dalzell, 225.

40. DIC, 283.

41. For Caswell's story see DeWolf, *passim*.

42. Robinson, 69.

43. Beckert, 242-273.

44. "Factory Stopped," *Brunswick Telegraph*, May 17, 1861, 2.

45. "Cotton Storehouse," *Brunswick Telegraph*, May 18, 1860, 2.

46. Gilman, 341.

47. Mass. BSL, *Third Annual Report* (Boston, 1872), 377.

48. Roby 1990, 57-58; Weil 1989, 25; Rumilly, 37.

49. For Lavallée and Mallet see Rumilly, 36-39. Mallet offered a stirring defense of Riel in a series of resolutions at the Rutland, Vermont General Convention of French-Canadians of the United States in June 1886, welcomed by the delegates "with thunderous applause." Cf. Gatineau, 175-77.

50. For the "chaos" in the New England textile industry brought on by the war see Moran, 68.

51. *Report on Condition of Woman and Child Wage-Earners in the United States*, 61st Cong., 2d sess., 1910, S. Doc. 645, vol. 9, 82-83.

52. DIC, 284.

53. Roby 1990, 49.

54. Weil 1989, 37-41.

55. Weil 1989, 37-38.

56. Weil 1989, 39; For the *Canadien* recruiters cf. also Brault, 55; Roby 1990, 49.

57. Quoted by Frances H. Early, in Quintal ed., *Steeples and Smokestacks*, 90. For Marin's work cf. also Weil 1989, 39; Roby 1990, 49.

58. Weil 1989, 40.

59. Philippe Lemay and Louis Pare [*French Canadian Textile Worker*], New Hampshire, Manuscript/Mixed Material. Retrieved from the Library of Congress, https://www.loc.gov/item/wpalh001099/ (accessed March 28, 2017). Interview conducted in the late 1930s for the U.S. Work Projects Administration's Federal Writer's Project.

60. Weil 1989, 24 (Table 1.2). Compare the somewhat different numbers for "net emigration" in Roby 2004, 12 (Table 2). Both sets of numbers agree that either the 1880s or the 1890s were the peak. For the "cyclical nature" of *Canadien* emigration see Roby 2004, 13, 19.

61. Rumilly, 40-41.

62. For instance, persons of French origin constituted 29 percent of the Canadian population in 1911; but there are 385,083 "French-Canadian" foreign born persons in the USA in 1910 vs. 819,554 "Other" Canadians. This was after a deceleration in the emigration of *Canadiens* in the 1900-1910 period. Data from Statistics Canada, *Historical Statistics of Canada*, Section A: Population and Migration, Table A125-163, Origins of the population, census dates, 1871 to 1971 (http://www.statcan.gc.ca/pub/11-516-x/sectiona/4147436-eng.htm, accessed September 5, 2017) and U.S. Census Bureau, *Statistical Abstract of the USA 1912*, "Area, Natural Resources, and Population," 65.

63. Anderson 40-41. She found that the Yankees in 1930s Burlington, VT preferred to live near English-Canadians more than any other group besides their own stating that "they are like our own people."

64. Statistics in this paragraph derived from Weil 1989, 26, cf. esp. Table 1.3.

65. Weil 1989, 26; Roby 2004, 22.

66. For the institutional network see Brault 68-82; Chartier, 42-54; Roby 2004, 21-28.

67. Brault, 95. Brault (92-97) gives a good description of the Franco-American parochial school.

68. See Raymond Duval, "Growing Up in Brunswick in the 1930s and 1940s" in Nelson Madore and Barry Rodrigue, eds., *Voyages: A Maine Franco-American Reader* (Gardiner, ME: Tilbury House, 2007), 129. Duval, raised in Brunswick's "Little Canada," states, "In 1940 you could walk anywhere in this large neighborhood and hear French spoken. We lived on Dunning Street, and my neighborhood was about 99 percent French-Canadian. French was the language in use, and I barely spoke English when I started school."

69. Brault, 64-65.

70. Roby 1990, 115 (Table 14, parishes per Roy), 127 (national societies).

71. Weil 1989, 99 (Table 3.3).

72. Roby 1990, 123.

73. Weil 1989, 24 (Table 1.2).

74. For this pattern of migration in extended family groups see Roby 1990, 51-54.

75. For the twinning of a region of Québec with a particular mill town, see Brault, 56, Roby 2004, 20. For Brunswick's connection to L'Islet and "four contiguous counties" in Québec, see William N. Locke, *Pronunciation of the French Spoken at Brunswick, Maine* (American Dialect Society, Number 12, 1949) 17.

76. For example, I have traced the Ouellet, Racine, Lavigueur, Paiement and MacDuff (*Canadien* despite the Scottish name) families of Brunswick to Roxton Falls through connections of kinship or proximity.

77. For employment statistics see Joshua L. Rosenbloom, "The Challenges of Economic Maturity: New England, 1880-1940," in Temin, ed., *Engines of Enterprise*, 155.

78. Peter Temin, "The Industrialization of New England, 1830-1880," in Temin ed., *Engines of Enterprise*, 122 (Table 3.1).

79. Roby 1990, 66-67 (Tables 9 and 10). Vermont is the outlier. In the Green Mountain State, only 18 percent of employed Franco-Americans worked in manufacturing in 1900.

80. Roby 1990, 48.

81. For the statistics in this paragraph see DIC, 36. This document includes the figures for Maine, Massachusetts, New Hampshire, Rhode Island and Connecticut. The figures for Vermont are from U.S. Department of Commerce and Labor, Bureau of the Census, *Special Reports, Occupations and the Twelfth Census*, 1904, 400-403 (Table 41). The figure for the total number of cotton mill operatives in the U.S. (246,391) is from *Special Reports, Occupations and the Twelfth Census*, xlvi (Table III). For the French-Canadian-born population of Connecticut in 1900 see U.S. Census Bureau, *Statistical Abstract of the United States*, 1910, "Area, Natural Resources and Population," 52, 55.

82. S. N. Dexter North, "American Textile Mills," in Chauncey M. Depew, ed., *One Hundred Years of American Commerce* (New York: Haynes, 1895), 2:477.

83. Roby 2004, 17.

84. Rosenbloom in Temin, ed., *Engines of Enterprise*, 155.

85. North in Depew, ed., 480.

86. Henry F. Bedford, ed., *Their Lives and Numbers* (Ithaca: Cornell University Press, 1995), 103.

87. For the family as an economic unit in rural Québec see Horace Miner, *St. Denis: A French-Canadian Parish* (Chicago: Phoenix Books, 1966), 63-65. See also Roby 1990, 69-85.

88. I worked briefly as a farmhand on a family-owned, commercial farm in

356 A DISTINCT ALIEN RACE

Western Massachusetts at harvest time and learned firsthand about this type of labor.

89. Yves Roby, "A Portrait of the Female Franco-American Worker" in Claire Quintal, ed., *Steeples and Smokestacks*, 550-51.

90. For the father's responsibility for the family's financial security see Roby in Claire Quintal, ed., *Steeples and Smokestacks*, 554.

91. Bruno Ramirez, "French Canadian Immigrants in the New England Cotton Industry: A Socioeconomic Profile," Labour / Le Travail 11 (1983): 139-40.

92. Dyke Hendrickson, *Quiet Presence: Stories of Franco-Americans in New England* (Portland, ME: Guy Gannett Publishing, 2003), 37.

93. Mass. BSL, *Thirteenth Annual Report* (Boston, 1882), 90.

94. For these early Labor actions and organizations see Beckert, 197.

95. Dickinson and Young, 188-89 (Grande Association), 131 (Knights of Labour).

96. For example, Frank K. Foster, a founder of the American Federation of Labor, disparaged Franco-Americans before a U.S. Senate committee. See United States, Congress, Senate, Committee on Education and Labor, *Report of the Committee of the Senate Upon the Relations Between Labor And Capital And Testimony Taken by the Committee* (Washington, D.C.: Government Printing Office, 1885), 66-68. See also Philip T. Silvia, Jr. "Neighbors From The North: French-Canadian Immigrants vs. Trade Unionism in Fall River, Massachusetts" in Quintal, ed., *Steeples and Smokestacks*, 145-163.

97. E.g. Moran, 191.

98. Dickinson and Young, 130.

99. "Strike," *Brunswick Telegraph*, August 12, 1881, 2.

100. For statistics on the 1881, 1886 and 1887 strikes in the Cabot mill see Maine Bureau of Industrial and Labor Statistics, *First Annual Report* (Augusta, 1888), 130-

34, 145. For the January 1887 strike see "Strike at the Cabot Mill," *Brunswick Telegraph*, January 14, 1887, 2.

101. "The Mill Strike at Suncook," *New York Times*, January 7, 1881.

102. "Cotton Hands On Strike," *New York Times*, March 11, 1886.

103. "Cotton Mills Shut Down," *New York Times*, June 29, 1887.

104. "Mill Workers," *Bath Independent*, January 22, 1898, 7; "Going Again," *Bath Independent*, March 26, 1898, 7.

105. "Nameless Frenchman Threatens Agent of Cabot Mill With Death," *Bath Independent*, February 12, 1898, 7.

106. "The Cotton Mill Strike," *New York Times*, February 13, 1898.

107. Roby 2004, 308-313; Moran, 134; Matthew Laflamme, "Franco-American and Lebanese Textile Workers in Waterville, Maine: La Survivance Economique" in Madore and Rodrigue, eds., *Voyages: A Maine Franco-American Reader*, 156-170.

108. Dalzell, 226.

109. Dalzell, 68-9.

110. Robinson, 204-210.

111. Cited in Moran, 160 and Dalzell, 35.

CHAPTER SIX: Franco-Americans Come to Brunswick

1. Everett, Charles Carroll, 1829-1900, Lectures in theology and correspondence: A Finding Aid, bMS 435, Andover-Harvard Theological Library, Harvard Divinity School, Harvard University, http://oasis.lib.harvard.edu/oasis/deliver/deepLink?_collection=oasis&uniqueId=div00435 (accessed September 5, 2017). See also *Publications of the Colonial Society of Massachusetts*, vol. 7, Transactions 1900-1902 (Boston: Colonial Society of Massachusetts, 1905), 337-40.

2. Brunswick, Maine, *Celebration of the One Hundred and Fiftieth Anniversary of the Incorporation of the Town of Brunswick, June 13, 1889* (Brunswick: Pejepscot Historical Society, 1889), 18-19.

3. Edward Chase Kirkland, *Brunswick's Golden Age* (Lewiston, Maine: C. Parker Loring, 1941), 21.

4. The following analysis of the Franco-American population of Brunswick is based on the manuscript U.S. Federal Census, Brunswick, Cumberland County, Maine 1840, 1850, 1860, 1870, 1880, and 1900.

5. I traced 1860 Brunswick's Franco-American families using databases of images of microfilmed Québec parishes registers on Ancestry.com and FamilySearch.org. I searched for a marriage of a couple with the first names in question, and a likely surname, and then compared the names and ages of each couple's children baptized in Québec, with the data in the 1860 Brunswick census. I then traced these families using the U.S. Federal Census (images available on these same sites) and images of the manuscript Canadian census from Library and Archives of Canada. Unfortunately, the 1852 Canadian Census is lost for many of the home parishes of these families.

6. Child labor statistics from the following Maine Bureau of Industrial and Labor Statistics Reports: *Eighth Annual Report* (Augusta, 1895), 214; *Ninth Annual Report* (Augusta, 1896), 206-07; *Thirteenth Annual Report* (Augusta, 1900), 180; *Fourteenth Annual Report* (Augusta, 1901), 149.

7. *Souvenir du 50ième Anniversaire de la Paroisse St. Jean Baptiste Brunswick, Maine 1877-1927* (Reproduced by Curtis Memorial Library, Brunswick, Maine, 1981), 55.

8. William N. Locke, "Notes on the Vocabulary of the French-Canadian Dialect Spoken in Brunswick, Maine," *The French Review* 19, no. 6 (1946): 416.

9. *Registres des Baptêmes, Mariages, Sépultures (1855-1874)*, Paroisse Notre Dame de Bonsecours, Co. L'Islet, Que. Canada, Drouin Institute (microfilm), at New England Historic and Genealogical Society Library, Boston. See for example the marriage of André Labbé and Eléonore

Gamache (M. 15), August 13, 1867; at the same parish, marriage of Charles Fortin and Adèle Lamard (M. 17), September 30, 1867.

10. "The Factory," *Brunswick Telegraph*, December 15, 1865, 2; Wheeler and Wheeler, 567.

11. *Souvenir du 50e Anniversaire de la Paroisse St. Jean Baptiste Brunswick, passim.*

12. *Souvenir du 50ième Anniversaire de la Paroisse St. Jean Baptiste Brunswick*, 15.

13. "Saint Jean de Baptiste [sic] Band Celebrates its Fiftieth Anniversary Next Monday," *Brunswick Record*, April 16, 1931, 7.

14. *Constitutions et Reglements, de la Société Saint Jean Baptiste de Brunswick, Me*, avec l'approbation de Mgr. James Augustine Healey, Lewiston, September 1889.

15. Richard 2008, 57-58. For one member in Brunswick, among many, see Obituary of Albina Ouellette Vermette, *Brunswick Record*, June 14, 1918, 12, which mentions her membership in this Montréal-based society.

16. "The Diphtheria," *Brunswick Telegraph*, July 30, 1886, 2.

17. Analysis for 1890 is missing because most of the manuscript census materials produced in that year were destroyed in a fire in the 1920s.

18. Calculations for 1900 include people in Brunswick who had at least one parent who is identified as originating in "Canada-French." In all but a very small number of cases a Brunswick resident in 1900 who had one French-Canadian parent had two.

19. See Locke 1949, 16 and the footnotes on this page. Locke gives the estimate of 41 percent in 1940 but his count also includes Topsham. See also Gerard J. Brault, "An Overview of Studies Relating to Franco-American Communities in New England" in Quintal ed., *Steeples and Smokestacks*, 77. Relying on Locke, Brault gives the Franco-American population as "nearly one half of the town's population" in 1940. *Souvenir du 50ième Anniversaire de la Paroisse St. Jean Baptiste Brunswick*, 55,

states that the town was roughly one-half Franco-American as of 1927.

20. Cited in William N. Locke, "The French Colony at Brunswick, Maine: A Historical Sketch," *Les Archives de Folklore* 7, no. 1 (1946): 104.

21. For the U.S. Armed Forces as an agent of cultural assimilation see Mary Mackinnon and Daniel Parent, "Resisting the Melting Pot: The Long Term Impact of Maintaining Identity for Franco-Americans in New England," Working Paper No. 75, Center for Labor Economics, University of California, Berkeley (June 2005), 24-28.

CHAPTER SEVEN: The Case of the Cabot Mill

1. State Board of Health of the State of Maine, *Second Annual Report for the Fiscal Year Ending Dec. 31, 1886* (Augusta: Sprague and Son, 1887), 28-30.

2. Centers for Disease Control (Atlanta, GA), "Typhoid Fever, General Information," April 25, 2014, https://www.cdc.gov/typhoid-fever/sources.html (accessed October 3, 2017).

3. Artur Galazkaa, "The Changing Epidemiology of Diphtheria in the Vaccine Era," *The Journal of Infectious Diseases* 181 (Suppl 1) (2000): S6.

4. "The Diphtheria," *Brunswick Telegraph*, July 30, 1886, 2.

5. Onésime Paré was born and baptized at the parish of Saint-Gervais, Bellechasse on June 1, 1854 (B. 62). He was the son of Pierre Paré and Perpétue Roy. Québec, registres paroissiaux catholiques, 1621-1979, database with images, FamilySearch.org (16 July 2014), *Saints-Gervais-et-Protais, Baptêmes, mariages, sépultures 1845-1868*, image 298 of 572, nos paroisses de Église Catholique, Québec (Catholic Church parishes, Quebec).

6. Suzanne Roy, Interview with Celestine Lavigne (July 7, 1977), Oral History, Franco-American Collection, University of Southern Maine, Lewiston, Maine.

7. "The Diphtheria," *Brunswick Telegraph*, July 30, 1886, 2.

8. "Cabot Company's Exemption From Taxation," *Brunswick Telegraph*, September 2, 1881, 2.

9. "Those Figures," *Brunswick Telegraph*, September 9, 1881, 2.

10. "The Diphtheria," *Brunswick Telegraph*, July 30, 1886, 2; "four in one house," see *Brunswick Telegraph*, July 23, 1886.

11. "Nuisances – One Hundred and Twelve Cases of Diphtheria in Two Months and a Half," *Brunswick Telegraph*, July 23, 1886, 2. The load was dumped on the corner of Mill and Cushing Streets.

12. "Nuisances – One Hundred and Twelve Cases of Diphtheria in Two Months and a Half," *Brunswick Telegraph*, July 23, 1886, 2.

13. "Nuisances – One Hundred and Twelve Cases of Diphtheria in Two Months and a Half," *Brunswick Telegraph*, July 23, 1886, 2.

14. Brunswick, Maine, Births 1879-1910, Deaths 1877-1910, Microfilm copy of Manuscript Town Vital Records, New England Historic and Genealogical Society Library, Boston, MA. See also the list of fatalities compiled in the *Brunswick Telegraph*, September 10, 1886, 2. The two children were Marie and Alexis Sainte-Marie who died of diphtheria on April 13, 1886 per the manuscript town vital town records.

15. "Diphtheria," *Brunswick Telegraph*, August 6, 1886, 2.

16. See items on the Cabot mill in the *Brunswick Telegraph*, May 28, 1853, 2; "Importing Operatives," June 25, 1853, 2; "Enlarging," January 17, 1854 and "Brunswick Water Power – The Cabot Manufacturing Company – and Our One Mill," May 6, 1859, 2. Tenney did not become editor of the *Telegraph* until 1857 (Wheeler and Wheeler, 309-10), but his coverage remains positive through the 1850s.

17. "Diphtheria," *Brunswick Telegraph*, September 17, 1886, 2.

18. "Diphtheria," *Brunswick Telegraph*, August 6, 1886, 2.

19. "Diphtheria," *Brunswick Telegraph*, September 3, 1886, 2.

20. "Diphtheria," *Brunswick Telegraph*, August 20, 1886, 2.

21. "Diphtheria," *Brunswick Telegraph*, September 3, 1886, 2.

22. "Diphtheria," *Brunswick Telegraph*, August 27, 1886, 2.

23. "Diphtheria," *Brunswick Telegraph*, August 6, 1886, 2.

24. "Diphtheria – And the Cabot Company," *Brunswick Telegraph*, August 13, 1886, 2.

25. "Diphtheria," *Brunswick Telegraph*, August 20, 1886, 2.

26. "Diphtheria," *Brunswick Telegraph*, August 27, 1886, 2.

27. G. Overcash Seilhamer, *Leslie's History of the Republican Party*, vol. 2 Biographical (New York: Judge Publishing Co. 1899?), 94-95.

28. "Diphtheria," *Brunswick Telegraph*, September 10, 1886, 2.

29. "Diphtheria," *Brunswick Telegraph*, September 3, 1886, 2. Tenney's emphasis.

30. "Diphtheria," *Brunswick Telegraph*, September 3, 1886, 2.

31. *Brunswick, Maine, Births 1879-1910, Deaths 1877-1910*, Microfilm copy of Manuscript Town Vital Records, New England Historic and Genealogical Society Library (Boston, MA).

32. State Board of Health of the State of Maine, *Second Annual Report for the Fiscal Year Ending Dec. 31, 1886* (Augusta: Sprague and Son, 1887), 24-25.

33. State Board of Health of the State of Maine, *Second Annual Report* for 1886, 28-30.

34. William N. Locke, "The French Colony at Brunswick, Maine: A Historical Sketch," 101.

35. "Diphtheria," *Brunswick Telegraph*, September 10, 1886, 2.

36. "Diphtheria," *Brunswick Telegraph*, August 27, 1886, 2.

37. "Report of the State Board of Health," *Brunswick Telegraph*, September 10, 1886, 2.

38. "Diphtheria and Typhoid Fever in Brunswick," *Brunswick Telegraph*, October 5, 1888, 2.

39. State Board of Health of the State of Maine, *Second Annual Report* for 1886, 24-31.

40. State Board of Health of the State of Maine, *Second Annual Report* for 1886, 120.

41. State Board of Health of the State of Maine, *Second Annual Report* for 1886, 73.

42. State Board of Health of the State of Maine, *Second Annual Report* for 1886, 73.

43. State Board of Health of the State of Maine, *Second Annual Report* for 1886, 135.

44. State Board of Health of the State of Maine, *Second Annual Report* for 1886, 134.

45. State Board of Health of the State of Maine, *Second Annual Report* for 1886, 98.

46. Franco-Americans comprised one-quarter of Lewiston's population in 1880 and were the largest foreign-born group. See Richard 2008, 19-20.

47. State Board of Health of the State of Maine, *Second Annual Report* for 1886, 131.

48. Rhea Côté Robbins, ed., *Canuck & Other Stories* (Brewer, ME: Rheta Press, 2006), 15-17.

49. Mass. BSL, *Thirteenth Annual Report* (Boston, 1882), 282-84.

50. William Bayard Hale, "Impotence of Churches in a Manufacturing Town," *Forum*, November 1894, 288-300.

51. Anderson, 241-42.

52. Anderson, 242.

53. Anderson, 237.

54. Anderson, 237-38.

55. Anderson, 243-44.

56. Anderson, 209.

57. Anderson 242.

58. Hamon, 19-22, 26-27.

59. Hamon, 16-17.

60. See discussion of Franco-American working class salaries below pp. 154-156.

61. For the Goodalls of Sanford see Moran, 166.

62. John J. Leane, *A History of Rumford, Maine, 1774-1972* (Rumford, ME: Rumford Publishing Co., 1972), 52-53.

63. Friedrich Nietzsche, *Beyond Good and Evil*, trans. R.J. Hollingdale (Harmondsworth, England: Penguin Books, 1982), 173.

CHAPTER EIGHT: A Rich Uncle from the States?

1. For a vivid account of such visits see Brault, 139-141.
2. Lavoie, "Chapitre 2, La montée du movement: Les paroisses nationales et le mode de vie des Franco-Américains."
3. Mass. BSL, *Sixth Annual Report* (Boston, 1875), 191-450 ("Condition of Workingmen's Families").
4. Mass. BSL, *Sixth Annual Report*, 337.
5. Mass. BSL, *Sixth Annual Report*, 314.
6. Mass. BSL, *Sixth Annual Report*, 314.
7. Mass. BSL, *Sixth Annual Report*, 236.
8. Mass. BSL, *Sixth Annual Report*, 305.
9. For the summary statistics (median income, median cost of living, and mean savings) I did not include the richest family in each group. For the percentages, I included all families in each sample.
10. "If [a Franco-American] has 10 dollars he spends 10. If he has 20 he spends 20." Hamon, 28.
11. Mass. BSL, *Sixth Annual Report*, 218.
12. Mass. BSL, *Seventeenth Annual Report* (Boston, 1886), 237-326.
13. Dickinson and Young, 91 and Miner, 142-43. Dickinson and Young discuss the rural diet before 1810, while Miner discusses the same in the 1930s. The dietary regimens in the two periods were similar, except for the introduction of potatoes and the prevalence of soup mentioned by Miner.
14. For this study see Maine Bureau of Industrial and Labor Statistics, *First Annual Report* (Augusta, 1888), 89-98.
15. Maine Bureau of Industrial and Labor Statistics, *First Annual Report*, 96; the report cites here the work of Edward Atkinson.
16. Maine Bureau of Industrial and Labor Statistics, *First Annual Report*, 98.
17. Richard 2008, 62.
18. "The Cotton Mill Strike," *New York Times*, February 13, 1898.
19. Allen Green, Mary MacKinnon and Chris Minns, "Conspicuous by their Absence: French Canadians and the Settlement of the Canadian West," *The Journal of Economic History* 65, no. 3 (2005): 841.
20. Philippe Lemay and Louis Pare [*French Canadian Textile Worker*], New Hampshire, Manuscript/Mixed Material. Retrieved from the Library of Congress, https://www.loc.gov/item/wpalh001099/ (accessed March 28, 2017).
21. For what I call "the standard theory" see Damien-Claude Bélanger and Claude Bélanger, "French Canadian Emigration to the United States, 1840-1930," Readings in Québec History (Marianopolis College: 2000), http://faculty.marianopolis.edu/c.belanger/quebechistory/readings/leaving.htm (accessed October 26, 2017). See also Yves Roby "The Economic Evolution of Québec and the Emigrant (1850-1929)" in Quintal ed., *Steeples and Smokestacks*, 7-19. Roby does not dwell on an early 19th century agricultural crisis. He does place the emphasis on indebted farmers.
22. Fernand Ouellet is usually associated with the view that the "mentality" of the *Canadien* farmers held them back agriculturally.
23. For Desjardins see Gaetan Frigon, "Prudent Beaudry" in Andre Pratte and Jonathan Kay, eds., *Legacy: How French Canadians Shaped North America* (Toronto: Signal, 2016), 74-76. For the story that he was inspired by the borrower compelled to pay $5000 see Jacquie McNish, "Desjardins' Quiet Revolution," *Globe and Mail* (Toronto), February 24, 2011. For the debate where Desjardins heard of the exorbitant interest see Canada, House of Commons Debates, 8th Parliament, 2nd Session: Vol. 1, Tuesday 6th April 1897, p. 550.
24. Roby 2004, 13.
25. Geographer Serge Courville is associated with this revisionist view. See for example the analysis of 19th century

Québec agriculture in Serge Courville, Jean-Claude Robert, Normand Séguin, *Atlas Historique du Québec, Le pays Laurentien au XIXe siècle: Les morphologies de base* (Sainte-Foy, QC: Les Presses de l'Université Laval, 1995), 49-76. For a brief review in English of the terms of the agricultural crisis debate see Morris Altman, "Land Tenure, Ethnicity, and the Condition of Agricultural Income and Productivity in Mid-Nineteenth-Century Québec," *Agricultural History* 72, no. 4 (1998): 712-16.

26. For 1831 see Vincent Geloso, Vadim Kufenko and Michael Hinton, "The Equally 'Bad' French and English Farmers of Québec: New TFP Measures From the 1831 Census," *Historical Methods: A Journal of Quantitative and Interdisciplinary History* 50, no. 3 (2017): 170-189. For 1852 see Frank Lewis and Marvin McInnis, "The Efficiency of the French-Canadian Farmer in the Nineteenth Century," *The Journal of Economic History* 40, no. 3 (1980): 497-514.

27. Altman, 708-62. Cf. esp. 711-12.

28. Dickinson and Young, 140-41.

29. That "economic recovery" from the alleged agricultural crisis was "well underway" by 1848, see Robert Armstrong, "The Efficiency of Québec Farmers in 1851," *Histoire Sociale – Social History* 17, no. 33 (mai- May 1984): 163; Lewis and McInnis, 500. Armstrong disputes the findings of Lewis and McInnis (1980) regarding the 1852 census data. Geloso (2017) defends Lewis and McInnis against these counterarguments.

30. Hendrickson, 51.

31. Timothy J. Hatton and Jeffrey G. Williamson, "What Fundamentals Drive World Migration?" NBER Working Paper Series, 9159, Cambridge, MA: National Bureau of Economic Research, 2002, 24. © 2002 by Timothy J. Hatton and Jeffrey G. Williamson.

32. Hatton and Williamson, 4. © 2002 by Timothy J. Hatton and Jeffrey G. Williamson.

33. Hatton and Williamson, 11. © 2002 by Timothy J. Hatton and Jeffrey G. Williamson.

34. Bélanger and Bélanger describe well the non-financial costs of emigration. See the section "Causes of French Canadian emigration to the United States" in their on-line article "French Canadian Emigration to the United States, 1840-1930," Readings in Québec History (Marianopolis College: 2000).

35. For the data cited in this paragraph see Green, MacKinnon and Minns, 841.

36. Draws on the 1851 Census of Canada which was actually conducted in 1852. Where authors refer to this as the 1851 Census, I have retained their usage.

37. Courville, Robert, and Séguin, 16 (Figure 11).

38. Warren S. Thompson and P. K. Whelpton, *Population Trends in the United States* (New York: McGraw-Hill, 1933), 120-21. Calculated from Table 33.

39. Philippe Lemay and Louis Pare [*French Canadian Textile Worker*], New Hampshire, Manuscript/Mixed Material. Retrieved from the Library of Congress, https://www.loc.gov/item/wpalh001099/ (accessed March 28, 2017).

40. For the reception of new immigrants in the mill towns see Brault, 56-59.

41. For the shifting attitudes of Québec elites to the emigration movement see Roby 2004, 30-53.

42. See the discussion of Irish vs. Italian immigration to the USA in Hatton and Williamson, 12. © 2002 by Timothy J. Hatton and Jeffrey G. Williamson.

43. Vincent Geloso and Mathieu Bédard, "Was Economic Growth Likely in Lower Canada?" *Journal of Private Enterprise*, forthcoming.

44. Green, MacKinnon and Minns, 831.

45. The Median salary for factory operatives in Québec in 1900-1901 was $377 and for common-laborers $300. For all workers it was $380. See Green, MacKinnon and Minns, 837.

46. For the repatriation project see Rumilly 63-66, 77-79, 84; Brault, 82-83; Roby 2004, 38-40.

47. Richard 2008, 59.

48. Ferdinand Gagnon and Fréderic Houde reproached the Canadian government for the amount of money spent to attract European immigrants, compared to the pittance dedicated to repatriation. See Rumilly, 65.

49. Canada, House of Commons Debates, 5th Parliament, 1st Session: Volume 1, 892-94.

50. Gatineau, 175-77; Robert G. Leblanc, "The Francophone 'Conquest' of New England: Geopolitical Conceptions and Imperial Ambition of French-Canadian Nationalists in the Nineteenth Century," *American Review of Canadian Studies* 15, no. 3 (1985): 299-300. Cf. also Jeremy Ravi Mumford, "Why Was Louis Riel, a United States Citizen, Hanged as a Canadian Traitor in 1885?" *The Canadian Historical Review* 88, no. 2 (June 2007): 237-262.

51. For a brief account of the Manitoba schools question see Mason Wade, *The French Canadians 1760-1967*, rev. ed. (Toronto: MacMillan, 1968), 1:435-40.

52. Rumilly, 84.

53. Michael J. Guignard, "The Franco-Americans of Biddeford, Maine" in Quintal, ed., *Steeples and Smokestacks*, 133-34.

54. Weil 1989, 109.

55. Dickinson and Young, 111 (Table 5), 203.

56. O.J. Firestone, "Development of Canada's Economy, 1850-1900" in *Trends in the American Economy in the Nineteenth Century* (Princeton: Princeton University Press, 1960), 223.

57. Bailey, 278-80, 373-75.

58. Firestone, 230.

59. Yvan Lamonde, *Histoire Sociale des Idées au Québec 1760-1896*, vol. 1 (Fides, 2000), 391-394.

60. Claude Bélanger, "Agriculturalism," Events, Issues and Concepts of Québec History, Québec History (Marianopolis College, 2006), http://faculty.marianop-olis.edu/c.belanger/quebechistory/events/agr.htm (accessed October 26, 2017).

61. J. I. Little, *Nationalism, Capitalism and Colonization in Nineteenth-Century Québec* (Montreal & Kingston: McGill-Queen's University Press, 1989), *passim*; Roby 2004, 46-47.

62. Little, 7.

63. Dickinson and Young, 209-210.

64. For the "colonization" movement as an alternative to the New England mill towns see Little, 4, 128.

CHAPTER NINE: Who Were the Immigrants?

1. In his naturalization papers, Charles Vermette claims that he entered the USA at Lancaster, New Hampshire, a town in the White Mountains then associated with the log drives on the Connecticut River. Oath of Naturalization, State of Maine, Cumberland County, Portland, September 5, 1888. National Archives at Boston; Waltham, Massachusetts; ARC Title: Copies of Petitions and Records of Naturalization in New England Courts, 1939 - ca. 1942; Record Group Title: Records of the Immigration and Naturalization Service, 1787-2004; Record Group Number: RG 85.

2. Youville Labonté, *Marriages of St. John the Baptist (1877-1979) and of St. Charles Borromeo (1930-1980), Brunswick, Maine* (n.p.: 1981).

3. Lavoie, "Chapitre 2, La montée du mouvement: Les paroisses nationales et le mode de vie des Franco-Américains."

4. DIC, 69.

5. DIC, 347.

6. DIC, 70.

7. DIC, 70.

8. DIC, 360.

9. Derived from table in DIC, 363.

10. DIC, 364.

11. DIC, 54.

12. Not all agricultural laborers for wages were *journaliers* (day-laborers). Some lived with farm families and were sometimes called "servants" (*serviteurs*) in the

Canadian census. In the data gathered by the DIC, there is no way to extract the "servants" from the agricultural day-laborers. It's my sense that most of the people listed by the DIC as agricultural laborers for wages were *journaliers* because there are so many more *journaliers* than *serviteurs* in the rural parishes. If the agricultural laborers for wages in the DIC study were primarily *serviteurs* then people of this occupation emigrated to the USA in a percentage disproportionate to their numbers in Québec which I think doubtful.

13. Pierre Poulin, "Les Journaliers Dans La Vallée Laurentienne: L'Example de la Paroisse de Saint-Jean Chrysostôme Entre 1831 et 1842" (Masters diss., Université Laval, 1995).

14. Miner, 88.

15. For the day-laborers see Miner, 39, 88, 111, 210, 218, 234, 253-54.

16. Miner, 39.

17. I conducted the following research through inspection of the photographed images of the manuscript census available on the Library and Archives Canada website: Census of Lower Canada 1831, St. Gervais, Bellechasse; St. Jean Port Joli, L'Islet and L'Islet, L'Islet; Census of Canada East 1861, St. Gervais, St. Jean Port Joli, and L'Islet. Also 1871 Census of Québec, Saint-Jean Port Joli, https://www.bac-lac.gc.ca/ENG/CENSUS/Pages/census.aspx (accessed November 19, 2017). I counted only those individuals whose occupation is listed in the census. Percentages were calculated from the total of all employed people. I did not include retirees or people living from their property or saved income (*rentiers/rentières*). In a small number of cases, the enumerator lists more than one occupation for a subject. I counted only the first-named occupation for that individual.

18. For Pierre Morin see J. H. Burgess, ed., *Franco-Americans of the State of Maine U.S.A. and their Achievements Historical, Descriptive and Biographical* (Lewiston,

ME: Royal Press, 1915), Maine History Documents, Paper 22, 121; "Pierre A. Morin Dies Former Selectman Retired Merchant," *Brunswick Record*, December 3, 1925, 7; U.S. Department of Justice, Immigration and Naturalization Service, Form No. 1-IP, *Naturalization Petition for Pierre A. Morin*, Certificate Number 18 – 190. Manuscript U.S. Federal Census of 1870, 1880, 1900, 1910, 1920 for Brunswick, Maine, Cumberland County, Ancestry.com.

19. "Meeting of the French-Canadians," *Brunswick Telegraph*, August 22, 1884, 3.

20. Burgess, ed., *Franco-Americans of the State of Maine*, 121.

21. "Pierre A. Morin Dies Former Selectman Retired Merchant," *Brunswick Record*, December 3, 1925, 7.

22. For example, see "Lettre pastorale, no. 26," *Mandements: lettres pastorales et circulaires des évêques de Québec*, vol. 1 (Québec: Imprimerie générale A. Coté, 1889), 166-171, https://archive.org/stream/mandementslettr06arcgoog (accessed October 26, 2017). Emigration here is connected not to poverty and its systemic causes but to the love of luxury and intemperance.

23. Canada, Senate Debates, 18th Parliament, 1st Session, vol. 1, 284.

CHAPTER TEN: They Came from L'Islet

1. Research conducted through inspection of the photographed images of the manuscript census available on the Library and Archives Canada website: Census of Canada East 1851 and 1861, L'Islet, L'Islet, https://www.bac-lac.gc.ca/ENG/CENSUS/Pages/census.aspx (accessed November 19, 2017).

2. The note appears on page 5 (3) of the 1851 Census of Canada East, L'Islet, County of L'Islet. http://data2.collectionscanada.gc.ca/e/e093/e002305794.jpg (accessed January 31, 2017).

3. Altman, 754.

4. The note appears on page 17 (33) of the 1851 Census of Canada East, L'Islet, County of L'Islet.

5. Dickinson and Young, 31.

6. For the role of the Seigneurs in industrialism in this period see Dickinson and Young, 170-73.

7. Firestone, 230.

8. See advertisements in *Brunswick Telegraph*, June 11, 1853, 3 and June 25, 1853, 3.

9. "The Habitant as an Ally," *New York Times*, January 13, 1889.

10. Pope Leo XIII addressed the social problems relating to industrialism and capitalist economies in his encyclical *Rerum Novarum: On Capital and Labor* (1891). While rejecting Socialism, Pope Leo is wary of unregulated capitalism and is concerned about the exploitation of the working class in the 19th century. For an English translation of Pope Leo's encyclical see: http://w2.vatican.va/content/leo-xiii/en/encyclicals/documents/hf_l-xiii_enc_15051891_rerum-novarum.html (accessed October 26, 2017).

CHAPTER ELEVEN: Franco-Americans and Americanism

1. Paul Johnson, *A History of the American People* (New York: HarperCollins, 1997), 87.

2. David Hawke, *The Colonial Experience* (Indianapolis: Bobbs-Merrill, 1966), 364, 367.

3. Johnson, 172.

4. Eric Kaufmann, "American Exceptionalism Reconsidered: Anglo-Saxon Ethnogenesis in the 'Universal' Nation, 1776-1850," *Journal of American Studies* 33, no. 3 (1999): 456.

5. Kaufmann, 437–57.

6. Kaufmann, 444.

7. Hamon, xi.

8. Hamon, 39-40.

9. Hamon, 32.

10. Richard 2008, 28. The notion of "three pillars of *la survivance*" is commonplace in the literature.

11. Gatineau, 6.

12. Gatineau, 413. Also cited in Armand Chartier, *The Franco-Americans of New England: A History* (Manchester, NH: ACA Assurance and Worcester: Institut Français, 2000), 64. Translation as it appears in Chartier.

13. Chartier, 186; Roby 2004, 286-87.

14. See Ferdinand Gagnon, *Sa Vie et Ses Oeuvres* (Worcester, MA: C.-F. Lawrence, 1886), 7-24. Benjamin Sulte wrote this biography of Gagnon.

15. Gagnon, 136.

16. Gagnon, 140. For the variant "Loyal but French-Canadian" see Richard 2008, 66.

17. Richard 2008, 66-9.

18. A 1942 article articulates this Franco-American concept of U.S. citizenship: "[The Franco-American] believes that culture is a thing apart from a land and should not be confused with allegiance and political loyalty. The culture or soul of the Canadian Frenchman is something to be cherished and preserved wherever it may be found. He believes that by retaining his French individuality and tradition, with all they imply, he can make his greatest contribution to the country of his adoption.... He can swear loyalty to the United States in English with honesty and conviction; but he prays, writes, sings, and talks in French....He explains that this is not to be interpreted as a state within a state, but that by conserving his customs, traditions, and language he enriches the community in which he lives." Thorsten V. Kalijarvi, "French Canadians in the United States," *Annals of the American Academy of Political and Social Science* 223 (1942): 134.

19. See for example the speech of Fr. M. Joseph Kerlidou of Burlington, Vermont at the Rutland Convention of 1886 in Gatineau, esp. 197-199 with its refrain of *"Nous sommes chez nous"* ("We are at home") in the USA.

20. Gatineau, 277.

21. Gatineau, 469.

22. Gatineau, 486.

23. Gatineau, 435.

24. Robert Perreault, "One Piece in the Great American Mosaic," in Albert S. Renaud ed., *A Franco-American Overview,*

vol. 1 (Cambridge, MA: National Assessment and Dissemination Center, ESEA Title VII), 33.

25. *Uniform Hours of Labor*, reprint ed. from *The Twelfth Annual Report of the Massachusetts Bureau of Statistics of Labor*, for 1881 (Boston, 1889), 150-51.

26. Mass. BSL, *Thirteenth Annual Report* (Boston, 1882), 4-9.

27. Mass. BSL, *Thirteenth Annual Report*, 9.

28. Senate Committee on Education and Labor, *Report of the Committee of the Senate Upon the Relations Between Labor And Capital And Testimony Taken by the Committee* (Washington, D.C.: Government Printing Office, 1885), vol. 1, 66-68.

29. Mass. BSL, *Thirteenth Annual Report*, 82.

30. Mass. BSL, *Thirteenth Annual Report*, 9-10.

31. Mass. BSL, *Thirteenth Annual Report*, 11-12.

32. Mass. BSL, *Thirteenth Annual Report*, 16.

33. Mass. BSL, *Thirteenth Annual Report*, 16.

34. Mass. BSL, *Thirteenth Annual Report*, 17.

35. Mass. BSL, *Thirteenth Annual Report*, 18.

36. Mass. BSL, *Thirteenth Annual Report*, 20-21.

37. Mass. BSL, *Thirteenth Annual Report*, 21.

38. Mass. BSL, *Thirteenth Annual Report*, 22-23.

CHAPTER TWELVE: Fears of Franco-American Conspiracy

1. *British-American Citizen*, December 28, 1889. Cited in Wade, 1:434.

2. The Albany convention was the 15th General Convention of the *Canadiens* of the United States. Cf. Gatineau, 6.

3. "French Canadian Interests," *New York Times*, August 6, 1884.

4. "Canadians in New England," *New York Times*, September 23, 1885.

5. In Maine, Catholic houses of worship were torched by Know Nothings in Bath and Lewiston and the Catholic priest at Ellsworth was tarred and feathered and driven out of town. See Richard 2008, 9-10.

6. DIC, 342.

7. "The French Canadian," *New York Times*, November 29, 1885.

8. "The Habitant as an Ally," *New York Times*, January 13, 1889.

9. Mass. BSL, *Thirteenth Annual Report*, 18-19.

10. "The French Canadians in New-England," *New York Times*, June 6, 1892.

11. Egbert C. Smyth, "The French-Canadians in New England," *Proceedings of the American Antiquarian Society*, October 1891, 335-36.

12. For a brief treatment of the *Frères Chasseurs* see Wade, 1:188-193; Dickinson and Young, 166-67. For the *Croisés* see Chartier, 144-48. There were also attempts to form Franco-American secret societies on the pattern of the Knights of Columbus (cf. Rumilly, 323).

13. Marcel Martel, *French Canada: An Account of its Creation and Break-up, 1850-1967*, The Canadian Historical Association, Canada's Ethnic Group Series, Booklet No. 24 (Ottawa, 1998), 10.

14. Smyth, 319.

15. Smyth, 320.

16. "French Canadians as Citizens," *New York Times*, May 31, 1895.

17. William MacDonald, "French Canadians in Maine," *The Nation*, October 15, 1896, 285.

18. MacDonald 1896, 286.

19. Maine Bureau of Labor and Industrial Statistics, *Second Annual Report* (Augusta, 1889), 129.

20. Maine Bureau of Labor and Industrial Statistics, *Second Annual Report*, 132.

21. MacDonald 1896, 286.

22. William MacDonald, "The French Canadians in New England," *The Quarterly Journal of Economics* 12, no. 3 (1898): 276-77.

23. MacDonald 1898, 279.

24. Rev. Calvin E. Amaron, *The Evangelization of the French Canadians of New England* (Lowell: Campbell & Hanscom, 1885), 7.

25. Amaron 1885, 15.

26. Amaron 1885, 9.

27. Amaron 1885, 3.

28. Amaron 1885, 10.

29. Amaron 1885, 11.

30. Amaron 1885, 14.

31. Amaron 1885, 12.

32. Rev. Calvin E. Amaron, *Your Heritage; or New England Threatened*, 2nd ed. (Springfield, Mass.: French Protestant College, 1891), 174-179.

33. Amaron's book is divided into the following parts, "Part I: The Invading Force," "Part II: The Allies and Engines of War of this Force," and "Part III: The Conquest of this Force."

34. Amaron 1891, 52-53, 89.

35. Amaron 1891, 12, 53.

36. Amaron 1891, 83.

37. Amaron 1891, 118.

38. Amaron 1891, 10, 64-65.

39. Amaron 1891, 41.

40. Amaron 1891, 40-41.

41. For the alleged perfect obedience of the Catholic rank and file see Amaron 1891, 52-55, 65-68, 90.

42. Amaron 1891, 86.

43. Amaron 1891, 166.

44. Amaron 1891, 153, 197-98.

45. Henry Lyman Morehouse, "The French Canadian in Québec and New England," *The Home Mission Monthly* (New York City: The American Baptist Home Mission Society, December 1893), 3.

46. Hamon, 120.

47. Morehouse, 11.

48. Morehouse, 26.

49. Morehouse, 27.

50. Morehouse, 27-28 for his statistics on the Home Baptist Missions.

51. Morehouse, 29-30.

52. Morehouse, 31.

53. Morehouse, 32.

54. Morehouse, 32. Amaron's book confirms the existence of the Congregationalists' publication.

55. Morehouse, 32.

56. Howard B. Grose, *Aliens or Americans?* (Dayton, OH: Home Missionary Society of the United Brethren Church, 1906), 316.

57. For a brief biography of Grose see "GROSE, Howard Benjamin" in *The Twentieth Century Biographical Dictionary of Notable Americans*, Rossiter Johnson and John Howard Brown, eds. (Boston: The Biographical Society, 1904), 4:468-469, https://archive.org/stream/twentiethcentur41unkngoog (accessed October 26, 2017).

58. Grose, 202, 272-73.

59. Grose, 273.

60. Grose 260.

61. Grose, 239. Here Grose is quoting an author named Richmond Mayo-Smith.

62. Grose, 236.

63. Grose, 257. Here Grose is quoting an author named Josiah Strong.

64. Grose, 240.

65. Brault, 70-73; Rumilly, 102-112, 146-158; Roby 2004, 123-139.

66. For the *fabrique* as it functioned in the 1930s see Miner, 54.

67. Rumilly, 432, 447-8.

68. Cf. Chartier 138-174 for an overview of the Sentinellist Crisis. There's a large literature on this event.

69. *Souvenir du 50ième Anniversaire de la Paroisse St. Jean Baptiste Brunswick*, 11.

70. Roby 2004, 132-33.

71. For Olivine Trudeau as organist/music director at St. John's in Brunswick see "Olys – Delehunty (Wedding Announcement) *Bath Independent*, June 10, 1882, 2; "Dedication of the Catholic Church," *The Brunswick Telegraph*, July 2, 1886, 3. She became music director as soon as Fr. Gorman came to St. John's. See *Souvenir du 50ième Anniversaire de la Paroisse St. Jean Baptiste Brunswick, Maine 1877-1927* (Reproduced by Curtis Memorial Library, Brunswick, Maine, 1981), 51.

72. Roby 2004, 132.

73. Roby 2004, 133.

74. Michael Guignard, "Maine's Corporation Sole Controversy," in Madore and Rodrigue, eds. *Voyages: A Maine Franco-American Reader*, 247-262. For Brunswick's

involvement cf. esp. 251-52. For a contemporary view of the Brunswick Convention of October 1909 see "La Convention de Brunswick, Me," *La Justice* (Biddeford), October 7, 1909, 2.

75. Michael J. Guignard, "The Corporation Sole Controversy," in Quintal, ed., *Steeples and Smokestacks*, 199. This is a different essay on the same topic by the same author as the note above. Cf. also Roby 2004, 186.

76. Roby 2004, 133.

77. Roby 2004, 125.

78. Roby 2004, 121-123.

79. The August 13, 1889 *New York Times* article from Montréal had this right.

80. Lamonde 2000, 287-292.

81. The *Institut Canadien* in Montreal was committed to a liberal, Enlightenment-inspired viewpoint and resisted church oversight. See e.g. the Guibord Affair, Lamonde 2000, 363-67; Wade, 1:347-49.

82. Weil 1989, 30-31.

83. Leblanc, 291.

84. Roby 2004, 49.

85. Roby 2004, 49.

86. Weil 1989, 31.

87. Roby 2004, 51.

88. Gatineau, 485.

89. Gatineau, 486.

90. Gatineau, 489.

91. Gatineau, 26.

92. "The Annexation of Canada to the United States – Important Meeting of French Canadians," *New York Times*, December 17, 1870, 4.

93. For *L'Avenir*, Batchelor, Dorion and Papineau see Michèle Lefebvre, "Le journal *L'Avenir* (1847-1852): engagé et impartial ?" *Mémoires du livre* 3, no. 1 (Automne 2011), https://www.erudit.org/fr/revues/memoires/2011-v3-n1-memoires1830163/1007574ar/ (accessed November 28, 2017); Lamonde 2000, 311-315.

94. "Convention of French Canadians at Springfield, Mass," *New York Times*, October 9, 1868.

95. For this belief see the article "The French Canadians," *New York Times*,

September 7, 1874. Cf. also the speech of the Mayor of Chicago at 18th National Convention of the French-Canadians of the United States in August 1893 (Gatineau, 291). The Mayor hopes that soon Canada will be annexed to the United States and then all of the *Canadiens* will become U.S. citizens. The delegates applauded the Mayor's speech at length. The annexation question was alive throughout the 19th century.

96. Hamon, 129.

97. Hamon, 131.

98. Hamon, 145.

99. Hamon 145.

100. Hamon, 131.

101. For this attitude of fatalism see the interview with Norman Dube in Hendrickson, 213.

102. Hamon, 144.

103. Leblanc, 291.

104. Hamon, 144.

105. For the family cycle and the matter of parents "establishing" their children see Miner, 81-90.

106. For Tardivel see Jean-François Fortier, "Jules-Paul Tardivel (1851-1905): À L'aube du Projet Indépendantiste du Québec," *Aspects Sociologiques*, vol. 11, no. 1 (Octobre 2004): 92-101; Lamonde 2000, 444-447.

107. Lamonde 2000, 447. The author emphasizes Tardivel's isolation.

108. For Bishop Laflèche's condemnation of emigration see Weil 1989, 29; for his criticism of the recruiters for the mills see Weil 1989, 40. For his more conciliatory views toward the Franco-Americans and their Providential mission see Gatineau, 155-56.

109. Roby 2004, 41.

110. For Laflèche at Springfield see Wade, 1:432-33.

CHAPTER THIRTEEN: Eugenics and the Alien in Our Midst

1. Roby 1990, 279-290; Roby 2004, 269-280.

2. For the post-WWI surge in "race riots" and Nativism see Johnson, 660-670. For

the effect of the nativist resurgence on Franco-Americans see Rumilly, 312-320; Roby 2004, 224-241; Weil 1989, 189-196.

3. Tom Marsh, *To The Promised Land: A History of Government and Politics in Oregon* (Corvallis, OR: Oregon State University Press, 2012), 146.

4. Nicholas Wright Gilham, *A Life of Sir Francis Galton* (New York: Oxford University Press, 2001), 207.

5. Gilham, 18, 324.

6. This theory is attributed to German scientist August Weismann although it had antecedents in the work of Francis Galton. For this theory cf. Nancy L. Gallagher, *Breeding Better Vermonters: The Eugenics Project in the Green Mountain State* (Hanover, NH: University Press of New England, 1999), 20-21.

7. For the distinction between positive and negative eugenics see Gilham, 1; Stefan Kühl, *The Nazi Connection: Eugenics, American Racism and German National Socialism* (New York: Oxford University Press, 1994), 5.

8. Madison Grant, *The Passing of The Great Race* (New York: Scribner's, 1916), 17-18.

9. Grant 1916, 23.

10. Grant 1916, 198.

11. Jonathan Spiro, *Defending the Master Race: Conservation, Eugenics, and the Legacy of Madison Grant* (Hanover: University Press of New England, 2009), 148.

12. Spiro, 355-56.

13. Kühl, 85; Spiro, 357.

14. Gilham, 2-3.

15. Spiro, xii.

16. For a review of Osborn's paleontological work see William K. Gregory, "Biographical Memoir of Henry Fairfield Osborn 1857-1935," National Academy of Sciences of the United States of America, Biographical Memoirs, vol. 19, Third Memoir, 1937, http://nasonline.org/publications/biographical-memoirs/memoir-pdfs/osborn-henry-f.pdf (accessed October 26, 2017). Cf. Spiro, 89 for Osborn's coinage of the name Tyrranosaurus Rex.

17. Spiro, 136-38; Gallagher, 66-70.

18. Grant 1916, 44-51; Spiro, 136.

19. Spiro, 156.

20. Spiro, 138-140.

21. Kühl, 15; Francesco Cordasco, ed., *Dictionary of American Immigration History* (Metuchen, NJ: The Scarecrow Press, 1990), 172-3.

22. Spiro, 127-28; Gallagher, 4.

23. Spiro, 236.

24. Gallagher, 84; Spiro, 236-40.

25. Spiro, 240.

26. Gilham, 2; Edwin Black, *War Against the Weak: Eugenics and America's Campaign to Create a Master Race* (New York: Four Walls Eight Windows), 2003. Cf. esp. 293-4.

27. Gilham, 356.

28. For Johnson's membership in the Klan see Linda Gordon, *The Second Coming of the KKK* (New York: Liveright, 2017), 164.

29. Cordasco ed., 485.

30. Cordasco, ed., 485; Spiro, 204.

31. Johnson, 670.

32. Spiro, 209.

33. Johnson, 670.

34. Spiro, 233.

35. Spiro, 226.

36. Cited in Cordasco, ed., 464.

37. Speech of April 9, 1924. *Cong. Rec.*, 68th Congress, 1st Sess., Washington DC: Government Printing Office, 1924, vol. 65, 5961–5962.

38. Gilham, 354.

39. Henry Friedlander, *The Origins of Nazi Genocide From Euthanasia to the Final Solution* (Chapel Hill: University of North Carolina Press, 1995), 7; Spiro, 220-233.

40. For the USA as a whole, see U.S. Census Bureau, *Statistical Abstract of the United States* 1933, "1. Area and Population," 26-27. I calculated the growth of the French-Canadian-born population as a percentage of "foreign-born whites" in New England between 1920 and 1930 by comparing the 1920 and 1930 U.S. Federal Census numbers found in two documents: U.S. Census Bureau, *Statistical Abstract of the United States* 1922, "Population," 63 and

U.S. Census Bureau, *Statistical Abstract of the United States* 1933, "1. Area and Population," 31. The proportion of the French-Canadian-born rose in every New England state by at least one percentage point between 1920 and 1930. In Vermont, the French-Canadian-born, as a percentage of "foreign-born whites," grew by eight percent between 1920 and 1930.

41. Gatineau, 428.

42. Cf. e.g. Gatineau 440, 445.

43. Grant 1916, 72.

44. Madison Grant, *The Passing of The Great Race*, Rev. ed. (New York: Scribner's, 1921), 11-12.

45. Grant 1921, 85. Emphasis added.

46. Spiro, 152-3.

47. *New York Times*, December 25, 1878, 4.

48. Maine Bureau of Industrial and Labor Statistics, *Second Annual Report* (Augusta, 1889), 120.

49. Anderson, 64.

50. Smyth, 324.

51. *Dictionary of Races or Peoples*, 61, 63.

52. Charles B. Davenport, "Race Crossing in Man," in Cold Spring Harbor Laboratory's Image Archive on the American Eugenics Movement, Harry H. Laughlin Papers, Truman State University, http://www.eugenicsarchive.org/eugenics/list2.pl (accessed September 8, 2017). Cf. esp. 5-6.

53. For Goethe see Kühl, 57.

54. C. M. Goethe letter to the Press about high Mexican birthrates, Cold Spring Harbor Laboratory's Image Archive on the American Eugenics Movement, Harry H. Laughlin Papers, Truman State University, http://www.eugenicsarchive.org/eugenics/list2.pl (accessed September 8, 2017).

55. Weil 1989, 190.

56. Robert C. Dexter, "The Gallic War in Rhode Island," *The Nation*, August 29, 1923, 215-16.

57. Robert Cloutman Dexter, "Fifty-Fifty Americans," *The World's Work*, August 1924, 366-371.

58. Dexter 1924, 367.

59. Dexter 1924, 371.

60. Dexter 1924, 371.

61. Robert Dexter, "The French-Canadian Invasion" in Madison Grant and Charles Stewart Davison, eds. *The Alien in Our Midst* (New York: Galton, 1930), 71.

62. Dexter, in Grant and Davison, eds., *The Alien in Our Midst*, 78.

63. Madison Grant, *The Conquest of a Continent or The Expansion of Races in America*, Rev. ed. (New York: Scribners's), 1934, 296.

64. Grant 1934, 283, 305.

65. Grant 1934, 356-7.

66. Gallagher, 39.

67. Gallagher, 10.

68. Spiro, 6 (Grant), 126 (Davenport), 171.

69. Gallagher, 95-97.

70. Gallagher, 96.

71. Gallagher, 75.

72. Gallagher, 81.

73. Gallagher, 80-85.

74. Gallagher, 185-86.

75. Lutz Kaelber, University of Vermont, "Eugenics: Compulsory Sterilization in 50 American States, Vermont" (from the presentation *"Eugenic sterilizations" in Comparative Perspective*, 2012 Social Science History Association), http://www.uvm.edu/~lkaelber/eugenics/VT/VT.html (accessed September 8, 2017).

76. Rowland E. Robinson, *Vermont: A Study of Independence* (Boston: Houghton Mifflin, 1892), 330-331.

77. Gallagher, 45-46.

78. Gallagher, 111-14.

79. Anderson, 8.

80. Gallagher, 113.

81. Dr. Perkins re French Canadians, Eugenics Survey of Vermont and the Vermont Commission on Country Life records, 1925-1956 (PRA-005), PRA-00016 (Folder 16), Vermont State Archives and Records Administration, Middlesex, VT.

82. Gallagher, 157.

83. Anderson, 29-30.

84. Anderson, 28-29.

85. For these forerunners see Spiro, 103-126.

86. Kühl, 39.

87. James Q. Whitman, *Hitler's American Model* (Princeton: Princeton University Press, 2017), 12, 46-47; Kühl, 25-26.

88. Kühl, 38.

89. Spiro, 357.

90. For the *Conquest of a Continent* in German, Grant's efforts to promote it to Rosenberg, and Fischer's introduction see Kühl, 74; Spiro, 359.

91. For these connections between the U.S. eugenicists and the Nazis cf. Spiro, 357-364; Cf. also Whitman 8-9; Friedlander, 4-9.

92. For Grant's book as evidence at Nuremberg see: Nuremberg - Document Viewer - Extract from a Book concerning Eugenics, Nuremberg Trials Project, Harvard Law School, June 2016, http://nuremberg. law.harvard.edu/documents/2703-extract-from-a-book?q=%2AMadison+-Grant#p.1 (accessed October 11, 2016).

93. Spiro, 382-83; Kühl, 101. For the influence of U.S. immigration, citizenship and anti-miscegenation legislation and court rulings on Nazi German law cf. Whitman, *passim*.

94. Spiro, 369. For Gregory's objections to U.S. eugenicists praise for Nazis cf. also Kühl, 67.

95. Kühl, 46-47, 67.

96. Spiro, 130.

97. Kühl, 24-25.

98. Kühl, 48.

99. For Laughlin's promotion of the Nazi propaganda film see Kühl, 48-50.

100. Grant 1916, 3-10; Spiro, 155-57.

101. For Coolidge see Gilham 354; cf. also Spiro 177-78.

CHAPTER FOURTEEN: A Klan For New England

1. National Association for the Advancement of Colored People, *Twelfth Annual Report* for the year 1921 (New York: NAACP, 1922), 63.

2. "Ku Klux Klan Brewing Racial and Religious Hate," *Philadelphia Evening Public Ledger*, September 12, 1921, 1. The New York *World* series was reprinted in newspapers nationwide. I have relied on the series as it was published in the *Philadelphia Evening Public Ledger*, which adds additional coverage.

3. "Defiance of Law by Klan Upheld by Ku Klux 'Wizard'; Sharp Warning by Gompers," *Philadelphia Evening Public Ledger*, September 20, 1921, 1, 18; David Annan, "The Ku Klux Klan" in Norman MacKenzie, ed., *Secret Societies* (New York: Crescent Books, 1967), 266-274.

4. For Dixon, Griffith and *Birth of a Nation* see Melvyn Stokes, *D.W. Griffith's The Birth of a Nation: A History of "The Most Controversial Motion Picture of All Time"* (New York: Oxford University Press, 2007), *passim*. For the background of Dixon and Griffith, and the development of Griffith as a filmmaker cf. esp. 27-80.

5. Roland G. Fryer Jr. and Steven D. Levitt, "Hatred and Profits: Under the Hood of the Ku Klux Klan," *The Quarterly Journal of Economics* 127, no. 4 (2012): 1886; Linda Gordon, *The Second Coming of the KKK* (New York: Liveright, 2017), 11.

6. Leonard Dinnerstein, *The Leo Frank Case* (New York: Columbia University Press, 1968).

7. "Ku Klux Klan Brewing Racial and Religious Hate," *Philadelphia Evening Public Ledger*, September 12, 1921, 1.

8. Gordon, 12.

9. Dinnerstein, 150. Dinnerstein claims that "Knights of Mary Phagan" who lynched Frank were among the charter members of the Second Klan.

10. For details of the initiation on Stone Mountain see "Klan 'Emperor' Predicts Vengeance for Foes," *Philadelphia Evening Public Ledger*, September 14, 1921, 1, 6.

11. "Ku Klux Klan Chiefs in Bitter Clash as 'Empire' Nears Fall," *Philadelphia Evening Public Ledger*, September 26, 1921, 1, 18.

12. Thomas R. Pegram, *One Hundred Percent American* (Chicago: Ivan R. Dee, 2011), 7; Marsh, 147; Gordon, 13. Pegram claims

there were 2000 Klan members before 1920. Marsh says 5000, while Gordon says "only a few hundred."

13. "Ku Klux Klan Lobby Fights to Kill Probe of Order by Congress," *Philadelphia Evening Public Ledger*, September 27, 1921, 1, 12.

14. "Ku Klux Klan Brewing Racial and Religious Hate," *Philadelphia Evening Public Ledger*, September 12, 1921, 1, 6.

15. "Ku Klux Klan Lobby Fights to Kill Probe of Order by Congress," *Philadelphia Evening Public Ledger*, September 27, 1921, 1, 12.

16. "Ku Klux Klan Brewing Racial and Religious Hate," *Philadelphia Evening Public Ledger*, September 12, 1921, 1.

17. "E. Y. Clark and Mrs. Tyler Resign as K.K.K. Officials," *Philadelphia Evening Public Ledger*, September 22, 1921, 1.

18. Pegram, 23.

19. Pegram, 47.

20. Pegram, 12.

21. William Joseph Simmons, *The Klan Unmasked* (Atlanta: William E. Thompson, 1923), 23. My emphasis.

22. Simmons, 87.

23. Simmons, 81.

24. Simmons, 240.

25. Simmons, 76.

26. Simmons, 219-229.

27. "See Press Agentry in Ku Klux Move," *Philadelphia Evening Public Ledger*, September 29, 1921, 15.

28. Simmons, 170-1.

29. "Carefully Guarded List of Klan Kleagles Shows Growth of Ku Klux Klan in the U.S.," *Philadelphia Evening Public Ledger*, September 15, 1921, 6.

30. "Carefully Guarded List of Klan Kleagles Shows Growth of Ku Klux Klan in the U.S.," *Philadelphia Evening Public Ledger*, September 15, 1921, 6.

31. "Labor Leader Warns Unions Against Ku Klux," *Philadelphia Evening Public Ledger*, September 16, 1921, 1, 13.

32. Gordon, 65. The article "'Emperor' Uses Klan to Split American Loyalty," *Philadelphia Evening Public Ledger*, September 15, 1921, 1, claims there were 214 Kleagles by June 1921.

33. Fryer and Levitt, 1908.

34. "President Lauded for Ku Klux Probe by Negro Leaders," *Philadelphia Evening Public Ledger*, September 28, 1921, 1.

35. Marsh, 147.

36. For the Klan's targeting of local power brokers see also "Congressmen Bound to Ku Klux by Oaths is 'Emperor's' Boast," *Philadelphia Evening Public Ledger*, September 21, 1921, 1; Marsh, 147. For its recruitment of police see Gordon, 103, 186.

37. Pegram, 27-29.

38. Finn J. D. John, "How the Ku Klux Klan Took Over the State in 1922," *Yamhill Valley* (Oregon) *News Register*, https://newsregister.com/article?article-Title=how-the-ku-klux-klan-took-over-the-state-in-1922--1370448297--8076 (October 8, 2017). Relying on Marsh and others, John gives an account of Klan sales tactics.

39. For the offer of free membership to clergymen and outreach to fraternal orders see Pegram, 8; Gordon, 15, 186.

40. Gordon, 15.

41. Pegram, 8; Gordon 3, 13, 15.

42. The Klan took over Lanier University. See "Ku Klux Dollars Give Wizard Home," *Philadelphia Evening Public Ledger*, September 24, 1921, 4.

43. For accounts of the split of the $10 fee see "Protestant Churchmen Open Fire on Ku Klux Klan as U.S. Probers Start Work," *Philadelphia Evening Public Ledger*, September 24, 1921, 1; Fryer and Levitt, 1908; Pegram, 16; Gordon 64-65; Charles C. Alexander, "Kleagles and Cash: The Ku Klux Klan as a Business Organization, 1915-1930," *The Business History Review* 39, no. 3 (Autumn 1965): 352; Mark Paul Richard, *Not a Catholic Nation* (Amherst: University of Massachusetts Press, 2015), 8-9.

44. Fryer and Levitt, 1891.

45. "'Emperor' Controls Klan's Millions," *Philadelphia Evening Public Ledger*, September 26, 1921, 18; Fryer and Levitt, 1908;

Gordon, 66. Fryer and Levitt state that the outfits cost $2.00 to manufacture and that the Klan reduced the price to the consumer to $5.00 over time. Gordon claims the outfits cost $4.00 to manufacturer which dropped to $2.00 over time.

46. "Roosevelt Fund Sues Klan Kleagle," *Philadelphia Evening Public Ledger*, September 27, 1921, 12.

47. Fryer and Levitt, 1891.

48. Alexander, 359 (2.5 million by May 1923 and 3 million "active Klansmen in 1924"); Fryer and Levitt, 1883 (Klan "claimed four million members" at its height); Pegram, 26 (4 or 5 million at the peak).

49. Alexander, 356 (3500 new members per day).

50. "$50,000 Weekly Tinkles into Strong Box of Ku Klux Leaders," *Philadelphia Evening Public Ledger*, September 20, 1921, 18.

51. "Ku Klux Tries to Grab Control of Courts and City Officials," *Philadelphia Evening Public Ledger*, September 21, 1921, 1; "Congressmen Take Ku Klux Klan Oaths," *Philadelphia Evening Public Ledger*, September 21, 1921, 23.

52. "Klux Leaders Caught in Resort," *Philadelphia Evening Public Ledger*, September 19, 1921, 1.

53. "This Order is not organized as an adjunct to any other movement." Cf. *Kloran, or, Ritual of the Women of the Ku Klux Klan*, Imperial Headquarters Women of the Ku Klux Klan (Little Rock: AK, 1928), 39. Cf. also Gordon, 113, 126-27.

54. For the WKKK see Kathleen M. Blee, "Women in the 1920s Ku Klux Klan Movement," *Feminist Studies* 17, no. 1 (1991): 57-77. Cf. also Gordon, 109-137.

55. "Klux Leaders Caught in Resort," *Philadelphia Evening Public Ledger*, September 19, 1921, 1, 18 and "Roosevelt Fund Sues Klan Kleagle," September 27, 1921, 12; Gordon, 114.

56. "Imperial Kleagle Ousted by Church," *Philadelphia Evening Public Ledger*, October 1, 1921, 1, 4.

57. "Mrs. Tyler Scores Clarke as a Quitter," *Philadelphia Evening Public Ledger*, September 26, 1921, 18; Gordon, 114.

58. "Klan Outrages Kept from Public," *Philadelphia Evening Public Ledger*, September 24, 1921, 4.

59. "Klan Outrages Kept from Public," *Philadelphia Evening Public Ledger*, September 24, 1921, 4.

60. Pegram 9-10; Alexander, 354.

61. "Hays May Close Mails to K.K.K." *Philadelphia Evening Public Ledger*, September 22, 1921, 1 (FBI, Postmaster General) and "Daugherty Won't Call Wizard Now," September 24, 1921, 4 (Treasury Department and Prohibition Commissions).

62. For the effect of the *World* publicity see Kneebone, 1.

63. "Fire at Mrs. Tyler, Threaten Simmons," *New York Times*, October 12, 1921; Gordon, 114.

64. That the Klan customized its message to appeal to different regions of the country see Pegram, 16; Gordon, 68, 120, 147.

65. Richard 2015, 1.

66. Richard 2015, 4.

67. Richard 2015, 24.

68. Richard 2015, 183.

69. Richard 2015, 140.

70. Richard 2015, 72.

71. Department of Commerce and Labor, Bureau of the Census, *Statistical Abstract of the United States* 1910, "Area, Natural Resources and Population," 53.

72. The percentage of the "foreign-born white" population of New England calculated from Department of Commerce, Bureau of the Census, *Statistical Abstract of the United States 1922*, "Population," 46, 64.

73. Richard 2015, 62.

74. Richard 2015, 17.

75. Richard 2015, 28.

76. Richard 2015, 31.

77. Richard 2015, 31.

78. Richard 2015, 59.

79. Richard 2015, 144.

80. Richard 2015, 12.

81. Richard 2015, 17-18. Cf. also Pegram, 72; Gordon, 26.

82. Richard 2015, 85-89.

83. Richard 2015, 2-3, 38-39.

84. "Parade With Orangemen," *Fiery Cross*, October 3, 1924, 8.

85. Richard 2015, 86-87.

86. "Ku Klux Klan to Reorganize: Catholics O.K.," *Fiery Cross*, January 5, 1923, 3.

87. "Clarke Quits for the 'Good of the Order'," *Fiery Cross*, March 16, 1923, 2.

88. For this view see Richard 2015, 205.

89. Richard 2015, 34.

90. "Rome Aims to Control Immigration of Continent," *Fiery Cross*, January 9, 1925, 3.

91. Simmons, 126.

92. Simmons, 133.

93. For the Conscription Crisis in Quebec during the First World War see Wade, 2:708-780.

94. Rumilly 299-311 (esp. 309-11); Patrick Lacroix, "Americanization By Catholic Means: French-Canadian Nationalism and Trans-Nationalism, 1889-1901," *The Journal of the Gilded Age and Progressive Era* 16, no. 3 (2017): 296; Roby 2004, 229-232.

95. *Souvenir du 50ième Anniversaire de la Paroisse St. Jean Baptiste Brunswick, Maine 1877-1927*, 72-73.

96. Simmons, 114.

97. Simmons, 104.

98. Simmons, 104-105.

99. Roby 2004, 238; Richard 2015, 64.

100. C. Stewart Doty, "How Many Frenchman Does It Take To...?" in Madore and Rodrigue, eds., *Voyages: A Maine Franco-American Reader*, 336-37.

101. Richard 2015, 43-44. The Klan's alleged attempt to cross the bridge into Biddeford is a subject of Franco-American lore. I have followed Richard's account based on press reports, but I have heard several different versions of the tale.

102. Richard 2015, 44-48.

103. For the incidents in Dexter see Richard 2015, 36-38.

104. Nancy Sheehan, "Presentation looks at the Klan in Worcester County," *Worcester Telegram & Gazette*, January 6, 2012, http://www.telegram.com/article/20120106/NEWS/101069744 (accessed September 8, 2017). Dr. Eileen M. Angelini has researched this incident in Leominster.

105. Richard 2015, 112.

106. Richard 2015, 113.

107. Richard 2015, 111-112.

108. "Governor Sproul Denounces Klan," *Philadelphia Evening Public Ledger*, Sept 17, 1921, 6. For Protestant repudiation of the Klan see Pegram, 34. See also, "Ku Klux Klan Denounced in Boston City Council," *Philadelphia Evening Public Ledger*, Sept 13, 1921, 21.

109. Richard 2015, 79-82.

110. *Report of the Proceedings of the Forty-First Annual Convention of the American Federation of Labor*, Denver Colorado, June 13 to 25, Inclusive, 1921 (Washington, D.C.: Law Reporter Printing), 205-06.

111. Richard 2015, 27-29.

112. For the Klan's advocacy of King James Bible reading in schools cf. Pegram 109-112. For this issue in Maine see *La Justice*, August 29, 1924.

113. "Mesdames, Enregistrez-Vous et Votez," *La Justice*, August 29, 1924, 1.

114. "Brewster Carries Maine," *Fiery Cross*, September 12, 1924, 1.

115. Republican Brewster was the Klan's candidate in Maine in 1924. For the Klan's hold over the GOP in Oregon see Marsh, 145.

116. For the Klan and party politics see Gordon 164, 170. Cf. also Fryer and Levitt, 1915, 1916n33.

117. For the text of the Simian Act see Meyer v. Nebraska, 262 U.S. 390 (1923).

118. Gordon, 149-156. For the Oregon law see Pierce v. Society of Sisters, U.S. Supreme Court, 268 U.S. 510 (1925).

119. Richard 2015, 38.

120. Ross and Judy Paradis, "The Silent Playground" in Madore and Rodrigue, eds., *Voyages a Franco-American Reader*, 428-440.

121. For the Peck Act see Rumilly, 335-343.

122. Richard 2015, 136.

123. *Brunswick Record*, November 29, 1923, 7.

124. "Ku Klux Klan Holds Meeting in Brunswick," *Brunswick Record*, December 20, 1923, 1.

125. "Brunswick's New Board of Selectmen," *Lewiston Evening Journal*, March 9, 1915.

126. *Brunswick Record*, February 14, 1924, 6.

127. "White Robed Klan Cheered on March in Nation's Capital," *Washington Post*, August 9, 1925.

128. For Clarke's arrest see Athan G. Theoharis, ed., *FBI: A Comprehensive Reference Guide* (Phoenix, AZ, Oryx Press, 1999), 363; Gordon, 192.

129. For Stephenson's fall see Gordon, 192-94; Pegram 206-07; Fryer and Levitt, 1912; for a popular treatment see Karen Abbott, "'Murder Wasn't Very Pretty': The Rise and Fall of D.C. Stephenson," *Smithsonian* (Smithsonian.com), August 30, 2012.

130. Alexander, 365.

131. Richard 2015, 53.

132. Pegram, 20; Alexander, 365.

133. "Scenes at St. John's Day Parade," *Brunswick Record*, June 26, 1930, 1.

134. Richard 2015, 55.

135. Richard 2015, 77.

136. Cf. e.g. Fryer and Levitt, 1886, 1887 for this approach.

137. Pegram, 52.

CHAPTER FIFTEEN: Textiles Go South

1. Leblanc, 296.

2. Beckert, 171.

3. Beckert, 394.

4. Thomas R. Navin, *The Whitin Machine Works Since 1831: A Textile Machinery Company in an Industrial Village* (New York: Russell & Russell, 1969), 528-30.

5. Beckert, 393.

6. Navin, 341.

7. Beckert, 394.

8. For the reasons for the move South see Beckert 394-95; Moran, 228-30.

9. For the 1912 and 1934 strikes see Moran, 171-223, 231. The 1934 strike originated in the South.

10. Zinn, 396-97; Roby 2004, 310. Zinn gives the numbers of strikers as 2000.

11. Brault, 91.

12. An 1874 law limited the work day to ten hours per day for women and for children under the age of 18. Mass. BSL, *Labor Laws of Massachusetts: Part 1 From the Twenty-first Annual Report of the Massachusetts Bureau of Statistics* (Boston, 1890), 5.

13. Moran, 229.

14. For the technological development of textile production and its effect on the move to the South see Hekman, 697–717. For the electric mill and its impact see C.A. Chase, "Electric Power in the Textile Industry," *General Electric Review,* 18 (1915): 540-550.

15. Hendrickson, 65.

16. State of Maine, Bureau of Labor and Industrial Statistics, *Sixteenth Annual Report* for 1902 (Augusta: Kennebec Journal), 99; Moran, 230.

17. Hekman, 716.

18. Moran, 230; Beckert, 395.

19. Beckert, 394.

20. Brault, 90.

21. Richard 2008, 154.

22. Brault, 90-91; Moran, 225-26.

23. Laflamme in Madore and Rodrigue, eds., *Voyages: A Maine Franco-American Reader,* 158.

24. Moran, 227.

25. Moran, 238-39.

26. Beckert, 435. For Fall River as the "third largest" see Roby 2004, 155.

27. "Death of Benjamin Greene," *Brunswick Record*, March 18, 1904.

28. U.S. Federal Census 1900, Massachusetts, Norfolk County, Cohasset; Commonwealth of Massachusetts. Ancestry.com. 1900 United States Federal Census [database on-line]. Provo, UT, USA: Ancestry.com Operations Inc, 2004.

29. Town of Brookline, Return of a Death, Francis Cabot, no. 90, filed April 13, 1905. Ancestry.com. Massachusetts, Death

Records, 1841-1915 [database on-line]. Provo, UT, USA: Ancestry.com Operations, Inc., 2013.

30. Briggs, 652.

31. Briggs, 741-42. That Frederick P. Cabot took over as a Director of Francis Cabot's portfolio of mills see *Directory of Directors in the City of Boston and Vicinity*, 7th ed. (Boston: Ernest S. Woodaman, 1911) 70.

32. "Russell W. Eaton" (Obituary), *Transactions of ASME*, American Society of Mechanical Engineers 43 (1922): 1291.

33. For the construction of the new mill see *Brunswick Telegraph*, June 4, 1891, 2; July 28, 1892, 2; April 20, 1893, 2.

34. "The New Development in Topsham," *Brunswick Telegraph*, November 9, 1893, 2; and "Topsham Heights," Brunswick Telegraph, November 16, 1893, 2.

35. For the pedestrian bridge known as "the swinging bridge" or "le petit pont," see Juliana L'Heureux, "Brunswick: A Bridge and its History Un Pont et Son Histoire" in Madore and Rodrigue, eds., *Voyages: A Maine Franco-American Reader*, 517-19.

36. "Sewer Meeting at the Town Hall," July 3, 1893, printed handbill with handwritten note, Pejepscot Historical Society Collection, Brunswick, Maine. The text of the handbill was copied and incorporated into *Brunswick Town Meeting Minutes 1857-1924 (inc.)*, transcribed by Harry Shulman, Curtis Memorial Library, Brunswick, Maine, 213.

37. State of Maine, Bureau of Labor and Industrial Statistics, *Seventh Annual Report* for 1893 (Augusta: Burleigh and Flint, 1893), 191-92.

38. "Capt. Stover Makes It Unanimous," *Brunswick Telegraph*, June 14, 1895, 2.

39. "A Sewer System," *Brunswick Telegraph*, April 13, 1894, 2.

40. "Capt. Stover Makes It Unanimous," Brunswick Telegraph, June 14, 1895, 2.

41. Brunswick Village Corporation, Fourth Annual Report, 1896, Pejepscot Historical Society Collection, Brunswick, Maine. Cf. esp. 15-17.

42. Manley U. Adams was also known as Urial (Uriel, Uriah) M. Adams. For his early life see the birth record for Manley Urial Adams, Births in the Town of Spencer (Massachusetts, Town and Vital Records, 1620-1988 [database on-line] Provo, UT, USA: Ancestry.com Operations, Inc., 2011). He then appears as "Uriel Adams" in the Massachusetts State Census of 1855, Spencer, Worcester County (Massachusetts, State Census, 1855 [database on-line] Provo, UT, USA: Ancestry.com Operations, Inc., 2014). I believe he is the Uriah Adams who appears in the manuscript U.S. Federal Census of 1860, Providence, Smithfield, Rhode Island, 14 years old, born in Massachusetts living with machinist Edward Kilburn and his wife Elinora. For his Civil War service see Urial M. Adams of Lonsdale, RI, mustered in May 26, 1862, mustered out, September 2, 1862 (U.S., Adjutant General Military Records, 1631-1976 [database on-line]. Provo, UT, USA: Ancestry.com Operations, Inc., 2011.) For "Urial Adams" as a machinist in Lewiston see *Lewiston and Auburn Directory*, 1864, 55 (*The Lewiston and Auburn directory: containing the names of the inhabitants, their occupation and places of business, &c.* [database on-line] Provo, UT: Ancestry.com Operations Inc, 2005).

43. For Adams's business address and portfolio of mills see *Directory of Directors in the City of Boston and Vicinity*, 7th ed. (Boston: Ernest S. Woodaman, 1911), 13.

44. "Manley U. Adams" (Obituary), *Textile World Journal* 57, no. 8 (February 21, 1920): 69. "Obituary. Manley U. Adams," *American Wool & Cotton Reporter* 34, no. 10 (March 4, 1920): 47.

45. Cumberland County Registry of Deeds, Volume 872, Page 200, filed March 25, 1911. For the incorporation of the Cabot Manufacturing Company in Boston on February 18, 1911 see Commonwealth of Massachusetts, Secretary of the Commonwealth, Abstract of the Certificates of

Corporations Organized Under the General Laws of Massachusetts (Boston: Wright & Potter, 1912), 14.

46. "Manley U. Adams" (Obituary), *Textile World Journal* 57, no. 8 (February 21, 1920): 69. "Obituary. Manley U. Adams," *American Wool & Cotton Reporter* 34, no. 10 (March 4, 1920): 47; "Russell W. Eaton" (Obituary), *Transactions of ASME*, American Society of Mechanical Engineers 43 (1922): 1291.

47. "Acquires Control," *Fibre and Fabric*, January 3, 1920, 13.

48. "Farewell May Change Hands," *Textile World Journal* 57, no. 1 (January 3, 1920): 25.

49. For Nathaniel Farwell see Geneva Kirk and Gridley Barrows, *Historic Lewiston, Its Government*. (Lewiston, ME: Lewiston Historical Commission, 1982), 19-20. For the importance of the Grand Trunk connection to Franco-American Lewiston see Richard 2008, 12.

50. "John Whittemore Farwell (Obituary), *Proceedings of the American Antiquarian Society* (Worcester, MA) 39, pt. 2 (October 1929): 240-42.

51. "Obituaries: Nathaniel Farwell Ayer," *Proceedings of the American Antiquarian Society* (Worcester, MA) 58, pt. 2 (October 1948): 203-04.

52. "Personal Page," *Textile World Journal* 57, no. 11 (March 13, 1920): 31.

53. "William Worsnop," in Harrie B. Coe ed. *Maine Biographies, Reprinted in Two Volumes* (Baltimore: Genealogical Publishing Company, Inc., 2002), 1:100.

54. "Cabot Employees Vote Not to Return To Work," *Brunswick Record*, August 13, 1920, 1.

55. For the length of Worsnop's tenure at the mill see "Closing of Brunswick's Verney Mill May Be Imminent," *Brunswick Record*, May 19, 1955, 7.

56. "Record Presents Complete Analysis of the Cabot Mill Situation," *Brunswick Record*, January 27, 1938, 1.

57. For the three-part series on the Cabot mill's woes see "Record Presents Complete Analysis of the Cabot Mill Situation," *Brunswick Record*, January 27, 1938, 1; "Cabot Spending Real Money to Make Mill Here One of Best in Country," *Brunswick Record*, February 3, 1938, 1; "Reduction in Cabot Mill's Local Taxes Sought as Aid to Recovery," *Brunswick Record*, February 3, 1938, 1.

58. Yves Roby, "A Portrait of the Female Franco-American Worker (1865-1930)" in Quintal, ed. *Steeples and Smokestacks*, 557. Roby cites Michael J. Guignard, *La Foi – la Langue – la Culture: The Franco-Americans of Biddeford, Maine* (n.p.: Michael J. Guignard, 1982), 114. I confirmed the provenance of this quotation from an anonymous Cabot company executive through an e-mail exchange with Michael J. Guignard, April 8-11, 2017.

59. Moran, 237.

60. For Ziskind see "Jews in the Textile Industry," *Rhode Island Jewish Historical Notes* 6, no. 2 (November 1972): 278-281; "Jacob Ziskind," *National Cyclopaedia of American Biography*, vol. 38 (New York: James T. White, 1953), 56-57; Moran, 237-38.

61. "Employees Buying Houses From Cabot," *Brunswick Record*, November 7, 1940, 1.

62. Cumberland County Registry of Deeds, Volume 1622, Page 218, filed November 21, 1940.

63. Cumberland County Registry of Deeds, Volume 1702, Page 151, filed December 21, 1942.

64. Ziskind was also involved in a Verney Corporation of Canada. Whether Ziskind's connection to Verney was prior to the sale of the Cabot Company or subsequent to it remains unclear.

65. "Obituaries: Nathaniel Farwell Ayer," *Proceedings of the American Antiquarian Society* (Worcester, MA) 58, pt. 2 (October 1948): 204. That Ziskind retained the Cabot name see "Jews in the Textile Industry," *Rhode Island Jewish Historical Notes* 6, no. 2 (November 1972): 280. Text mentions the Stevens Mill of Fall River operating "under Cabot Manufacturing."

66. "Cabot Mill Purchased by New Hampshire Man," *Brunswick Record*, December 24, 1942, 1.

67. "Closing of Brunswick's Verney Mill May Be Imminent," *Brunswick Record*, May 19, 1955, 1.

68. "Closing of Brunswick's Verney Mill May Be Imminent," Brunswick Record, May 19, 1955, 1.

69. "Closing of Brunswick's Verney Mill May Be Imminent," *Brunswick Record* May 19, 1955, 1.

70. Town of Brunswick, Population and Demographic Plan Analysis (Appendix A), Comprehensive Plan Update, Planning Decisions & Town of Brunswick Staff, July 23, 2004, A5.

71. "Closing of Brunswick's Verney Mill May Be Imminent," *Brunswick Record*, May 19, 1955, 1.

72. James P. Allen, "Franco-Americans in Maine: A Geographical Perspective," *Acadiensis* 4, no. 1 (1974): 58.

73. "Standard Romper Company to Occupy Space in Verney Mill," *Brunswick Record*, January 5, 1956. States that the Verney mill had closed the previous June.

74. Cumberland County Registry of Deeds, Volume 2262, Page 367, filed November 19, 1955.

75. "Standard Romper Company to Occupy Space in Verney Mill," *Brunswick Record*, January 5, 1956, 1.

76. Town of Brunswick, Population and Demographic Plan Analysis (Appendix A), Comprehensive Plan Update, Planning Decisions & Town of Brunswick Staff, July 23, 2004, A5.

CHAPTER SIXTEEN: Drifting Away from Little Canada in Body and Mind

1. Rumilly, 100.

2. Roby 2004, 326-32.

3. Roby 2004, 328-331.

4. Chartier, 385. For a recent reappraisal of Metalious see Ardis Cameron, *Unbuttoning America: A Biography of Peyton Place* (New York: Columbia University Press, 2015).

5. "Historian Will Durant Dies; Author of 'Civilization' Series," *New York Times*, November 9, 1981.

6. Cf. Roby 2004, 289, 426-27, 444-45. The second half of Roby's (2004) work is this story of the decline of Francophone institutions, a death by a thousand cuts.

7. For the drift of Maine's Franco-Americans toward Portland in the 20th century see Allen, 65, although he's referring to a somewhat later period.

8. Roby 2004, 466.

9. Thorsten V. Kalijarvi, "French Canadians in the United States," *The Annals of the American Academy of Political and Social Science* 223 (1942): 132.

10. For the effect of military service see Mackinnon and Parent, 24-29.

11. For example, Marie-Joëlle Parent, "Sur les Traces des Franco-Américains," 28 mai 2014, *Le Journal de Montréal* http://www.journaldemontreal.com/2014/05/28/sur-les-traces-des-franco-americains (accessed March 26, 2017); Michel Lapierre, "Histoire - La tragédie du Québec étatsunien," *Le Devoir*, 11 août 2007, http://vigile.Québec/Histoire-La-tragedie-du-Québec (accessed March 26, 2017); Rémi Francœur, "Le dernier Franco-Américain?" *Le Huffington Post, Québec,* January 3, 2016, http://Québec.huffingtonpost.ca/remi-francoeur/le-dernier-franco-americain_b_9360238.html (accessed March 26, 2017).

12. Peter Behrens, "Welcome to the Town of Ghosts," *Montreal Gazette*, 10 October 1998, B7. Cited in Richard 2008, 248.

13. Cf. Richard 2008, *passim*. The notion that negotiation rather than assimilation is a better way to understand the Franco-American experience is a major thesis of Richard's book.

14. Anniina Simula, "Les Franco-Américains de la Nouvelle Angleterre: communauté discursive et rôle de la langue française" (Mémoire de maîtrise, Département d'études

françaises, Université de Turku, 2008). Cf. esp. 70-73.

15. Hendrickson, 151, 99, 168, 213.

CHAPTER SEVENTEEN: A Distinct Alien Race No Longer

1. Anderson, 6.

2. Anderson, 144.

3. Anderson, 148.

4. Anderson, 22.

5. Cf. esp. Anderson's discussion of inter-racial marriage 191-201.

6. Anderson, 61.

7. Anderson, 185.

8. Anderson, 64.

9. Anderson, 54.

10. Anderson, 248.

11. Anderson, 40, 187-201.

12. Blake McKelvey, *The Emergence of Metropolitan America 1915-1966* (New Brunswick, NJ: Rutgers University Press, 1968), 131-36, 181-87.

13. Leon Bouvier, "The Socio-Economic Status of the French Canadians in the United States," Suzanne A. Hatfield, trans., in Madeleine Giguère, ed. *A Franco-American Overview: New England (Part 2)*, vol. 4 (Cambridge, MA: National Assessment and Dissemination Center, ESEA Title VII., 1981), 117-122.

14. Mackinnon and Parent, 16, 20, 22-24.

15. Jacob Albert, Tony Brinkley, Yvon Labbé and Christian Potholm, "Contemporary Attitudes of Maine's Franco Americans," Occasional Papers, Orono, ME: University of Maine, Spring 2013.

16. For the Mainers who had a bachelor's degree or higher see U.S. Census Bureau, 2012 American Community Survey, "Educational Attainment, 2012 American Community Survey 1-Year Estimates" (Maine). https://factfinder.census.gov (accessed October 5, 2017).

CHAPTER EIGHTEEN: Franco-Americans and Québécois

1. These quotations are paraphrases from memory.

2. For the events of the Quiet Revolution see Dickinson and Young, 305-344.

3. Dickinson and Young, 324.

4. Dickinson and Young, 360.

5. For Beaulieu see Chartier, 232-34.

6. Roby 2004, 483, 513-16. Note the contrasting views of Brault (182-83) who sees FAROG as "one of the most refreshing Franco-American phenomena in years" and Chartier (344-47) who sees it as part of the "'me' generation" and its "cult of the 'self'." Chartier characterizes the *FAROG Forum* as obsessed "with the negative aspect of things" and possessing a tone of "effrontery that sometimes smacked of arrogance."

7. Chartier, 361, 369.

8. Hendrickson, 219-20.

9. I interviewed Yvon Labbé about these events in which he participated in September of 2015.

10. Roby 2004, 507-08.

11. Roby 2004, 508.

12. Author's interview with Yvon Labbé September 2015.

13. Roby 2004, 465.

14. For French (of France) emigration to the USA see James S. Olson and Heather Olson Beal, *The Ethnic Dimension in American History*, 4th ed. (Hoboken: John Wiley & Sons, 2011), 56.

15. Étienne Rivard, "L'immigration Franco-européenne aux États-Unis, 1899-1910," La Francophonie Nord-Americaine, 172, *Atlas Historique du Québec*, https://atlas.cieq. ca/la-francophonie-nord-americaine/l-immigration-franco-europeenne-aux-etats-unis-1899-1910.pdf (accessed October 4, 2017).

16. U.S. Census Bureau, *Statistical Abstract of the United States* 1910, "Area, Natural Resources and Population," 55-56.

17. U.S. Census Bureau, *Statistical Abstract of the United States* 1933, 26.

Index

Songs Upon the Rivers
The Buried History of the French-speaking Canadiens *and Métis*
From the Great Lakes and the Mississippi across to the Pacific
Robert Foxcurran, Michel Bouchard, and Sébastien Malette

The Question of Separatism
Quebec and the Struggle over Sovereignty
Jane Jacobs

A People's History of Quebec
Jacques Lacoursière & Robin Philpot

The History of Montréal
The Story of a Great North American City
Paul-André Linteau

The Complete Muhammad Ali
Ishmael Reed

The Einstein File
The FBI's Secret War on the World's Most Famous Scientist
Fred Jerome (with Forewords by Ajamu Baraka and David Suzuki)

America's Gift
What the World Owes to the America's and their First Inhabitants
Käthe Roth & Denis Vaugeois

Through the Mill
Girls and Women in the Quebec Cotton Textile Industry (1881-1951)
Gail Cuthbert Brandt (October 2018)

Printed by Imprimerie Gauvin
Gatineau, Québec